OCR Ancient History

GCSE

COMPONENT 2

ALSO AVAILABLE FROM BLOOMSBURY

OCR Classical Civilisation GCSE Route 1: Myth and Religion,
Ben Greenley, Dan Menashe and James Renshaw

OCR Classical Civilisation GCSE Route 2: Women in the Ancient World,
Robert Hancock-Jones, Dan Menashe and James Renshaw

OCR Classical Civilisation AS and A Level Component 11: The World of the Hero,
Sally Knights

OCR Classical Civilisation AS and A Level Components 21 and 22: Greek Theatre and Imperial Image,
Robert Hancock-Jones, James Renshaw and Laura Swift

OCR Classical Civilisation A Level Components 23 and 24: Invention of the Barbarian and Greek Art,
Athina Mitropoulos, Laura Snook and Alastair Thorley

OCR Classical Civilisation A Level Components 31 and 34: Greek Religion and Democracy and the Athenians,
Athina Mitropoulos, Tim Morrison, James Renshaw and Julietta Steinhauer

*OCR Classical Civilisation A Level Components 32 and 33:
Love and Relationships and Politics of the Late Republic*,
Matthew Barr, Lucy Cresswell and Alastair Thorley

OCR Ancient History GCSE Component 1: Greece and Persia,
Sam Baddeley, Paul Fowler, Lucy Nicholas and James Renshaw

OCR Ancient History AS and A Level Component 1: Greece,
Charlie Cottam, David L. S. Hodgkinson, Steve Matthews, Lucy Nicholas and James Renshaw

OCR Ancient History AS and A Level Component 2: Rome,
Robert Cromarty, James Harrison and Steve Matthews

Books published for the OCR specifications in GCSE and AS / A Level Latin and Classical Greek are also available, including editions of every set text for A Level. Please see our website
www.bloomsbury.com/uk/education/secondary/classics

This resource is endorsed by OCR for use with specification OCR GCSE (9–1) Ancient History (J198). In order to gain OCR endorsement, this resource has undergone an independent quality check. Any references to assessment and/or assessment preparation are the publisher's interpretation of the specification requirements and are not endorsed by OCR. OCR recommends that a range of teaching and learning resources are used in preparing learners for assessment. OCR has not paid for the production of this resource, nor does OCR receive any royalties from its sale. For more information about the endorsement process, please visit the OCR website, www.ocr.org.uk.

OCR Ancient History

GCSE

COMPONENT 2:
Rome

PAUL FOWLER
CHRISTOPHER GROCOCK
JAMES MELVILLE

GENERAL EDITOR:
JAMES RENSHAW

Bloomsbury Academic
An imprint of Bloomsbury Publishing Plc

BLOOMSBURY
LONDON · OXFORD · NEW YORK · NEW DELHI · SYDNEY

Bloomsbury Academic

An imprint of Bloomsbury Publishing Plc

50 Bedford Square	1385 Broadway
London	New York
WC1B 3DP	NY 10018
UK	USA

www.bloomsbury.com

BLOOMSBURY and the Diana logo are trademarks of Bloomsbury Publishing Plc

First published 2017

© Paul Fowler, Christopher Grocock and James Melville, 2017

Paul Fowler, Christopher Grocock and James Melville have asserted their right under the Copyright, Designs and Patents Act, 1988, to be identified as Author of this work.

All rights reserved. No part of this publication may be reproduced or transmitted in any form or by any means, electronic or mechanical, including photocopying, recording, or any information storage or retrieval system, without prior permission in writing from the publishers.

No responsibility for loss caused to any individual or organization acting on or refraining from action as a result of the material in this publication can be accepted by Bloomsbury or the author.

British Library Cataloguing-in-Publication Data
A catalogue record for this book is available from the British Library.

ISBN: PB: 978-1-3500-1519-7
ePDF: 978-1-3500-1521-0
ePub: 978-1-3500-1520-3

Library of Congress Cataloging-in-Publication Data
A catalog record for this book is available from the Library of Congress.

Cover design by Terry Woodley and Olivia D'Cruz
Cover image © Getty/Tibor Bognar

Typeset by RefineCatch Limited, Bungay, Suffolk
Printed and bound in Great Britain

To find out more about our authors and books visit www.bloomsbury.com. Here you will find extracts, author interviews, details of forthcoming events and the option to sign up for our newsletters.

ACKNOWLEDGEMENTS

The authors divided the text between them as follows:

Chapters 1 and 2: The Foundations of Rome and Hannibal and the Second Punic War by Paul Fowler
Chapter 3: Cleopatra: Rome and Egypt by James Melville
Chapter 4: Britannia: From Conquest to Province by Christopher Grocock

The authors would like to thank the many anonymous reviewers at universities, schools and OCR who read and commented on drafts of this text. All errors remain their own.

CONTENTS

Introduction | vii
How to Use this Book | viii

PART 1   **LONGER PERIOD STUDY: THE FOUNDATIONS OF ROME: FROM KINGSHIP TO REPUBLIC, 753–440 BC** | 1

Introduction | 2

- **1.1** The Legendary Kings and the Origins of Rome, 753–616 BC | 5
- **1.2** The Etruscan Kings, 616–509 BC | 24
- **1.3** Origins of the Republic, 509–494 BC | 39
- **1.4** Securing the Republic, 494–440 BC | 51

What to Expect in the Exam: Section A | 69

PART 2   **DEPTH STUDIES** | 79

Introduction to the Depth Study options | 80

DEPTH STUDY 1: HANNIBAL AND THE SECOND PUNIC WAR, 218–201 BC | 81

Introduction to Hannibal and the Second Punic War, 218–201 BC | 82

- **2.1** Reasons for the Outbreak of the Second Punic War | 84
- **2.2** The Nature and Dynamics of Hannibal's Leadership | 93
- **2.3** The Changing Nature of Rome's Response to Hannibal | 116
- **2.4** How Did Rome Defeat Carthage? | 128

What to Expect in the Exam: Section B | 140

DEPTH STUDY 2: CLEOPATRA: ROME AND EGYPT, 69–30 BC | 149

Introduction to Cleopatra: Rome and Egypt, 69–30 BC | 150

- **3.1** Cleopatra as Queen of Egypt | 153
- **3.2** Cleopatra's Relationship with Julius Caesar, 48–44 BC | 167
- **3.3** Cleopatra's Relationship with Mark Antony, 41–30 BC | 181
- **3.4** The Battle of Actium and its Significance for Egypt and Rome | 194

What to Expect in the Exam: Section C | 207

Contents

DEPTH STUDY 3: BRITANNIA: FROM CONQUEST TO PROVINCE, AD 43–c. 84 | 215

Introduction to Britannia: from Conquest to Province, AD 43–c. 84 | 216

- **4.1** Claudius' Invasion of Britain, AD 43 | 222
- **4.2** The Romans in Britain | 245
- **4.3** Romanisation and Further Resistance | 259

What to Expect in the Exam: Section D | 278

Glossary | 287
Sources of Quotations | 290
Sources of Illustrations | 291
Index | 292

INTRODUCTION

Welcome to your textbook for OCR GCSE Ancient History.

This book has been created to support the Roman half of the new OCR GCSE (9–1) specification. It contains the Longer Period Study 'The Foundations of Rome: from Kingship to Republic, 753–440 BC' and you will study this chapter followed by a choice of one out of the three Depth Studies: 'Hannibal and the Second Punic War, 218–201 BC', 'Cleopatra: Rome and Egypt, 69–30 BC' and 'Britannia: from Conquest to Province, AD 43–c. 84'.

Through your reading of this textbook and your wider study in class, you will be able to gain a broad understanding of military, political, religious, social and cultural aspects of the history of the ancient world. You will read and analyse ancient source material, and study certain debates by modern scholars related to this material. This will enable you to develop the skills to formulate coherent arguments about key issues and concepts.

The specification requires you to respond to the prescribed source material and assess its content through analysis and evaluation. The box features (see pp. viii–ix) are designed to build up your skills and knowledge, while exam tips, practice questions, and chapters on assessment will prepare you for taking your final examinations.

A Companion Website, available at www.bloomsbury.com/anc-hist-gcse, supports this textbook with further information, resources and updates. If you have any suggestions for improvement and additional resources please get in touch by writing to contact@bloomsbury.com

HOW TO USE THIS BOOK

The layout design and box features of this book are designed to aid your learning.

COLOUR

The colour blue is used to highlight prescribed source quotations, box features that focus on assessment preparation and exam skills.

ICONS

The Prescribed Source icon **PS** flags a quotation or image that is a source prescribed in the specification.

The Stretch and Challenge icon **S&C** indicates that an exercise extends beyond the core content of the specification.

The Companion Website icon **CW** highlights where extra material can be found on the Bloomsbury Companion Website www.bloomsbury.com/anc-hist-gcse.

BOX FEATURES

In the margins you will find feature boxes giving short factfiles of key events, individuals and places.

Other features either **recommend** teaching material or highlight **prescribed** content and **assessment** tips and information.

Recommended teaching material is found in the following box features:

Activities
Debates
Explore Further
Further Reading
Modern Parallels
Study Questions
Topic Reviews

Prescribed content and assessment-focused tips and information are found in the following box features:

- Exam Overviews
- Exam Tips
- Practice Questions
- Prescribed Sources

Material that extends beyond the specification is found in the Stretch and Challenge box features. Remember that the specification requires students to study extra sources and material not listed in the specification, so S&C information and exercises will provide a good place for you to start.

A NOTE ON QUESTIONS

Discussion prompts found in Topic Review boxes and Study Question boxes are not worded in the form you will find on the exam papers. They are intended to encourage investigation and revision of the material, but do not reflect the questions you will answer in the exam. Practice Questions at the end of each topic, and the questions found in the 'What to Expect in the Exam' chapters do mirror the format and wording you will encounter in the exam.

GLOSSARY

At the back of the book you will find a full glossary of key words. These words are also defined on pages in margin features.

Spellings of names and texts are formatted in line with the OCR specification.

On the Companion Website you will find a colour-coded glossary that highlights which components the words come from.

IMAGES

Illustrations give you the opportunity to see the ancient visual material you are required to study. Images of the prescribed visual/material sources are flagged with the PS icon, but other images illustrate other relevant aspects of the ancient world. Often what survives from the ancient world does not provide us with ways to illustrate what we study. Thus, art, drawings and reconstructions from later periods and the modern day may be used to illustrate this book. Don't forget that these are not sources like your prescribed texts and visual material – they are later interpretations of aspects of antiquity and do not represent evidence for analysis.

How to use this book

TRANSLATIONS

If not otherwise specified, translations are copyright OCR. Documents of translations covering the prescribed sources for each component are available from the OCR website and include OCR and other translations of the texts.

COMPANION WEBSITE

Resources will include

- links to the text of Prescribed Literary Sources
- further images and information on Prescribed Visual/Material Sources
- annotated further reading
- links to websites that give useful contextual material for study
- quizzes on key topics and themes
- worksheets to supplement Activity box features in the book

DON'T FORGET

Look out for cross references to other pages in the book – this is where you will find further information and be able to link concepts or themes.

PART 1
LONGER PERIOD STUDY: THE FOUNDATIONS OF ROME: FROM KINGSHIP TO REPUBLIC, 753–440 BC

Introduction

Just over a quarter of your GCSE in Ancient History involves a Roman Period Study. You will learn about the earliest history of Rome as told by ancient historians, and you will think about how to distinguish myth from fact. OCR has not set any particular sources for you to read, so the ones you will encounter in this textbook are only a suggestion: you should use the skills you build to read other texts and sources about this period of history.

EXAM OVERVIEW — J198/02 SECTION A

Your assessment for the Period Study will be:

27.5% of the GCSE	60 mins out of 1hr 45mins for the whole paper	60 marks out of 105 marks for the whole paper*

* This includes 5 marks are available for spelling, punctuation, grammar and appropriate historical terminology (SPaG).

30 marks will test AO1: demonstrate knowledge and understanding of the key features and characteristics of the historical periods studied.

15 marks will test AO2: analyse and explain historical events and historical periods to arrive at substantiated judgements.

10 marks will test AO3: use, analyse and evaluate ancient sources within their historical context.

EXAM TIP: THE DIFFERENCE BETWEEN EVALUATION AND ANALYSIS

Analysis is the ability to explore the value or weight of a particular piece of evidence or event. Evaluation is the ability to weigh up a number of facts and sources in combination to make a decision about how far something is important.

USING ANCIENT HISTORIANS TO STUDY THE FOUNDATIONS OF ROME

Historians are confident about only three things.

1. We do not know for certain how Rome was founded, we only have theories and possibilities.
2. The ancient accounts of this period are a mixture of legend, myth and fiction.
3. The archaeology we possess is limited and produces more questions than answers.

It may seem strange to be studying a topic we know very little about. This is a common obstacle when studying Ancient History. Most periods have an incomplete archaeological record which makes it very difficult to make sense of the past.

This component concentrates upon the work of Livy and Dionysius. In their opinion Rome developed from a small settlement of soldiers into a thriving city with a **Republic**. The archaeological record does not fully agree with their version of events. Unfortunately, archaeology does not provide us with a complete history.

Modern historians use Livy and Dionysius, cautiously, to provide an approximate chronology to the foundation of Rome. The **foundation chronology** they provide is not historical fact but a historical **narrative**. Modern historians call their story **the literary tradition**.

Historians debate the **weight** of the literary tradition. Some value the ancient historians because they had access to evidence which no longer exists. Others argue that the ancient sources they use have been manipulated or made up by earlier historians like Fabius Pictor. In their opinion Livy's and Dionysius' histories are **interpretations**. In other words, they alter the ancient sources to achieve personal aims.

What will I study?

In the first two sections, you will explore the role of the legendary kings. Romulus, the legendary founder of Rome, is supposed to have created Rome's basic structure. This included dividing the city into two orders called **patricians** and **plebeians**. Over time, other kings would add to this structure until the removal of Tarquinius Superbus in 509 BC.

In the final two sections, you explore the early history of the Republic. In section three you will explore how Rome fought to remain independent. Then in the final section how these wars of independence developed into a conflict between the two orders.

Themes

To help students understand this longer Period Study, there are four themes.
They are:

Political change: As you study each component you will discover how the Roman historians describe the development of Ancient Rome's government. It is important to remember that this account is not necessarily factual, but rather, how the ancients believed the Roman government developed between 753 and 440 BC.

---

republic a country without a king; the word derives from the Latin – res publica – the 'public matter' or the people's government

foundation chronology a popular theory that the Roman writer Fabius Pictor created a foundation timeline to organise the history of Rome, by mixing together the different sources he had found with his own narrative

narrative used by all authors to help readers follow their story and ancient historians similarly used story-lines to help explain the changes and developments introduced in Rome

literary tradition accounts of Rome's foundation by ancient historians such as Dionysius and Livy; very little of older sources such as Cato and Pictor survives

weight the historical value of a source

interpretations the different ways historians have viewed the past

patricians a difficult group to define accurately, Livy and Dionysius refer to them as men belonging to Rome's oldest families, many being rich landowners

plebeians Roman citizens who did not belong to the patrician families

Part One Longer Period Study

> **divine intervention** the interference (good and bad) of gods in human affairs
>
> **Conflict of the Orders** the conflict between the patricians and the plebeians

Social and religious change: **Divine intervention** and the development of Rome's religious structures is a key theme in the first two sections. After the downfall of the kings, Livy focuses upon the social and political changes brought about by the **Conflict of the Orders** between the plebeian and patrician orders.

Impact of warfare and military change: Warfare is a crucial part of Rome's history. Modern historians are convinced that most of the battles and tactics described by Livy are part of his narrative, rather than an accurate account of how Rome subdued its neighbours. The archaeological record does, however, show periods of widespread destruction in the city of Rome around 500 BC.

Separating myth from reality: The 'legendary' nature of this whole period can be very daunting to any student. This final theme will introduce you to the influences upon the literary tradition. For example, Livy believed that his history should celebrate the Glory of Rome and the achievements of its early heroes. He also wrote stories which contained moral lessons. Livy had lived through the Roman civil wars of the first century. He believed that Rome was in decline and in danger of collapse because of the dangers of greed, **sedition** and ambition.

> **sedition** encouraging others to challenge the government

TIMELINE OF ROME'S FOUNDATION ACCORDING TO THE ROMAN HISTORIANS

Date (BC)	
753–716	Romulus
715–673	Numa Pompilius
673–642	Tullus Hostilius
642–616	Ancus Marcius
616–579	Lucius Tarquinius Priscus
578–535	Servius Tullius
535–509	Lucius Tarquinius Superbus
509	Establishment of Roman Republic. Consuls created. Battle of Silvia Arsia
c. 508	Roman – Etruscan Wars begin. Lars Porsena invades Rome
501	Creation of dictator to deal with national emergencies
c. 496	Battle of Lake Regilius. Rome defeats Lucius Tarquinius Superbus
494	First Secession of the Plebeians and creation of plebeian tribune
471	Volero Uprising.
451–449	First and Second Decemvirate. Second Secession. Creation of Twelve Tables.

1.1 The Legendary Kings and the Origins of Rome, 753–617 BC

TIMESPAN OVERVIEW

- the nature and origin of the historical evidence for this period, including archaeological and geographical issues
- the Aeneas and Romulus foundation myths
- Romulus' political initiatives
- Romulus' religious initiatives
- Romulus' organisation of the Roman army
- Romulus' conflicts with neighbouring communities
- Rome's relationship with the Sabines
- the role of the Senate
- Romulus' death and the succession of Numa
- Numa's religious reforms
- Numa's diplomacy and religious policies
- the legal system in the reign of Tullus Hostilius
- Tullus Hostilius' conflict with Alba Longa
- Ancus Marcius' expansion of Rome

There are no prescribed sources for this component, but the following suggested readings and archaeological evidence are covered in this chapter:

- Livy, *The History of Rome*, Preface, Book 1, sections 1–2, 4–10, 12–14, 16–21, 23–33
- Dionysius, *Roman Antiquities*, Book 1, sections 85–8; Book 2, sections 9, 14, 21–3

- Amphora depicting Aeneas
- The citadel of Luni Sul Mignone
- The Capitoline She-wolf
- Drawing of the tho Bolsena Mirror
- The Lapis Niger Stele
- Villanovan funerary urn
- Roman sesterce showing the temple of Janus

Part One Longer Period Study

> **EXAM TIP: SECOND-ORDER CONCEPTS**
>
> In your exam, Question 4 asks you to use second-order concepts. These are used by historians to analyse the past. As you read this section make sure you that you look out for opportunities to consider the following second-order concepts: change and continuity; cause; consequence; significance; similarity and difference

This topic covers the earliest history of Rome, from its founding to the time of the Kings. The descriptions of the lives of the four legendary kings Romulus, Numa, Tullus and Ancus are fictional. Each king was given a personality and role to help the Roman historians create a narrative about Rome's origins.

Romulus was the great founding father of Rome. Numa developed religion. Tullus, the conqueror, revived Rome's military reputation. Ancus, the just, balanced military expansion with law and order.

ACTIVITY

Theme 4: Separating Myth from Reality

Read Livy's Preface.

- Summarise what Livy claims are his aims in writing his history.
- Can you find examples of:
  - Concerns about first century Rome.
  - Patriotism: Celebrating the Glory of Rome.

Mars the Roman god of warfare and conflict

HOW USEFUL ARE THE ROMAN FOUNDATION MYTHS?

Why did Livy and the Roman historians use legends?

The foundation myths are unlikely to contain many facts. Livy, for example informs us in his Preface that many of his sources are legendary.

> The accounts of Rome's earliest history which have been passed down are mainly poetic tales, rather than reliable records of historical events. I, however, have no intention to challenge these tales. The ancients must be allowed to make the foundation of their cities more impressive by adding the divine to human history. It is not for me to criticise those who want to claim their cities were founded by gods. The Romans, for example, claim **Mars** as the father of Romulus, its founder. I am sure that the great cities Rome has conquered would have little trouble in accepting this.
>
> Livy, *The History of Rome* Preface (adapted)

Livy reminds us throughout his history that he has his doubts about these early sources. He includes them because they are part of the Roman story.

It is important to remember that Livy is using many sources to write his history.

Livy's most influential source is likely to be Fabius Pictor. He was a Roman historian, writing at the end of the third century. Modern historians suspect that Pictor drew together all of the sources available at the time to create a timeline of Roman history.

This helped preserve some of the earliest Roman sources. It also created many mistakes and errors in early Roman history. It is obvious that there were numerous gaps in the historical record, and Pictor seems to have filled these gaps in as best as he could. Livy identifies some of the mistakes Pictor makes. Modern archaeology has revealed many more.

Livy was influenced by **Stoicism**. The challenge of writing about all of Rome's history was Livy's life work. Livy, however, did not write his history to celebrate

Stoicism an Ancient Greek school of philosophy that believed that virtue is based upon knowledge

Stoicism. Instead Livy seems interested in human behaviour and how it affected the world.

Dionysius, the other historian we shall use, wanted to copy the famous Greek historian Herodotus and create a great history. Both Dionysius and Herodotus came from Halicarnassus, a Greek island. Like Herodotus, Dionysius wanted to demonstrate the influence of Greek ideas. Dionysius' history suggested that the Romans were descended from Greece, and shared many Greek qualities.

> **KEY EVENT**
>
> **Second Punic War** war between Rome and Carthage, from 218 to 203

> ***Iliad*** epic Greek poem which describes the 'legendary' war between Greece and the Trojans
>
> **oral history** historical information which is not recorded in writing, but passed down in folk tales, stories, poems or songs, and often mixing fact with fiction to make the event more interesting

AENEAS

Why was Aeneas added to the foundation myth?

The inclusion of Aeneas in the foundation myth is an excellent example of the role of legend in the literary tradition. Roman historians wanted to link the foundation of Rome with Homer's *Iliad*. Aeneas, a survivor from the Trojan Wars, was chosen because his story linked Rome with another great military power.

The earliest mention of Aeneas' influence upon the foundation of Rome is by a Greek author Hellanicus. By the late fourth century, Roman authors began to develop Hellanicus' ideas. The growing influence of Greek philosophy upon the Roman elite after the **Second Punic War** saw the story of Aeneas added to the Foundation narrative.

An important element of Aeneas' story are his adventures in **Carthage**. When Aeneas visited Carthage and fell in love with its queen, Dido. Duty demanded Aeneas leave Carthage. This broke Dido's heart and she committed suicide. The Punic Wars were considered an important turning point in the development of Rome. It is possible that this short story was added to help illustrate why Rome and Carthage went to war.

By the time Livy and Dionysius were writing in the first century BC, Aeneas had become an important part of the foundation myth. Men like Julius Caesar and Augustus would have enjoyed hearing, no matter how fantastical, that Rome had links to the heroes of **Troy**. Aeneas' depiction in Greek pottery and poetry is of a strong warrior who wandered across the Ancient World.

> **KEY PLACES**
>
> **Carthage** a powerful city in Africa which controlled trade across the Mediterranean until the third century and lost control of the western Mediterranean to Rome after the Punic Wars
>
> **Troy** ancient civilisation at the heart of the mythical Trojan Wars, around the end of the thirteenth or early twelfth century

According to Livy (1.1), Aeneas and his army were Trojan refugees who travelled across the ancient world overcoming obstacles and trials. When Aeneas and his men arrived in Italy they stole food to survive. King Latinus tried to drive Aeneas out of Italy but formed a strong friendship after meeting him in battle. King Latinus offered Aeneas his daughter, Lavinia, as his wife.

Aeneas' marriage united the Trojans with King Latinus' tribe. To celebrate his marriage, Aeneas built a new settlement called Lavinium. Over time, Aeneas united his Trojan settlement with other local tribes from Latium to create a group of people known as the Latins. Livy continues by explaining how Aeneas' son, Ascanius, eventually created another settlement called Alba Longa. According to legend Romulus, the founder of Rome, descended from the kings of Alba Longa.

FIGURE 1.1
Greek amphora showing Aeneas saving his father from the destruction of Troy.

Part One Longer Period Study

FIGURE 1.2
Map of Latium and Rome's neighbours. Latium is modern day Lazio.

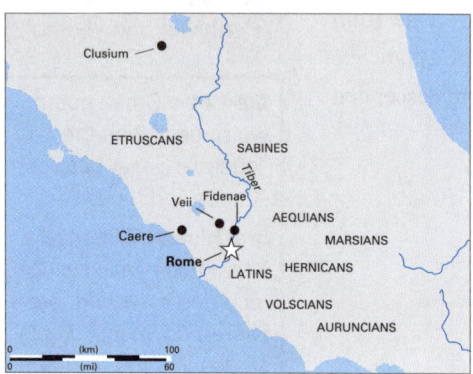

Aeneas supposedly founded Lavinium in the twelfth century BC. Archaeology has revealed only small settlements of **subsistence** farmers belonging to the **Apennine culture**. There is no conclusive archaeological evidence of the advanced civilisations described by Livy, in Lavinium or Alba Longa, during the Bronze Age. There are, however, examples of hill citadels or acropoli across Latium, such as the Luni Sul Mignone.

Lavinium, however, was a real city. It became an important town in Latium during the seventh to fifth century BC. Its foundation was probably part of the spread of **Villanovan civilisation** between the tenth and seventh century BC. It was not, therefore, created by Aeneas. The ancient historians, therefore, are using their limited knowledge of ancient Italy to recreate the past.

KEY INDIVIDUAL

Aeneas fictional King of Lavinium and survivor of the Trojan War. Ancestor of Romulus, the first king of Rome

subsistence farming when communities make just enough food to feed themselves and their families

Apennine culture central European and Italian culture from the late Bronze Age (fifteenth–fourteenth century BC)

Villanovan civilisation an early Iron Age culture of the tenth–sixth centuries BC which cremated their dead and were skilled in metal work, and which were destroyed by the Etruscan civilisation

S&C Alba Longa

Fabius Pictor probably created the chronology of the Roman kings. Aeneas was introduced to the foundation myth before Pictor was writing. Pictor's research would have shown a 400-year gap between the foundation of Lavinium in 1150 and Rome in 753.

We suspect that Fabius Pictor filled the 400-year gap by inventing Alba Longa and its kings.

FIGURE 1.3
Luni Sul Mignone. The remains of a Latium citadel c. 1300–800 BC.

HOW WAS ROME FOUNDED?

The Legend of Romulus and Remus

The legend, according to Livy (1.3–1.4) tells us that Romulus' grandfather, King Numitor of Alba Longa, was removed from power by his brother Amulius. Once Amulius became king, he murdered Numitor's son and made Numitor's daughter, Rhea, a **Vestal Virgin**. Her entry into the priesthood would prevent Rhea from having any children to challenge Amulius' control of Alba Longa. Pregnant Vestal Virgins would be executed along with their unborn children.

> In my opinion the gods intervened to save Numitor. Fate could not stop the world's mightiest empire from developing. Rhea Silva, Numitor's daughter, lost her virginity and gave birth to the twins Romulus and Remus. To avoid execution, she told Amulius that a god, Mars, had made her pregnant. In a fury Amulius imprisoned Rhea and ordered the twins be drowned in the river Tiber.
>
> Livy *The History of Rome* 1.4 (adapted)

The twins survived. Discovered by a she-wolf, the two boys were nursed until a poor shepherd Faustulus discovered them. Faustulus and his wife, Larentia, suspected they were royalty, but raised them as their own (Livy 1.5). When they became men, Romulus and Remus were admired and followed by the farmhands who worked on the Alban Hills. Eventually they began to ambush robbers and steal their loot to distribute amongst the poor.

One gang of robbers wanted revenge so they ambushed Romulus and Remus during a festival. Romulus fought his way free, but Remus was captured and taken to Amulius. The Alban king worked out that Remus was one of his brother's grandsons. If this was true, then his control of Alba Longa was under threat.

Romulus organised his friends into an army to free Remus. Romulus killed Amulius and restored king Numitor to his throne.

1.1 The Legendary Kings and the Origins of Rome, 753–617 BC

Study questions

Theme 4: Separating Myth from Reality

1 Summarise two of the reasons Aeneas was added to the foundation myth.

Read Livy's account of Aeneas, Livy 1.1–1.2

2 Summarise the main events in Aeneas story.

Vestal Virgin celibate female priestesses who played an important role in Roman society by protecting Rome's sacred flame

FIGURE 1.4
The Capitoline She-wolf with the boys Romulus and Remus.

FIGURE 1.5
The Bolsena Mirror, an Etruscan mirror from Porsena c. 340 BC.

The Bolsena Mirror

The Bolsena Mirror seems to show Romulus and Remus with the she-wolf. It is important because it suggests that the legend of Romulus and Remus was well established by the fourth century BC.

Porsena, however, was an Etruscan city not a Roman one. Was the She-wolf legend an Etruscan tradition which Rome adopted? Livy suggests Romulus adopted many Etruscan customs. Could Livy have mentioned this because he was aware of an Etruscan myth which was similar to the Romulus myth?

Some modern historians like Mazzoni and Wiseman believe this picture only looks like Romulus and Remus, but shows an unrelated Etruscan myth.

Part One Longer Period Study

Foundation of Rome

Romulus' success inspired the shepherds to follow the twins, and Numitor gave them land to create their own settlement. The twins could not decide who would create the city. Livy explains what happens next.

augury the Roman tradition of using birds to read the future, or seek divine support for a decision

> At this point the family curse – the desire for power – came between them. From innocent beginnings their relationship developed into conflict. There was no way to separate the twins, so they decided to use **augury** to decide who would build the city. Romulus went to the Palatine Hill and Remus to the Aventine. . . Remus' supporters claimed that they saw six vultures first. Then Romulus' supporters announced that he had seen twelve. . . Remus' supporters argued they had been chosen first, Romulus' supporters claimed they had seen more vultures. This war of words turned quickly to anger, and then to bloodshed. In the heat of the battle, Remus was killed. The more common story claims that Remus mocked his brother's claims and jumped over Romulus' incomplete city walls. This act angered Romulus who murdered his brother then stated,' This will be the fate of anyone who tries to cross my walls.' In this way Romulus became the sole king of Rome.
>
> Livy, *The History of Rome* 1.6–1.7 (adapted)

Was the Foundation Myth Made by Rome's Enemies?

Some modern historians have found this story problematic. Strasburger went so far as to argue that Rome's enemies created the foundation myth. Most historians believe this was unlikely and there is no surviving evidence to suggest the Ancient Romans disliked the story. Most accounts describe Romulus as a leader who put his city above family ties.

We will find out how Brutus, the founder of the Republic, behaved in a similar manner on p. 44. He executed his sons for threatening Rome.

Explore Further

Mary Beard's *SPQR* (pp. 57–60) provides an excellent overview to the story of Romulus and Remus.

For a detailed overview read Mary Beard's, *Confronting the Classics*, ch. 6, 'Who wanted Remus dead?'

Study questions

Theme 4: Separating Myth from Reality

Read Livy's and Dionysius' accounts of the conflict between Romulus and Remus

Livy 1.6–1.7
Dionysius 1.85–1.88

1 Summarise Livy's and Dionysius' version of events. Mention
   - the removal of Numitor by Amulius
   - Rhea's pregnancy
   - Romulus' and Remus' upbringing
   - the removal of Amulius
   - the creation of Rome
2 In what ways are the two versions different?

1.1 The Legendary Kings and the Origins of Rome, 753–617 BC

IS THERE ANY EVIDENCE TO SUPPORT THE FOUNDATION MYTH?

Historians can say confidently that there was no Romulus and Remus.

Recent excavations at the **Roman Forum** have revealed that Rome is much older than 753 BC. The findings, examined by the modern historian Fulminante, suggest that the first Roman settlers arrived in the thirteenth or twelfth century BC.

Romulus, reputedly, founded Rome in the eighth century. However, by this time Rome was already a large town, going through a process of **urbanisation**.

KEY PLACE

Roman Forum the oldest market place in Rome

urbanisation development of a town as people move from the countryside to take up crafts and trades

Theme 4: Separating Myth from Reality: The Lapis Niger Stele

FIGURE 1.6
The Lapis Niger Stele, c. 570–550 BC. The word 'recei' is in the second column from the right, read PECEI from bottom to top.

An inscription found upon a **stele** under the Lapis Niger, or Black Stone, offers very convincing evidence that there were Roman kings. Upon this stele, which was found in the Roman Forum, is the word 'recei' which links to the word rex or king.

The stele is dated from 570–550 BC, and it is part of the earliest known sanctuary in Rome from the sixth or even the seventh century. The stele declares that the site is sacred, and that the king and his assistant played an important role in religious processions. As one third of the stele is damaged we cannot complete the inscription.

Historians believe that the sanctuary was possibly used by the king to perform rituals before a meeting at the **Comitium** or a festival at the Roman Forum. While the Lapis Niger proves that Rome had kings, it does not prove that Romulus or the other legendary kings existed.

stele/stela (pl. **stelae**) an upright stone or wooden column bearing an inscription or design. Usually used as a gravestone

comitium the open-air space where Roman citizens would meet to discuss important matters

ACTIVITY

Some historians have claimed that the Lapis Niger helps us understand the role of kings in Ancient Rome.

Using the information on the previous page and your own research complete this table:

Useful for helping us understand	Its limitations and problems

ROMULUS 753–714 BC

Romulus' story is legendary for many reasons:

- The chronology is not accurate. Rome was probably founded in the twelfth or thirteenth century. The Roman historians claim that Rome was created on 21 April 753 BC. A very precise date chosen for religious rather than historical reasons.
- The claim that only four kings ruled between 753 and 617 BC is highly unlikely, especially if we consider the violent nature of the age.
- Fabius Pictor and other Roman historians believed Rome's systems were added to over time. Nothing was removed. The Republic kept Romulus' systems. It just replaced the king with magistrates. In reality, the systems the literary tradition described were probably developed over a greater period of time.

POLITICAL INITIATIVES

We know that Romulus is legendary and did not create the Senate, patron-client system, the assembly or any laws to govern the people. You might be wondering why we are studying a legend, not historical fact.

Primarily, the legend of Romulus tells us a lot about the spirit of the Roman people. Historians, study the story because we do not have a better account and it tells us how the ancients believed Rome's traditions and systems developed.

This is one of the reasons why there are so many differences between Dionysius' account of an advanced political system based upon Greek traditions and Livy's basic no-nonsense system.

MODERN PARALLELS   Wikipedia

The development of the foundation myth over time is similar to the development of Wikipedia. Wikipedia is open-source, which means that anyone can add or change an entry. That is why Wikipedia should never be considered to be accurate, but rather as a starting point.

Historians use Roman historians like Livy and Dionysius in the same way. They might begin with their account but then they use archaeology to check its accuracy.

1.1 The Legendary Kings and the Origins of Rome, 753–617 BC

What did the Roman historians claim Romulus created?

Asylum: Roman citizenship had been granted to many different cultures by the third century BC. It should not be surprising that Rome's concept of citizenship was attributed to Romulus. Dionysius claims that Romulus built a temple in 'the space between the two groves' for asylum seekers wanting to escape tyrannies There is little doubt that Dionysius' asylum seekers were Greek refugees. In contrast, Livy claims Romulus invited criminals and outcasts.

Safety: Before building his 'city' Romulus built walls and fortified the Palatine hill. Foundation ditches for wooden walls have been found in Rome which date from the eighth century BC. Some have suggested that this supports the existence of Romulus. Historians refute this. City walls were essential in the eighth century BC. The discovery of Roman walls does not prove the existence of Romulus, but it does support the urbanisation of Rome.

Representation: The most far-fetched claim of the Roman historians was the creation of a complex system of political representation. At the heart of this system was the patron-client system. One hundred of Rome's best men, called patriarchs, would act as patrons offering leadership and guidance to the rest of Rome's population, the plebeians, who would serve as clients. In exchange for legal protection, clients would perform tasks, such as fighting under the command of the patriarchs. In this way, Romulus was supposed to have created a form of representative government, 200 years before Greek democracy.

> Romulus decreed that the patricians would help him run Rome. They would become priests, magistrates and judges. Romulus declared that the plebeians would become farmers and tradesmen. They did not have the intelligence or the free-time to become involved in public office.
>
> Dionysius, *Roman Antiquities* 2.9 (adapted)

The Senate: One hundred patriarchs also served in Romulus' Senate. They advised the king and were appointed for life. These patriarchs would give the king an insight into the concerns and needs of his people. Livy tells us Romulus struggled to find enough patriarchs to serve him. The king remained the most important member of Romulus' government. He ruled by **decree**, declared war and negotiated with other kingdoms. To show his power over ordinary people, Romulus adopted Etruscan customs such as **lictors**.

Livy's description of Romulus is interesting because he tells a story about how the Senate murdered Romulus because he was acting like a **tyrant** (1.16). The Senate is portrayed by Livy as an important check to the kings power. After Romulus' death, the Senate decided they would appoint one of their number to act as an interrex. The interrex would, supposedly, manage the appointment of the next king. In this way, Livy claims, the Senate gave **imperium** to future kings.

Democracy: Dionysius' account is confused. On one hand, he describes Rome's small population. Dionysius then describes an advanced political system which required a very

---

Senate a council or assembly of Rome's 'best men' during the time of the kings; became a council of retired magistrates who advised consuls from 509, and from 27 advised emperors. Controlled Rome's finances during the Republic

rule by decree passing laws and judgements without listening to others or to previous laws, which suggests a leader or king has total power

lictors Roman bodyguards who protected the king or consul and carried fasces, which symbolised power

tyrant king or leader who abuses their powers to rule unfairly (the original meaning was not negative, however, and simply meant a ruler with sole power)

imperium in Ancient Rome this gave kings the power to rule or govern. In the Republic, it gave consuls the power to control the army

Part One Longer Period Study

> **Study questions**
>
> Theme 1: Political Change
>
> Read Livy's account of Romulus' political initiatives
>
> Livy 1.8
>
> 1. Summarise the different political systems introduced by Romulus?
> 2. In your opinion, do you think Livy admires Romulus' political initiatives?

> **EXPLORE FURTHER**
>
> Read Dionysius' account of Romulus' political initiatives in Book 2.4–2.14.
>
> - Identify the similarities and differences with Livy's accounts.
> - Can you explain why they might be different?

large population. For example, he claims that Romulus divided the people into three tribes. Each tribe was then divided further into ten curiae or sub-regions which sent elected representatives to a council called the Comitia Curiata (see p. 32 – Servian Reforms). Within these divisions the patricians and plebeians were to be allocated jobs and duties.

Livy's account is much simpler. After Romulus agreed to share power with the Sabine king Tatius, Rome was divided into thirty curiae. Livy does not mention the Comitia Curiata until the Sack of Rome in 390 BC. He does, however, imply political participation during Priscus' selection as king and Servius Tullius' reforms.

Under Romulus and the other kings each citizen, regardless of status, had one vote.

Livy, *The History of Rome* 1.43

Some historians doubt if the Comitia Curiata ever existed, and it appears as if Livy struggled with the idea too.

RELIGIOUS INITIATIVES

Livy suggested that Romulus adopted the customs of local cities such as Alba Longa. Dionysius claims that Romulus assessed Greek practices and chose the best traditions for his new city. Neither of these assumptions are correct. Archaeology suggests that Roman religion developed over a long period of time influenced by many other cultures. These may have included Greek, Etruscan, Apennine, Latial Villanovan and urnfield cultures.

FIGURE 1.7
Map showing the location of Italian cities near the Tiber c. seventh century BC. The Villanovan culture influence was north of the river Tiber. The Latial or Latin culture influenced cities to the south of the river Tiber. Rome appears to have been influenced by both cultures.

The Casa Romuli or 'Hut of Romulus' on the Palatine hill, was shaped like a Villanovan hut. Its existence illustrated the influence of northern cultures upon Rome. Archaeology seems to suggest that by 800 BC Rome had adopted the more advanced burial rites of the Latial culture from the south of the Tiber.

Livy outlines Romulus' religion in a few sentences. Romulus, Livy claims, built a temple to Jupiter to commemorate military success; (1.12) was influenced by the Greek legend of Heracles (1.7) and Romulus' transformation into a god (1.16.)

Dionysius, in comparison, describes a complex Greek system of religion, with tribal customs and religious ceremonies.

FIGURE 1.8
Villanovan culture funerary urn, which was based upon their simple mud and straw homes.

> **Study questions**
> Theme 2: Social and Religious Change
>
> **1** Summarise what archaeology tells us about the development of religion in Rome.
>
> Read Livy Book 1.7, 10, 12 and 16
> Dionysius 2.21–2.23
>
> **2** Summarise the religious initiatives described by:
>   ○ Livy
>   ○ Dionysius
> **3** Summarise the main differences between the two versions.

MILITARY INITIATIVES

Dionysius explains how Romulus organised Rome's army.

> Whenever the king needed to lead an army from Rome, he did not need a tribune to be selected from the tribes, or a centurion by the centuries, or a commander of the horse. Nor did Romulus need to personally divide the army into centuries or tell the men their post. Such was his organisation that when Romulus gave instructions to the tribunes, they passed them to the centurions and so on. Romulus' army was so well organised that when he summoned his army they appeared with arms at the designated post and time.
>
> Dionysius, *Roman Antiquities* 2.14 (adapted)

According to Dionysius the **military tribune** organised the call to arms for each tribe. A **centurion** would command each unit, called a **century**, of the Roman army. Typically, between sixty and one hundred men. This system is described as efficient and well organised.

In reality the armies of this period would have been small bands of men.

The **celeres** are described as Romulus' most loyal soldiers and they acted as his bodyguard in battle. Over time, a celeres unit may have developed, but it was a cavalry unit drawn from the **eques**.

military tribune men who organised military service (not to be confused with the **plebeian tribunes** of later Roman history)

centurion a commander of a century

century a unit in the Roman army. It is unlikely that this system was in place until the Republic

celeres a Roman cavalry unit believed to have developed from Romulus' bodyguard

eques, equites (pl.) a social class named because they were men who received a horse from the Roman state and formed the Roman cavalry

It is likely that the Roman historians used legions, centuries and celeres units to describe Romulus' army, because these terms were more familiar to the educated Roman elite.

We suspect that no details about eighth-century Roman tactics were available to the Roman historians, so historians like Livy relied upon much later battles for inspiration for their stories. For example, Livy's description of Rome's war with the city of Fidenae contains some of the same tactics used by the Carthaginian leader, Hannibal, during his invasion of Italy in the third century BC.

'RAPE' OF THE SABINE WOMEN

Livy (1.9) tells us that the greatest obstacle facing Romulus was the lack of women in his new city. To solve the problem, Romulus appealed to his neighbours for help. He wanted to arrange marriage between some of his leading men and their women. They all refused. Romulus organised a festival with games and invited many neighbouring cities including the Sabines. During the festival Rome abducted young Sabine women. It is important to note that the word 'rapio' or 'rape' does not mean the same as the modern word. In fact, it means 'I seize.'

Livy (1.10) then suggested Romulus visited as many of the women to reassure them. He told them that they would be married and enjoy the wealth of their husbands. Apparently, this pleased the women and they settled down in their new home.

The Sabines were outraged and prepared for war. However, the Sabine king, Titus Tatius, spent nine months preparing for war and creating alliances. Conveniently just enough time for the Sabine women to have children.

One of Titus' allies, the city of Caenina, did not wait for Titus and **plundered** the outskirts of Rome. Romulus marched into Caenina and massacred their army. After killing the leader Acro, Romulus reputedly began the tradition of spoila opima, the first spoils. He then built a temple to Jupiter Feretrius to display the armour, weapons and riches which made up these spoils. No archaeological evidence remains of the temple.

When Rome was invaded by the Sabines, much of the city was taken. Rome's leading general, Hostius Hostilius, was murdered and the Roman army panicked. Romulus

plunder to loot or steal at a time of war

Study questions
Theme 3: Impact of Warfare and Military Change

1 Summarise the key events of Romulus' defeat of the Caenina.
2 Summarise the key events of the Sabine invasion of Rome.
3 How does Romulus use his victory over the Caenina for propaganda purposes?

Study questions
Theme 3: Impact of Warfare and Military Change

Read Dionysius' description of how Romulus' army is organised
Dionysius Book 2.14 (or the extract above)

1 Summarise the key features of Romulus' army.

Read Livy's account of Romulus' war with Fidenae
Livy 1.14–1.15

2 Make a list of the tactics used by Romulus to defeat the city of Fidenae.

> **Study questions**
>
> Theme 2: Social and Religious Change
>
> Read Livy's account of the Rape of the Sabine women
> Livy 1.9–1.10 and 1.13
>
> 1 Why was the lack of women a problem for Rome?
> 2 What did Romulus do to reassure the abducted women?
> 3 In what ways does Livy describe the Sabine women?
> 4 Who shares power with Romulus after the Sabine war? Do you think this increases or decreases Romulus' reputation as a great king?

prayed to Jupiter, and retook the citadel with a small group of men. As Romulus regrouped, the Sabine women entered the battlefield with their children.

> If you cannot accept the ties between Romans and Sabines created by our marriage, then turn your weapons on us. If Rome wins we will be orphans, if the Sabines win then we will be widows.
>
> Livy, *The History of Rome* 1.13 (adapted)

The two cities agreed to end the conflict. Romulus agreed to share power with Titus Tatius. To cement this relationship, the Forum was built in the space where the Palatine Hill and Capitoline Hill met. Many Sabines became Roman citizens.

Archaeology does not support this story. The Roman Forum was developed as a meeting place between the tenth and eighth century BC. The marshy area between Palatine and Capitoline had previously been used as a necropolis or burial place. Discoveries in 2009 suggest that construction took place as early as the eleventh century to channel water from an **aquifer** under the Capitoline Hill.

FIGURE 1.9
The Sabine women stop the war between their husbands and their families.

aquifer a rock formation which can be used to supply water

NUMA 715–673 BC

Numa's appointment as king

In the foundation myth, Numa is the king of Rome who introduced religion and civilisation. When he died Rome had been at peace for over forty years.

> By introducing the gods into the government and daily life of Rome, Numa was able to change the character of the Roman people. They no longer concentrated on warfare, but instead dedicated their lives to the gods and filled their hearts with brotherly love. As a consequence, Rome's neighbours believed that it would anger the gods to attack a city which was so devoted to the gods.
>
> Livy, *The History of Rome* 1.21

FIGURE 1.10
Numa Pompilius, as imagined on a Roman coin minted by Gnaeus Calpurnius Piso during the reign of Emperor Augustus.

Part One Longer Period Study

> **interregnum** a period of time between two reigns when the normal government is suspended
>
> **piety** being religious

According to Livy (1.17), the death of Romulus provided the Senate with the opportunity to take power for themselves. This period became known as the **interregnum.** For one year the Senate tried to rule, but it caused civil unrest because it served the needs of the patricians.

To end civil disorder, the Senate chose Numa. He was a Sabine nobleman who had a reputation for **piety** and justice.

NUMA'S RELIGIOUS INITIATIVES

> **Study questions**
> Theme 1: Political Change
>
> Read Livy's account of how Numa became king Livy 1.17–1.18
>
> 1 Summarise the main reasons the interregnum failed to rule Rome.
> 2 Summarise the reasons Livy gives for Numa's appointment as king.

Dionysius emphasises Numa's piety. According to his account, Numa married a goddess named Egeria. She advised him how to govern Rome with the help of religion.

Livy summarises Numa's relationship with Egeria.

> There was a grove watered by a fountain of never-failing water that poured from a shaded grotto in its centre. Numa often made solitary visits there to meet, as he said, with the goddess; he consecrated this grove to the **Camenae** because it was there that they conferred with his spouse Egeria.
>
> Livy, *The History of Rome* 1.21

Numa established several priesthoods and religious officials.

> **Camenae** in Roman mythology they were the goddesses of childbirth, fountains with the ability to tell the future. Vestal Virgins were involved in festivals to celebrate them
>
> **flamen** a Roman priest who performed rituals for a particular god
>
> **pontiff** a Roman high priest who regulated religious practices

- Numa allegedly created a priesthood for Mars, Romulus and Quirinus. Quirinus was Romulus' divine name and Mars was Romulus father. The idea of a religious trinity including the son, father and a spirit would be borrowed by other religions including Christianity.
- Romulus also created the **flamen** Dialis as the priest of Jupiter. This priest would make sure that the king performed his sacred duties even in times of war.
- Numa created the **pontiff**. This new official would be chosen from the Senate and looked after religious practices in Rome.
- He introduced the Vestal Virgins into Rome and set aside public funds to make sure their temple was well managed.
- The archaeological record of this period is sketchy at best. There is some evidence that Etruscan ideas began to influence Roman religion in the sixth century BC, at least fifty years after Numa died.
- Livy also suggested Numa created a lunar calendar. Mommsen and Cornell both believe that there may have been a seventh century BC lunar calendar as urbanisation increased literacy and scientific thought.

Numa's diplomacy

Livy claimed (1.21) that Numa ended conflict with religion. It is difficult to imagine that this would encourage all of Rome's neighbours to make peace with Rome.

Dionysius suggests that poor men from the asylum were planning a revolt. Rather than crushing the plotters, Numa gave the homeless men some of Romulus' land to end the conflict.

1.1 The Legendary Kings and the Origins of Rome, 753–617 BC

As you will discover in Section 4, this reads like a story from the Conflict of the Orders. Its inclusion in Numa's reign is completely **anachronistic** and gives the impression eighth century BC Rome is similar to Rome during the Republic.

Dionysius suggests Numa improved the status of the Roman Forum by placing the hearth of the Vestal Virgins there. He also divided Rome into districts and appointed an official to inspect them. Any labourer or worker neglecting their land would be reported so that the king could intervene. Plutarch, another Roman historian writing in the first century, tells us that Numa established blacksmiths, musicians and other crafts within the city. This is partially supported by the evidence of urbanisation around the Roman Forum.

Another element of Numa's story is the construction of the Temple of Janus. Its doors were to be kept shut during times of peace and left open when Rome was at war. Livy suggests (1.19) that the temple doors were always open except during Numa's reign, after the First Punic War and when Augustus ended the civil war. While archaeologists cannot find any remains of the temple. Livy tell us that it did exist in the first century BC.

> **anachronistic** a description of an event which uses features or people who are not alive or available at that time

> **Study questions**
> Theme 2: Social and Religious Change
>
> Read Livy's account of Numa's religious initiatives Livy 1.19–1.20
>
> 1 Summarise the ways Numa uses religion to control the Roman people.
> 2 Summarise the religious initiatives introduced by Numa.

> **Study question**
> Theme 1: Political Change
>
> Read Livy's account of Numa's use of diplomacy
> Livy 1.19
>
> Summarise the ways Numa makes Rome peaceful.

EXAM TIP: CHANGE

In your exam, Question 4 will be linked to a source. You will need to use the source and your own knowledge, in combination, to show the extent of change.
The activity box will help you develop the skills you need to answer questions on change in the exam.

ACTIVITY

Reread pp. 11–19 on Romulus and Numa. Complete the table below:

Characteristics of the Roman people during Romulus' reign	Characteristics of the Roman people during Numa's reign

To complete the table, identify the different ways Livy describes the attitudes of the Roman people to war, women, religion and each other.

- Discuss with the rest of your class the extent of change introduced by Numa. Is the amount of change the same, or do some attitudes change more than others?

FIGURE 1.11
Roman sesterce showing the temple of Janus with its doors shut.

TULLUS HOSTILIUS 673–642 BC AND ANCUS MARCIUS 642–617 BC

The third and fourth legendary kings introduced the last pieces of Rome's heritage. The Roman historians use Tullus to reintroduce Rome's military character. Ancus, on the other hand, is used to reconcile Numa's civilising influence with Tullus' military attitude.

Who was Tullus Hostilius?

Tullus Hostilius was depicted as a dynamic and inspirational leader who shook Rome from 'idleness'. Tullus was presented as more 'aggressive than Romulus'.

During Numa's reign, the Etruscan army and navy had expanded. After Numa's death Rome's neighbours prepared for war. Tullus helped Rome meet the Etruscan challenge.

Archaeological records suggest the Etruscan culture was expanding during the seventh century BC. It is possible Numa was used to describe a period of peace in Rome, while Tullus a period of war.

War with Alba

A border dispute with Alba was to become Tullus' first test. The Romans and the Albans had been close allies for some time. The Alban king, Gaius Cluilius, wanted compensation for the damage caused by Roman cattle raiders. Both kings refused to compromise and their armies were mobilised for war.

When the Albans set up camp on the outskirts of Rome, their king, Cluilius, died. A dictator called Mettius was appointed in his place. Mettius attempted diplomacy. He reminded Tullus that their two cities shared a common Trojan heritage. It was in both cities interests to avoid war.

The story of the Three Albans

Mettius and Tullus agreed to settle their differences with a battle between two teams of triplets. The Horatii would fight for Rome and the Curiatii for Alba. Livy's (1.25) exciting account of the battle describes how Rome quickly lost two of their triplets. When all seemed lost, the final Roman triplet isolated each of the three remaining Alban triplets so that he could kill them one by one. This handed Rome victory and control of Alba.

Mettius did not accept defeat and formed a secret alliance with the Etruscan cities of Veii and Fidenae (Livy 1.27–1.28). Mettius and the Albans lined up with Tullus to fight the Etruscans, but when the battle started the Albans did not join the Romans on the battlefield. Tullus was aware of Mettius' betrayal and inspired his army to defeat the Etruscans.

After the battle, Tullus exposed Mettius' plan to destroy Rome and executed him by tying the Sabine leader between four chariots which ripped his body apart.

Alba Longa, as we have already seen, was invented to link Aeneas to the Roman foundation story. With Mettius' death, the Roman historians conveniently destroyed the fictional city of Alba Longa and resettled the Albans in Rome.

1.1 The Legendary Kings and the Origins of Rome, 753–617 BC

> **Study questions**
>
> Theme 3: Impact of War and Military Change
>
> Read Livy's account of the Three Albans
> Livy 1.22–1.25, 1.27–1.29
>
> 1 What does Livy tell us caused the war between Rome and Alba Longa?
> 2 Why does Mettius claim Rome and Alba should not fight?
> 3 Summarise the key events from the story of the Three Albans. Underline the sections which make the story more exciting.
> 4 Summarise the key events from the war with the cities of Veii and Fidenae.
> 5 Summarise how Alba Longa becomes a part of Rome.

Tullus' death

Tullus kept fighting and achieved many great victories including the Battle of Malitosa Forest against the Sabines. When plague struck Rome, Tullus refused to allow his armies to rest and take care of their families. This led to unrest and division in Rome. Many people openly criticised Tullus and praised Numa's peaceful nature. When he failed to perform his religious duties correctly, the gods punished him and killed him with a thunderbolt. His reign had ended after thirty-two years.

Tullus' legal initiatives

Livy (1.26) also shares an important story which introduces the idea of a right to an appeal. After the Battle of the Horatii and the Curiatii, the surviving Roman triplet murdered his sister. His sister had been betrothed to one of the murdered Alban triplets. According to Livy, Tullus avoided passing judgement on the young man and asked two patrician judges to hear his case. Both found him guilty, but in the face of civil unrest the judges allowed his case to be heard by the people. He was freed on appeal.

Tullus' political initiatives

When Tullus became king, he gave land to homeless citizens and built new farms. Tullus also expanded Rome with his victories over Alba and the Sabines. He built a new settlement on the Caelian hill for the Albans and created new tribes, or districts, for each of the Alban groups including the Curiatii. To accommodate the new enlarged Senate he built a new Senate House called the Curia Hostilia.

> **Study questions**
>
> Theme 1: Political Change
>
> Read Livy's political and legal initiatives
> Livy 1.26 and 1.30
>
> 1 Summarise the murder trial of the surviving Horatii triplet.
> 2 In what way does Livy describe Tullus' character in this story.
> 3 Summarise Tullus' political changes mentioned in Book 1.30.

Ancus' character

Livy (1.32) tells us that Ancus realised he needed to adopt the character of Romulus and his grandfather, Numa. The Roman people were in need of religious guidance after plague and war, but they were also needed a warrior to lead them against Rome's enemies.

Part One Longer Period Study

Ancus' achievements

Ancus told his pontiff, Gaius Papirus, to publish laws and religious rites on oak boards across the city. If Numa's teachings were to be re-introduced, then the citizens needed to know their responsibilities.

Ancus also gave the people a greater say in foreign affairs. **Envoys** would visit the enemy and demand justice. If justice was denied, then the envoy would ask each tribe to vote. If a majority of tribes agreed, then war would be declared.

Ancus successfully defended Rome. He invited citizens who lived outside the city to settle on the Aventine hill. He captured the Latin city of Politorium and destroyed it so that it could not be used in the future to attack Rome. He destroyed the Latin threat in the Battle of Medullia.

Ancus invited the Latins to become Roman citizens. The Admurciae district between the Aventine and Palatine was created to help them settle in the city.

Rome was also extended over the river Tiber. A bridge was built to connect Janiculum hill to the city and a wall built around it. Very few settled here during Ancus' reign, but it made Rome more secure from attack. These new fortifications protected the city from attack by the river. The port of Ostia and a salt works were also supposed to have been built on the Tiber at this time.

> **envoys** representatives sent between cities or countries to improve relationships or prevent conflict

> **Study question**
> Read Livy's account of Ancus' reign
> Livy 1.32–1.33
>
> Summarise Ancus':
> ○ military achievements
> ○ political achievements
> ○ religious achievements
> ○ expansion of Rome

EXAM TIP: SIGNIFICANCE

In your exam, Question 4 may ask a question which will require you to assess the significance of an event or person. To answer this question effectively you will need to assess whether the event or person was a turning point or had a major impact upon an aspect of Rome's history.

These are usually iceberg questions. This means that you need to find other factors which also led to a significant change in the same aspect of Rome's history. You will then have to compare these factors and make a judgement about how significant the person or event identified by the question is.

Question four will be linked to a source. Make sure you use the source **and** your own knowledge to make a judgement about its significance.

Your conclusion should state 'how far' it was significant.

The activity will help you develop the skills you need to answer questions on similarity and difference in an exam.

ACTIVITY

Revisit the four legendary kings on pp. 11–21. Choose four significant contributions from each king. Complete the table below.

Romulus	Numa	Hostilius	Ancus

As a class discuss who you think was the most significant king from this period.

1.1 The Legendary Kings and the Origins of Rome, 753–617 BC

TIMESPAN REVIEW

Boost your knowledge

Describe:

a. Livy's approach to history as shown in the Preface
b. the foundation myth including Aeneas, Romulus and Remus
c. Romulus' reign including his political and religious intiatives, military record and the 'rape' of the Sabine women
d. Numa's, Tullus' and Ancus' reigns

Stretch your understanding

Explain:

a. what Aeneas, Romulus and Remus tell us about Roman values
b. if Romulus was a great king
c. how Numa civilised Rome
d. the changes introduced by Tullus and Ancus

PRACTICE QUESTIONS

1 a. Identify **two** initiatives which were said to have been introduced by Ancus Marcius which improved Rome. [2]
   b. Identify **two** ways Romulus is said to have organised the people of Rome. [2]
2. Outline how Tullus Hostilius is said to have destroyed Alba Longa. [6]

1.2 The Etruscan Kings, 616–509 BC

> **TIMESPAN OVERVIEW**
>
> - the manner in which each monarch gained power
> - the enlargement of the equites and nobility to strengthen the Etruscan kings
> - Servius Tullius' reforms
> - the development of the city of Rome
> - the influence of omens ascribed to Servius Tullius
> - the popularity of the Tarquins among the plebeians
> - the tyranny of Tarquinius Superbus
> - the reorganisation of the army
> - the political and economic significance of Tarquinius Priscus and Servius Tullius' victories
> - the impact of Tarquinius Superbus' military recordthe nature and origin of the historical evidence for this period, including both the literary and archaeological sources
>
> **There are no prescribed sources for this component, but the following suggested readings and archaeological evidence are covered in this chapter:**
>
> - Livy, *The History of Rome*, Book 1, sections 34–45, 47–58
> - Dionysius, *Roman Antiquities*, Book 3, sections 48, 67–68; Book 4, sections 21, 43–44
>
> - Apollo of Veii

According to the foundation story, an Etruscan, Lucius Tarquinius Priscus, became the fifth king of Rome. He began a series of reforms and changes to Rome which would enlarge the size of the city and its army. His adopted son Servius Tullius continued Priscus' work and also introduced the census to radically reform the way Roman society and its army was organised. Servius, however, was unable to complete his work when one of Priscus' children, Tarquinius Superbus, removed him from power. Superbus may have increased Rome's status through an ambitious building programme and successful wars, but he also ruled as a tyrant. The nature of his rule would eventually lead to his downfall.

WHO WERE THE ETRUSCAN KINGS?

Etruscan culture had a significant impact upon Italy between the eighth and sixth centuries. The Greek historian, Herodotus, claimed that the Etruscans were settlers who had travelled from the Near East to colonise Italy.

Modern archaeology tells us that the Etruscan's belonged to Central Europe's **urnfield culture**. The Near East influence Herodotus identified came from Greek traders who brought the **orientalising culture** into Italy.

During the orientalising period, the Etruscans adopted Greek art, architecture and burial practices. The Etruscan's also developed a far-reaching trade network which had links with Egypt, Greece, Phoenicia and, of course, Rome. These trade links might explain why Livy believed Etruscan practices, like lictors and Vestal Virgins, were introduced by Romulus in the eighth century.

> **urnfield culture** a culture that spread from central Europe into Italy before the ninth century; its name comes from the custom of cremating the dead and placing their ashes in urns
>
> **orientalising culture** during the late eighth century, art and technology from places like Syria in the Near East influenced Greek culture, as can be seen in the pottery and metalwork of the period

FIGURE 1.12

Map showing Etruscan expansion between 750 and 500.

> **Reassessing the Value of the Literary Tradition**
>
> Many modern historians believe Demaratus was added to the foundation myth in the fourth century at a time when Roman historians were looking for links to Greek history.
>
> Livy was suspicious of some of these traditions. He confidently dismissed the claim Pythagoras educated Numa. Livy correctly (1.18) identified that both men lived a century apart.
>
> Zevi suggests that some of these Greek links may have some historical value. Zevi, for example, has investigated the story of Demaratus using Greek sources. He identified a number of references to a Demaratus-like character who brought Greek culture to the Etruscans. He also discovered some evidence exploring the seizure of Tarquinius Superbus' personal wealth by Rome.
>
> None of the evidence is conclusive, but it does suggest that historians cannot be completely dismissive about the literary tradition.

Origins of the Etruscan kings

The Etruscan kings were Greeks who came from the Etruscan city, Tarquinii.

Livy claims the fifth king of Rome descended from Demaratus who fled Corinth in 657. Demaratus then created a trade empire in Tarquinii.

According to the story, Demaratus brought Greek craftsmen, engineers and traders to Italy. The archaeological record, certainly agrees with this statement. Etruscan culture spread in the seventh century.

Demaratus' role is less clear. See Stretch and Challenge box.

> **EXPLORE FURTHER**
>
> For a good introduction to the Etruscan kings, Mary Beard's *SPQR*, pp. 109–24 is an excellent starting point.

TARQUINIUS PRISCUS 616–578

Priscus' succession

When Demaratus died his eldest son, Lucumo, inherited his wealth. Livy suggested that he could not stand for office because he was half-Greek. Lucumo knew that Numa, a Sabine, had become king of Rome after winning the support of the Senate. Lucumo's wife, Tanaquil, was an Etruscan noblewoman who encouraged him to move to Rome.

According to Livy (1.34), when Lucumo saw the gates of Rome an eagle flew down and snatched his cap. After circling above Lucumo for some time, it then placed it back on his head. Tanaquil, who had experience of interpreting omens, saw this as an opportunity for her husband to secure the throne of Rome.

Dionysius continues the story.

Lucumo was overjoyed at the omen and immediately sought an audience with king Ancus Marcius. Whereby he told the king that he had more money than any man would need, and would be honoured to give much of his wealth to the Roman people. Ancus was delighted by Lucumo's gesture and assigned him and his followers to one of the curiae, and a plot of land to establish his estate. Ancus suggested that he adopt a Roman name. Lucumo agreed and became Lucius Tarquinius Priscus. He quickly won the hearts of the Roman people and the king. He was a great horseman and fought bravely in the wars he funded for the king. He had good judgement and won the support of the patricians and plebeians by investing so much money and affection into his adopted city.

Dionysius, Roman Antiquities 3.48 (adapted)

Dionysius suggested that Priscus' charitable nature and military record helped him become the fifth king of Rome. In contrast, Livy (1.34–1.35) suggested **ambitus** was significant.

> **ambitus** used by ancient Romans to describe behaviour of men who used political corruption or bribery to gain power

Ambitus or ambitio was used by the ancient Romans to describe political corruption. The Latin word ambitus developed into the English word ambition. Anyone guilty of ambitus was using bribery or unethical persuasion to win power. Livy frequently used ambitus to explain the motivation of his characters.

In the foundation myth, Priscus is associated with ambitus for two reasons: **largesse** and the removal of Ancus' children from Rome to clear his way to power. Of these two reasons, Livy's main concern is that Priscus used his father's wealth to win the support of the Roman people, in particular the plebeians.

> **largesse** giving gifts or money to people

Ancus' children would eventually murder Priscus many years later in an attempt to seize control of Rome from a foreigner.

> **Study questions**
> Theme 1: Political Change
>
> Read Livy's account of Priscus' succession to the Roman throne
> Livy 1.34–1.35
>
> 1 Summarise the events which led to Priscus becoming king of Rome.
> 2 List any examples of ambitus or largesse from Livy's account.

Priscus' reforms

FIGURE 1.13
Second century AD depiction of a chariot race which may have been introduced into the Circus Maximus during Priscus' reign.

Political change

Livy and Dionysius described a number of important political initiatives.

- Priscus added one hundred of his men to the Senate to consolidate his power. Livy (1.35) describes the hundred men as 'lesser families'. Dionysius, on the other hand, presents the hundred men as good warriors or excellent administrators.
- The Circus Maximus was built by Priscus with the spoils of war. Livy hinted that the stadium had political significance. Priscus granted a number of patricians the right to build their own twelve feet high fori or seating areas.
- At the age of eighty Priscus was murdered by Ancus Marcius' sons.

Social change

- The construction of the Circus Maximus allowed Priscus to increase the number of festivals and games in Rome. Etruscan boxing and chariot racing were among the entertainments provided.
- The Forum was extended. Shops and colonnades were also constructed. Archaeological findings agree. The Roman Forum underwent a period of expansion at this time. Whether this was because of an Etruscan influence or Etruscan trade is not clear.
- The construction of an open-air sewer was commenced by Priscus. This would become the Cloaca Maximus under his son Superbus. Archaeology supports this. The Etruscans were excellent engineers and had developed technology to improve sanitation in their cities.

Religious change

- Priscus increased the number of Vestal Virgins to six.
- Priscus introduced harsher punishments for Vestals who broke their vow of chastity.

FIGURE 1.14
Apollo of Veii. Terracotta sculpture by the Etruscan artist Vulca from c. 550–520.

> **S & C** **Greek influence on Roman Religion**
>
> There is good evidence that Greek religion was beginning to permeate into Italian and, potentially, Roman religion by the sixth century.
>
> The worship of Apollo is a very good example. He was one of the few Roman gods who shared the same name as the Greek equivalent. Apollo was worshipped for many reasons throughout the Ancient World such as prophecy and medicine.
>
> We have evidence that the cult of Apollo spread across Italy in the sixth century. Both the Temple of Apollo at Veii and Pompeii are believed to have been built at that time. In Rome, the earliest surviving temple to Apollo is to Apollo Medicus from 433. His temple was built after a plague had devastated Rome.

> **Study questions**
> Theme 1 and 2: Political, and Social and Religious Changes
>
> Read Livy's account of Priscus' reforms
> Livy 1.35–1.36
>
> 1 Summarise Priscus':
>   o political initiatives
>   o social initiatives
>   o religious initiatives
> 2 Complete the following table:
>
> | Priscus' initiatives which gave him more power | Priscus' initiatives which were introduced to improve Rome |
> |---|---|
> | | |

> **ACTIVITY**
> Look again at question 2 in the box on the left. Some initiatives may fit into both categories. Discuss, as a class, why this might be the case.
> Did Priscus' improvements make him more powerful? Try to find evidence for both sides of the argument.

How successful was Priscus' military record?

Livy and Dionysius agree that Priscus was a great military commander. Shortly after Ancus' death, Priscus successfully defeated several Latin cities. He also enjoyed military success against Etruscan and Sabine cities, and punished the Veii. Priscus was exerting Rome's influence over the region.

When Priscus was strengthening the walls around Rome, a Sabine army crossed the Anio river and threatened the city. To meet the threat, Priscus demanded several new centuries. Attus Navius, an augur, stopped him by demonstrating the gods did not support his plan.

> **Study questions**
> Theme 3: Impact of Warfare and Military Changes
>
> Read Livy's account of Priscus military record
> Livy 1.36–1.38
>
> 1 Make a list of Priscus' military successes and his reforms of the Roman army.
> 2 Summarise the ways the augur Attus Navius prevented Priscus from creating new centuries.
>
> Extension: Complete the table below to summarise Priscus' achievements.
>
> | Evidence that Priscus was a great king | Evidence that Priscus was a great general |
> |---|---|
> | | |

Livy implied the omens did not support Priscus because he wanted to name the new centuries after himself.

Despite this setback, Priscus managed to increase the number of his men. He doubled the number of men in each century and added 1,200 horsemen. Priscus went on to defeat the Sabines.

This story is significant for two reasons. It suggests that the patrician families chosen by Romulus used their influence to oppose him. It also implies that Priscus created Rome's first separate cavalry unit known as the supplementary ones.

SERVIUS TULLIUS 578–535

Supernatural origins of Servius Tullius

Servius' story is steeped in mythology and legend. In one of these myths Servius is depicted as a young slave whose head was surrounded in flame while he slept. This miracle was witnessed by Priscus' wife and she stated that this young man would save the royal family in its hour of need. Priscus raised Servius as his son and married him to one of his daughters.

Livy (1.39) does not believe this account. Instead he argues that Tullius was the child of Servius Tullius, the leading general of Corniculum. When the general was killed his pregnant wife was brought to Rome and lived with Tanaquil, as her friend. In this way, Livy disputes the claim that Servius was a slave. Another myth suggested that Servius was conceived when his mother was impregnated by a divine phallus which rose from the fire.

Servius' succession

According to Livy, when Priscus was assassinated there was chaos at the king's court. Tanaquil, Priscus' wife, closed the palace and summoned Servius to her. Together they planned to avenge Priscus' death and Tanaquil urged him to take the throne.

> Take the throne son, if you are man enough. Do not allow your father in laws murderers to take control of the city. The gods have chosen you, when you were a child they encircled your head with flame. Just as they chose your father, a foreigner, they have chosen you. Do not worry about your birth, just think about the man you have become.
>
> Livy, *The History of Rome* 1.41 (adapted)

Tanaquil helped Servius to become king. She told the leading men of Rome that her husband was unwell. They agreed to follow Priscus' wishes and install Servius as a temporary king until he recovered. When Priscus' death was revealed, Servius became king. He was the first king, since Romulus, not to be chosen by the people. This story is an important plot device in the decline of the kings. Servius' route to kingship is another step away from Romulus' system.

S&C Was Servius Tullius a Warlord?

Emperor Claudius' speech to his senators in AD 48 provides another interpretation of Servius Tullius. A bronze tablet found at Lyon contains Claudius' speech to encourage the Senate to accept Gauls into the Senate. During his speech, Claudius mentions the Etruscan version of how Servius Tullius became king.

Servius, whose real name was Mastarna, was a great Etruscan soldier. He won fame and fortune fighting with a great warlord called Caelius. When Caelius died, Mastarna took control of his army and created a settlement on the Caelian hill. This gave him a great deal of influence. After changing his name to Servius he ruled Rome for many years.

There is no evidence that this story is any more accurate than Livy's. It is interesting for another reason. Many historians, including Beard and Cornell, suggest that Italian cities were unlikely to have stable governments like the ones described in the foundation myths. Instead, powerful warlords with large mercenary armies could have competed for control of Italian cities at this time creating political chaos.

> **Study questions**
> Theme 4: Separating Myth from Reality
>
> Read Livy's account of Servius' birth and succession to the Roman throne
> Livy 1.39–1.41
>
> 1 In what way does Livy suggest that the stories of Servius' childhood are legendary?
> 2 Why might Livy want to present Servius as the son of a great general rather than a slave?
> 3 Summarise the events which led to Servius becoming king of Rome.

THE SERVIAN REFORMS

Some of the reforms credited to Servius include:

- the census. Designed to share military burdens according to wealth
- development of the equites
- introduction of a new voting system
- introduction of the tribal system
- extension of the city and the Servian Wall
- the Temple of Diana
- tackling plebeian poverty caused by warfare and debt

Political changes

The **census** introduced a class system to decide how much each individual should contribute to the military. Livy described how the population was divided into five classes according to their wealth and what weapons they would have to provide. Here is a short extract.

> Men whose possessions were worth 100,000 asses, or more, were divided into 80 centuries. 40 of these centuries were for older men who had to defend the city. The other 40 centuries were made up of young fit men who would fight for Rome's glory outside the city. The men in this First Class needed a helmet, round shield, greaves and breastplate made of bronze. They also needed a long spear and a sword.
>
> *Livy, The History of Rome* 1.43

> **census** a survey to determine the wealth, and consequently the class, of each Roman citizen; used to determine military service

> **ACTIVITY**
>
> As a class, discuss whether you believe Livy's claim that Servius was going to abdicate and hand over power to the people (1.48).
>
> As a class, discuss why you think Livy's and Dionysius' views on Servius' reforms are so different.

> **Study questions**
> Theme 1: Social and Political Change
>
> Read Livy's account of Servius' reforms in Book 1.42, 1.43 and 1.48.
>
> **1** Summarise the key features of the census and the new voting system introduced by Servius.
> **2** List the ways Livy praised the census and the new voting system.
>
> Read the following extract from Dionysius, *Roman Antiquities* Book 4.21
>
>> In establishing this political system (the census), handed power to the rich. Tullius outwitted the people, as I said, without their noticing it and excluded the poor from any part in public affairs. For they all thought that they had an equal share in the government because every man was asked his opinion; . . . but they were deceived in this, . . . the poor, who were very numerous, had but one vote and were the last called last, and by then the decision had already been made.
>
> **3** How does Dionysius' view of the census differ from Livy's?

According to Livy the equites were also created as part of the census. Equites were given a state horse and would join the cavalry unit. Belonging to this unit was prestigious and it is implied that it helped promote successful plebeian families.

By sharing the burden of military service Servius would be remembered 'as the one who established all distinctions and ranks in society whereby groups are differentiated from one another by station and wealth'.

To compensate the rich, Servius changed the voting system. According to legend, Romulus gave each citizen an equal vote in the **Comitia Curia**. After the introduction of the Servian census, votes were cast according to wealth. Those who contributed the most money would vote first, those who contributed the least would vote last. In practice, this took the vote from the poorest as decisions would be made before they had cast their vote.

The Servian reforms are an important turning point in Livy's narrative. Livy argued that the introduction of the class system and the census was 'an invaluable institution for a nation destined to be so great'. Livy also suggested that Servius 'intended to abdicate' and hand power to the people.

> **Comitia Curiata** a political assembly divided into thirty groups or curiae who were split among the three tribes of the period of the first king, Romulus. Modern historians are unclear if this council ever existed

Social changes

Livy also described how Servius introduced a new tribal system in Rome to help him manage the census. These tribes did not describe an ethnic group, but rather where a citizen lived in Rome. Rome was divided into four areas

To encourage further growth, Servius added two new areas to the city, the Quirinal and Viminal hills. He also extended the Esquiline. As part of his extension, Servius was believed to have begun the construction of the Servian wall. We have no evidence that any construction of this type took place in the sixth century. Archaeological

1.2 The Etruscan Kings, 616–509 BC

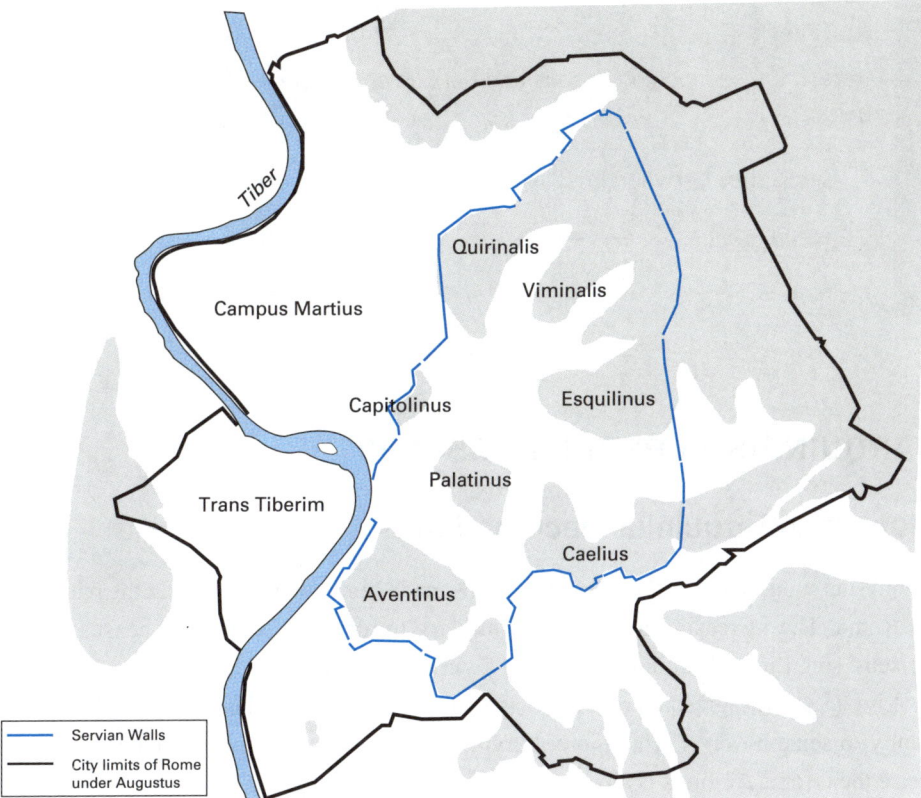

FIGURE 1.15
The seven hills of Rome showing one potential route of the fourth century Servian wall.

investigation dates the construction of the Servian wall to the Roman Republic in the fourth century.

Religious changes

Livy (1.45) also describes the importance of the temple of Diana in Rome. The temple was a joint project between Rome and a number of Latin cities. Its purpose was to strengthen the ties between the Latin cities. Livy suggested it was used by Rome to cement its position as the most powerful city in the area.

The Activity will help you develop the skills you need to answer questions on similarity and difference in an exam.

EXAM TIP: SIMILARITY VS DIFFERENCE

In your exam, Question 4 uses a source and may ask a question which focuses upon similarity and difference. Make sure you use the source **and** your own knowledge to find some comparisons.

Your conclusion should state 'how far' they were different/similar.

Study questions
Theme 2: Social and Religious Change

Read Livy 1.44–1.45

1 Summarise how Servius extended Rome and improved its defences.
2 Summarise the ways Servius used religion to strengthen Rome.

Part One Longer Period Study

> **ACTIVITY**
>
> Reread the sections on Priscus and Servius on pp. 26–32. Complete the table below.
>
> | Similarities between Priscus and Servius | Differences between Priscus and Servius |
> |---|---|
> | | |

TARQUINIUS SUPERBUS 535–509

How does Tarquinius become king?

Dionysius suggested that the Servian reforms made him unpopular among the patricians of Rome. The increasing financial and military burdens caused by the census helped Priscus' son, Lucius Tarquinius Superbus, win the support of the patricians.

Livy (1.47) disagrees. Servius' old age gave Lucius Tarquinius Superbus the opportunity to seize power. Furthermore, Servius' daughter, Tullia, encouraged Superbus to seize the throne. Ambitus is an important theme in this story.

Livy describes the coup:

> Superbus approached many of the senators whom his father, Priscus, had created and demanded their loyalty. He won the support of other younger, inexperienced senators with gifts and flattery. Once he had enough support he marched into the Senate with a small army and sat on the throne and demanded that the Senate meet its new king, Lucius Tarquinius Superbus. His co-conspirators arrived promptly, the other senators appeared out of curiosity or fear.
>
> Superbus began by attacking the elderly Servius Tullius . . . Superbus claimed that Rome had allowed a slave to become king. Worst of all he had become king by the plotting of a woman, without a vote from the people or the support of the Senate. This slave-king, he went on to argue, had stolen land from the patricians to reward the dregs of society. His census had poisoned Rome because personal wealth was public knowledge. This had led to jealousy and hate.
>
> Servius burst into the Senate and demanded that his son-in-law explain himself. Superbus hissed in reply, 'the son of a king will always better a slave'. With that he used his youthfulness to grab Servius around the waist and lift him above his head before carrying him out of the room and hurling him down the Senate steps.
>
> Before Servius could return to the palace, Superbus' men killed him. One account suggested that it was his own daughter, Tullia, who murdered Servius. On her way home she had seen the dying body of her father . . . In a maddening rage she drove the chariot over him.

Livy, *The History of Rome* 1.47–1.48 (adapted)

> **DEBATE** How Old was Lucius Tarquinius Superbus?
>
> Dionysius is convinced that Tarquinius Superbus was the son of Tarquinius Priscus. If he is correct, then Superbus was at least seventy when he threw Servius down the steps of the Senate and ninety when he fought at the Battle of Lake Regilius (6.21).
>
> Livy (1.46) recognises this problem and offers a simple solution. Tarquinius Superbus must be Priscus' grandson. There is, however, no evidence to prove this.
>
> Some historians believe that the problem was created by Fabius Pictor. Pictor may have had access to sources about Servius Tullius and Tarquinius Superbus which did not fit into his timeline so he just made them live longer.

Study questions

Theme 4: Separating Myth from Reality

Read Livy's account of Servius death
Livy 1.47–1.48

1. Summarise the ways Tarquinius Superbus encouraged the patricians to oppose Servius.
2. Summarise Tarquinius Superbus' attack upon Servius' kingship.
3. Summarise the key events which lead to Tarquinius Superbus' succession.

What is a tyrant?

The tyrannies of Greece would have been well documented in the histories that the Roman historians were trying to copy. These all-powerful kings used their control of the people to build great cities and amass personal wealth. Tarquinius Superbus is presented in the same way.

Political changes

Livy emphasises Superbus' use of murder and violence to keep power.

- He seized the throne by force, never received the approval of the Senate and used bodyguards to protect him from assassination attempts. Dionysius described Superbus as a man who 'surrounded himself with dangerous men armed with swords and spears' and who would only appear 'unannounced so that no-one could plan his murder'. This is a departure from the previous kings.
- As king, Superbus presided over all capital crimes. Anyone who threatened Superbus' control of Rome would be accused of a capital crime and sentenced to death. In this way, he removed Servius' supporters and established his tyranny.
- The Senate's influence decreased until it was not consulted at all.
- Superbus refused to bury Servius.
- According to Dionysius, the plebeians were badly treated.
- Superbus removed the census.
- He banned religious ceremonies which could allow groups of men to plot against him.
- To prevent the plebeians from opposing him, he turned them into labourers. They were forced to modernise the Circus Maximus, Cloaca Maxima and to construct several temples.
- Livy (1.56) is more balanced. He implies that the building programme provided jobs, albeit unpleasant, and his military expansion created colonies for some to acquire new land.

Study questions

Theme 1: Political Change

Read Livy's account of Superbus' tyranny and complete the table below. Book 1.49 and 1.56

Threats to Superbus' power	Superbus' tactics to keep power

Read Dionysius 4.43–4.44 and add extra details to your table.

1 List the ways Superbus controls the plebeians.
2 Summarise the attitudes of the patricians described in the passage.

The Sibylline Oracles

Read Dionysius 4.62. It tells an interesting tale to illustrate Superbus' tyranny. When an old woman visited Rome with nine books of oracles, Tarquinius refused to pay the asking price. The old woman burnt three of the books. Once again she offered to sell the books. Still at the original price. Tarquinius refused, and the old woman burnt another three books. To save the last three books from destruction Tarquinius paid for nine books but only received three.

FIGURE 1.16 German medieval woodcut illustration showing Tarquinius with the old woman burning books.

He then appointed three men to take care of them. One of these men tried to sell the books. Tarquinius punished him by sewing him inside a leather bag. He then threw the bag into the sea.

What does this story tell us about Superbus' character?

Military successes

Outside of domestic politics, Superbus is viewed more sympathetically.

- Superbus is described as an effective diplomat and general.
- Dionysius and Livy agree that he enlarged Rome's empire. He created two colonies. One at Signia and one at Circeii.
- His son Sextus' conquest of the city of Gabii is an important achievement. Sextus pretended to flee Rome, and quickly rose through the ranks in Gabii's political structure. Once in a position of power he murdered the leading men of Gabii and seized control of the city.
- Superbus also defeated the Volsci. Although, Livy states this victory started a 200-year war with the Volsci.

Religious and social change

Superbus significantly improved the infrastructure of Rome.

- He completed the Cloaca Maximus which improved sanitation within the city.
- He extended the Circus Maximus.
- He built a number of temples across Rome.

Excavations at Sant' Omobono indicate that this was a period of rapid expansion. There are many seventh- or sixth-century temples, and the remains of the Cloaca Maximus suggest that a canal was also constructed in this period.

> **Study questions**
>
> Theme 3: Impact of Warfare and Military Change
>
> Read Livy's account of Lucius Tarquinius Superbus reign and military record Livy 1.50–1.56
>
> 1. Make a list of Lucius Tarquinius Superbus' military successes and achievements.
> 2. Why might Superbus be seen as a great general? Justify your decision.

> **ACTIVITY**
>
> Reread the section on Tarquinius Superbus from pp. 34–37 and complete this table:
>
> | Evidence that Tarquinius Superbus was a tyrannical king | Evidence that Tarquinius Superbus was a successful king |
> |---|---|
> | | |
>
> Discuss as a class whether Tarquinius Superbus' tyrannical reputation is deserved.

Part One Longer Period Study

TIMESPAN REVIEW

Boost your knowledge

Describe:

a. Priscus' strategies for becoming king of Rome and his reforms
b. the myths surrounding Servius and how he became king
c. Servian reforms
d. Tarquinius Superbus' reign comparing his seizure of power, tyranny, military successes and building programme.

Stretch your understanding

Explain:

a. the impact of ambitus on Priscus' and Superbus' reigns
b. the role of warfare during the Etruscan kings' reigns
c. compare Priscus', Servius' and Tarquinius' character and role in Livy's narrative
d. the importance of reform during the Etruscan kings reigns

PRACTICE QUESTIONS

Passage A

Sextus had managed to secure the support of the Gabii by pretending to plot the downfall of Rome and his father. Once Sextus was confident he had gained the trust of the Gabii, he sent one of his servants to his father to ask him what to do next. Tarquinius Superbus was cautious, he could not risk anything. So Tarquinius led the servant into his garden. As they walked through the garden Tarquinius came to some poppies. As he walked back to his palace he knocked all of the heads off the tallest poppies. Although Sextus' messenger was confused. Sextus knew what his father meant immediately. He was to murder the most influential men in Gabii. To achieve this, he called the men of Gabii to a meeting. He informed them that his messenger had visited his father. His servant had learned his father wished to murder him and had managed to convince some Gabii traitors to deliver him to Rome. The men of Gabii asked if he knew who the traitors were. Sextus told them that it was Antistius Petro the great Gabii general.

Dionysius, *Roman Antiquities* 4.46

1. Using details from Passage A and your own knowledge, what can we learn about the nature of Tarquinius Superbus reign? [10]
2. Using details from Passage A and your own knowledge, explain why Tarquinius Superbus was a successful general. [15]

1.3 Origins of the Republic, 509–494 BC

> **TIMESPAN OVERVIEW**
>
> - the removal of Tarquinius Superbus
> - the creation of the early Republic
> - the development of the Consulship and the Senate
> - impact of the foundation of the Republic upon the plebeian and patrician class
> - tensions developing between the plebeian and patrician class
> - Military challenges to the early Republic and the Roman response
> - the Battle of Silvia Arsia, the invasion of Lars Porsena and the Battle of Lake Regilius
> - the nature and origin of the historical evidence for this period
>
> **There are no prescribed sources for this component, but the following suggested readings and archaeological evidence are covered in this chapter:**
>
> - Livy, *The History of Rome*, Book 1, sections 56–60; Book 2, sections 1–2, 6–15, 19–22
>
> - The Capitoline Brutus
> - The Lapis Satricanus

The removal of Tarquinius Superbus by Lucius Junius Brutus led to the establishment of the Roman Republic. The transition from King to Republic was not an easy one. The king was replaced by the consul, who shared leadership of the army. These consuls had to deal with civil unrest within Rome from Superbus' supporters, and the invasion from Superbus' allies. Livy shares a gripping story about how the early Republic overcame these threats to secure the future of Rome.

WHAT WERE THE ORDERS

Romulus introduced the two orders. Patricians were men whose birth and heritage gave them access to the political system. Plebeians were those who could not stand for a magistracy or government position. It is unclear when the two orders really became established in Rome, but it seems to have been fairly well established by the third century BC.

It is vital that you do not confuse the orders with the social classes Servius introduced. The class system, introduced by the census, was according to wealth not birth.

The plebeians

The plebeians are the easiest group to categorise. They were Roman citizens who did not belong to the patrician class.

Plebeians made up most of the Roman population in this period. Most rural plebeians were labourers or farmers. According to Livy and Dionysius, the biggest issue facing many plebeians was access to land. This may have been true by the second and first century BC, but not in the fifth century BC.

Urban plebeians were skilled workers with their shops attached to their homes, as in the later Republic. For example, archaeologists have found remains of terraced homes under the horrea vespasiani (Vespasian's market). In front of these homes are a number of shops from the sixth century BC.

They worked hard to pay their taxes and feed their families. Many plebeians had to serve in the Roman army which may have been called a **legion** at this time. Military service was very important for the Roman government. Without a very large well-trained army, Rome would not have become so powerful. Withholding military service in the fourth century was used to achieve reform.

The plebeians would have made up most of the army, it is unlikely that they would have been **velites** at this time. Instead evidence suggests the plebeians were organised into a large **hoplite** force. Some wealthier plebeians may have belonged to the eques class. They would have been given a horse by the state, and would have fought in the Roman cavalry.

legion unit of the Roman army (used to describe early Roman armies by ancient historians even though there is no evidence for this unit until the fourth and third centuries BC)

velites Roman light infantry, recruited from the poorest plebeians, and given limited training to use javelins and in hand-to-hand fighting (used to describe early plebeian armies by ancient historians even though there is no evidence for this unit until the fourth and third centuries BC)

hoplite citizen-soldiers of Ancient Greek city states, and probably the system adopted by Rome in the fifth century

S&C: Were the Roman Plebeians Politically Aware in the Fifth Century BC?

Trade is believed to have helped raise the political awareness of the Roman plebeian class. This, reputedly, led to Greek ideas such as democracy and religion spreading through Rome's urban population during the fifth century BC.

Critics of this theory state that Rome did not have a seaport until Ostia was built in the fifth century BC. Excavations have revealed a small outpost at Ostia connected to Rome by a very small sixth century road. This could not support international trade, which suggests Roman plebeians had limited access to Greek ideas.

The expansion of the Roman Forum, on the other hand, suggests that trade was rapidly expanding, but not necessarily with other countries. The vast number of Etruscan artefacts found at Roman archaeological sites from the sixth century BC onwards, suggest that Roman trade was limited to Italian cities. These Italian cities did have strong Greek links and some modern historians partially agree with Livy's assertion that Rome imported Etruscan political and religious customs.

The patricians

The patricians are much harder to categorise. According to Livy and Dionysius, they descended from the noblest families who settled in Romulus' Rome. One hundred of these earliest patricians made up the Senate. During the period of the legendary and Etruscan kings, membership of the patricians is described as fluid. Dionysius implies that Tarquinius Priscus was admitted into the patrician order by King Ancus when he arrived in Rome.

Livy and Dionysius share stories about ex-plebeians who had been elevated to the patrician class. We are not sure how this elevation happened. Was it through marriage or adoption into a patrician family? Was there a process where rich or successful plebeians were admitted into the patrician order?

We believe that at some time there was a closing of the patrician class. It is possible that when the Republic developed, the leading families wanted to protect their power structures. If access to the patrician class was open, then there would be fewer opportunities to become **magistrates**.

The patrician families had an important role to play in the Roman state. They provided the generals and administrators who would manage army and public affairs. We call these individuals magistrates. Becoming a consul was the highest honour a patrician could achieve. It would grant them access to the Senate for life and would allow them to command Rome's armies.

magistrate an elected office-holder who had responsibility in the Roman state

DOWNFALL OF THE ROMAN KINGS

Rape of Lucretia

Livy's story (1.56–1.59) about the downfall of the Roman kings begins with a drinking game.

> **EXPLORE FURTHER**
>
> Read Beard's *SPQR*, pp. 139–41 to explore the problems with the Ancient Romans' accounts of the early Republic.

Why Don't We Know How Rome Became a Republic?

In Chapter One you read about the inscription on a stele from under the Lapis Niger or Black Stone. This inscription, from the mid-sixth century or earlier, is the strongest evidence available that Rome was controlled by kings.

There is no evidence to tell us when Rome's kings were replaced, or what replaced them. The earliest definitive written evidence of the Republic is from c. 280 BC. On the sarcophagus of Lucius Cornelius Scipio Barbatus there is an epitaph. It describes him as a consul and describes his achievements. This leaves over 300 years between the inscription on the stele near the Black Stone, and Barbatus' epitaph.

Despite this lack of evidence no one seriously believes that the literary tradition is accurate. As a consequence, there are many conflicting theories.

Beard summarises the problems that historians face. It is evident that the foundation of the Republic took place over many years. The existence of **dictators**, **praetors** and **consuls** within the late Roman Republic hint at this transition.

dictator a magistrate appointed for six months to deal with a national emergency or crisis and in full control of the army and government during that time

praetor Roman magistrate who supported the consuls – usually as an army commander

consul one of two annually elected magistrates who shared leadership of the Roman army and influenced political decisions in Rome

Part One Longer Period Study

> **KEY INDIVIDUAL**
> **Lucius Junius Brutus**
> **Dates:** 545–505 BC
>
> Grandson of Rome's fifth king, Lucius Tarquinius Priscus. Used his position as tribune of the celeres to remove the Tarquins after the rape of Lucretia. Established the Republic and became one of Rome's first consuls.
>
> As consul, he would demand that all Roman citizens swear an oath to resist the restoration of a king. He would also increase the size of the Senate to 300, and create a new office of rex sacrorum to carry out the religious duties of the king.
>
> To magnify his sense of duty, the Roman historians tell us that Brutus executed his two sons and two step-brothers for trying to help Tarquinius Superbus reclaim his power. Brutus eventually dies defending Rome from the Tarquins at the Battle of Silvia Arsia.

Tarquinius Superbus' sons and their cousin, Collatinus, were drinking heavily during the siege of Ardea. This led to a debate about their wives' virtues. Tarquinius Collatinus was so positive he would win that he convinced the men to ride home and spy on their wives. They found the royal princesses drinking heavily, but Lucretia, Collatinus' wife, was working hard with her maids. Collatinus, pleased with his victory, asked his two cousins to join him for another drink.

According to Livy, Lucius Tarquinius Sextus was now drunk with lust. He decided he had to rape the chaste and loyal Lucretia. A few days passed before Sextus returned alone to Lucretia's home. Lucretia welcomed him to the guest room, but at night Sextus attacked her.

At first he threatened to kill her if she did not sleep with him. She refused. Sextus would not give up. He threatened to destroy her husband's reputation by exposing her as an adulterer. Sextus told Lucretia he would rape and murder her. Then, to cover his crime, he would tell the world he had discovered Lucretia with a male slave, and had killed them both. In this way, he would satisfy his lust and destroy her husband. Lucretia submitted in order to save her husband's career.

When Sextus left, Lucretia sent for her father and husband. Her husband, Collatinus, brought Lucius Junius Brutus. Her father, Spurius Lucretius, came with Publius Valerius. When the men arrived she told them of Sextus' crime. She made them vow revenge before driving a knife into her chest.

Livy describes the impact Lucretia's death had upon Brutus.

> Seizing the knife from the fair Lucretia's breast Brutus swore revenge. 'By your pure blood, defiled by the cruel prince Sextus; I vow to remove your father Lucius Tarquinius Superbus, his evil wife Tullia, and all of their children. Rome shall no longer be corrupted by kings.'
>
> Livy, *The History of Rome* 1.59 (adapted)

FIGURE 1.17
A sixteenth-century bronze statuette showing the Rape of Lucretia.

1.3 Origins of the Republic, 509–494 BC

Brutus creates the Roman Republic

Livy used the character of Brutus to turn the private tragedy into a political one. Junius Brutus was one of King Tarquinius Priscus' grandsons. Being Superbus' nephew provided no protection for Brutus. Brutus' brother was murdered by the tyrant, and to escape death, Brutus pretended to have low intelligence and was uninterested in power. 'Brutus' can be translated into 'fool'.

Livy suggested that Brutus behaved like a fool because he was very ambitious. During his mission to the Delphic Oracle with Superbus' sons, Livy (1.56) describes Brutus kissing the ground after hearing the Oracle state that the first envoy to kiss their mother would become the next king of Rome. Lucretia's death enabled Brutus to inspire the Roman people to help him remove Tarquinius Superbus.

Brutus was the tribune of the celeres at this time. This gave him control of the kings' bodyguard and the power to call an assembly. At the assembly, Brutus delivers his revolutionary speech outlining the crimes of Tarquinius Superbus and demands his immediate exile. The people of Rome agreed. On his return, Lucius Tarquinius Superbus was refused entry into Rome. Superbus and most of his family went into exile, except Sextus who returned to Gabii.

EXAM TIP: CAUSE

In your exam, Question 4 may ask a question which will ask you to assess what caused a major event to occur. It may also ask you to compare how far two different people or two different events led to a major event.

Question 4 will be linked to a source. Make sure you use the source **and** your own knowledge to make these comparisons

The Activity 'Cause' will help you develop the skills you need to answer questions on similarity and difference in an exam.

ACTIVITY Cause

Complete the table below.
Find evidence to explain which event caused the exile of Tarquinius Superbus.

Superbus' tyranny	Lucretia	Brutus' leadership

As a class, discuss how each factor may link, and which you believe was the most important cause of Superbus' exile.

Study questions
Theme 1: Political Change

Study Livy's account of the Rape of Lucretia and how Brutus exiles Tarquinius Superbus Livy 1.56–1.59

1 Summarise the key events of Brutus' visit to Delphi.
2 Summarise the character of:
   ○ Lucretia
   ○ Sextus
   ○ Brutus
3 Summarise the events which lead to Lucretia's death and the exile of Tarquinius Superbus.

ACTIVITY

As a class discuss whether you think Brutus is driven by ambitus or patriotism?

THE ROMAN REPUBLIC

The archaeological record provides some limited evidence that Rome experienced a period of upheaval at the end of the sixth century. Soil samples from the period show a great deal of destruction in the city. This could have been the result of many things, including invasion, fire or revolution. There is no conclusive evidence which supports the literary narrative of the foundation of the Roman Republic.

The Tarquin conspiracy

Exiling Superbus did not guarantee the survival of the Republic. Tarquinius Superbus was still an influential man and Brutus expected him to attack Rome.

After gaining the support of the Roman army, Brutus suggested that Collinatus should step down as consul. Collinatus agreed; he realised that for the Republic to succeed all members of the Tarquin family should leave Rome. Publius Valerius Publicola replaced him as consul.

Tarquinius Superbus sent members of the royal family to demand the return of his property. The Senate agreed that Superbus' possessions should be returned. Brutus told the Senate to refuse the request, he wanted to seize Superbus' land as compensation for his tyrannical actions against the people of Rome. The Senate rejected Brutus' request.

While the Senate debated Superbus' case, Superbus' family approached leading patricians to join a conspiracy to murder Brutus. Publius Valerius discovered the plot and arrested the conspirators. Brutus discovered his sons were involved in the plot. To protect the Republic, Brutus ordered their execution. After the Tarquin conspiracy was discovered the Senate voted to seize Superbus' land.

FIGURE 1.18
The Capitoline Brutus. This is traditionally identified as a portrait of Brutus. Sculpted in the fourth to third century BC. Modern historians are convinced that the founder of the Roman Republic is mythical like Romulus, or inserted into the story by a Roman historian's patron.

Study questions
Theme 4: Separating Myth from Reality

Read Livy's account of the foundation of the Roman Republic
Livy 1.59–1.60 and 2.1–2.2

1. Summarise the events which led to the creation of the Roman Republic.
2. Summarise the key events of the Tarquin conspiracy.

Dionysius' and the Creation of the Republic

Dionysius invented a conference where Brutus' co-conspirators discussed alternative forms of government for Rome. Dionysius asserted that Brutus dismissed them all in favour of the system of government created by the kings.

> Time is short and any attempt to change it in the time available to us would be dangerous. If we want to change the government let us do it later when we have removed the tyrant. In my opinion there is no better constitution than the one handed down by Romulus, Numa and the succeeding kings. We know that kings often abuse their power and become tyrants. If we can take precautions to prevent this, then we shall prevail.
>
> Dionysius, *Roman Antiquities* 4.73 (adapted)

As a consequence, the Republic replaced the king with two consuls, and a priest to carry out the king's religious duties. Brutus and Collatinus would become Rome's first two consuls.

WHAT WERE THE MAIN FEATURES OF THE NEW REPUBLIC?

After the removal of the kings, magistrates inherited the powers and responsibilities of the kings. They were given attendants called **lictors** to protect them. Each lictor carried fasces to show the power of the magistrate.

Consuls controlled the army and were the most important magistrates in the Roman Republic. Elected for one year, they were given the task of protecting Rome or seeking glory. Although they replaced the king, law-making, building programmes and taxation were controlled by other institutions.

Two consuls were appointed to prevent any one man having too much power. If one consul disagreed with the other, then they could intervene and block the others decision. Sharing power in this way would, hopefully, prevent another tyrant taking control of Rome. Patricians could be elected as consul more than once, but not in successive years.

Consuls also performed auspices before battles. These religious ceremonies were used to try to predict the outcome of a battle.

Censors were also elected from the assembly. They were elected for five years and were responsible for the administration of Rome. They performed the census, drew up who could attend the Senate and decided contracts for public work. Tarquinius Priscus allegedly introduced them to carry out a census every year. The census would decide which class every Roman citizen belonged to. During the Republic they were also asked to maintain public morals and organise state building projects. Censors were not given lictors to protect them.

Dictators were only appointed in times of emergency. They had total power and replaced the consuls. They could assemble armies and manage the state to defend Rome or overcome an emergency. Limits were placed upon dictators. They only held the position for six months. They also had a deputy called the **Master of the Horse** who held the dictator to account and made sure that they did not abuse their powers.

The Senate is said to have been created by Romulus. During the Republic, senators held their position for life and were retired magistrates. A senator had to be a landowner and usually came from the most powerful families. To most Romans they were probably seen as a council of elders and their most important role was giving advice to the consuls and kings. The Senate controlled the treasury, but they also had an important role in planning the development of the city and its relationships with its neighbours.

FIGURE 1.19
An illustration of Roman lictors carrying the fasces.

censor the administrator of Rome which kept an eye on finances and the people and would also decide membership of the different classes

Master of the Horse dictator's deputy appointed to keep a check on his power and to ensure it was not used to create a tyranny

HOW DID THE EARLY REPUBLIC SURVIVE INVASION AND WAR?

Wars of Independence

According to the literary tradition, the new Republic was well organised and prepared for war. Despite this, Lucius Tarquinius Superbus had strong allies who would help him reclaim his throne. Rome would have to defend the new Republic from Superbus and his allies.

Part One Longer Period Study

The Latin League was one of the organisations which helped Superbus. The League was a collection of Latin cities which co-operated to maintain peace and encourage trade. Livy (1.52) suggests that Tarquin Superbus was the League's most powerful member until his exile.

Another significant ally of Tarquinius Superbus was Lars Porsena of Clusium.

The Battle of Silvia Arsia

The failure of the Tarquin conspiracy did not deter Tarquinius Superbus. He approached the Etruscan city of Veii and promised to help them seek revenge against the Roman army. The men of Tarquinii volunteered a force as well. They had supported the Tarquin royal family for decades.

The newly-appointed consul, Valerius, was given control of the Roman army. Brutus commanded the cavalry. They met the Veian and Tarquinian forces at Silvia Arsia in 509 or 508 BC.

Tarquinius Superbus and his son Arruns commanded the Etruscan forces and they planned to use their knowledge of Roman warfare to their advantage. Arruns searched the battlefield for lictors, knowing the consuls would be nearby. Arruns plan was successful. When he saw Brutus surrounded by lictors, he turned his horse to strike him down. Brutus joined him in battle and the two men killed each other.

Valerius eventually drove the Tarquinii army back, but suffered heavy losses. On his return to Rome he arranged a state funeral for Brutus, but did not immediately seek a replacement consul.

Valerius Publicola

Valerius' leadership had given Rome a victory at Silvia Arsius. His failure to appoint a co-consul led to widespread concerns that Valerius wanted to become a king. To calm the Roman people, Valerius called an election and Marcus Horatius was chosen as his colleague.

Valerius then introduced a number of laws to guarantee fair prices for the plebeians. He also gave the plebeians a right to appeal against any magistrate who was unfairly prosecuting them. These actions gave Valerius the nickname Publicola or Friend of the People.

> **Study questions**
> Theme 3: Impact of Warfare and Military Change
>
> Read Livy's account of the Battle of Silvia Arsia
> Livy 2.6–2.7
>
> 1. Summarise Rome's preparations and the key events from the Battle of Silvia Arsia.
> 2. Summarise the 'miracle of Silvia Arsia'. Does Livy believe in the miracle?
> 3. Summarise the consequences of the Battle of Silvia Arsia.

> **KEY INDIVIDUAL**
> **Publius Valerius Publicola**
> **Dates:** 503–461 BC
> Roman consul who helped defend Rome from the exiled king Tarquinius Superbus

> **Study questions**
> Theme 1: Political Change
>
> Read Livy's account of Valerius Publicola's preparation for war
> Livy 2.7–2.9
>
> 1. Summarise the preparations introduced by Valerius to help the people of Rome prepare for war.
> 2. Make a list of the problems the plebeians were facing in the build-up to war. These problems will become a crisis in chapter 4.

The Stone of Satricum

The Lapis Satricanus or the Stone of Satricum has a reference to a Publius Valerius inscribed on it. As with most evidence from this period it is inconclusive. Firstly, it was found in Satricum, which was not part of Rome at this time. Furthermore, it could be another Valerius. Despite these issues, many historians consider the possibility that Publius Valerius might be real. Jan Bremner argues that the companions who dedicated this stone might have been a group of young soldiers. It is not unreasonable to suggest that Valerius Publius could have been an important Roman.

FIGURE 1.20

The Lapis Satricanus from c. 500 BC. The inscription reads 'The (?) dedicated this, as companions of Publius Valerius, to Mars'.

Valerius was elected consul again. He began strengthening Rome's walls and rebuilding his legions. The two consuls also made sure that the plebeians' animals were moved into the mountains to keep them safe during this period of war. Furthermore, a law was passed to make sure that the plebeians did not have to contribute to the first year of the next war.

Lars Porsena

Tarquinius Superbus approached Lars Porsena, the king of Clusium, for help. Porsena demanded Rome restore Tarquinius Superbus as king of Rome, or return his possessions. Rome refused, so Clusium declared war on Rome.

Lars Porsena's army quickly took control of the Janiculum. Rome positioned its army in front of the bridge which crossed the Tiber into Rome. The defence of the city was presented by Livy as a final stand.

Rome's armies could not prevent Lars Porsena from gaining the upper hand. Many of Rome's finest men were killed or injured. To avoid a massacre three men volunteered to defend the bridge into the city.

One of these men was Horatius Cocles. A distant relative of the surviving Roman triplet who defeated the Three Albans. This story is no coincidence. Horatius Cocles fought bravely to protect the bridge and allow the Roman army to retreat. The last Roman soldier to cross the bridge destroyed it, leaving Horatius Cocles to swim across the river to safety. Livy suggests he received a spear through his buttocks for his troubles. Polybius, in the earliest known version, says he drowned. A much more likely outcome if you leap into a fast-flowing river in full armour.

KEY INDIVIDUAL

Lars Porsena

Dates: late sixth to early fifth century

Fictional king of Clusium who almost conquers Rome, but makes peace after the bravery of Gaius Mucius

FIGURE 1.21
A sixteenth-century engraving of Horatius Cocles defending the bridge.

Study questions
Theme 4: Separating Myth from Reality

Read Livy's account of Horatius Cocles
Livy 2.10

1. Summarise the key events from Lars Porsena invasion of Rome.
2. Summarise the actions of Horatius Cocles to defend Rome.
3. How do you think Livy has used this story to celebrate the Glory of Rome?

KEY INDIVIDUAL

Gaius Mucius Scaevola
Dates: late sixth–fifth century

Fictional character who tried to assassinate Lars Porsena and whose bravery secured peace for Rome

The defeat of the Roman army was decisive. Livy describes desperate plebeians deserting the city to support Tarquinius Superbus. The consuls appealed to the Latin League for help. The League announced they could not get involved when there was a dispute between some of its members.

The situation was desperate. The scene was set for another Roman hero called Gaius Mucius Scaevola. He allegedly saved Rome from destruction.

Gaius Mucius approached the Senate and presented them with his plan to assassinate Porsena. He would use his knowledge of Etruscan customs to make his way into Porsena's tent and murder him.

The only flaw to Mucius' plan was that he did not know what Porsena looked like. He successfully entered Porsena's tent, but murdered the king's secretary rather than the king. Mucius was quickly arrested and brought in front of Porsena. Here Mucius told Porsena that he was the first of 300 men who would try to kill him. This forced Porsena to rethink his strategy. He offered Rome a compromise. Porsena would end the war if Rome guaranteed Veii's independence and provide hostages to Clusium.

Livy then describes the bravery of a female hostage Cloelia. She escaped from captivity by leading several other hostages to safety by swimming the Tiber under heavy enemy fire. Despite Cloelia's actions threatening the peace agreement, Porsena eventually

> **Study questions**
>
> Theme 4: Separating Myth from Reality
>
> Read Livy's account of Gaius Mucius and the peace with Lars Porsena
> Livy 2.12–2.13
>
> 1 Summarise the bravery of:
>   - Gaius Mucius
>   - Cloelia
> 2 How do you think Livy has used these two stories to celebrate the Glory of Rome?
> 3 Summarise the reasons why Lars Porsena made peace.
> 4 Summarise the key terms of the treaty between Rome and Clusium.

agreed to allow Cloelia her freedom and a select number of other hostages. Cloelia's decisions to rescue children earned her recognition with a statue on the Sacred Way.

Lars Porsena kept his peace treaty and Rome was able to regain control over its neighbours, including the Sabines in 499 BC.

The end of the Wars of Independence

Constant war began to have an impact upon the plebeians of Rome. To deal with the crisis the Senate decided to create a dictator and a Master of the Horse to replace the consuls. Dionysius stated that Larcius was the first dictator. He updated the census to ensure military levies were fair.

Aulus Postumius, Rome's second dictator, was asked in 496 BC to deal with a new threat from the Latin League.

Tarquinius Superbus, if we believe Dionysius (6.21), was over ninety years old at this time, but fought like a much younger man. At the Battle of Lake Regilius, Superbus and his son managed to destroy much of the Roman army.

Postumius used his personal bodyguard to bolster the Roman forces and capture the Latin camp. During the battle, Superbus and his son were injured. As a consequence of this battle, Rome re-joined the Latin League and signed a peace treaty with them. This ended the threat from the Etruscan Kings.

As we shall see in the next chapter, the Wars of Independence are used in the narrative to explain the origins of the Conflict of Orders.

> **Study questions**
>
> Theme 3: Impact of Warfare and Military Change
>
> Read Livy's account of the Battle of Lake Regilius
> Livy 2.19–2.22
>
> 1 Summarise Rome's preparations for the Battle of Lake Regilius.
> 2 Summarise the key events of the battle and Postumius' actions.
> 3 Summarise the key features of Rome's membership of the Latin League.

Part One Longer Period Study

TIMESPAN REVIEW

Boost your knowledge

Describe:

a. the key events leading to the exile of Tarquinius Superbus – include Lucretia and Brutus
b. the key features of the early Roman Republic – consuls, Senate, censors
c. the actions taken by Publicola to protect the plebeians from the impact of War
d. the battles of Silvia Arsia, Lars Porsena and Lake Regilius – include Brutus, Valerius, Cocles, Mucius and Postumius roles in the defence of Rome

Stretch your understanding

Explain:

a. Lucretia's, Brutus', Cocles', Mucius' and Postumius' character and role in Livy's narrative
b. how the Roman Republic survives the Wars of Independence – include the importance of heroes, organisation, military strength and unity
c. why the differences between patricians and plebeians may lead to conflict
d. how the Roman Republic was developed to prevent a tyrant from taking power

PRACTICE QUESTIONS

1. a. Identify **two** ways Lucius Junius Brutus is said to have encouraged the people of Rome to revolt against Tarquinius Superbus. [2]
   b. Identify **two** events from the Wars of Independence 508–494 BC? [2]
2. Outline the actions said to have been taken by Publius Valerius in 508 BC to prepare for war with Tarquinius Superbus. [6]

1.4 Securing the Republic, 494–440 BC

> **TIMESPAN OVERVIEW**
>
> - impact of war upon Roman politics
> - power of the patricians relative to the plebeians
> - problems facing the plebeian class
> - the development of plebeian influence on government
> - the impact of Appius Claudius and his family upon patrician and plebeian relations
> - the military implications of the plebeian revolts and the role of soldiers in those revolts
> - Sicinius and the First Secession of the plebeians
> - Volero Publilius' uprising and the reforms of 471
> - First and Second Decemvirate
> - Second Secession and the Twelve Tables
> - Valerio-Horatian laws and the other reforms of the 440s
> - change and continuity in patrician and plebeian lives
> - the nature and origin of the historical evidence for this period
>
> **There are no prescribed sources for this component, but the following suggested readings are covered in this chapter:**
>
> Livy, *The History of Rome*, Book 2, sections 21, 23–35, 41, 54–58, 61
>
> - Book 3, sections 9, 31–54
> - Book 4, sections 1–7

After the defeat of the Tarquins, Rome should have secured its future. The wars had, however, impacted upon the lives of the plebeians. Debt and poverty caused unrest and the Senate refused to help relieve these problems. This led to the Conflict of the Orders which resulted in two plebeian secessions from Rome. To address the problem, plebeian tribunes and the Twelve Tables were created to help improve the lives of the plebeians.

THE CONFLICT OF THE ORDERS

The **Conflict of Orders** story is based upon events from the later Roman Republic. The strongest echoes are from the second century. The Second Punic War militarised the plebeians. Rich Romans bought plebeian land and introduced slave labour to farm it. As a consequence, by the end of the second century there were many poor Roman citizens. Livy and Dionysius would have seen how men like Julius Caesar had been able to secure the support of poor citizens. Scarcity of reliable records before the fourth century, meant that both historians relied upon Late Republican politics to describe Early Republican politics.

Livy himself admits that the records from this time are uncertain.

> There are so many chronological uncertainties in the history of these years, with different authorities giving different lists of magistrates, that the great antiquity of the events and of the sources does not permit one to make out which consuls followed which or what events happened in what year.
>
> Livy, *The History of Rome* 2.21

> **plebeian tribune** powerful tribunes who represented the plebeian class and shared their concerns with the Senate, holding the Senate and consuls to account after the First Secession
>
> **land reform** governmental policy to distribute land among the poor
>
> **war veteran** a retired soldier

The biggest influence upon the description of the Conflict of the orders in the fifth century are Tiberius and Gaius Gracchus. They were plebeian magistrates called **plebeian tribunes** elected in 133 and 123. They used popular support to try and pass **land reform** laws which would redistribute the land among the poor and **war veterans**.

CAUSES OF PLEBEIAN UNREST

Warfare

Livy suggested Rome's Wars of Independence caused homelessness and indebtedness among the poor. With so many men fighting to protect Rome, farms and businesses struggled to make ends meet. Impoverished families had to borrow money to keep their farms afloat while the men fought. As a consequence, many plebeian soldiers and war veterans returned from the war to find themselves homeless or with large debts.

> **EXPLORE FURTHER**
>
> Read a brief overview of Tiberius Gracchus from Mary Beard's *SPQR*, pp. 221–7. This overview will help you identify how the Gracchi influenced Livy's account of the First and Second Secession.

Modern historians criticise Livy's claim that warfare caused the Conflict of Orders.

- **Subsistence farming** existed until Hannibal's invasion of Italy. If we believe Livy's account, the seizure of land by the rich happened in the fifth century. If this was the case, there would have been no land to seize in the early second century. Our sources from the second century BC are more reliable so we must conclude that Livy's claim is either exaggerated or made up.
- Another flaw with the story is that Livy offers a stereotypical view of war. In ancient Rome, warfare provided opportunities for many men. Looting was a profitable business, and the sale of slaves could help poor citizens quickly climb the social ladder. Many men sold their farms in the second century because they could make more money employed by the Roman army.
- Finally, the stories of the First and Second **Secession** are part legend. There is likely to be some truth in the story, but with limited evidence this is difficult to prove.

> **secession** name given to plebeian protests in the Republic when plebeians left the city to create a new settlement on the Aventine hill or other location

EXAM TIP: CONSEQUENCE

In your exam, Question 4 uses a source and may ask a question which focuses upon consequence. Make sure you use the source **and** your own knowledge to find several outcomes or impacts of the question focus.

Your conclusion should compare these impacts and make a decision about the most significant

The Activity will help you develop the skills you need to answer questions on similarity and difference in an exam.

ACTIVITY

Questions that focus on consequences will ask you to look at an event and identify different impacts. Reread the sections of Silvia Arsia (p. 46), Lars Porsena (pp. 47–48) and Lake Regilius (p. 49) and complete the following table which looks at the impact of the Wars of Independence.

Event	Impacts on Rome	How did it affect people's lives.
Silvia Arsia		
Lars Porsena		
Lake Regilius		

The decline of the patron-client relationship

Livy (2.23) suggests that plebeian and patrician relationships were strained. There was no system in place which would allow plebeians to express their concerns. The patricians did not look favourably upon plebeian demands for land and debt reform. Patricians such as Appius Claudius and his descendants represent patrician greed.

WHAT WAS THE CONFLICT OF ORDERS?

It described the period of unrest and tension between the plebeian and patrician orders between 494 and 287. Livy described how plebeians used non-violent protests to demand greater access to the political system.

The ancients called these protests secessions. Refusing to work or to live in the city forced the patricians to listen and introduce changes. Without the plebeians, Rome's military power was reduced. Rome would have no workforce.

DEBATE

Did Patron-Client Relationships Exist?

There is some debate about the nature of the patron-client relationship. For example, Fergus Millar, believes the relationship was actually a business agreement between families. Such as a farmer and a landowner, or a craftsman and merchant. Alexander Yakobson, disagrees. For him it was an important part of Roman culture and it tied different families together.

> **S&C** **The Sack of Rome 387**
>
> Roman historians believed that the original bronze tablets of the Twelve Tables (p. 65) were destroyed by the Gauls in the 387 sack of Rome. The legend claims that the Gauls set fire to Rome and destroyed most of the ancient records. Archaeology, however, disputes this version of events. There is evidence of widespread destruction around 507, not 387.
>
> As a consequence, some historians suspect the Sack of Rome may have been exaggerated or created by Fabius Pictor to explain the scarcity of evidence before the fourth century.

FIGURE 1.22
A nineteenth century depiction of the Twelve Tables.

EXPLORE FURTHER

For a short overview of the Conflict of the Orders try Mary Beard's *SPQR*, pp. 146–53.

The Conflict of the Orders showed the patricians that they could not ignore the needs of the plebeians. Rome's power depended upon having a large number of soldiers to call upon. Rome knew it needed to have a loyal army which would defend the city and expand its empire.

THE FIRST SECESSION 494–492

Impact of the Battle of Lake Regilius

> While they [the plebeians] were fighting for freedom on the battlefield [at Regilius], their families were being imprisoned at home by those they were fighting to protect.
>
> Livy, *The History of Rome* 2.23 (adapted)

1.4 Securing the Republic, 494–440 BC

FIGURE 1.23
A nineteenth century interpretation of the story of the war veteran.

Livy (2.23) begins his story about the First Secession with the case of the war veteran.

In 495, a war veteran visited the Forum to ask for help. He told passers-by had been a commander in the army, but had been reduced to homelessness by war. His farm had been destroyed by the Sabines and his possessions stolen.

When the Senate demanded he pay a new war tax he had borrowed money to pay his share. The taxes were too high and he could not settle his debts: So his land was **repossessed** and his **creditor** demanded he be tortured and whipped. According to Livy, his story spread throughout the city causing outrage. The Forum was overrun by an angry mob and debtors who demanded justice. The two consuls, Publius Servius and Appius Claudius, averted a riot in the Forum. They could not, however, stop sedition spreading.

repossess taking the possessions of a person by force when they cannot afford to pay their debt

creditor a person lending money

Role of Publius Servilius and Appius Claudius

When the Senate met to discuss war debt and civil unrest it did not have a **quorum**. Livy suggested some senators stayed away because they did not want to help the plebeians. Without a quorum, the Senate could not take any action to help the debtors.

In his account, Livy (2.23–2.24) describes a debate between Appius Claudius and Servilius. It is very unlikely that Livy had access to a copy of the debate, or if the debate ever occurred. It is an important part of the story because it introduced the two divisions within the patricians.

On one side, Appius wanted to crush the plebeians. Servilius, however, represented compromise and unity. He wanted to avoid conflict by helping the poor with debt relief.

As the debate ended, Latin horsemen rode into the meeting and informed the crowd that a Volscan army was attacking Rome's allies. Servilius, vowed to fight against debt if the plebeians would fight for him.

quorum the number of people from a group needed to make a meeting official – without a quorum, a group like the Senate could not make a decision or recommendation

Part One Longer Period Study

S&C Why Are There Three Appius Claudius in this Period?

Appius Claudius and his two descendants were probably invented by the Roman historians to show how greed and immorality led to civil strife.

indict formal accusation that someone has committed a crime

> **KEY INDIVIDUALS**
>
> **Appius Claudius Sabinus Regillensis**
> Dates: Late sixth to fifth century
>
> Legendary consul who caused the First Secession because he refused to help starving war veterans and increased the tensions created by the debt crisis
>
> **Appius Claudius Regillensis (the younger)**
> Dates: Late sixth to fifth century
>
> His son was also known as Appius Claudius Regillensis. As consul in 471 he resisted changes to tribunal elections. Like his father, he was prepared to risk civil strife to protect his own interests. He was **indicted** in 470, but died before his trial could be concluded
>
> **Appius Claudius Crassus**
> Dates: fifth century–454
>
> Presented as the worst. He pretended to support the plebeians to create a tyranny. His greed and lust caused the Second Secession when he tried to abduct Virginia

Study questions
Theme 3: Impact of Warfare and Military Change

Read Livy's account of the causes of the Conflict of Orders Livy 2.23–2.27

1. Summarise the story of the war veteran.
2. Summarise the problems facing the poor.
3. How does Livy describe Appius Claudius? Why does he oppose debt relief?
4. How does Livy describe Servilius? Why does he support debt relief?
5. Summarise the actions of the Senate which cause further unrest.

Servilius quickly assembled an army with plebeian assistance. Appius, however, used his powers as consul to wage a war against the debtors. Men who fought with Servilius were placed in chains when they returned to Rome.

Appius blamed Servilius. Appius told the war veterans that Servilius had no right to cancel debts without the support of the Senate. The debtors who fought for Rome demanded Servilius help, but the consul could not intervene.

THE FIRST SECESSION

Livy (2.26) created a vivid portrayal of a city in turmoil. Appius' actions caused civil unrest. Lawlessness gripped Rome. Groups of plebeians freed debtors from their chains. Senators were attacked. The consuls Verginius and Vetusius could not assemble an army. The plebeians began meeting in secret on Esquiline and Aventine hills.

The unrest encouraged Rome's enemies because they realised the consuls could not assemble any armies. Rome's rivals took this opportunity to attack its Latin allies.

The Senate quickly organised an emergency meeting to find a solution. Titus Larcius took up the case of the plebeians. He believed helping the plebeians would end the unrest so the consuls could create an army. Otherwise there was a chance Rome would be permanently divided.

Dictator Valerius

Appius Claudius told the Senate that they should not be bullied by criminals. If the Senate cancelled plebeian debt, their demands would not end until they controlled Rome.

He proposed that a dictator be appointed to crush the rebellion. The Senate agreed, appointing Publius Valerius as dictator.

Much to Appius Claudius' anger, Valerius appealed to the people. He reassured them that he did not seek power, but would put their case and recommendations to the Senate. His speech was so powerful that he managed to assemble ten legions to defeat the Sabine, Aequi and Volsci threat.

On his return to Rome, the victorious dictator asked the Senate to consider debt relief. The Senate refused and Valerius resigned his position. The plebeians hailed him as a hero, but realised that they had made no more progress in their fight against poverty.

Sicinius and the First Secession 494 BC

The Senate had pushed Rome to the brink of civil war. The consuls refused to demobilise the army and pretended that they were still at war. The army knew the war was over and feared they would be used to wage war upon the plebeians.

Sicinius, one of the soldiers who had fought for the dictator, told the army that they needed to act in a way which would strike fear into the heart of the patricians. Sicinius suggested a secession. If they occupied the Sacred Mount and inspired **seditious** plebeians to join them, then success could be theirs.

When the people of Rome heard about the occupation of the Sacred Mount, many citizens fled the city, some to join the soldiers on the Sacred Mount, others to escape imminent civil war. Armed patricians tried, unsuccessfully, to prevent the plebeians from leaving the city.

The Sacred Mount settlement raided outlying farms to secure food and provisions for themselves. The Senate sent ambassadors to the Sacred Mount to hear the plebeians'

> **Study questions**
> Theme 1: Political Change
>
> Read Livy's account of the growing lawlessness in Rome
> Livy 2.28–2.31
>
> 1. Summarise the three viewpoints expressed by the Senate about the civil unrest in 2.29.
> 2. Why do the plebeians agree to support Valerius?
> 3. Why does Valerius resign the dictatorship?

seditious keen to start or participate in an uprising

Sicinius Bellutus

Very little is known about Sicinius. Unlike other characters in this story, he is given very little back story. This may be because he was made up, or he could be an historical echo.

We can assume, from the literary tradition, that he was an influential soldier, perhaps a commander in a century. According to Dionysius (6.45) he convinces the army to seize the army standards. Standards were symbols of honour in the Roman army, and any consul losing a standard would be weakened and shamed. Sicinius role in the Secession appears to be pivotal and he is appointed leader of the deserting soldiers.

Sicinius was appointed one of the first plebeian tribunes. We have very little evidence of whether he was successful or not. Livy (2.34) only mentions him again when he criticises Sicinius for abusing his power.

Part One Longer Period Study

> **Study questions**
> Theme 1: Political Change
>
> Read the account of the First Secession from Livy Livy 2.32–2.33
>
> 1 Summarise the actions of the Senate after the resignation of Valerius.
> 2 Summarise the actions of Sicinius and the plebeians.
> 3 Summarise Menenius Agrippa's role in convincing the plebeians to negotiate with the Senate.
> 4 Summarise the outcome of the negotiations.

> **S&C Was the Secession Violent?**
>
> Dionysius (6.46) described those that joined Sicinius as criminals and evil men.
> Livy (2.32) presents them as surprisingly quiet.
> One reason for this could be that they were using different sources, the other might be their different beliefs. Dionysius was very critical of the plebeians. Livy on the other hand valued peace and blamed aristocratic greed for many of Rome's problems.

demands. The plebeians repeated their request for debt relief and refused to enter negotiations until these requests were met.

The Senate had no solution. When two new consuls were elected, they asked Menenius Agrippa to speak with the Plebeians on the Sacred Mount. Menenius was a patrician who had descended from an honourable plebeian family.

Menenius encouraged the plebeians to enter into negotiations after telling them the story about the body politic.

> Once upon a time a man's body did not work in unison. Instead each organ had its own voice and own ambitions. They complained that they fed the stomach, but it did nothing but enjoy their labours. So they agreed to starve the stomach. The body began to waste away. The organs realised that they all relied upon each other.
>
> Livy, *The History of Rome* 2.32 (adapted)

Menenius convinced the plebeians to enter into negotiations. Appius Claudius refused to compromise or negotiate. He told the Senate to replace the plebeians with workers from Rome's Latin allies.

Brutus Lucius Junius and Sicinius presented the case for the plebeians. They reassured the plebeians that the Senate wanted to help them. While speaking to the Senate, they proposed the creation of plebeian magistrates called tribunes. Tribunes would have the power to fight against injustice and inform the Senate about plebeian problems.

> **DEBATE Did the First Secession Achieve Anything?**
>
> Plebeian tribunes provided access to the political system. The role of the tribune is unclear, and it probably developed over time.
> Livy suggested that the tribunes achieved very little except cause civil unrest. Livy's annual reports about civil unrest caused by the plebeian tribunes are a common feature of his book.
>
> > Lucius Furius and Gaius Manlius were the next consuls. Command against the Veii fell to Manlius, but no war ensued... Discord at home immediately followed peace abroad. The plebs were in uproar because the tribunes were agitating for a new land law.
> >
> > Livy, *The History of Rome* 2.54 (adapted)

WHY HAD THE TRIBUNES FAILED TO IMPROVE THE LIVES OF THE PLEBIANS BY 462 BC?

Coriolanus

The First Secession caused famine. Marcius Coriolanus argued that the plebeians had caused the famine, and they should starve. The tribunes **indicted** Coriolanus and ordered him to be put on trial. Coriolanus ignored the threats of the tribunes, he believed they only had the power to help the oppressed, not to punish senators.

The tribunes used their position to **incite** the plebeians to use mob violence if Coriolanus was not punished. The senators agreed to offer Coriolanus as a **scapegoat** and set fair food prices. Rather than face trial Coriolanus fled to Volsci and encouraged them to wage war upon Rome.

Spurius Cassius and the demand for an agrarian law

According to Livy land redistribution was wanted by the plebeians. The tribunes realised this and they proposed a series of **agrarian laws**.

The consul Spurius Cassius tried to use this demand to establish a tyranny. After signing a peace treaty with the Hernici in 486 BC he acquired 60 per cent of their land. Cassius wanted to split the land between the plebeians and the Latins.

Cassius was attacked on all sides. The senators accused him of wanting to become a tyrant by bribing the poor and the Latins. The plebeians became suspicious. When Spurius Cassius tried to use surplus grain to buy plebeian support, his plan backfired. Livy suggested he was executed in 485.

Volero Publilius

In 473, Volero Publilius, a plebeian, refused to join the army as an ordinary soldier because he had once been a commander. To avoid arrest he told the people that the tribunes were too scared or too friendly with the Senate to help the people. The mob turned on the lictors and he escaped.

The Senate assembled to decide how to punish Volero. The elder senators urged caution and Volero was freed.

Volero successfully campaigned to become the next tribune in 472. He demanded a change to the tribune voting system. Livy (2.56) suggested that Volero was right to demand reform, rather than incite sedition.

> **The Assassination of Gnaeus Genucius**
>
> Gnaeus Genucius fought for an agrarian law. He indicted the consuls who had resisted the law once they left their magistracy in 473. Members of the Senate met in secret to discuss the problem and decided to take extreme action. On the day of the indictment Gnaeus failed to turn up. He was discovered murdered in his home. Read the fully story in Livy 2.54.

---

incite to encourage people to use violence

scapegoat a person or group of people blamed for something that has happened

Study questions
Theme 1: Political Change

Read Livy's account of Coriolanus exile
Book 2.34–2.35

1. Summarise the impact of the First Secession upon the plebeians.
2. Summarise the events leading to Coriolanus indictment.
3. What happened at the trial of Coriolanus?
4. In what ways does this story demonstrate political change in Rome?

agrarian law a redistribution of land or a change of the way land is farmed

Study questions
Theme 1: Political Change

Read Livy's account of Spurius Cassius
Book 2.41

1. Summarise the events leading to Spurius Cassius' execution.
2. In what ways does this story demonstrate political change in Rome?

Part One Longer Period Study

> **Study questions**
> Theme 1: Political Change
>
> Read Livy's account of Volero Publilius Book 2.55–2.58, 2.61
>
> 1 How does Livy describe Volero Publilius when he resists arrest?
> 2 How does Livy describe Volero Publilius when he requests a change to the voting system for tribunes?
> 3 Summarise the key events in the story of Volero Publilius.
> 4 How does Livy describe Appius Claudius?
> 5 Summarise the key events from the trial of Appius Claudius from 2.61.

According to Livy, Volero's request frightened the Senate. If Volero's proposals were accepted, then the patricians would have no influence over the election of tribunes. Anyone could become a tribune.

Appius Claudius' son, also known as Appius Claudius, was elected as consul. Volero and Appius clashed violently. To prevent civil unrest, Appius Claudius was coerced into accepting the law.

The indictment of Appius Claudius

In 470, Appius Claudius was indicted by the tribunes. Appius refused to acknowledge the charges against him. This caused widespread unrest. The trial was suspended until a later date to avoid further conflict. During the suspension Appius died.

The Volero reforms had strengthened the tribunes. The reduction of senatorial influence allowed the plebeians to elect people who were more likely to represent them.

Gaius Terentilius and the demand to limit consular power

Quintus Fabius proposed in 467 that land taken from the Volsci could be used to create a colony for the plebeians. By creating a colony, Fabius was able to offer new land to Roman plebeians. Reducing the demand for land reform weakened the influence of the tribunes.

Gaius Terentilius Harsa adopted a new approach. The absence of the consuls gave him an opportunity to demand constitutional reform. Terentilius demanded a written constitution to define and limit the powers of the consul. Terentilius claimed that consuls abused their powers and acted with more freedom than kings.

Quintus Fabius attacked Terentilius and called him a traitor. Fabius asked Terentilius to present his ideas to the consuls when they returned. The Senate agreed that Terentilius' ideas were worth investigating, but they would not vote on the matter until they had more information. This gave the Senate the excuse not to do anything.

> **Study questions**
> Theme 1: Political Change
>
> Read the speech of Gaius Terentilius Harsa from Livy 3.9
>
> 1 Summarise the aims of Terentilius.
> 2 Summarise Quintus Fabius' reply.

EXAM TIP: CHANGE AND CONTINUITY

In your exam, Question 4 may ask you to assess how much an aspect of Rome had changed or stayed the same between two dates or events. We looked at change on p. 19.

Many change questions may ask you to explore the extent of change. To do this you will need to look for examples of continuity **and** change. The best answers will find examples of change and areas which have not changed (continuity).

The Activity will help you develop the skills you need to answer questions on change and continuity.

ACTIVITY

Reread this section. To what extent had nothing changed between the end of the Wars and Independence and 460?

Progress since the story of the war veteran	Obstacles which prevented change	Continuity from the story of the war veteran

As a class debate how far you think Rome's political systems had changed by 460.

THE FIRST AND SECOND DECEMVIRATE?

The creation of the Decemvirate

Livy tells us (3.31–3.32) that the tribunes realised that Terentilius' demands were never going to be met. In 454, a new spirit of co-operation began. The newly-elected tribunes agreed to drop Terentilius' demands if the senators allowed the plebeians to participate in the selection of lawgivers. The Senate agreed to the request and sent ambassadors to Athens to investigate its laws. Athens at this time had created a democracy which gave all citizens equal rights. The laws of Solon they were investigating were believed to have helped create the Athenian democracy.

On their return in 452 BC, the Senate created the Decemvirate, a council of ten men, to create a new law code. The Decemvirate replaced the tribunes and consul. Its members came from the patrician class.

The rule of the First Decemvirate

The Decemvirate of 451 was described by Livy (3.33) as just and fair.

Appius Claudius Crassus, the grandson of Appius Claudius, helped create the first Ten Tables of laws. Claudius Crassus had become the hero of the plebeians. Claudius Crassus was, however, deceiving the poor to become a tyrant.

When the Decemvirate published its laws, people flocked to see them. Despite widespread approval, the Roman historians claimed the people wanted two more tables.

It was agreed that ten more men would be chosen to complete the tables. Livy makes it clear that the plebeians were so relieved by the work of the Decemvirate that they did not demand the return of the tribunes.

Study questions
Theme 1: Political Change

Read Livy's account of the First Decemvirate Book 3.33

1 Make a list of the different ways the Decemvirate rule Rome fairly.
2 Make a list of the different tactics used by Appius Claudius Crassus to win the support of the plebeians.
3 Make a list of the different reactions to the Ten Tables.

> **Study questions**
> Theme 1: Political Change
>
> Read Livy's account of the Second Decemvirate Livy 3.36–3.37
>
> 1 Summarise the events leading to the creation of the Second Decemvirate.
> 2 Make a list of the different ways the Second Decemvirate was tyrannical.
> 3 Make a list of the different ways the people of Rome reacted to the Second Decemvirate.

> **KEY INDIVIDUALS**
>
> **Lucius Valerius Potitus and Marcus Horatius Barbatus**
>
> **Dates**: fifth century
>
> Consuls who helped reform plebeian rights after the Second Secession

The tyranny of the Second Decemvirate

Appius Claudius Crassus' popularity among the plebeians concerned many senators. They feared he wanted to control the Second Decemvirate. To prevent this, Crassus' opponents put him in charge of the selection process. They foolishly believed he would not be arrogant enough to use this power to elect himself.

Crassus manipulated the selection process to appoint himself and nine allies. Livy (3.36 and 3.39) describes them as the ten Tarquins. The new Decemvirate of 450 was tyrannical. They met in secret and appointed twelve lictors each to act as bodyguards.

Crassus used his new powers to attack the plebeians. Trials were held in the homes of his friends to attack the plebeians and remove Crassus' enemies. In 449, the Decemvirate announced their intention to rule for another year.

The Second Decemvirate did create two new tables of laws (Livy 3.37) which protected the patricians. For example, it included a law which banned inter-marriage between plebeians and patricians.

Valerius' and Horatius' Opposition to the Decemvirate

The use of tyranny had allowed Crassus and the Second Decemvirate to rule Rome unchallenged. When a Sabine army attacked a Roman colony and the Aequi attacked Algidus, the Decemvirate (Livy 3.38) called a meeting of the Senate to assemble an army.

No senators attended the meeting and the plebeians refused to enlist in the army. Crassus used his lictors to force a quorum of senators to attend. Crassus told the Senate they could only vote to approve military action.

Lucius Valerius Potitus and Marcus Horatius Barbatus told the Decemvirate that they were acting like kings (Livy 3.39), and they would share the same fate as Tarquinius Superbus.

The majority of the Senate, however, were more fearful of plebeian unrest than the Decemvirate. The Senate voted for an army. This new army had no heart and suffered many heavy defeats (Livy 3.42).

The abduction of Virginia

The downfall of the Second Decemvirate is almost an exact copy of the downfall of the Tarquins. Livy (3.44–3.49) describes how the abduction of Virginia leads to the Second Secession.

Crassus lusted after a plebeian girl named Virginia. He knew she was engaged to Lucius Icilius, a former tribune. When Virginia refused his advances, Crassus asked his client, Marcus Claudius to claim she was a runaway slave. This would allow Crassus to put her on trial.

At the trial, Virginia demanded time to contact her father, Lucius Verginius, who was fighting at Algidus. Crassus agreed to wait if Virginia accompanied him home.

Lucius Icilius fought his way through Crassus' lictors and told the crowd that Crassus wanted to rape Virginia. The crowd turned against Crassus. He let Virginia leave and ordered her to return the next day.

Icilius immediately left for Algidus and managed to tell Verginius of his daughter's situation.

The following day Crassus dismissed Verginius' and Icilius' evidence. Crassus declared that Viginia was a slave and that Verginius was a traitor.

Before Crassus' lictors could seize Virginia her father took extreme action. He asked Crassus for permission to speak to Virginia's nurse and check if Virginia was really his daughter. Crassus agreed. Taking the opportunity, Verginius seized a knife from a butcher and ran towards his daughter.

> Taking his daughter in his arms Verginius said, 'I am preserving your freedom and liberty in the only way I can'. Taking the butcher's knife he plunged it into his daughter's chest. Then he turned to look Crassus in the eyes, and he roared 'with my daughter's blood I curse you'.

Livy, *The History of Rome* 3.47 (adapted)

Verginius escaped from Rome and returned to his camp at Algidus. Valerius and Horatius demanded the Senate recall the tribunes and consuls. The Senate refused. They feared Verginius would mobilise the army against them. The Decemvirate provided the Senate protection.

FIGURE 1.24
A German medieval woodcut illustration of Virginia's trial.

> **ACTIVITY**
>
> As a class discuss why the Roman historians use the death of an innocent woman to end a tyranny?
>
> Mary Beard claims that the death of Virginia is more shocking than the rape of Lucretia. As a class discuss whether you agree.

> **Study questions**
>
> Theme 4: Separating Myth from Reality
>
> Read Livy's account of the Abduction of Virginia
> Livy 3.44–3.49
>
> **1** Summarise the events which led to Virginia's death.
>
> Reread the chapters on the Rape of Lucretia and the abduction of Virginia
>
> **2** Complete the table below.
>
> | Similarities between the two stories | Differences between the two stories |
> |---|---|
> | | |

THE SECOND SECESSION 449 BC

Verginius and the Second Secession

When Verginius returned to his camp his fellow soldiers were alarmed to see their comrade covered in blood. Livy tells us that Verginius addressed the soldiers.

> Verginius turned to his comrades, his hands outstretched, and asked them not to punish him. He had loved his daughter more than his own life, but could not live with himself if he allowed his daughter to be defiled by the tyrant. He told the crowd he had contemplated suicide, but hoped that his fellow soldiers might help him avenge her death. After all they all had wives, daughters and sisters. Crassus' lust would not have ended with his daughter. Unchecked it would have worsened and he would have dishonoured and defiled many more women. If needed he would fight alone, but hoped that others would help him protect their own children from his daughter's fate.
>
> Livy, *The History of Rome* 3.50 (adapted)

Verginius' speech encouraged many soldiers to leave the battlefield and join a Second Secession on the Aventine hill. Icilius followed Verginius' example and encouraged the army fighting the Sabines to join the Secession.

Impact of the Secession

Members of the Senate were alarmed. The Senate sent envoys to the Aventine to try to find a prompt solution. The soldiers stated that they would only talk to Valerius and Horatius.

Valerius and Horatius used this to their advantage. They would not meet the soldiers until the Decemvirate handed power back to the consuls. The Decemvirate refused.

Once the soldiers heard that Valerius and Horatius were being ignored they took their families with them to the Sacred Mount. Livy describes Rome as a ghost town. Livy is drawing upon a similar event from his lifetime, when Julius Caesar marched on Rome in 49 BC.

The Second Secession left the Decemvirate no choice. They agreed to disband if protected from prosecution. Valerius and Horatius met with the leaders of the Secession. They demanded the restoration of the tribunes and the indictment of the Decemvirate.

The two senators urged caution. They respected the desire of the plebeians to seek a shield to protect themselves from injustice, but could not support their desire to wield a sword against the Decemvirate. Valerius wanted to end the relentless war between the two orders.

Valerio-Horatian Laws

Valerius' and Horatius' success in organising a compromise was met with relief across Rome.

An immediate election was organised to take place on the Aventine hill. Verginius and Icilius were two of the ten tribunes elected. Icilius' first action was to propose that no revenge or reprisals be sought against the Decemvirate.

Valerius and Horatius were elected as the new consuls and they immediately used their powers to pass laws to protect the plebeian order. These laws became known as the Valerio-Horatian Laws.

- The right to appeal was restored and strengthened. Before 449 BC, consuls and other magistrates had the power to create courts which had no right of appeal. The Valerio-Horatian Laws ended this practice.
- **Inviolability** of the tribunes, and their assistants the aediles, was restored.

Despite their promises to not seek revenge against the Decemvirate, the tribunes indicted Crassus. Aware of his imminent death Crassus committed suicide. The other members of the Second Decemvirate went into exile or committed suicide.

The Twelve Tables

Before raising armies to destroy the Sabine and Aequi threat, Valerius and Horatius published the Twelve Tables.

The Twelve Tables were available to all in precise and simple language, and in this regard gave the Roman citizen basic civil rights. They did not, however, establish the idea that 'everyone was equal before the law'.

Here is a brief summary of their content:

- attendance in court
- theft
- lending and debtors
- family law and the rights of fathers
- inheritance
- possession, ownership and slavery
- criminal acts
- property law

> **Study questions**
> Theme 1: Political Change
>
> Read Livy's account about the end of the Second Secession Livy 3.53–3.54
>
> **1** Make a list of the concerns and demands of the patricians and plebeians.
> **2** How similar are the two lists? What reasons do you think there are for this?
> **3** How significant are Valerius and Horatius in securing a settlement between the patrician and plebeian groups?

> **inviolability** legal protection from violence or harm

Part One Longer Period Study

> **ACTIVITY**
>
> As a class, consider if there is any evidence that attitudes had changed since the story of the war veteran.

- public law and treason
- religious law
- Tables 11 and 12 created by the Second Decemvirate to protect patricians

LEGAL CHANGES IN ROME TO 440 BC

The Twelve Tables and the Valerio-Horatian Laws were flawed. Very little had actually changed and the two orders still distrusted each other. Over the next nine years, a number of important changes were made.

Gaius Canuleius managed to lift the ban on marriage between patricians and plebeians in 445. But according to Livy (4.1) he went much further. The Twelve Tables and the Valero-Horatian Laws had not eased tensions, but had encouraged the plebeians to demand more. Livy suggested (4.3–4.5) that Gaius Canuleius used his popular support to not only remove the marriage ban, but to argue that plebeians should have the right to stand for election as consul in 445.

Livy (4.2) argued that the Senate feared this development. To ease the popular unrest, the Senate offered a compromise (Livy 4.6). They would allow plebeians to become military tribunes. This new role would give elected plebeians or patricians the power to command armies and seek the same glory as a victorious consul.

> **Study question**
>
> Theme 2: Social and Religious Change
>
> Read Livy's reasons for the division between the patricians and plebeians Livy 4.1–4.6
>
> Complete this table by summarising the views of Quinctius and Canuleius.
>
> | Consul Titus Quinctius' (Bk 4.2) views of the plebeians | Gaius Canuleius' (Bk 4.3–4.5) views on the patricians |
> |---|---|
> | | |

> **Study question**
>
> Theme 4: Separating Myth from Reality
>
> Read Livy 4.5
>
> To what extent do you think this speech reflects Livy's views?

1.4 Securing the Republic, 494–440 BC

TIMESPAN REVIEW

Boost your knowledge

Describe:

a. the First Secession. Include the impact of war, the war veteran and the creation of the tribune
b. actions taken by the tribunes to improve plebeian rights. Agrarian and voting reform
c. the cases of Coriolanus, Appius Claudius and Spurius Cassius
d. the two Decemvirates, the Twelve Tables and the Volero-Horatian Laws

Stretch your understanding

Explain:

a. why Livy believed war caused the First Secession
b. Appius Cassius', Menenius', Volero Publilius' and Claudius Crassus' character and role in Livy's narrative
c. why the Conflict of the Two Orders could not be resolved
d. the limitations of the Twelve Tables and the Volero-Horatian Laws

PRACTICE QUESTIONS

Passage B

The battle was on: the consuls and the Senate on the one side, Canuleius and the plebeians on the other. Both sides blamed each other. The consuls swore that the lunatic excesses of the tribunes proved they were deliberately provoking war. A war far more deadly than with a foreign enemy. 'All Roman citizens share responsibility,' the Senate said, 'for the present situation. But we cannot allow the magnificent aura which surrounded the Senate in our fathers' day, to have disappeared when we pass it to our children! Think how the plebeians will be able to brag of their increased power and influence! There can never be an end to this unhappy process as long as sedition against the government is honoured. Do you realise. . . what Canuleius is trying to do? If he succeeds. . . he will contaminate the blood of our ancient and noble families. . . that no one will know who he is and where he came from!

Livy, *The History of Rome* 4.2

1. Using details from Passage B and your own knowledge, what can we learn about the relationship between the plebeians and patricians in 445 BC? [10]
2. Using details from Passage B and your own knowledge, explain how far the rivalry between the patricians and plebeians had changed between 473 and 440 BC. [15]

Further Reading

General texts on the period

Beard, Mary, *SPQR* (London: Profile, 2016).

Boardman, John (ed.), *The Oxford History of the Roman World* (Oxford: Oxford University Press, 2001).

Cary M. and H.H Scullard, *A History of Rome* (Basingstoke: Palgrave Macmillan, 1980), 3rd ed.

Faulkner, Neil, *Rome: Empire of the Eagles, 753 BC–AD 476* (Abingdon: Routledge, 2013).

Hornblower, Simon and Tony Spawforth, *The Oxford Companion to Classical Civilisation* (Oxford: Oxford University Press, 2014).

Mackay, Christopher S., *Ancient Rome: A Military and Political History* (Cambridge: Cambridge University Press, 2005), pp. 3–40.

Renshaw, James, *In Search of the Romans* (London: Bristol Classical, 2008).

Scullard, H.H., *A History of the Roman World: 753 to 146 BC* (Abingdon: Routledge, 2012), 4th ed.

Southern, Patricia, *Ancient Rome: The Republic 753–30BC* (Stroud: Amberley Publishing, 2011), p. 11–68.

Focused texts

Claridge, Amanda, *Oxford Archaeological Guides: Rome* (Oxford: Oxford University Press, 2010), 2nd ed.

Cornell, Tim, *The Beginnings of Rome* (Abingdon: Routledge, 1995).

Flower, Harriet *Cambridge Companions to the Ancient World: The Cambridge Companion to the Roman Republic* (Cambridge: Cambridge University Press, 2004).

Fraschetti, Ausgusto, *The Foundation of Rome* (Edinburgh: Edinburgh University Press, 2005), trans. Marian Hill and Kevin Windle.

Grandazzi, Alexandre, *The Foundation of Rome: Myth and History* (Ithaca: Cornell, 1997) trans. Jane Marie Todd.

Mazzoni, Cristina, *She-wolf: The Story of a Roman Icon* (Cambridge: Cambridge University Press, 2010).

Mellor, Ronald, *The Roman Historians* (Abingdon: Routledge, 1999).

Serres, Michel, *Rome: The First Book of Foundations* (London: Bloomsbury, 2015), trans. Randolph Burks.

Smith, Christopher, *The Etruscans: A Very Short Introduction* (Oxford: Oxford University Press, 1996).

Sorek, Susan, *Ancient Historians: A Student Handbook* (London: Bloomsbury, 2012), pp.105–12.

Southern, Patricia, *The Roman Army: History 753 BC–AD 476* (Stroud: Amberley Publishing, 2016).

Documentaries

Beard, Mary, *Meet the Romans* (BBC/IMC Vision, 2012).

Beard, Mary, *Ultimate Rome* (BBC/IMC Vision, 2016).

Ancient sources

Electronic versions can be found online.

Dionysius of Halicarnasus, *Roman Antiquities*: Books 1–9.

Livy, *The Rise of Rome: Books 1–5* (Oxford University Press: Oxford, 1998), trans. T.J. Luce.

Mellor, Ronald, *The Historians of Ancient Rome: An Anthology of the Major Writings* (Abingdon: Routledge, 2012).

What to Expect in the Exam: Section A

PERIOD STUDY: THE FOUNDATIONS OF ROME: FROM KINGSHIP TO REPUBLIC, 753–440 BC

This chapter aims to show you the types of questions you are likely to get in Section A of the Rome and its Neighbours exam. It offers some advice on how to answer the questions and will help you avoid common errors. Remember, Section A is compulsory and you must answer all the questions in this section. After this chapter, you will find advice on the three optional depth studies.

General exam skills

When you are sitting the examination, read the instructions carefully so that you realise which questions are compulsory and which are from optional Depth Studies. Remember that the questions on the examination will range in difficulty; some of them are designed to be challenging, and so do not worry if you cannot think of an answer immediately. The following pieces of advice may seem obvious, but you should not underestimate their importance:

- the examination lasts 105 minutes and is worth 105 marks. Don't assume this means you should spend a minute per mark: in reality, a lot of short questions will take less than a mark a minute and you should spend longer than a mark a minute on the longer questions
- if you see a question that you do not know the answer to, move on to another question and don't waste time thinking. Leave enough time to go back to it as during the examination you might well remember the answer
- stick to the question: if you are asked for facts, do not give opinions and vice versa.
- do not try to answer a slightly different question if you wish another had been set, or if you have practised a similar one before at school.

The examination

Section A on the Roman period study is compulsory. Section A is worth 60 out of the 105 marks on offer. Remember that your exam is 105 minutes long so you need to make sure you organise your time accordingly.

This component of the GCSE examination is designed to test your knowledge, understanding and evaluation of the Foundations of Rome 753–440 BC.

Part One Longer Period Study

There are three Assessment Objectives in your Ancient History GCSE. Questions will be designed to test these areas. These Assessment Objectives are explained in the table below:

	Assessment Objective
AO1	Demonstrate knowledge and understanding of the key features and characteristics of the historical periods studied
AO2	Analyse and explain historical events and historical periods to arrive at substantiated judgements
AO3	Use, analyse and evaluate ancient sources within their historical context to make judgements and draw conclusions about: • historical events and historical periods studied • how the portrayal of events by ancient writers/sources relates to the historical contexts in which they were written/produced

Be aware that there is some overlap with these Ancient History Assessment Objectives. As you will see in the table on the next page, questions 3, 4 and 5 assess multiple assessment objectives. For example, AO2 and AO3 both require you to make 'judgements' on the 'historical events and historical periods'.

In terms of knowledge and understanding, you should be able to demonstrate:

- a good grasp of the foundation myth, its key characters and events
- a good understanding of the key characters and events which led to significant developments or turning points
- knowledge of Rome's political, religious and social structures; and how the foundation myth suggested they developed over time;
- an awareness of the similarities and differences between the archaeological record and the different versions of the foundation myth

When analysing and evaluating your evidence in order to make judgements, you should be able to:

- compare and contrast key individuals and events across the full period
- analyse and evaluate the causes and consequences of key events from across the full period
- look at change and continuity, including the rate of change and the relative success of different developments
- support your arguments with relevant knowledge and understanding to come to a substantiated judgement

When dealing with the unseen source, you should be able to:

- read and comprehend the unseen written extract or visual source
- draw inferences from the unseen written extract or visual source about the issue in the question

What to Expect in the Exam: Section A

- analyse and evaluate the unseen written extract or visual source to make valid judgements about the period or event it describes.

QUESTION TYPES

There are five different types of question. The table below shows how they are assessed.

Question	Type of question	AO1 marks	AO2 marks	AO3 marks	SPaG marks	Total marks
1	Discrete factual knowledge	4	–	–	–	**4**
2	Outline . . .	6	–	–	–	**6**
3	Features/characteristics of a period, event or individual	5	–	5	–	**10**
4	Second-order concepts	5	5	5	–	**15**
5	Essay	10	10	–	5	**25**

Question 1 will test your knowledge. This question will be divided into 2–3 sub-questions.

Question 2 will ask you to develop several features and/or characteristics of an important event, development or individual.

Question 3 and 4 will supply you with an unseen source. Question 3 will ask you to comprehend the source and identify key features from the source. You will also need to use your own knowledge to develop your answer. Question 4 will require you to use the source alongside your own knowledge to tackle a second-order concept.

Question 5 is an essay question which will explore your ability to construct a line of argument and support it with knowledge, analysis and evaluation. There are 5 marks awarded for spelling, punctuation and grammar and the use of specialist terminology (SPaG) in this question.

Question 1 – knowledge questions

There will be 4 marks available for question 1, all testing factual knowledge (AO1). The 4 marks will be broken down into a series of short-answer questions, typically worth 1, 2 or 3 marks.

These questions will usually start with one of the following stems:

- State . . .

Part One Longer Period Study

- Identify...
- Name...
- Give...

For example: *Name **two** plebeians who demanded political reform.* [2]

- **Answers may include:** Gnaeus Genucius [1] and Sicinius Bellutus [1] are two possible answers.

You do not have to write in full sentences, and the answer should be brief.

Question 2: outline questions

There will be 6 marks available for question 2. Knowledge and understanding (AO1) is being assessed.

This question will start with the following stem:

- Outline...

For example: *Outline the main features of Aeneas' role in the 'Foundation story.'* [6]

Answers may include:

- Romulus and Remus were descended from Aeneas
- Aeneas visited Carthage and broke the heart of its queen Dido
- Aeneas' son founded Alba Longa. The city of Romulus' birth

When writing your outline you will identify several features and/or characteristics and develop them with relevant and developed knowledge. You should write in continuous prose, not bullet points.

Make sure that your outline is focused upon the question.

Question 3: source-based question: What can we learn...

Questions 3 and 4 both use the same unseen source. The unseen source could be a short extract from an ancient historian or a visual source from the archaeological record. You are not expected to have seen the unseen source before you sit your exam.

Question 3 will assess your ability to draw out information from the unseen source (AO3) and supplement it with additional knowledge that you can recall (AO1). You will therefore need to identify features from the source, and analyse or evaluate what this source tells us about the issue in the question. You should also develop your points by referring to your wider knowledge of the topic, this could be relevant information which is not referred to in the source. This information will then be used to evaluate the importance of the event/ individual or period highlighted in the question (AO1 and AO3).

The question will start with the following stem:

Using details from Passage A and your own knowledge, what can we learn about . . .

Here's an example:

Passage A
There Verginius created even greater unrest than he had in the city. For as he approached, he was seen to be accompanied by nearly four hundred men from the city, who had joined him because of the outrage they felt for the shocking way he had been treated. The entire camp was even more stirred by the sight of his drawn sword and bloodstained clothing. Moreover, the sight of men in civilian dress everywhere in the camp made their number seem somewhat greater than it really was. When those he encountered asked what was the matter, he stood silently weeping for a time, but after a crowd had gathered round and was waiting in anxious silence, he told them everything as it had happened. Then with palms upraised to heaven and appealing to them as fellow soldiers, he begged them not to find him responsible for Appius Claudius crime and not to reject him as the murderer of his own child. His daughter's life had been dearer to him than his own, but she could not live that life as a free and pure woman. When he saw her being hurried off like a slave to be raped, he thought it better to lose her to death than to abuse.

Livy, *The History of Rome*, Book 3.50

For example: *Using details from Passage A and your own knowledge, what can we learn about the role of Verginius in the Second Secession?* [10]

Answers may include:

From the passage:

- Verginius' inspired 400 men to leave Rome. This shows he was influential.
- He had murdered his daughter, Virginia, to protect her from slavery and the lust of Appius Claudius. Verginius was one of the first men to oppose the power of Appius Claudius.

From your own knowledge:

- Appius Claudius abused the powers of the second Decemvirate to try to abduct Verginius' daughter. This appalled the people of Rome.
- Verginius inspired the soldiers fighting in Algidus to secede and abandon Rome. This led to the down fall of the second Decemvirate.

When answering question 3 you must remember that this question is only worth 10 out of 60 marks so make sure you organise your time accordingly.

- After reading the passage, try to identify several key features from the passage and/or key features from your own knowledge. You will need to evaluate these features and identify their importance or significance.
- To develop a sophisticated evaluation of the passage, make sure that you use the features you have identified from the source and your own knowledge to make a judgement about the role of Verginius in the Second Secession.

Part One Longer Period Study

- **You do not need to evaluate the sources reliability,** but you will be credited if it is relevant to the question and the passage.

Question 4: source-based question: second-order concepts

Second-order concepts are used in this exam to test your ability to evaluate and analyse.

In GCSE Ancient History you will need to use the unseen source in order to answer a question on any one of the following: change and continuity, similarity and difference, significance, cause and consequence.

This question combines all three Assessment Objectives (AO1, AO2 and AO3.) It requires you to develop the content of the unseen source with your own knowledge to create an argument. To achieve this, you need to organise the features you have identified to provide a balanced answer to the question. For example, you could organise this information into a comparison of several causes or a comparison of similarity and difference. This question is worth 15 marks. 5 points will be awarded for AO1, AO2 and AO3.

The questions **may** look something like this:

- **Change and continuity.** These questions **may** ask you to explore an event or an aspect of Rome's development (such as political structures) and explain how much change there was between two points.
- *e.g. Using details from Passage/Source A and your own knowledge, explain how far x changed during y?*
- The best answers will identify examples of change and continuity and make a judgement about how far it changed.

- **Similarity and difference.** These questions **may** ask you to explore an aspect of the foundation myth and explain if individuals or events responded to it in a similar or different way.
- *e.g. Using details from Passage/Source A and your own knowledge, explain whether x's response was different/similar to y?*
- The best answers will identify similar and different approaches and then make a judgement about how far they were similar or different.

- **Significance.** These questions **may** ask you to explore the importance of an individual or event upon the 'Foundation myth'.
- *e.g. Using details from Passage/Source A and your own knowledge, explain the significance of x to y?*
- The best answers will be able to place the event within the context of the period and make a judgement about how far this event shaped Rome. You may compare the event with another event or individual, but don't lose focus of the question.

- **Cause.** These questions **may** ask you to explain how an event happened or why an individual took a particular course of action.
- *e.g. Using details from Passage/Source A and your own knowledge, explain what caused x?*

- The best answers will identify a number of causes and compare them. You may want to discuss how the causes combined to create the outcome identified in the question or explain why one was more significant.

- **Consequence.** These questions **may** ask you to explain the impact of an event or individual.
- *e.g. Using details from Passage/Source A and your own knowledge, explain the impact of x?*
- The best answers will identify a number of consequences and compare them. You may want to discuss how the consequences combined to lead to a particular outcome. You could also explain why one consequence was more significant.

Here is an example of how to answer a second-order concept question. As in your exam we will be using the same passage as on page xx: Livy 3:50:

Using details from Passage/Source A and your own knowledge, explain what caused the second secession? [15]

Possible answers may include:

From the passage and developed using knowledge:

- He appealed to the soldiers at Algidus to help him seek revenge against Appius Claudius. This meant that the Second Decemvirate would lose its army and be unable to fight Rome's enemies the Veii. He was also the first man to oppose the Second Decemvirate.
- He spread the word about Appius Claudius tyranny and treatment of his daughter Virginia. This led to widespread discontent among the citizens of Rome, including Horatius and Valerius.
- He had been forced to murder his daughter, Virginia, when Appius Claudius refused to listen to his evidence about her Roman citizenship. This shocked the people of Rome who witnessed the trial and 400 followed him to Algidus.

General advice

- Remember this question asks you to use your knowledge to identify, develop and assess key features from the passage to make a judgement about the second-order concept.
- Identify several possible features. These must be supported by the source and/or your own knowledge
- You must make sure that each of these features is linked to the question and its importance evaluated.
- Most significantly you must reach a substantiated judgement.
- Remember that question 4 is worth 15 out of a possible 60 marks, make sure that you organise your time accordingly.

Part One Longer Period Study

Question 5: essay question

The final question is an essay question which assesses knowledge and understanding (AO1) and analysis and explanation (AO2) are both worth 10 marks each. An extra 5 marks are awarded for SPaG.

When your essay is assessed you will be marked according to its best fit. This means that you need to meet broadly the expectations of each level to achieve it. If you wrote an essay with lots of detailed evidence, but failed to address the 'how far' or 'to what extent' part of the question then you would fail to achieve a high mark as you are as you are not fully addressing the analysis and explanation part of the question.

Your essay question will be much broader than question 4 and may expect you to draw upon material from across the whole period.

The following is an example of a possible essay question:

- 'Romulus shared more qualities with Tarquinius Superbus than any other king in the period 753–509 BC.' How far do you agree with this view? [20] + [5 SPaG]

Answer

(This is not an exhaustive list but it is designed to give you a flavour of what you might choose.)

Romulus and Superbus shared qualities

- Both were suspected of tyranny and removed from power; both committed murder to become king
- They were both builders. Romulus built the city. Superbus the Cloaca Maximus and temples.
- Both were good military commanders.

Romulus and Superbus were different

- Romulus became a god. Superbus an enemy of Rome.
- Romulus created political structures which created unity. Superbus divided Rome.
- Romulus listened to the advice of the Senate, Superbus did not.

Romulus shared more qualities with another king

- Romulus was more like Servius – both reformed Roman society to create unity. Romulus created the orders, Servius the class system. Both had 'mythical' conceptions (Romulus – Mars; Servius – Flaming Phallus).
- Romulus was more like Tullus Hostilius. Great military leaders. Both struck down by lightning.

Key points:

- There is no set answer and you can agree or disagree with the statement. The best answers will explore the extent you agree or disagree. You will therefore accept that there is evidence to support both sides, but one has more weight or is more

likely in your opinion.
- Make a quick plan which organises the key features you can identify into a table which supports and challenges the statement in the question.
- Identify two sides of the argument and make a decision about which is more likely in your opinion. This will allow you to develop a substantiated argument. NB. You do not need more than two sides of the argument but more sophisticated answers may have them.
- Support both sides of the argument with relevant knowledge. This information needs to be factual by drawing upon key features and individuals.
- Avoid retelling the story. Describing one or two important features from the story as an anecdote, however, is good practice.
- Make sure that you keep referring back to the statement and explain how significant the key features you have identified from your knowledge are. This link should explore how far the evidence agrees with the statement.
- After exploring each side of the argument try to evaluate all the evidence which challenges or supports the statement in combination.
- You will not have a lot of time to answer these questions and so it is always best to use your most important arguments first in case you find yourself running out of time.
- Ultimately make your conclusion **logical**, and supported by evidence from your whole answer, not just one part of it.

PART 2
DEPTH STUDIES

Introduction to the Depth Study options

Just under a quarter of your GCSE in Ancient History involves the study of a particular topic in greater detail.

OCR offers the choice between three options:

Hannibal and the Second Punic War, 218–201 BC	J198/02 Section B
Cleopatra: Rome and Egypt, 69–30 BC	J198/02 Section C
Britannia: from Conquest to Province, AD 43–c. 84	J198/02 Section D

The following pages of this textbook guide you through the content of all three of these options, but you will only study one. A booklet of translations of the prescribed sources is provided by OCR and is available online for downloading and printing. **CW**

All three Depth Studies develop what you have learned in the Longer Period Study about Rome. The events studied in Hannibal and the Second Punic War are some 250 years after the end of the Longer Period Study and you will see how Rome has developed and increased in power since then as it faces the threat of Carthage. In Cleopatra you will study events during the first century BC that lead to the end of the Roman Republic and the start of the principate under Octavian/Augustus. In Britannia, you will learn how Rome continued to grow in power, expanding its empire westwards in the first century AD.

EXAM OVERVIEW — J198/02 SECTIONS B–D

Your assessment for the Depth Study option will be

22.5% of the GCSE	45 mins out of 1 hr 45 mins for the whole paper	45 marks out of 105 marks for the whole paper

15 marks will test AO1: demonstrate knowledge and understanding of the key features and characteristics of the historical periods studied.

10 marks will test AO2: analyse and explain historical events and historical periods to arrive at substantiated judgements.

20 marks will test AO3: use, analyse and evaluate ancient sources within their historical context.

DEPTH STUDY 1
Hannibal and the Second Punic War, 218–201 BC

Introduction to Hannibal and the Second Punic War, 218–201 BC

This depth study looks at:

- the origins of the Second Punic War
- Hannibal's leadership
- Rome's response to Hannibal's invasion
- Rome's eventual victory.

Carthage, on the north coast of Africa (modern Tunisia), had controlled the Mediterranean until the end of the First Punic War in 241. Rome, having secured control of mainland Italy, Sicily, Sardinia and Southern Europe, now looked to expand across the Mediterranean.

After the First Punic War, Carthage had been humbled by the Treaty of Lutatius. To recoup its losses, Carthage colonised Iberia and rebuilt their army. Whether Hannibal crossed the Alps to seek revenge or defend Carthage from Roman aggression we will never know. Whatever the reason, Hannibal's invasion of Italy lasted for fourteen years.

Hannibal was helped by poor Roman leadership. This gave Hannibal the opportunity to secure outstanding victories at Trebia, Trasimene and Cannae. Under the guidance of the dictator Fabius Maximus, however, Rome managed to rebuild. Eventually, Scipio Africanus was able to conquer Iberia and then Carthage.

Throughout this component you will learn to explore the fine margins between success and failure and how the different attitudes of Roman and Carthaginian governments influenced the final outcome of the war.

EXAM OVERVIEW

Your examination for Hannibal will require you to show knowledge and understanding of the material you have studied. This component is worth 45 marks – 15 based on AO1 skills, 10 on AO2, and 20 on AO3.

Question 6 will consist of a number of short factual questions worth a total of five marks.

Questions 7 and 8 will require you to study a passage of text or visual source.

Question 7 will be a comprehension question, whereas question 8 will need you to evaluate the source. Each question is worth 5 marks.

Question 9 will ask will ask you a use second-order concepts such as continuity, change, cause, consequence, significance or similarity and difference within specified situations. This question is worth 10 marks.

Finally, question 10 is a longer essay-style question worth 20 marks.

TIMELINE OF THE SECOND PUNIC WAR

Date (BC)	
247	Hannibal Barca born in Carthage
241	Rome defeats Carthage in the First Punic War
237–236	Hasdrubal Barca and his family travel to Iberia (ancient Spain)
230	Hamilcar Barca killed. Hasdrubal replaces him
227	Hasdrubal establishes New Carthage as the Carthaginian capital, Iberia
226	Ebro Treaty between Rome and Carthage
221	Hasdrubal assassinated. Hannibal elected as his successor
219	Roman ally Saguntum captured by Hannibal
218	Hannibal crosses the Alps. Rome defeated at Ticinus and Trebia
217	Battle of Trasimene. Fabius Maximus becomes Dictator
216	Battle of Cannae. Capua becomes Hannibal's headquarters
211	Hannibal's failed march on Rome and Capua is retaken by Rome. Publius Cornelius Scipio is killed
209	New Carthage taken by Scipio Africanus
207	Hasdrubal Barca is killed at the Battle of the Metaurus
206	Scipio Africanus defeats the Carthaginian army in Iberia
205	Mago Barca invades Northern Italy
204	Scipio invades Africa
203	Mago Barca dies. Hannibal is ordered to leave Italy and defend Carthage
202	Battle of Zama. Second Punic War ends
196	Hannibal reforms Carthage
195	Hannibal is exiled to Syria
183	Hannibal commits suicide in Bithynia

2.1 Reasons for the Outbreak of the Second Punic War

TOPIC OVERVIEW

- the impact of the First Punic War on the balance of power between Rome and Carthage
- the impact of the Treaty of Lutatius on Carthage
- the significance of the colonisation of Iberia by Hamilcar and Hasdrubal
- the development of a war party within Carthage demanding revenge or renegotiation of the Treaty of Lutatius
- Hannibal's personal motivations for war against Rome, including the influence of Hamilcar and the threat of Roman expansion into Iberia

The prescribed source for this topic is:

- Polybius, *Histories*, Book 3, sections 8–12

WHY WERE ROME AND CARTHAGE RIVALS?

Carthage was one of the most heavily fortified cities in the ancient world. Its position on the coast of Africa (see Fig. 2.2) was helped by two harbours. Both were heavily defended. One was built for trade, the other for its warships. Its military harbour had a dual use. It deterred invaders, and made merchants feel safe in the city. As well as holding a strong position at home, Carthage controlled a large portion of the western Mediterranean, including the islands of Sardinia, Corsica and Sicily.

By 264 BC, Rome had unified Italy under its control. The Roman Senate wanted to expand its trade into the Mediterranean. An agreement signed with Carthage in 348 meant that Rome, like most Mediterranean traders, had to pay harbour dues to Carthage. Such dues helped maintain Carthage's dominance of the Mediterranean.

Carthage's defeat in Sicily would change this relationship. Rome saw an opportunity to take control of Sicily. In 264, Rome invaded Sicily which led to the First Punic War. The war continued until 241 when Rome's fleet destroyed the Carthaginian navy during the Battle of the Agates Islands.

2.1 Reasons for the Outbreak of the Second Punic War

FIGURE 2.1
Reconstruction of Carthage's military harbour after the Second Punic War.

The Treaty of Lutatius was agreed in 241 by the Roman consul, Gaius Lutatius Catulus, and Gesco, the deputy of a Carthaginian general, Hamilcar Barca. The agreement was a significant shift in power within the Mediterranean Sea. Polybius informs us that Carthage was ordered to leave Sicily, hand over all war prisoners and pay 3,200 talents of silver over twenty years. This 3,200 talents would have weighed about 83,000 kilogrammes. In return, Carthage kept its other overseas territories, including the islands of Sardinia and Corsica.

Carthage had started the First Punic War as the masters of the western Mediterranean; by the end they had lost their dominance over the area. To add to Carthage's problems, they were immediately involved in another war called the Truceless War. This was a revolt of Carthaginian mercenaries in Africa and it took three years to subdue.

Hanno the Great, a Carthaginian politician, had refused to pay the mercenaries after losing the First Punic War. The **mercenary** army decided to gain its revenge by trying to take control of African cities under Carthage's control. Hamilcar Barca eventually stopped the revolt and restored order to Carthage.

While Carthage was involved in the Truceless War, Rome extended its influence in the Mediterranean. Rome used Carthage's problems to take Corsica and Sardinia from them. These two islands had been under Carthage's control. Roman historians, such as Polybius, tell us that Hamilcar Barca and many other leading Carthaginians saw this as an act of war, and they argued Rome had broken the Treaty of Lutatius because they had invaded Carthaginian territory. Carthage was, however, in no position to declare war on Rome or to demand compensation. Polybius believed this may have led to the start of the Second Punic War.

WHAT WAS THE IMPACT OF HAMILCAR BARCA?

Hamilcar Barca belonged to the powerful Carthaginian family the Barcids. His success in the First Punic War had gained his family the nickname Barca which means Thunderbolt. During the First Punic War he showed his effectiveness as a general. Sent

> **KEY INDIVIDUAL**
>
> **Hamilcar Barca**
> **Dates:** *c.* 275–228
> Carthaginian general
> Father of Hannibal. Hamilcar was a huge influence on his son. He commanded Carthaginian forces during the First Punic War and started the conquest of Spain. He died in battle during the campaigns in Spain

> **mercenary** hired soldier who will fight in return for payment

> **Study questions**
> 1. Why was Carthage so powerful before the First Punic War?
> 2. How did Rome weaken Carthage in the First Punic War?
> 3. What was the impact of the Treaty of Lutatius on Carthage?
> 4. What was the impact of the Truceless Wars on Carthage?

Part Two Depth Study 1: Hannibal and the Second Punic War

FIGURE 2.2
Map of the Mediterranean at the time of the Second Punic War.

to Sicily with no army, he managed to regroup the Carthaginian mercenaries and begin to force the Roman army out of Sicily. Carthage's defeat at the Aegates Islands in 241 cut off Hamilcar's supplies, however, and he was eventually ordered to negotiate a truce with Rome. We are told that Hamilcar refused and sent his deputy, Gesco, instead.

Introduction to Polybius' history

Polybius' account of the Punic Wars is one of the most significant sources we have from this period. He lived through the latter part of the Punic Wars, and travelled extensively around the Roman world. A fact which Polybius believed separated good and bad historians:

> For since many events occur simultaneously in different places and it is impossible for . . . him to have seen with his own eyes all the different places in the world and observed their particular features, the only course which remains to a historian is to question as many people as possible.
>
> Polybius, *Histories* 12.4c

> But once a man takes up the role of a historian he must discard all considerations of hatreds and loyalties . . . For just as a living creature, if it is deprived of its eyesight, is rendered completely helpless, so if a history is deprived of truth, we are left with nothing but an idle, unprofitable tale.
>
> Polybius, *Histories* 1.14

Polybius' experience of warfare and political life provides invaluable insights into Roman military and political life. No doubt he gained access to leading Roman aristocrats from his friend and supporter Publius Scipio, son of Aemilius Paullus. In 151, Scipio Aemilianus volunteered for service in Spain and Polybius joined him. Here he

> **EXPLORE FURTHER**
> **The First Punic War and Hamilcar Barca**
>
> Read Polybius *Histories* Book 1.56–1.60 to find out more about Hamilcar's role in the First Punic War

2.1 Reasons for the Outbreak of the Second Punic War

> **PRESCRIBED SOURCE**
>
> ***Histories,*** **Book 3, sections 8–12**
>
> **Date:** 2nd century
>
> **Author:** Polybius (*c.* 200–117)
>
> **Genre:** history
>
> **Significance:** a near contemporary source for the Punic Wars, written by a Greek historian
>
> **Content of the prescribed sections:** Polybius' assessment of Fabius Pictor and the causes of the Second Punic War
>
> **Read it here:** OCR Source Booklet

> **EXAM TIP: REVISING PRESCRIBED TEXTS**
>
> It is always a good idea to read the prescribed texts carefully and write a brief synopsis or overview of each one. It is also useful to write a few sentences evaluating each prescribed source. Is the text/source accurate; where did the author find this information; and finally, does it have a different interpretation to other ancient historians?
>
> It is also a good idea to underline difficult words, or unfamiliar names. You could then create a glossary to help improve your understanding.

FIGURE 2.3
Carthaginian silver dishekel minted in Iberia (modern Spain). Some scholars believe that the head is Hamilcar Barca, but it may depict a god. The reverse shows a Carthaginian War Elephant

met Masinissa, the King of Numidia, and other eye-witnesses. Like most historians Polybius has an agenda. His history seems to favour the aristocratic families in Rome, and uses Hannibal's invasion as a cautionary tale to his countrymen, the Greeks.

The creation of a war party

According to Polybius, the Treaty of Lutatius was one of the most significant factors in the development of the Second Punic War (Polybius 3.10). Hamilcar Barca had wanted revenge, but his hands were tied by the Truceless War. Once the mercenary rebellion was ended, Hamilcar Barca's political supporters in Carthage wanted to revive Carthage's fortunes. These men, he implied, went on to create a war party in Carthage. We must not confuse this term with modern political parties, but rather think of this as a group of aristocratic men who wanted to revive Carthage's empire by attacking Rome. Polybius implied that Hamilcar's opponents were not concerned by the loss of the overseas colonies. They had made their fortunes from expanding into Africa.

Hamilcar travelled to southern **Iberia** (modern Spain) with a mercenary army to create a new Carthaginian colony. Modern scholars suspect that Carthage had once controlled much of Iberia. Archaeologists have uncovered an extensive earlier settlement

> **KEY PLACE**
>
> **Iberia** located in modern Spain, Iberia was colonised by Carthage after the First Punic War. It provided mercenary soldiers and silver to Carthage. Its loss during the Second Punic War significantly weakened Carthage's ability to match Rome's military might

Part Two Depth Study 1: Hannibal and the Second Punic War

> **Cassius Dio Fragment**
>
> An interesting fragment from the Roman historian Cassius Dio tells us that in 231 BC a Roman delegation went to Iberia to meet with Hamilcar. The Romans were concerned by Hamilcar's expansion into the area. Hamilcar's response apparently pleased the Romans and they returned home. He told the Romans that he was fighting to gather enough money to pay Rome's war compensation. This story does not survive in any other Roman historian's account. If it is true, however, it either challenges the view that Hamilcar wanted revenge or shows him to be a clever deceiver of the Romans by pretending to them, at least, that he did not want revenge.

Study questions

1 Why was Hamilcar an effective general?
2 How did Hamilcar help rebuild Carthage after the First Punic War?
3 Why do we know so little about Carthage's government?

> **The Carthaginian Government**
>
> Very little reliable evidence exists to tell us about the Carthaginian political system. The scholar Pedro A. Barcelo suggests that the Carthaginian government was very similar to Rome's. Power rested in the hands of rich landowners. Barcelo believes that alliances would be created between different families in order to exercise power and influence over the government.
>
> Barcelo encourages caution. Most of our evidence is from Roman authors who knew next to nothing about Carthage and may have used Roman systems to explain what was happening outside Rome. For example, Polybius (6.51 and 6.56) suggest that Carthage and Rome's governments are very similar.

on the southern peninsula of Spain. According to Polybius (PS 3.10), Hamilcar travelled to Iberia to strengthen Carthage and ready it for war.

There is no convincing evidence that Hamilcar invaded Iberia so he could seek revenge against Rome, other than a story attributed to Hannibal by Polybius (PS 3.11–3.12). As a young boy, Hannibal was reputed to have promised his father to seek revenge against Rome. This story is the only fragment which suggests that Carthage wanted revenge on Rome after the Treaty of Lutatius (see p. 85) and before the siege of Saguntum (see pp. 95–96).

Hamilcar was probably more interested in empire-building than seeking revenge. The military base he established on the site of the Phoenician colony of Gades (modern Cádiz, on the south coast of Spain), allowed him to expand into mainland Iberia. First of all, Hamilcar seized the silver mines of Andalusia to fund his military ambitions. This funded the development of a well-disciplined and flexible army. In 228 BC, Hamilcar died, possibly from drowning.

Hamilcar had established the foundations of a new empire, which would provide his son, **Hannibal,** with the means to attack Italy.

KEY INDIVIDUAL
Hannibal
Dates: c. 247–183/181
Carthaginian general
Considered one of the greatest military leaders ever. Hannibal led the Carthaginian army against Rome in the Second Punic War

HASDRUBAL THE FAIR AND THE CONQUEST OF IBERIA

According to Polybius (PS 3.8–3.9) Fabius Pictor believed Hasdrubal the Fair was the main cause of the Second Punic War. After failing to create a tyranny in Carthage he travelled to Spain and created an empire there instead. Rather than Hamilcar it was Hasdrubal the Fair who taught Hannibal to hate the Romans. Polybius, like most modern historians, challenged this interpretation.

Hasdrubal the Fair had followed Hamilcar to Iberia. After Hamilcar had set up his base in Gades and captured the silver mines of Andalusia, Hasdrubal the Fair had helped him extend their influence. Archaeology from the area suggests that the silver mines were used to mint coins almost immediately. The mines allowed Hamilcar and Hasdrubal to pay their mercenary armies and the Iberian allies they made. After Hamilcar's death in 228 BC, Hasdrubal took command.

Soon Hasdrubal the Fair had an army of 50,000. He wanted to make sure Carthage's control of Iberia would be permanent. He was more approachable than Hamilcar, and paid his troops well. Hasdrubal also married a local Iberian princess, to create a permanent tie. The foundation of a new Carthaginian capital called New Carthage in 228 was arguably Hasdrubal's most significant achievement. Hasdrubal cemented Carthage's new South Iberian empire by colonising the area.

These developments caused more distress in Rome than Hamilcar's raids across the Iberian countryside. Hasdrubal the Fair was creating an empire in Iberia. Rome set up a meeting with Hasdrubal the Fair and negotiated the Treaty of Ebro in 226. Hasdrubal agreed that, if Rome did not interfere, he would limit his expansion to the south banks of the River Ebro (which flows through what is now north-eastern Spain). It is likely that this is when Rome developed an alliance, or relationship, with the people of Saguntum

> **KEY INDIVIDUAL**
> **Hasdrubal the Fair**
> **Dates:** *c.* 270–221
> Carthaginian general who succeeded Hamilcar in leading the Spanish campaigns

> **S & C**
> Quintus Fabius Pictor was the earliest known Roman historian. It is likely he was the son of Gaius Fabius Pictor. Some scholars believe he fought against the Gauls in 225 and witnessed much of the Second Punic War. It is also suggested that he was appointed to travel to the oracle at Delphi in 216, for advice after the Roman defeat at the Battle of Cannae. We know from surviving extracts that he was very patriotic and possibly created much of the narrative of early Rome's early history. His description of Hannibal and Hasdrubal would have been prejudiced. After the Second Punic War many Roman historians, such as Pictor, wanted to use the siege of Saguntum to claim Carthage had started the conflict.

> **ACTIVITY**
> Read Polybius 3.8 **PS** and answer the questions below.
> In your prescribed text, Polybius analyses the account written by an earlier historian, Fabius Pictor (see S&C box above). Pictor's work does not survive, but Polybius' analysis of his history is interesting for many reasons. Here we will look at Pictor's treatment of Hasdrubal the Fair.
>
> - Summarise Polybius' account of Fabius Pictor's description of Hasdrubal the Fair.
> - How does Polybius challenge Fabius Pictor?

(a city on the east coast of Spain). Their strategic position on the Ebro would act as a deterrent to Carthaginian expansion in the north.

Hasdrubal preferred diplomacy to war. His tactics had strengthened Carthage's control over the area. He had also secured Rome's consent for the extension of the Carthaginian Empire. In 221, however, Hasdrubal was killed by a Gallic assassin because he had crucified his master.

At the age of twenty-six, Hannibal Barca was chosen to lead the Iberian army. His succession would eventually lead to the start of the Second Punic War.

WHAT MOTIVATED HANNIBAL TO ATTACK ROME?

According to one ancient tradition, Hannibal's father was the most important influence on the young general. At the age of nine, Hannibal had joined his father in Iberia. Hannibal was educated on the Iberian battlefield his father fought on. Here he witnessed his father's speeches, his father's tactics, and he experienced the lows and highs of warfare. Few doubt that spending his childhood on the bloody Iberian battlefield helped create the great general.

The historian Livy makes an interesting claim in his *History of Rome*. He argues that had Hamilcar Barca lived longer he would have invaded Rome. According to Polybius and Fabius Pictor, it was the 'Wrath of Hamilcar' which drove Hannibal to war with Rome.

FIGURE 2.4
French engraving of Hannibal's oath to destroy Rome.

2.1 Reasons for the Outbreak of the Second Punic War

Polybius (PS 3.10) makes it clear there were three distinct reasons Hannibal wanted to invade Rome.

- His father made him vow to seek revenge
- He, like many Carthaginians, was angered by the Roman seizure of Sardinia
- He was encouraged by Carthage's success in Iberia, to invade Italy.

Another theory is that Hannibal was ambitious. Hasdrubal had created a stable Iberian government of which Hannibal could take advantage. He also had a very experienced and well-trained army who shared his ambitions. After the Battle of Saguntum, Hannibal asked his men if they wished to ride on to Rome or remain in Spain. Most of them agreed to invade Rome to seek their fortunes.

Other historians believe that Hannibal's invasion of Italy was defensive. It is plausible that Rome used the siege of Saguntum to declare war on Carthage and Iberia. Rome was potentially fearful of Carthage's recovery and saw the attack on Saguntum as an opportunity to crush Carthage while it had a young and inexperienced general in charge of its Iberian army.

If this is true, then Hannibal's trek across the Pyrenees and the Alps could have been designed to protect Africa and Iberia from Roman invasion.

It is unlikely we will ever know what drove Hannibal to invade Rome. The ancient historians provide us with interesting theories, and their closer proximity to events means that their views have some weight.

ACTIVITY

Read Polybius PS 3.8–3.12 and answer the questions below.

- Why does Polybius believe Hamilcar wanted revenge on Rome?
- Briefly describe the story about Hannibal's oath to seek revenge against Rome.
- What are the strengths and weaknesses of this story?

EXAM TIP: SECOND-ORDER CONCEPTS

During this Depth Study, you will be required to reflect on second-order historical concepts, just as you were in the period study (see pp. 19, 22, 33, 43, 53 and 60). Remember to think about the following second-order concepts: continuity, change, cause, consequence, significance, similarity and difference.

Part Two Depth Study 1: Hannibal and the Second Punic War

TOPIC REVIEW

Boost your knowledge

Describe:

a. the rivalry between Carthage and Rome
b. the Treaty of Lutiatius
c. the conquest and colonisation of Iberia by Carthage
d. the different reasons Carthage's leaders may have had to invade Italy

Stretch your understanding

Explain:

a. the impact of the First Punic War on Rome and Carthage
b. how the Barcids conquered Iberia
c. why Hannibal decided to invade Italy

PRACTICE QUESTIONS

1 a. Name the Carthaginian general who founded the Iberian city of New Carthage. [1]
   b. Identify **two** ways Rome weakened Carthaginian supremacy of the western Mediterranean after the First Punic War. [2]
   c. Identify **two** ways the conquest of Iberia helped Carthage recover from defeat in the First Punic War. [2]
2.   What was the impact of the Treaty of Lutiatius upon the relationship between Rome and Carthage? [10]

2.2 The Nature and Dynamics of Hannibal's Leadership

> **TOPIC OVERVIEW**
>
> - Hannibal's leadership and tactics during the Siege of Saguntum
> - the battles on the Rhone and the crossing of the Alps
> - Hannibal's leadership and tactics during the invasion of Italy
> - Trebia
> - Trasimene
> - Cannae
> - Hannibal's failure to march on Rome and inability to counter Fabian tactics
> - Hannibal's failure to make peace with Rome and to retain alliances with Italian tribes made after Cannae
> - Hannibal's failure to keep supply routes open with Iberia and Carthage
>
> **The prescribed sources for this topic are:**
>
> - Polybius, *Histories,* Book 3, sections 15–16, 20, 33–34, 44, 50–56, 77–79, 81–86
> - Livy, *The History of Rome,* Book 21, sections 22, 26–29, 32–35 and 54
> - Book 22, sections 44–48 and 51
> - Book 23, section 29

After the siege of Saguntum, Hannibal marched to Italy through the Alps. Within five months he had travelled from New Carthage to Italy. Crossing the Alps was a gamble which took its toll on the Carthaginian army. Hannibal reached Italy with 26,000 of the 102,000 men that had left New Carthage. Despite this Hannibal, enjoyed significant victories against the Roman armies at Ticinus, Trebia, Trasimene and Cannae. After Cannae, Hannibal established himself in Capua and tried to win Italian allies. Hannibal failed to secure his victory peace and never won enough support from the Italian cities. After fourteen years, Hannibal was forced to leave Italy.

Part Two Depth Study 1: Hannibal and the Second Punic War

FIGURE 2.5
Map of Iberia 219 BC.

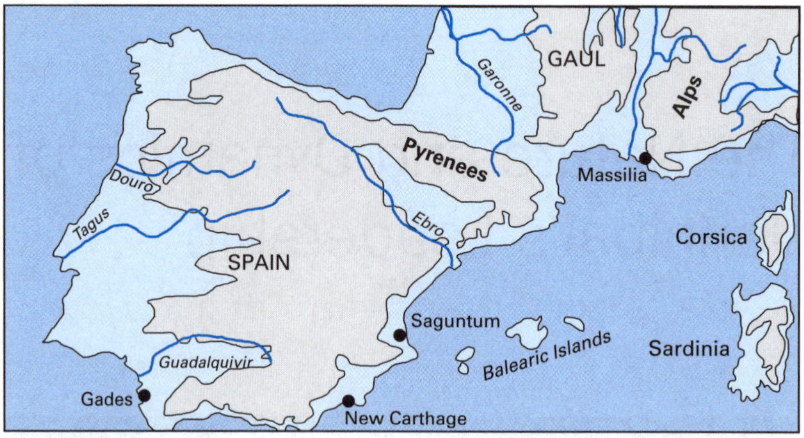

PRESCRIBED SOURCE

Histories, Book 3, sections 15–16, 20, 33–34, 44, 50–56, 77–79, 81–86

Date: second century BC

Author: Polybius (c. 200–117 BC)

Genre: history

Significance: a near contemporary source for the Punic Wars, written by a Greek historian

Content of the prescribed sections: the importance of Saguntum and Hannibal's invasion of Italy until the Battle of Cannae

Read it here: OCR Source Booklet

HANNIBAL'S LEADERSHIP DURING THE SIEGE OF SAGUNTUM

Hannibal's conquest of Iberia

After Hasdrubal's death in 221 BC, Hannibal called an assembly of his men. At the age of 26, he was chosen to lead Carthage's Iberian army. Livy argues that once Hannibal took control he instantly set his sights on invading Italy. He decided to attack Saguntum to break the Treaty of Ebro, and then march on Rome by crossing the Alps.

Livy and Polybius tell us that, despite his ambition, Hannibal did not immediately march towards Rome. Securing control of Iberia was his first priority. Hasdrubal's death reputedly led to unrest in Iberia. Polybius makes it clear that Hannibal dealt with this threat first rather than marching straight on Saguntum. Hannibal won a resounding victory at Tagus, by using his war elephants to trample upon the Iberian armies as they crossed the river. According to Polybius, Hannibal then ordered his cavalry to destroy the 100,000 strong Iberian army (Polybius 3.14).

Saguntum was a fertile area and the last powerful independent city state in Iberia. Polybius believes that Saguntum sent ambassadors to Rome. (**PS** Polybius 3.15) In reply, the Roman Senate sent representatives to remind Hannibal of the Treaty of Ebro and to respect the independence of Saguntum. Hannibal refused. He argued that the Saguntines were using their Roman alliance to cause unrest in Iberia. It was his duty, Hannibal claimed, to protect his allies. Polybius tells us the Roman ambassadors received the same response in Carthage.

Introduction to Livy's account of the Second Punic War

Livy was a Roman historian writing at the end of the first century. His history of Rome covered the foundations of the city through to the Roman civil war and the creation of the Empire. As you would have seen in the Period Study (p. 6) his Preface set out his ambitions. One of Livy's ambitions was to celebrate the glory of Rome. Anyone reading his account of the Second Punic War would have no doubt that Hannibal was the enemy. Despite this, there are moments when Livy shows grudging respect towards Hannibal.

ACTIVITY

Read **PS** Polybius 3.15

- Summarise Hannibal's and the Carthaginian Senate's response to Rome's ambassadors

2.2 The Nature and Dynamics of Hannibal's Leadership

> **PRESCRIBED SOURCE**
>
> ***The History of Rome,*** **Book 21, sections 22, 26–29, 32–35 and 54; Book 22, sections 44–48 and 51; Book 23, section 29**
>
> **Date:** late first century BC
>
> **Author:** Livy (*c.* 64/59 BC–AD 17)
>
> **Genre:** history
>
> **Significance:** major source for early Roman history charting the foundations of Rome until the collapse of the Republic.
>
> **Content of the prescribed sections:** Hannibal's invasion of Italy and the battles of Trebia, Cannae, and Ebro
>
> **Read it here:** OCR Source Booklet

The most significant flaws in Livy's account are his poor geography. He has Hannibal travelling in the wrong direction after crossing the Rhone. He also shares Polybius' aristocratic prejudice and attacks Flaminius and Varro, while praising Paullus and Sempronius. Finally, his accounts of the wars are more simplified and exaggerated than Polybius' version. For the general reader, this improves the story and creates a gripping tale. Livy, however, used histories and records which are no longer available to write his account. Livy rejected elements of Polybius' story because he felt his sources were more accurate. A very good example of this is the length of the siege at Saguntum.

The siege of Saguntum

Livy provides the fullest account of the siege of Saguntum (Livy 21.7–21.14). Most modern scholars doubt the authenticity of the account because of its similarity with first century siege tactics and the lack of potential sources Livy could have used. Polybius gives a simpler account: Hannibal may have starved the people of Saguntum until they surrendered.

Despite these reservations, both historians provide an insight into how the ancient sources represented Hannibal's leadership.

- To inspire his army, Hannibal distributed money from the sale of slaves among his troops.
- He also took his turn operating the **siege works** alongside his men.
- Hannibal was resilient. Despite failing to destroy the city walls, and becoming wounded by a javelin in the thigh he maintained his determination to succeed.
- Once Hannibal broke through the city walls he still faced significant resistance. The Saguntines used a large flaming javelin called a falarica to inflict heavy

> **ACTIVITY**
>
> - Summarise Hannibal's leadership during the siege of Saguntum
>
> Read the accounts of the Siege of Saguntum by Polybius (PS 3.17) and Livy (21.7–21.8)
>
> - How does Polybius describe Hannibal's leadership during the siege in 3.17?
> - How does Livy describe Hannibal's leadership and actions during the siege?

casualites. The falarcia could pierce armour and set fire to an enemy with its tar-tipped spear. Hannibal destroyed the resistance by using African miners to destroy as much of the city's walls as possible.

- To protect his men, Hannibal built a fort inside the city while he waited for the Saguntines to surrender.
- Hannibal's terms were harsh. If the Saguntines gave their wealth to Hannibal, surrendered their arms and settled in a new place of Hannibal's choosing, then they could live. Otherwise their women and children would be sold into slavery, and all of the men's throats cut.
- The people of Saguntum refused to accept. Hannibal's men set fire to the city. Many committed suicide by remaining in their burning homes. Those who survived were sold into slavery and their valuables used to fund Hannibal's invasion of Rome.
- It is likely that Livy deliberately represented Hannibal in a bad light. For this reason, Hannibal and his men are described taking pleasure in the suffering of others. Hannibal's troops are not brave Roman legionaries. Instead they are mercenaries motivated by gold.

TO WHAT EXTENT WAS HANNIBAL RESPONSIBLE FOR THE SECOND PUNIC WAR?

The Roman Senate, Polybius informs us (PS 3.16) feared the worst and prepared for conflict with Carthage. Rome, however, was already at war with the Illyrians and Hannibal's speedy victory over Saguntum in eight months meant its preparations were not complete. Livy disagrees and states that the siege either started earlier than this, or the siege was shorter.

Polybius believes that Hannibal attacked Saguntum to seek revenge for the Roman capture of Sicily. (Polybius 3.13) Many historians believe Polybius wanted the reader to accept Hannibal's guilt in starting the war.

> **DEBATE**
>
> Many modern historians challenge Polybius' interpretation of Hannibal as the aggressor. Some argue that Hannibal crossed the Alps into Italy to protect Carthage and Iberia from Roman forces. Hannibal suspected Rome had mobilised legions to invade Iberia and Africa. If he attacked Italy, Rome's legions would be recalled.

> The Carthaginians bitterly resented their defeat in the war for Sicily . . . and they were further provoked by the affair of Sardinia and the size of the increased indemnity which they had finally been compelled to agree to pay. Accordingly, after they had subdued the greater part of Spain they were ready to seize any opportunities that presented themselves for retaliating against Rome.
>
> Polybius, *Histories* 3.13

Once Saguntum was captured, Rome gave Carthage a simple ultimatum (PS Polybius 3.20). Surrender Hannibal or fight. The Carthaginians refused to recognise the charges against them. Hasdrubal had signed the Treaty of Ebro, not Carthage. Hasdrubal was dead so the treaty was no longer valid. Furthermore, Rome had broken the treaty of Lutatius when it seized Sicily. Rome was the aggressor according to the Carthaginian Senate.

2.2 The Nature and Dynamics of Hannibal's Leadership

> **Study questions**
>
> Read **PS** Polybius 3.13, 3.16 and 3.20 and answer the questions below.
>
> 1 What does Polybius' claim was Hannibal's real reason for invading Saguntum?
> 2 Why does Polybius claim Rome dealt with the threat from Illyria first?
> 3 What does Polybius tell us about Rome's decision to invade Carthage?
> 4 Why does Carthage refuse to negotiate with Rome?

KEY INDIVIDUAL

Publius Cornelius Scipio
Date: unknown–211 BC

Roman consul and commander

Sent to attack Hannibal in Iberia. Arrived too late due to an uprising of the Boii in Gaul. Defeated at the Battle of Ticinus. Key general in Rome's invasion of Iberia until his death

After the response from the Carthaginian Senate, Rome created six **legions** to travel to Iberia, Africa and Sicily. Publius Cornelius Scipio was sent to attack Carthage's forces in Iberia. Tiberius Sempronius Longus was sent to attack Carthage in Africa and Sicily.

FROM SAGUNTUM TO ITALY: HANNIBAL'S LEADERSHIP

Hannibal and Rome's preparations

After securing victory in Saguntum, Hannibal readied himself for his march on Rome. According to Polybius, Hannibal spent the early months of 218 BC at New Carthage (**PS** Polybius 3.33). He sent his Iberian soldiers home and passed control of Iberia to his brother, Hasdrubal Barca. In the spring, Iberian soldiers were sent to garrison Carthage's possessions in Africa. Likewise, African soldiers were sent to Iberia to garrison the newly conquered cities there. By doing this Hannibal would remove the threat of revolution while he was away.

Polybius claims that his own travels gave him proof of this (**PS** Polybius 3.33). He argues that he found a bronze tablet in Cape Lacinium (southern Italy), set up by Hannibal, which included a detailed list of where soldiers were sent during the Second Punic War.

Hannibal also sent spies and messengers ahead to form alliances with the **Celtic** tribes he would encounter as he travelled through **Gaul** on his way to Rome (**PS** Poybius 3.34). These spies were likely to be scouting the route for suitable battlefields, should the Romans attack. As spring approached, Hannibal had formed strong alliances with some Celtic tribes in Gaul including Magilius, the leader of the Boii. He had also secured the support of his troops to march upon Rome.

Rome's attempts to secure allies in Iberia were less successful. According to Livy (21.19), one Iberian tribe called the Volciani informed the Roman ambassadors that they had no intention of betraying Carthage. The leader of the Volciani stated:

> To the Spanish people the ruins of Saguntum are a fierce warning . . . no-one should trust the honour of the Romans.
>
> Livy, *The History of Rome* 21.19

The Celtic tribes between Iberia and Italy also refused to help Rome. They preferred to remain neutral in a war between such powerful nations.

KEY INDIVIDUAL

Hasdrubal Barca
Date: 245–207 BC

Carthaginian commander

Given control of Iberia's forces before Hannibal's march to Italy. Defended Iberia until his death in 207

Celtic the culture which dominated the area known as Gaul during this period

KEY PLACE

Gaul a region of Western Europe that was made up from many Celtic tribes. It included much of present day France, Northern Italy and Germany. Many of these Celtic tribes, such as the Boii, welcomed Hannibal's invasion of Italy

To make matters worse for Rome, a Celtic tribe known as the Boii attacked the Roman fourth legion. Cornelius Scipio was ordered to reinforce them, before travelling to Iberia. Rather than deal with the rebellion himself, Cornelius Scipio sent a large section of the army, with his deputy to deal with the Boii. Having lost most of his army, Scipio sailed to Iberia and sent a request to the Senate for a new legion.

These Roman setbacks gave Hannibal an early advantage. Livy (PS 21.22) claims that Hannibal set off across the river Ebro after a powerful dream told him he would cross the Alps into Italy. According to Polybius (3.35), Hannibal's army included 90,000 foot-soldiers and 12,000 horsemen. Despite some fierce resistance from the Iberian cities north of the Ebro, Hannibal quickly made his way to the Pyrenees. Before crossing these mountains, Hannibal left Hanno with 10,000 men to control northern Iberia and, if necessary, to provide reinforcements. His army was already reduced to 80,000 and he had not yet reached the Alps.

> ### ACTIVITY
>
> Read and compare Livy PS 21.22 and Polybius PS 3.33–3.34.
>
> - Read Livy's account. Summarise Livy's account of Hannibal's preparations after the siege of Saguntum. Does Livy present Hannibal as an effective leader?
> - Summarise Hannibal's dream. Why do you think Livy includes this, but Polybius does not?
> - How many troops does Polybius suggest Hannibal takes with him to invade Italy in 3.33? Where does Polybius find these figures?
> - Summarise Hannibal's final preparations in 3.34.

The Rhone crossing

The journey across the Pyrenees was relatively trouble free. Hannibal's messengers had used gifts and conferences to reassure the local tribes he was their friend. The Gallic tribes had told Rome they planned to remain neutral, and they told Hannibal they would not attack him either.

So when Cornelius Scipio finally arrived in Massilia (modern Marseilles), a few miles from the Rhone, he was shocked to discover Hannibal had already crossed the Pyrenees and reached the Rhone. Scipio took the decision to rest his small army and to search the area for a suitable battlefield. He had no time to wait for reinforcements.

According to Polybius, crossing the Rhone near Massilia was a considerable problem for Hannibal. In particular, how was he going to get his elephants across? Hannibal ordered his army to buy as many canoes and boats as they could from local tribes. These boats were tied together to ferry the cavalry and elephants across. Livy, however, paints a very different picture. His account suggests the elephants just swam across. As the Carthaginians put the finishing touches to their preparations, the Volcae, a local tribe, set up camp on the opposite side of the river. Livy describes the Battle of the Rhone crossing in PS 21.26–21.28.

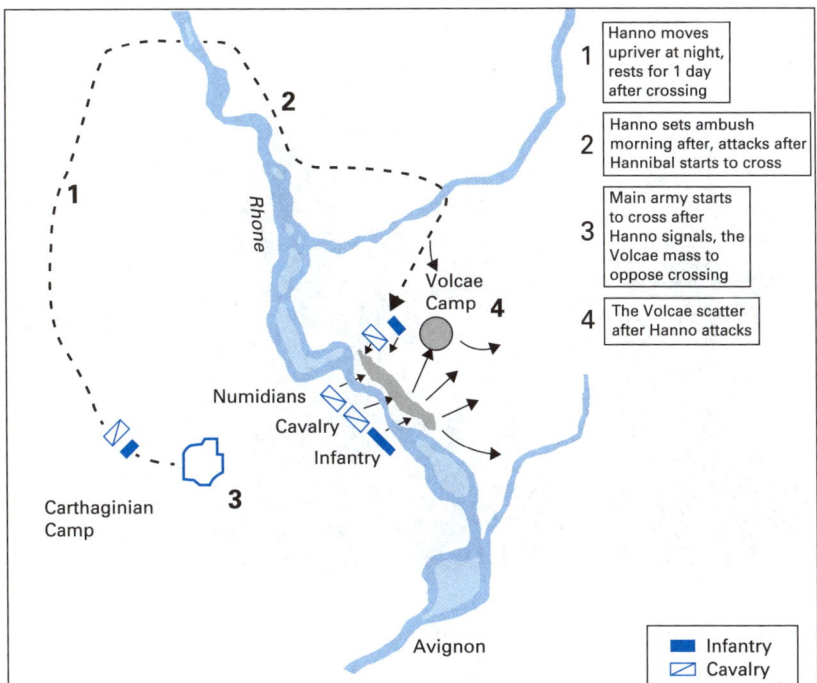

FIGURE 2.6
Plan of the Battle of the Rhone.

Undeterred, Hannibal sent Hanno with a small group of men to find an alternative crossing point. Under nightfall, they crossed the Rhone and moved into position behind the Volcae. Hannibal filled his boats with light cavalry and his canoes with light infantry. When Hanno was in position they would attack. Seeing the Carthaginians preparing to cross, the Volcae made their way to the river's edge in order to kill Hannibal's men as they landed.

When Hannibal saw an agreed smoke signal, he ordered his men to row across the river as fast as they could. Under the misconception that the Carthaginians were racing them to the river's edge, the Volcae ran towards the oncoming boats. Screaming and shouting, the Volcae did not see Hanno take their camp until it was too late. Hanno struck the unsuspecting tribe and they found themselves trapped between two armies. Within a few minutes the threat had disappeared as the Volcae fled for their lives. Hannibal could now ferry his war elephants cross the river.

The Battle of the Raiding Parties

Livy describes the first Battle of the Second Punic War in (PS) 21.29. As Hannibal's elephants were crossing the Rhone, Cornelius Scipio sent a small force of 300 Roman cavalry to spy on the Carthaginians. Hearing of Scipio's plan, Hannibal sent 500 of his finest Numidian cavalry to intercept them. After heavy losses on both sides the Numidian cavalry retreated and joined Hannibal on his march across the Alps. The cavalry was ordered to remain some distance behind Hannibal's main force to protect them.

Encouraged by his victory over the Numidian cavalry, the Roman cavalry informed Cornelius Scipio that they did not have much time left to attack Hannibal. Livy tells us ((PS) 21.32) that Cornelius Scipio quickly sailed up the Rhone, but when he arrived he

FIGURE 2.7
Hannibal's elephants crossing the Rhone, inspired by Polybius' account. Henri Motte, 1878.

ACTIVITY

Read Livy 🅿🆂 21.26–21.29 and answer the following questions.

- Why was Cornelius Scipio unable to prevent Hannibal from crossing the Rhone?
- Summarise Hannibal's crossing of the Rhone.
- Summarise the Battle of the Raiding Parties in 21.29.
- Does this show good leadership?

found the camp abandoned. Cornelius Scipio saw no reason to stay and sailed back to Italy. He intended to march north and meet Hannibal when he arrived in Italy.

CROSSING THE ALPS

Why did Hannibal cross the Alps when it would have been easier to sail to Italy?

Sailing to Italy was not a viable option for Hannibal. Carthage had been a powerful naval power, but the Treaty of Lutatius had given Rome control of the Mediterranean and would have easily defeated Hannibal who had no, or little, experience of naval warfare.

Transporting a large army to Italy by sea during the autumn was probably more dangerous than using a pass through the Alps. Ancient boats could not safely travel in open seas, but had to sail close to the coast. Weather conditions in September to October would not have been favourable for a large military fleet. Any attempt to sail to Italy would risk Hannibal's entire army without fighting a single battle.

Hannibal's plan to defeat Rome by crossing the Alps was simple. He would invade Rome by land and cut Rome off from its allies. By travelling across the Pyrenees and the Alps he hoped to create a supply line to bring reinforcements and food from Iberia. After winning a few battles, Hannibal hoped to convince the Celtic and the Italian cities to fight for their independence. Inciting revolt would make it easier to force Rome to accept a peace treaty which would give control of the Mediterranean back to Carthage.

Hannibal's conference at the foot of the Alps

Before setting off towards the Alps, Hannibal introduced his troops to his ally Magilus. Magilus was the chieftain of the Boii. Magilus encouraged Hannibal to abandon his plans of fighting Cornelius Scipio at the Rhone, and to concentrate upon his invasion of Italy. In Magilus' view, attacking Scipio would risk Hannibal's large army. Instead he would act as guide to the Carthaginian army across the Alps and into Italy. Livy's account of this discussion and Hannibal's speech can be found in 21.29–21.30. Livy, as a storyteller, frequently creates speeches to present his own opinions and to define his characters. Polybius describes the same event in PS 3.44. He illustrates Hannibal's leadership.

> Then the Celts, having said all this, withdrew. After them, Hannibal himself reminded the soldiers of their past successes. He said they had experienced many perils and dangers but had never failed when they had followed his judgment and advice. Next he told them to be courageous and confident because they saw that the hardest part of their task had been achieved, now that they had forced a crossing of the river and could see with their own eyes the good will of their allies and their willingness to support them. He encouraged and begged them not to deal with matters which were his concern. They should obey their general's orders, and be brave men and worthy of their past achievements.
>
> Polybius, *Histories* 3.44

There is a great deal of debate as to whether Polybius had inside information regarding the Carthaginian forces. Some historians believe that Polybius had read about Hannibal's crossing from Sosylus of Lacedaemon, who claimed to have travelled with Hannibal and wrote the lost book *The Deeds of Hannibal*. Other historians suggest, in accordance to Polybius' journalistic style, he may have interviewed Numidians who had fought alongside Hannibal. There are others who are dubious about the authenticity and reliability of the men Polybius interviewed. After all, there was nothing stopping Polybius' eyewitnesses exaggerating their experiences for the Greek traveller who wanted stories about Hannibal.

Study question

Livy describes the same event in PS 21.32–21.33. Read this alongside Polybius account in PS 3.50–3.51. Then complete this table and the question which follows.

	Livy's account	Polybius account
Hannibal's leadership		
Hannibal's tactics		
Language to describe the events		

1 What are the main differences between the two versions? Why do you think these differences exist?

Study questions

Read Polybius PS 3.44 and answer the following questions.

1 Why do the Celts from Northern Italy near the River Po hate the Romans?
2 What do the Celts tell Hannibal and his men about the Alps?
3 How does Hannibal motivate his men to begin the march across the Alps? Is this a good example of Hannibal's leadership?

The Allobrogian tribes

Hannibal's first stop on his march across the Alps was in an area known as The Island. It was a very fertile area. Polybius (3.49) tells us that Hannibal made this stop to support Brancus, a local leader, against his brother and rival for the tribal leadership. After securing Brancus' position, Hannibal received guides and supplies to help his troops cross the Alps.

FIGURE 2.8
Reconstruction of Hannibal's crossing of the Alps.

Hannibal now began his ascent. Polybius describes Hannibal's first major test in 3.50–3.51. A number of local tribes called the Allobrogians took this opportunity to attack. They positioned their troops along the pass Hannibal's army would have to climb. Hannibal's guides informed him of the threat and told him that the Allobrogian soldiers only guarded the pass during daylight hours. With this information Hannibal camped at the base of the pass a short distance from the enemy.

2.2 The Nature and Dynamics of Hannibal's Leadership

> **Study question**
>
> Read Livy (PS) 21.34 alongside Polybius account in (PS) 3.52–3.53. Then complete this table and the question which follows.
>
> | | Livy's account | Polybius account |
> |---|---|---|
> | Hannibal's leadership | | |
> | Hannibal's tactics | | |
> | Language to describe the events | | |
>
> **1** What are the main differences between the two versions? Why do you think these differences exist?

At night, Hannibal led a small force to take the barbarians' positions at the end of the pass. Feeling more secure, Hannibal began cautiously to move his pack animals and horsemen towards the exit. When the Allobrogian armies realised that Hannibal had taken their positions, they considered retreating. Realising Hannibal had sent his animals through first, they changed their minds. Hannibal had provided an opportunity for them to steal his supplies. The attack caused panic among Hannibal's pack animals and many fell to their deaths.

Hannibal's leadership was being severely tested. Hannibal moved to the front of the pass, took control of his troops and attacked the Allobrogians from higher ground. Despite suffering heavy losses, Hannibal drove the barbarians towards their town. With a small force Hannibal followed them and destroyed their settlement. Hannibal took Allobrogian pack animals and supplies to replenish those he had lost.

Livy ((PS) 21.34) and Polybius ((PS) 3.52–3.53) describe another challenge to Hannibal's army when they met another tribe from the region. This tribe claimed they wanted to form an alliance with the Carthaginians. To prove their loyalty, they offered gifts and hostages to Hannibal. Hannibal cautiously accepted their friendship. He calculated that refusing their help would result in war, but he did not trust them. To protect his main force, he placed his pack animals at the front again and his heavy infantry to the rear.

These precautions saved Hannibal from a massacre. The barbarians had placed their main force a few miles ahead above a pass. As Hannibal's army marched underneath they threw stones and boulders at the animals. Such was the panic, Hannibal retreated to higher ground with the main part of his army to protect them. The following day the barbarians had retreated after taking a large amount of supplies from Hannibal's army. Hannibal re-joined his cavalry and continued his ascent.

Polybius ((PS) 3.54) and Livy ((PS) 21.35) describe Hannibal's final ascent; on the ninth day he camped at the top of the Alps to allow the survivors of his army to catch up. Before departing on the eleventh day he brought his army together to raise their spirits. He showed them Italy in the distance and informed them that soon they would enjoy the hospitality of the Celtic tribes.

> **ACTIVITY**
> - Summarise the key events from Hannibal's crossing of the Alps.
> - From Livy's and Polybius' accounts, do you think Hannibal anticipated how dangerous the crossing would be?

Polybius (PS 3.55–3.56) and Livy (21.36) both describe the descent as treacherous. Snowfall and worsening weather conditions made it dangerous. Many animals fell to their deaths as they made their way down. To make matters worse, a landslide had destroyed the path. Hannibal attempted to take a detour, but the conditions were so icy that it was impossible to do so without further loss of life. With no other option, Hannibal ordered his men to rebuild the path and create a track for the army to pass. Livy shares another story. A landslide had blocked the path. To create a pass Hannibal used wine and fire to destroy the rocks and continue with their descent.

Polybius (PS 3.56) claims that the column at Lacinium told him that, after crossing the Alps, Hannibal's army had been reduced to 6,000 horsemen, 20,000 infantry and thirty-seven elephants. Although the journey from New Carthage had taken five months, it was the last fifteen days which had most severely weakened Hannibal's military power.

WAS HANNIBAL'S LEADERSHIP THE DECISIVE FACTOR IN THE WAR WITH ROME 218–216 BC?

Crossing the Alps had tested Hannibal's leadership. According to Livy and Polybius, Hannibal had to intervene several times to maintain his men's morale. If travelling from the Rhone to Italy had cost him 36,000 men and many horses, as Livy argues, we can see why. Livy claims his figures are accurate because they came from a Roman historian who had been a prisoner of war and had talked to Hannibal. Polybius, on the other hand, uses the column he found at Lacinium to claim that Hannibal had lost about 4,000 horses and 18,000 men. Whatever the true figure, it was a significant loss which, as Polybius suggests, would have left the men 'dejected'.

Polybius (3.60) shares an interesting story about how Hannibal dealt with his men's low spirits. For a few days he concentrated on resting the men, before mobilising them for war with Cornelius Scipio. The Taurini tribe had rejected Hannibal's request for an alliance, so he invaded their town and murdered everyone who refused to surrender. Such a tactic achieved two objectives. It caused fear among the other Celtic tribes who lived in northern Italy encouraging many of them to support Hannibal. It also raised the spirits of Hannibal's army.

Hannibal and Cornelius Scipio positioned their troops near Ticinus, a tributary of the river Po. Both armies were exhausted. Cornelius Scipio's Roman troops had sailed from Gaul and marched from Rome. Hannibal's Carthaginian and Iberian troops had marched from Iberia and crossed the Alps; but they were well supported by fresh Celtic troops.

The Battle of Ticinus: November 218 BC

The first conflict between Hannibal and Cornelius Scipio was inconclusive, but it gave Hannibal an important foothold in Italy.

Both men sent large raiding parties to spy on each other. Both generals then judged their meeting to be an excellent opportunity to gain an advantage and decided to engage.

Hannibal's 4,000–6,000 horsemen were evenly matched by a similar number of Roman horsemen and **velites.** To motivate his troops (Livy 21.45), Hannibal promised tax-free land, citizenship to his allies and freedom to the slaves who fought for him. He knew the importance of an early victory to inspire his troops.

Polybius informs us (3.65) Hannibal's flexibility and leadership gave him a significant advantage over his opponent. While Cornelius Scipio ordered his men to make a slow and steady advance, Hannibal seized the opportunity to close the gap between the two armies. As a consequence, the velites were unable to throw their javelins. Fearing for their lives, they fled through the Roman lines causing confusion among the Roman army.

The Roman army managed to regroup when the Roman cavalry drew the Numidian cavalry away from the main Roman force. The Numidian cavalry eventually managed to **outflank** and surround the Roman cavalry. Completely surrounded, the Roman cavalry dismounted and had to fight on foot to escape Hannibal's trap. In this confusion, Cornelius Scipio was badly injured. His son, the future Scipio Africanus, saved his father.

Cornelius Scipio realised that his defeat had given Hannibal the upper hand. He ordered his men to leave camp and to retreat beyond the River Po. Hannibal's victory at Ticinus had a significant impact upon Rome's Celtic allies. Encouraged by Hannibal's actions, the Gauls who had fought with Cornelius Scipio at Ticinus mutinied. Of Rome's Celtic allies, 2,200 murdered many Roman soldiers as they slept. Cutting off the heads of their victims, they marched to Hannibal's camp and asked to join his army. Hannibal, however, did not trust men who would change loyalty so promptly. Hannibal decided to send them around northern Italy looking for other allies who could fight with him.

outflank move round the side of an enemy force to outmanoeuvre them on both sides (of an army)

Study questions

1 Summarise the key events in the Battle of Ticinus.
2 How significant is this battle to Hannibal's plans to force Rome to surrender?

EXPLORE FURTHER

Read Polybius 3.65 for a fuller account of the Battle of Ticinus

The Battle of Trebia: December 218 BC

Scipio's injury forced him to wait until his co-consul, Sempronius, arrived with reinforcements. Sempronius' troops managed to surprise a small detachment of Hannibal's cavalry on his way to Scipio's camp. Livy (PS 21.52–21.53) tells us that Sempronius and Scipio discussed their next course of action.

Cornelius Scipio favoured waiting. According to Polybius (3.70) he believed the Carthaginians would lose their Celtic allies over the winter. More importantly, the Roman recruits were inexperienced and were not as battle-hardened as the Carthaginian force. Rome did not need to fight now, but Hannibal did.

Sempronius, on the other hand, like many consuls, wanted a victory for personal reasons. The pinnacle of a Roman's political career was to gain consulship and win a convincing victory for the glory of Rome. Sempronius' consulship would expire at the end of the month, and he had wasted most of his command sailing to Sicily. Confident of victory after defeating a small force of Numidian and Celtic cavalry, Sempronius prepared for battle.

Hannibal saw an opportunity. If he won a decisive victory, then he could attract the support of more Celtic tribes. Livy (PS 21.54) describes Hannibal's preparations. Hannibal asked his brother, Mago, to create a small force of 1,000 cavalry and infantry.

KEY INDIVIDUAL

Tiberius Sempronius Longus
Dates: *c.* 260–210 BC
Roman consul and commander

Initially sent against Carthaginian forces in Sicily and Africa, he joined the war in Italy in 218 BC and fought at the Battle of Trebia before returning to Rome at the end of his consulship.

FIGURE 2.9
Plan of the Battle of Trebia.

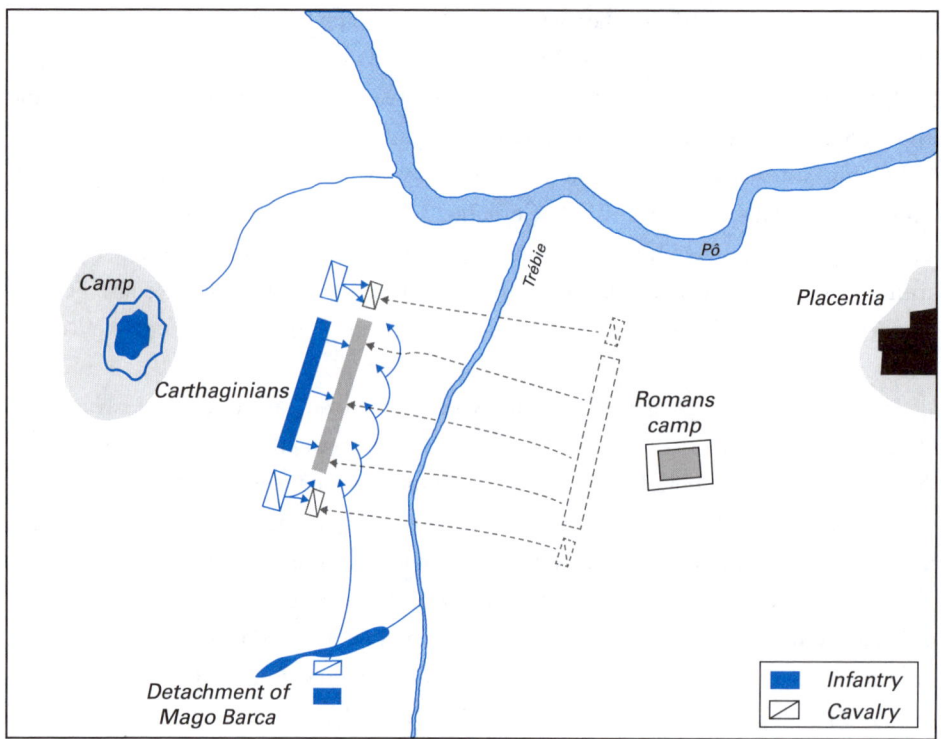

Under nightfall they were to hide from the Roman army. When he gave the signal they would attack the Roman army from behind. Many modern scholars believe that Livy is trying to diminish Hannibal's successes by presenting his tactics as underhand.

To lure Sempronius into battle Hannibal ordered the Numidian cavalry to march across the river Trebia. Here they would taunt Sempronius into battle by throwing spears at the Roman guards, and then feign retreat once they were sure the Roman army would follow. To tip the balance of the battle in his favour, Hannibal ordered his cavalry to cross before the Roman army had eaten their breakfast.

Sempronius fell into the trap. He ordered the Roman infantry to assemble and to follow the Numidian cavalry into the river. Whereas the Carthaginian horses were well protected from the cold, the Roman army was paralysed by the temperatures in the river. To make matters worse, they had not eaten and the Roman army tired quickly.

Hannibal, on the other hand, had ordered his army to eat a good breakfast and to cover themselves in oil to protect them from the cold. His army had grown in size as well. Many Gauls had joined him against the Romans. Ten thousand horsemen and thirty-seven elephants **flanked** Hannibal's 28,000 foot soldiers. The frozen and tiring Roman army had 38,000 infantry and 4,000 horsemen. Livy (21.55–21.56) describes a dramatic battle, whereas Polybius' version (3.72–3.74) depicts Hannibal's strategic manoeuvres.

As soon as the Roman army reached Hannibal's front line the Numidian cavalry turned around and attacked them. After taking significant losses, Sempronius ordered his

flanked on either side of an army's line

2.2 The Nature and Dynamics of Hannibal's Leadership

velites to retreat. Hannibal then ordered his cavalry and elephants to attack the Roman cavalry. The elephants scared the Roman horses and they fled the battlefield. Sensing victory was near Hannibal decided to bring Mago into play. Hannibal allowed the Roman infantry to push his main force back. This ordered retreat manoeuvred the Roman troops past Mago's position and allowed 1,000 horsemen and 1,000 foot soldiers to attack the Roman army from the rear. Hannibal's Carthaginian infantry immediately stopped its retreat. The Roman army was surrounded and exhausted, Sempronius could not prevent what remained of the Roman army breaking formation and fleeing to the river.

Hannibal ordered his men to massacre the Roman troops. Sempronius helped his 10,000 Roman **principes** escape by punching their way through Hannibal's centre towards the city of Piacenza. Rome's allies and velites were left behind to be massacred.

Hannibal's preparation and use of psychological warfare had provided him with the first significant victory he needed to win support from the Gauls. Hannibal also increased his pressure upon Rome's allies. All the captured Gauls were given their freedom by Hannibal. He reminded them that he was only interested in conquering Rome, and if they joined him they would be fighting for their freedom.

> **principes** the main Roman infantry: heavily armoured legionaries who formed the core of any Roman army

Study questions
Read Livy PS 21.54 and answer the following questions.

1. Summarise Hannibal's and Sempronius' preparations.
2. Summarise the tactics used by Hannibal to secure victory.
3. Do you think Livy is making excuses for the Roman soldiers? Explain your answer.

The Battle of Trasimene: June 217 BC

The onset of winter meant Hannibal could not take advantage of his victory. Scipio and Sempronius set up winter camps in two nearby cities. In the open countryside, the cold winter hit Hannibal's troops hard. Hannibal lost all but one of his elephants.

Rome created four new legions to fight him. The new year meant two new consuls were elected. Gaius Flaminius and Gnaeus Servilius. They reorganised Rome's defences and created a large fleet to make sure Carthage could not try and take control of the seas. Livy describes (21.60–21.61) how Publius Cornelius Scipio's command of the fleet brought Rome victories against Hanno and Hasdrubal in Iberia and destroyed Carthage's Spanish navy.

Servilius was sent to replace Cornelius Scipio, and Flaminius was ordered to use what remained of Sempronius' army to protect Rome from an attack by Hannibal. Hannibal's spies informed him of Rome's actions. They also told him that Flaminius was a weak general. Despite Flaminius' poor command, he was a popular consul. He delivered great speeches to the Roman people telling them he would quickly destroy Hannibal's army and protect the countryside.

> **KEY INDIVIDUALS**
>
> **Gaius Flaminius Nepos**
> Dates: c. 266–217 BC
>
> Roman politician and consul
>
> A 'new man' who as tribune of the plebs had given land to poor families destroyed by the first Punic War. During the Second Punic War he was appointed consul and raised four legions to meet Hannibal at Lake Trasimene
>
> **Gnaeus Servilius Geminus**
> Dates: c. unknown–216 BC
>
> Roman consul and commander
>
> Appointed consul in 217, Servilius was unable to prevent Rome's defeat at Trasimene due to Hannibal's march through the marshlands of Etruria. Servilius led the Roman navy in the Mediterranean for the remainder of 217. He returned to Rome in 216 and died in the Battle of Cannae

Part Two Depth Study 1: Hannibal and the Second Punic War

> **ACTIVITY**
>
> Read Polybius **PS** 3.77–3.79 and answer the following questions.
>
> - Summarise Hannibal's management of the Gauls.
> - Make a list of the strengths and weaknesses of Hannibal's leadership during his march through the marshy region of Etruria.
> - Read Polybius 3.80. How does he depict Flaminius?

To take advantage of the new consul Hannibal decided to march through marshland and surprise Flaminius. The main routes to Rome were well defended, so Hannibal decided to take the one route Rome would not expect him to take. Polybius (**PS** 3.77–3.79 and 3.80) explores the problems Hannibal confronts when dealing with his Celtic allies and crossing the marshy region of Etruria.

The march was hard and many of his Celtic troops died from exhaustion. The conditions were so harsh that Hannibal lost an eye from an infection. Despite these setbacks, Hannibal found himself a few miles from Flaminius' camp at Arretium. His march had cut Flaminius off from Rome, and given him the advantage of surprise. Servilius was some distance from Flaminius' army, and Hannibal could, if he wished, march on Rome.

Polybius (**PS** 3.81–3.82) outlines Hannibal's ability to take advantage of Flaminius' character. To enrage Flaminius, Hannibal ordered his men to destroy the Italian countryside between their camps. To maximise the impact upon Flaminius, Hannibal ordered his men to set fire to homes and crops. Witnessing the destruction around him, Flaminius lost his temper. His advisors told him to wait until Servilius could join him. Flaminius refused to listen and ordered his men to march after Hannibal.

Hannibal's spies had told him of a battlefield which would give him a significant advantage over the Roman army. (**PS** Polybius 3.82–3.83) At Lake Trasimene, there was a small plain which was surrounded by high ground. If Hannibal could lure Flaminius into the pass, his army could ambush the Roman army. Keeping his army between Flaminius and Rome, Hannibal moved towards Trasimene burning the countryside as he did so.

Seeing Flaminius' troops close behind him, Hannibal set his trap. He created a false camp at the end of the pass. A small part of his infantry would be positioned here to make it look as if Hannibal had taken a wrong turn and trapped himself in the pass. His cavalry,

FIGURE 2.10
Plan of the Battle of Trasimene.

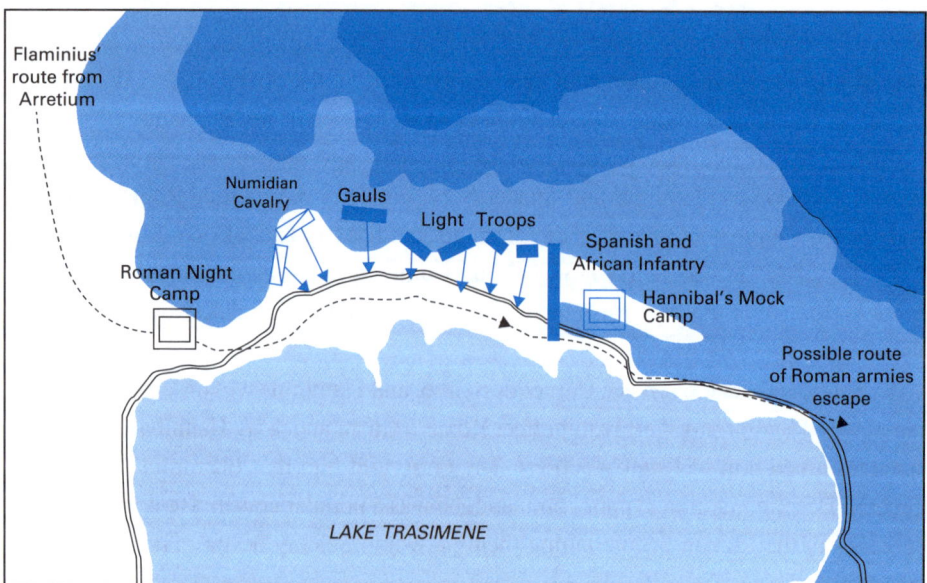

however, would be hidden just beyond the entrance to the pass. Behind them he placed the rest of his troops to trap the Roman army against the lake.

Polybius tells us (PS 3.84) that on the morning of the battle a thick mist had descended over the lake, reducing visibility. The Roman army marched into the pass, unaware that Hannibal's army was waiting to attack. As the Roman army marched past the Numidian cavalry Hannibal gave his order to attack.

Carthaginian troops attacked the Roman army from all sides. In the confusion, Flaminius was murdered by a group of Celtic troops. Many Roman soldiers ran into the lake in a desperate attempt to escape the massacre. This only made it easier for the Numidian cavalry to kill them. In a few hours over 15,000 Roman soldiers were dead.

Six thousand Roman troops bravely fought their way to the Carthaginian camp, but there was nothing there. When they reached the higher ground and turned around they could see the battlefield behind them. Realising there was nothing they could do, they marched on.

Hannibal was in no mood to allow anyone to escape. Polybius describes (PS 3.85) how he sent Maharbal and his Numidian cavalry to round them up and return them to the battlefield. After they had surrendered to Maharbal, Hannibal gave the order for them to be sold as slaves. Hannibal, on the other hand, lost 2,500 men, most of whom were Celtic soldiers.

The defeat at Trasimene caused further panic in Rome (Polybius PS 3.86). The Senate realised that it needed to appoint a dictator to plan Rome's defence. Quintus Fabius Maximus was appointed and he adopted the so-called Fabian strategy (see p. 119) to frustrate Hannibal and deny him another victory by never engaging in open battle.

The Battle of Cannae: August 216 BC

Fabius' strategy had allowed Rome to rebuild after the Battle of Trasimene. After his six-month tenure as dictator had finished, Gaius Terentius Varro and Lucius Aemilius Paullus, were appointed as consuls. Eight legions were assembled and combined to form one army under the command of both consuls. It was the largest army Rome had ever assembled. In another break with tradition the two armies were combined.

> **KEY INDIVIDUAL**
>
> **Maharbal**
> Dates: *c.* unknown–212?
>
> Carthaginian cavalry commander
>
> Fought alongside Hannibal in the Second Punic War. Deputised for Hannibal during the siege of Saguntum. After Cannae he urged Hannibal to attack Rome. The last known mention of Maharbal is in the siege of Capua in 212

> **Study questions**
>
> Read Polybius PS 3.81–3.86 and answer the following questions. What are Polybius' views on Hannibal and Flaminius leadership?
>
> 1 How does Hannibal use psychological warfare to convince Flaminius to fight at Trasimene?
> 2 Summarise the key events at the Battle of Trasimene.
> 3 What does the Battle of Trasimene tell us about Hannibal's leadership?

> **S&C Tensions in Hannibal's Army**
>
> Hannibal's cavalry commander from 219 to approximately 215 was called Maharbal. Many scholars believe he belonged to a prominent Carthaginian family. During the Battle of Trasimene, he offered 6,000 Roman soldiers safety after they surrendered to him. Hannibal, however, was displeased with this and overturned Maharbal's decision and sold them into slavery. After the next battle, at Cannae, Hannibal is said to have refused to take Maharbal's advice to march on Rome. According to Livy, Maharbal replied with the famous line, 'You know how to win a battle, Hannibal, but not a war.'

KEY INDIVIDUALS

Gaius Terentius Varro
Dates: mid third–second century BC
Roman consul and commander

Appointed consul in 216, Varro is associated with the 'new men' and is blamed for defeat at Cannae. He had a successful career after Cannae and served as an ambassador to Africa and Carthage in 200

Lucius Aemillius Paullus
Dates: unknown–216 BC
Roman consul and commander

Appointed consul in 216. Shared leadership of the Roman army at Cannae. He died in the battle. His daughter would marry Publius Cornelius Scipio Africanus

slingers Carthaginian troops from the Balearic Islands who used small slings to propel small projectiles at their enemy

Rome entered 216 BC with a core army of 40,000 troops and about 2,400 horsemen. In addition, Rome would have had many more thousands of allies fighting with them. Hannibal now had approximately 35,000 men and 10,000 horsemen.

Fabius Maximus had restricted Hannibal's raids, which left the Carthaginians with low supply levels. While Rome created its new army, Hannibal seized the initiative and took control of the supply depot at Cannae. This gave Hannibal two advantages. He could now feed his men. He could also control the local area as the depot was an important strategic point on the eastern coast of Italy.

Keen to seize the initiative back from Hannibal, the two consuls marched towards the Carthaginian army. Livy describes (22.41) an early success for Varro against a small Carthaginian raiding party. This gave the Roman army much needed confidence. Varro, however, made the same mistake as Sempronius at Trebia. He believed that this small victory proved he was more than a match for Hannibal and he pushed for action. Polybius tells us (PS 3.111–3.112) Paullus and Varro decided to set up camp on the Aufidus river, six miles from Hannibal's location.

Livy states (PS 22.44–22.45) that Paullus was cautious and wanted to consider the Roman army's decisions carefully. Varro was incensed by his partner's inaction and unsuccessfully tried to force battle during Paullus' day of command.

Hannibal knew that the Roman infantry was its strength. He could see from the number of the Roman **legions** that Varro and Paullus intended to use superior numbers to overpower the Carthaginian army.

Livy describes Hannibal's formation in PS 22.46. He lined his army up in small units, infantry at the front and Balearic **slingers** behind them. He placed himself at the front to manage his army. Then behind him in the centre he placed his Iberian and Celtic troops. On the two wings he placed his experienced African infantry. Finally, he positioned his cavalry on each side of his army.

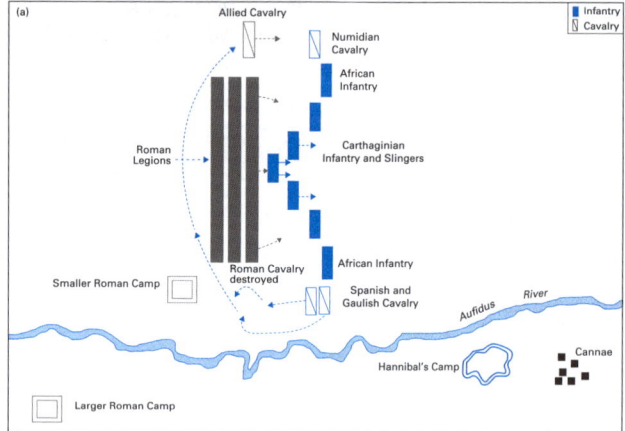 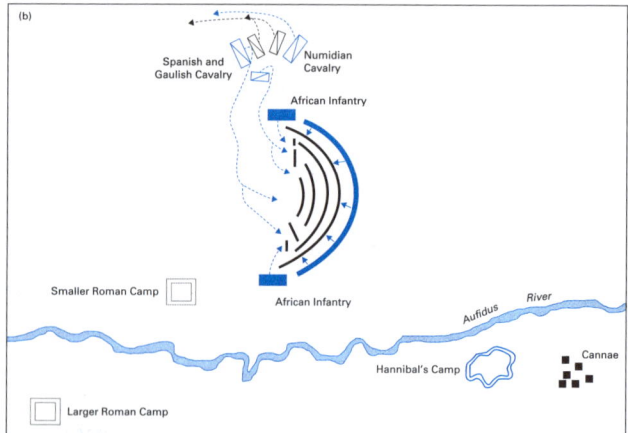

FIGURE 2.11
Approximation of how Hannibal lined up against the much larger Roman force before the battle of Cannae (left) and how he forced the Roman army into a crescent shape (right), which allowed him to surround it.

Hannibal's cavalry played a crucial role in the battle, according to Livy (PS 22.47) they forced the Roman cavalry to retreat after close quarters fighting. This allowed Hannibal to put his plans into action.

Hannibal's knew his infantry would be forced backwards by the Roman infantry. As the Roman legions punched through the lines of Iberian and Celtic troops, Hannibal ordered them to partially withdraw. In time this led to a concave or crescent shape developing which bent the Roman army out of formation.

As the crescent shape formed, Hannibal's African infantry positioned themselves on the flanks of the advancing Roman army. The Roman army had no idea that they were falling into a trap. They could only see Hannibal's Celtic and Iberian troops tiring and being slowly forced back.

Livy then describes the second phase of fighting (PS 22.48.) The Celtic and Iberian infantry quickly retreated so they were behind the African infantry. The Roman legions soon found themselves attacked on the flanks by Hannibal's fresh African troops.

Hannibal's best troops were now free to face the tiring Roman army. While the Iberian and Celtic troops created a semi-circular wall to prevent the Roman army escaping. What followed was 'butchery rather than a battle'.

To complete the massacre, Hannibal had earlier ordered a small number of his Numidian cavalry to lay a trap. Five hundred of them pretended to retreat, threw their shields to the floor and dismounted. The Romans accepted their surrender and they were moved into the Roman line. Once the African infantry faced the tired Roman legions, the Numidians took out their concealed swords and murdered the Romans from behind.

> **Study questions**
>
> Read Polybius PS 3.111–3.112 and answer the following question.
>
> 1. How does Polybius describe the Roman army's preparations?
>
> Read Livy PS 22.44–22.48 and answer the following questions.
>
> 2. How did the battlefield disadvantage the Roman army?
> 3. Summarise Livy's account of the Battle of Cannae?
> 4. Why do you think Livy describes the fighting as 'butchery rather than battle'?

FIGURE 2.12

The Death of Aemilius Paullus at the Battle of Cannae.

Hannibal showed no mercy. He ordered his cavalry to hunt down the retreating Romans and to slaughter them.

According to Livy, over 20,000 Romans and 20,000 of their allies were killed in the battle. Among the dead were the consuls Paullus, Sempronius and Servilius. Polybius suggests over 70,000 Romans were killed. Most historians agree that Livy's figures are more reliable. Livy was probably using Quintus Fabius Pictor's figures. Pictor fought in the Second Punic War and his insights into Roman tactics are very useful.

WHY WAS HANNIBAL UNABLE TO DEFEAT ROME?

Did Hannibal fail to take advantage of Cannae?

Hannibal had now defeated sixteen legions and approximately 80,000 Roman allies. Rome had lost one-fifth of its male population. A number of southern Italian cities, such as Capua, joined forces with Hannibal. Syracuse took advantage of Rome's weakness and agreed to help Hannibal by declaring war upon the Romans. Livy (PS 22.51) suggests that the Battle of Cannae was actually Hannibal's biggest mistake.

> Maharbal, his cavalry commander would have none of it, urging him not to waste a moment. 'I'll tell you what this battle has really achieved,' he declared, 'when in five days' time you are feasting on the Capitol. Follow up quickly. I'll go ahead with the cavalry, and before they even realise we are coming, the Romans will discover we've arrived.' For Hannibal it all seemed far too optimistic, an almost inconceivable possibility. He commended Maharbal for his imaginative idea, but said he needed time to think it through. Maharbal's reply was short and to the point. 'The gods do not give all their gifts to any one man. You can win a battle, Hannibal. But you have no idea how to exploit it.'
>
> That single day's delay, by common consent, proved the salvation of Rome and her empire.
>
> Livy, *The History of Rome* 22.51

Hannibal did not feel confident enough to attack Rome. He had crossed the Alps without siege equipment. His Iberian and African troops were tiring. Hannibal remained loyal to his strategy:

- defeat the Roman legions
- encourage the Italian cities to abandon Rome and side with Carthage to gain independence or protection
- enforce a victory peace upon Rome.

Livy (22.58) tells us that after Cannae, Rome showed no sign of wanting to negotiate a truce. Carthalo, a Carthaginian ambassador, led a delegation to Rome to demand a truce. The Roman Senate refused and immediately issued an order mobilising all men to prepare for war in the defence of Rome.

FIGURE 2.13
Tarentum coins probably minted during 219–212 when the city was allied to Hannibal.

Hannibal's campaign 215–204

Hannibal's strategy after Cannae was to isolate Rome and win over its allies in southern Italy. If Carthage could form alliances with the cities of Italy then Rome's army and wealth would slowly deteriorate.

After Cannae, Hannibal's policy was successful. Greek cities in Sicily revolted against Roman rule. Philip V of Macedon and Hannibal signed an alliance in 215 (Polybius 7.9) and this led to the start of the First Macedonian War. Hannibal also created an alliance of Greek city states in southern Italy. These included Arpi, Herdonia, Capua and, in 212, Tarentum. His most significant ally was Capua. It was the second largest city in Italy. The Capuans saw Hannibal's invasion as an opportunity to replace Rome as the most powerful city in Italy. Capua gave Hannibal access to fresh troops and a harbour to bring in supplies from Carthage and his allies. Hannibal's early successes had also established an independent Gaul in northern Italy.

Hannibal continued to enjoy great successes between 215–212, but Rome's return to a defensive strategy frustrated Hannibal. The Roman general, Marcus Claudius Marcellus, prevented Hannibal from taking the city of Nola, which would have given Hannibal control of Campania. Hanno the Elder introduced a second Carthaginian army into southern Italy. Hanno the Elder, however, did not enjoy the same success as Hannibal and his army would be destroyed by 212.

The year 212 was the high point of Hannibal's invasion. Tarentum joined Hannibal. Hannibal forced the Romans to abandon the siege of Capua which enabled new Numidian cavalry to join Hannibal. Hannibal massacred the Romans at Silarus and Herdonia.

After 211 Hannibal suffered several set-backs. Livy's account of Hannibal's siege of Rome suggests that by 211 BC Hannibal's confidence was beginning to wane. Extreme weather conditions prevented Hannibal from attacking Rome's walls and Hannibal began to think the gods had turned against him. (PS Livy 26.11).

Livy suggests that Hannibal's decision to attack Rome led to unrest within his army (PS Livy 26.12). Hanno the Elder, who led the defence of Capua, tried to send a message to Hannibal, asking him to abandon Rome.

> The Romans' persistence in carrying out the siege of Capua, however, was not equal to Hannibal's in defending it. For across Samnium, Apulia, and Lucania he hurried into the land of the Bruttii, to the strait and to Regium, at such a speed that it was almost as if he was to overwhelm them unawares with his sudden arrival. Capua, although it had been besieged no less viciously at that time, was aware nevertheless of Flaccus' arrival, and began to wonder why Hannibal had not returned at the same time. Then, through conversation with the enemy, they learned that they had been deserted and abandoned, and that the Carthaginians had given up any hope of holding Capua. The proconsuls also released a declaration, which was heralded and distributed amongst the enemy in accordance with a senatorial decree: that there would be no punishment for any Capuan citizen who changed sides before a certain date.
>
> Livy, *The History of Rome* 26.12

ACTIVITY

Read Livy PS 22.51

- Summarise Livy's account of the discussion between Maharbal and Hannibal after Cannae.
- Why does Livy believe Hannibal made a mistake?

Read Livy 22.58

- Do you think this extract supports or challenges Livy's view in 22.51? Explain your answer.

KEY INDIVIDUAL

Marcus Claudius Marcellus
Dates: 268–208

Roman consul and commander

Fought in the First Punic War, helped defeat the Gauls in 225 and was given command of an expedition to Sicily in 216. After Cannae, he successfully led the remnants of Rome's legions at Nola to prevent Hannibal's march through Italy for the first time. As consul, he successfully crushed rebellions in Sicily and Syracuse between 214 and 212. He was appointed consul five times before his death in 208 by a Numidian ambush. Credited by Plutarch with restoring the tradition of spoila opia – the ultimate spoils, whereby a Roman general kills the leader of the opposing army prior to a battle.

FIGURE 2.14
Coin possibly depicting Hasdrubal or a local god.

ACTIVITY

- Create a timeline showing Hannibal's actions between 215–204

Study question

Read Livy (PS) 26.11–26.12

Why does Hannibal fail to protect Capua?

Unfortunately, the Numidians who agreed to take the message were captured and tortured by the Roman forces. Capua fell before Hannibal could return.

Hannibal's attack upon Rome, failed to convince Rome's consuls to abandon the siege of Capua. Within a year Capua had fallen and Hannibal lost his most powerful Italian ally.

In 209, Marcellus and Fabius seized control of Tarentum. Hannibal now lacked a significant harbour and hoped to receive reinforcements from his brother, Hasdrubal, who planned to cross the Alps. Hasdrubal's army was defeated and his decapitated head was thrown into Hannibal's camp in southern Italy. After defeat in Iberia, Mago also tried to reinforce Hannibal. Unfortunately, Mago became trapped in northern Italy, while Hannibal was trapped in southern Italy. Both men were recalled to Carthage when Scipio Africanus attacked Africa.

Carthage loses Iberia

In spring 217 BC, before the Battle of Trasimene, Rome had managed to take control of the Iberian seas. Hannibal's brother, Hasdrubal Barca planned a secret naval attack upon Rome's base north of the Ebro river. To Hasdrubal's surprise the Roman navy was ready for him and it destroyed Carthage's Iberian navy. This gave Rome control of the seas around Iberia again. Hasdrubal's defeat encouraged many Iberian cities to rebel against Carthage.

Hasdrubal was dragged into an Iberian War. Fabius Maximus sent Publius Scipio Cornelius in Autumn 217 BC to support the rebels and prevent Iberian supplies and reinforcements reaching Rome.

A significant problem for Carthage was that the new Iberian armies assembled by Hasdrubal did not want to fight. Victory over Rome in Iberia would mean marchng to Italy. Rome appears to have been more successful in gaining Iberian allies, than Hannibal was at gaining Italian allies. This is a significant turning point in the war. Hannibal was becoming increasingly reliant upon the men he could assemble in Italy.

In 216 BC, Hasdrubal was defeated at the Battle of the River Ebro (Livy (PS) 23.29). The Carthaginian Senate panicked. Carthage relied on Iberia's silver mines to fund their military ambitions and develop their city. Carthage decided to send Mago to defend Iberia and its silver mines, rather than reinforce Hannibal in Italy. Carthage never recaptured Iberia. When Cornelius Scipo's son, the famous general Scipio Africanus, was sent to Iberia, in 210 BC, he captured New Carthage and by 205 BC had driven Carthage out of Iberia.

ACTIVITY

Read Livy (PS) 23.29 and answer the following question.

- Summarise the reasons Hasdrubal lost the Battle of Ebro.
- Summarise the impact of Hasdrubal's defeat.

2.2 The Nature and Dynamics of Hannibal's Leadership

TOPIC REVIEW

Boost your knowledge

Describe:

a. Hannibal's leadership and tactics at Saguntum
b. Hannibal's leadership and tactics during the march from Saguntum to Italy
c. Hannibal's leadership and tactics at Ticinus, Trebia, Trasimene and Cannae
d. Hannibal's failure to defeat Rome and conquer Italy

Stretch your understanding

Explain:

a. Why Hannibal crossed the Alps
b. the strengths and weaknesses of Hannibal's leadership
c. how effective Hannibal's tactics were
d. how Hannibal wanted to defeat Italy and why he failed

PRACTICE QUESTIONS

Passage A

Between the armies there was a river, enclosed on both sides by high banks, which were strewn all over with marsh grass, bushes, and brambles; the kind which generally cover uncultivated land. When Hannibal himself rode over the ground and saw that it offered sufficient cover even for cavalry, he said to his brother, Mago: 'This will be the place which you will occupy. Pick out 100 foot soldiers and 100 cavalrymen, and come to me with them at first watch. Now is the time to rest.' He spoke, and dismissed the council. Shortly afterwards, Mago arrived with his chosen band of men. Hannibal said: 'I see a strong group of men, but I think your numbers should be equally strong to match your valour. Each of you must go and choose nine men like yourselves from the ranks and companies. Mago will show you the place which you are to occupy; you have an enemy who is blind to these plans.' So, Mago having been sent out with his 1,000 cavalrymen and 1,000 foot soldiers, Hannibal instructed the Numidian cavalry to cross the River Trebia at first light.

Livy *The History of Rome* 21.54

1. What can we learn from Passage A about Hannibal's preparations for the Battle of Trebia? [5]
2. Using details from Passage A, evaluate how accurate you think Livy's account of these events is. [5]

2.3 The Changing Nature of Rome's Response to Hannibal

> **TOPIC OVERVIEW**
>
> - the leadership of Sempronius, Flaminius, Servillius, Varro and Paulus
> - Roman mistakes in the campaign and the reasons for them
> - the impact of Fabius Maximus upon Roman tactics, including his appointment as dictator and the use of religion to improve Roman confidence
> - Minucius' failure and Fabius' success in isolating Hannibal from his allies and cutting off his supply routes
> - Scipio Africanus' appointment and successful campaign in Iberia
> - debate in Senate between Scipio Africanus and Fabius Maximus
> - Scipio's invasion of Africa to draw Hannibal out of Rome
> - the impact of Scipio Africanus on Roman tactics
>
> **The prescribed sources for this topic are:**
>
> - Livy, *The History of Rome*, Book 22, sections 7–8, 23–26
> - Polybius, *Histories*, Book 3, sections 87–89
> - Plutarch, *Life of Fabius Maximus*, 5
> - Dedication for Quintus Fabius Maximus

Rome's response to Hannibal's invasion of Italy was arrogant. Hannibal punished Roman armies at Ticinus, Trebia and Lake Trasimene. He had routed the Roman army which caused panic in Rome. To protect Rome a dictator, Quintus Fabius Maximus, tried to contain Hannibal in the south of Italy. Once his term of office was up, the Roman Senate demanded victory. Instead, at the Battle of Cannae, Rome suffered its greatest defeat of the Second Punic War. Rome opened a new front in Iberia which stretched Carthage's resources to breaking point. The invasion of Iberia also produced one of Rome's greatest general's Publius Cornelius Scipio Africanus.

WHY WAS ROME UNABLE TO DEFEAT HANNIBAL BETWEEN 218 AND 216 BC?

Hannibal's use of psychological warfare, geography and innovative tactics help explain why the Carthaginian army fought so well. What they do not tell us is why Rome's generals were so ineffective against Hannibal.

Publius Cornelius Scipio, at Ticinus

Although a popular consul who appeared to understand how to attack Hannibal, Cornelius Scipio failed to prevent Hannibal leaving Iberia and invading Italy. His first mistake was underestimating Hannibal.

When he eventually arrived at Massilia in 218 BC, he was shocked that Hannibal had already travelled through the Pyrenees. He believed that the local Celtic tribes would have put up more resistance and slowed down his journey. Hannibal, however, had sent ambassadors ahead of him to secure their support with gifts and promises of neutrality. Scipio made the same mistake when he discovered that Hannibal had managed to cross the Alps and had reached northern Italy by November 218 BC.

Hannibal knew that taking unexpected routes would put his enemies on the back foot. He used a similar tactic in the Spring of 217 BC to surprise Sempronius and Flaminius. By marching through the marshlands in Etruria, he isolated Sempronius in the north of Italy and cut Flaminius off from Rome.

The second mistake Cornelius Scipio made was during the Battle of Ticinus. His enthusiasm to fight Hannibal encouraged him to engage the Carthaginians without his full army. This mistake nearly cost him his life and he had to retreat to recover his strength. His enthusiasm to fight and his failure to know his enemy gave Hannibal much needed confidence to raise the morale of his tired troops.

Tiberius Sempronius Longus, at Trebia

Cornelius Scipio's co-consul arrived shortly after the Battle of Ticinus. Sempronius, like Scipio, wanted to engage Hannibal quickly. He had enjoyed a small victory over a Carthaginian raiding party and believed his army could easily defeat Hannibal.

Sempronius ignored Scipio's advice to wait until the spring. A break would allow the Roman troops to be trained to counter the Numidian cavalry. His consulship was coming to an end, and he hoped to use the victory to improve his reputation in Rome.

Polybius (3.72) portrays Sempronius as arrogant and overconfident. Foolishly ordering his men to attack Hannibal's Numidian cavalry when they taunted him before the before the Battle of Trebia. This was a fatal mistake. His army had not eaten and froze in the icy river. Sempronius' Roman javelin throwers were ineffective and at a significant disadvantage. The Carthaginian army, on the other hand, had eaten and covered themselves in oil to keep warm (Livy 21.51). Livy (PS 21.54), suggests Sempronius' army was beaten by the weather and Hannibal's cunning, rather than Sempronius' arrogance.

Galus Flaminius and Gnaeus Servilius at Trasimene

Despite the defeat at Trebia, the Roman Senate was calm and the new consuls were given clear instructions. Servilius would replace Scipio in northern Italy and try to contain Hannibal. Flaminius would act as a final defence protecting Rome from attack. This strategy was sound, but Hannibal's march south avoided the Roman army by heading through marshland in Etruria.

> **Study questions**
>
> 1. Summarise Cornelius Scipio and Tiberius Sempronius responses to Hannibal's invasion of Italy.
>
> Read Livy 21.46 and 47
>
> 2. How does Livy make excuses for Cornelius Scipio's defeat?
>
> Read Livy 21.53–56 (PS 21.54)
>
> 3. How does Livy present Sempronius in this extract?
> 4. What excuses does Livy offer to explain Rome's defeat at Trebia?

Hannibal's actions took Servilius out of the picture, and his reinforcements arrived too late to prevent a Roman defeat at Lake Trasimene. Flaminius' leadership is given by Polybius and Livy as the main reason for defeat in the Battle of Trasimene.

Flaminius is presented as a politician who seeks popular support. He is presented as a rash man who is driven by personal ambition by Polybius (PS 3.81–3.82). His concern for how his actions would be seen in Rome meant that he failed to think rationally about how best to prepare for war. Livy (22.6), however, is more sympathetic and describes his death as heroic.

Hannibal's destruction of the countryside pushed Flaminius into a temper. Rather than using reason and strategy to plan Rome's defence he rushed headlong into a trap. Flaminius' actions were so rash that he failed to send spies to check the area for an ambush. The outcome was a Roman massacre which cost Flaminius his life.

Study questions

1 Summarise Gaius Flaminius' and Gnaeus Servilius' responses to Hannibal's invasion of Italy.

Read Livy 22.3–6

2 Explain whether you believe Livy represents Flaminius as hot-headed or patriotic.
3 How does Livy portray Flaminius during the battle?
4 What similarities and differences can you see between Livy's account of Flaminius' command and Polybius' account in 3.81–3.84?

FIGURE 2.15
Hannibal counting the rings of the Roman knights who died at the Battle of Cannae by Sébastien Slodtz 1704.

Lucius Aemilius Paullus and Gaius Terentius Varro at Cannae

The characterisation by ancient historians of Roman consuls in this period follows a very similar pattern; a reasoning and cautious consul, joined by a rash and arrogant consul. It is more plausible to believe Paullus and Varro were given distinct orders to seek out Hannibal and defeat him.

According to Livy (22.39), Fabius Maximus discussed the upcoming war with Paullus. Fabius Maximus warned Paullus that he faced two enemies. Of these two enemies, Varro was more of a threat than Hannibal, he was a madman who had promised the citizens of Rome an easy victory. This characterisation is probably a later addition. Varro, like Flaminius, became a scapegoat for Rome's defeat.

Varro was confident of victory. Then again, why wouldn't he be? Rome had a superior force. They were fighting on the broad plain of Cannae, a location which suited Roman tactics. Varro's belief that Rome's legions could punch through the Carthaginian line and cause chaos had worked for Roman generals in the past. This would be the first battleground not dictated by Hannibal.

But Varro did not anticipate that Hannibal had positioned his army so that dust would blow in the Roman army's faces. He did not anticipate that Hannibal would use his

2.3 The Changing Nature of Rome's Response to Hannibal

> **S&C**
>
> ### Are Flaminius and Varro Criticised Because They are Novus Homo?
>
> Reading Polybius' and Livy's accounts of Trasimene and Cannae will leave you with a clear message. The two consuls Flaminius and Varro were weak and flawed generals who led Rome to the brink of defeat.
>
> Many modern scholars believe that they are the victims of ancient slander. Each was a novus homo, literally 'new man'. This means that they were consuls whose families had only recently gained fortune and influence in Roman politics.
>
> It is important to remember that consuls were supposed to lead Roman armies to glory. Flaminius and Varro were therefore following tradition and expectation.
>
> Flaminius died for his country at Trasimene. Varro received a public vote of thanks for salvaging the situation at Cannae and was given many important tasks and commands later in the war.

> **PRESCRIBED SOURCE**
>
> ***The History of Rome*** **Book 22, sections 7–8, 23–26**
>
> **Date:** late first century BC
>
> **Author:** Livy (c. 64/59 BC–AD17)
>
> **Genre:** history
>
> **Significance:** major source for early Roman history and mythological–historical account of the foundation of Rome
>
> **Content of the prescribed sections:** the Battle of Trasimene and the following Fabian strategy
>
> **Read it here:** OCR Source Booklet **CW**

cavalry to surround and destroy the Roman army. In this regard the ancient historians' criticisms of Varro have weight. His underestimation of Hannibal's strategic mind led to a Roman massacre. However, Varro was not as rash as they claim. His plan of action had taken into account many of the factors which had led to defeat at Trebia and Trasimene. These were not the actions of a madman, but of a general who was outwitted by Hannibal.

> **Study questions**
>
> Read Livy 22.44 and 22.49
>
> 1. To what extent does Livy believe the rivalry between Paullus and Varro helped Hannibal win the Battle of Cannae?
> 2. How does Livy describe the fall of Paullus?
> 3. What do you think Livy means when he says 'Whether by chance or design, Varro managed to make his way to Venusia'?

WAS THE FABIAN STRATEGY EFFECTIVE?

Fabius Maximus was no stranger to Roman politics. He held the consulship at least five times (233, 228, 215, 214 and 209), and held the position of dictator twice (221 and 217). During his first consulship he had defeated the Ligurians in northern Italy. This victory cemented his reputation as a great general. It is widely believed that he served during the First Punic War.

After the defeat at Trasimene, the Roman Senate wanted a safe pair of hands to prevent panic from spreading through Rome. Fabius Maximus was chosen to be **dictator** and Marcus Minucius was chosen as his **Master of the Horse**. Minucius was Fabius' political rival.

Fabius Maximus' first action as dictator was to bring calm to Rome. Plutarch and Livy both inform us that Flaminius ignored religious customs when he was appointed consul.

> **KEY INDIVIDUAL**
>
> **Quintus Fabius Maximus**
>
> **Dates:** c. 280–203 BC)
>
> Roman general and consul
>
> Five times consul, Fabius is best known for adopting a particular strategy in the Second Punic War, aiming to wear Hannibal down by a war of attrition. The success of this strategy ultimately led to the end of the war, because Hannibal was unable to defeat Rome and was eventually recalled to Carthage

Part Two Depth Study 1: Hannibal and the Second Punic War

> **PRESCRIBED SOURCE**
>
> *Histories*, Book 3, sections 87–89
>
> **Date:** second century BC
>
> **Author:** Polybius (*c*. 200–117 BC)
>
> **Genre:** history
>
> **Significance:** a vital source for the history of the rise of Rome, written by a Greek historian
>
> **Content of the prescribed sections:** the significance of the Fabian strategy
>
> **Read it here:** OCR Source Booklet CW

> **ACTIVITY**
>
> - Summarise the events which led to the appointment of Fabius Maximus as dictator
>
> Read Livy PS 22.7–22.8 and answer the following questions.
>
> - Why does Livy tell us he uses Fabius Pictor's account?
> - How does Livy portray Rome after Trasimene?
> - How did Hannibal's relocation to Umbria affect Rome?
> - Many modern historians suggest that Trasimene, rather than victory at Cannae, was Hannibal's greatest opportunity to seize Rome. What evidence does Livy provide to support this claim?

As a consequence, when Flaminius was killed and the Roman army defeated, there was a feeling that the gods had deserted Rome.

Fabius organised several religious sacrifices to try and convince the public that the gods' support had been regained. He also ordered each citizen to spend 333 sestertii and 333 denarii. We do not know if Fabius believed these acts had appeased the gods. We do know that these sacrifices had a significant propaganda effect on the citizens of Rome.

Fabian strategy

Defeats at Ticinus, Trebia and Trasimene had weakened Rome's military power by the summer of 217 BC. Fabius Maximus realised that Rome needed to regroup and find a new strategy to deal with Hannibal. Fabius Maximus decided that he needed to find a way to wear Hannibal down. If he could win a number of small battles and cut off his supply routes, this would weaken Hannibal and his allies.

To achieve this, Fabius promoted a war of **attrition**. First, Fabius followed Hannibal wherever he went. Secondly, Fabius would only attack Hannibal's raiding parties. He kept his distance from the main Carthaginian force to prevent a full-scale battle. Finally, he used a 'scorched earth policy' which destroyed the Roman countryside to prevent Hannibal from taking any Roman supplies to feed his army. Fabius Maximus knew that Rome was rich and could always plant new crops and repair damaged homes. Rome also had many more men than Hannibal, but this did not mean that they should be sacrificed. This strategy meant that Hannibal was always on edge, unsure of where his army would gain their supplies. Polybius, Plutarch and Livy all agree that this strategy was a success.

> **attrition** warfare designed to reduce the number of men in the opposing army little by little, employed by Fabius and later Marcellus against Hannibal

> **Fabius Maximus Cunctator**
>
> His strategy earned Fabius Maximus the nickname 'Cunctator', which meant delayer.

Ager Falernus

In the summer of 417 BC, Hannibal's guides told him he could spend the summer collecting supplies from an area known as Ager Falernus. He could also seek more allies against Rome. Fabius just watched while Hannibal raided the area. This appalled the Roman public and the army.

2.3 The Changing Nature of Rome's Response to Hannibal

> **ACTIVITY**
>
> - Summarise Fabius Maximus strategy
>
> Read Polybius **PS** 3.87–3.89 and answer the following questions.
>
> - Does Polybius add any evidence to support the view that Trasimene was a missed opportunity for Hannibal?
> - What does Polybius tell us about the role of a dictator?
> - Why did Fabius Maximus not engage Hannibal?
> - What did Fabius Maximus believe were Rome's strengths?

In reality, Fabius was setting a trap. Fabius Maximus had lured Hannibal into the Ager Falernus because the area was surrounded by fast-flowing rivers. Fabius controlled all the exits and he planned to starve Hannibal into surrender.

Fabius Maximus' strategy was heavily criticised by his Master of the Horse. Minucius turned many of the new recruits against Fabius.

> They made Fabius an object of mockery and nicknamed him Hannibal's 'minder' (literally: pedagogue – child's slave attendant). By contrast, they had the highest regard for Minucius as being the sort of "real" general that Rome deserved.
>
> As a result he became increasingly arrogant and reckless, jeering at all their hilltop encampments and suggesting that the dictator was always providing splendid theatrical settings, from which they could watch the destruction of Italy by fire and sword.
>
> Plutarch, *Life of Fabius Maximus* 5

Despite accusations of cowardice and an army at odds with him, Fabius stuck to his strategy. Hannibal took advantage of the unrest in the Roman ranks and began a policy of destroying everyone's land except Fabius'. Furthermore, Livy (**PS** 22.23) tells us that Fabius Maximus exchanged prisoners of war with Hannibal without the Senate's permission. When this news reached Rome, Minucius' allies used it to claim Fabius had made a secret pact with Hannibal to weaken Rome.

Hannibal, however, knew Fabius had him trapped and made a desperate attempt to escape. At night, Hannibal drove a few cows towards the hills near Fabius' position. Fabius was convinced this was a trick, so he decided not to act. Fabius' determination not to be tricked played into Hannibal's hands. Behind the cows were Hannibal's entire army which easily overpowered the Roman soldiers guarding the exit from Ager Falernus.

Fabius Maximus was recalled to defend his strategy after the disaster of Ager Falernus. Before leaving, he put Minucius in charge of the army with clear instructions to continue his strategy. To disobey his orders would be treason. No sooner had Fabius left the command, Minucius prepared for battle. Livy states (**PS** 22.24) that within two days, Hannibal had sent a large part of his army on a raid. Minucius attacked what remained of Hannibal's camp and massacred a few hundred men. When news of the victory reached Rome, Livy writes (**PS** 22.25–22.26) that the public demanded that Municius should be made dictator. Fabius Maximus was incensed by Municius' actions. Instead of removing

FIGURE 2.16
Fabius Cunctator (Quintus Fabius Maximus Verrucosus). Statue from the Schönbrunn Gardens, Vienna.

PRESCRIBED SOURCE

***Parallel Lives: Life of Fabius Maximus*, 5**

Date: early second century AD

Author: Plutarch (*c*. AD 46–120)

Genre: biography

Significance: paired biographies of Greeks and Romans providing important historical information

Content of the prescribed sections: explanation of the Fabian strategy

Read it here: OCR Source Booklet **CW**

> **ACTIVITY**
>
> Summarise what happened at Ager Falernus and its impact.
>
> Read Plutarch's *Life of Fabius Maximus*, chapter 5, and answer the following questions.
>
> - Why does Plutarch believe Hannibal respected Fabius Maximus?
> - What is Fabius' response to these criticisms?
>
> Read Livy **PS** 22.23–26
>
> - How does Hannibal damage Fabius' reputation?
> - How does Fabius' defend his tactics?

Munucius for treason, Fabius had to accept Minucius as his equal and share control of the army. Fabius ceded, but demanded the legions be divided between them.

Geronium

Fabius and Minucius went their separate ways. Minucius prepared to attack Hannibal at Larinum. Hannibal placed his army on a field near Geronium. It was perfect for setting a trap because there were many hollows where large numbers of soldiers could hide without being noticed. Hannibal then moved a small force of men into Minucius' view.

Minucius took the bait. He failed to scout the area, and his four legions fell into Hannibal's trap. The Numidian cavalry met Minucius' troops and drew more of the Roman

> **PRESCRIBED SOURCE**
>
> **Dedication for Quintus Fabius Maximus**
>
> **Date:** after 209 BC
>
> **Medium:** inscription on stone
>
> **Location:** found at Arezzo, Italy
>
> **Significance:** a rare and important piece of surviving evidence giving details of the life, career and military achievements of Fabius
>
> **Read it here:** OCR Source Booklet **CW**

> **Study question**
>
> Below is a translation of the dedication for Quintus Fabius Maximus , which reads:
>
> > Quintus Fabius Maximus, the son of Quintus, dictator twice, consul five times, censor, interrex twice, curule aedile, quaestor twice, tribune of the soldiers twice, pontifex, augur. In his first consulship he overcame the Ligurians. After this he celebrated triumphs in his third and fourth consulships, when he checked Hannibal, daring because of his numerous victories, by doggedly following him. When Minucius was made Master of the Horse, with power equal to that of the dictator, according to the people's wish, Fabius as dictator came to the aid of the defeated army and, under the name (of dictator), was hailed as Father by the army of Minucius. As consul for the fifth time he captured Tarentum and held a triumph. He was regarded as the most cautious commander of his own age and the most expert in military affairs. He was enrolled in the Senate as princeps for two five-year terms.
>
> What does this tell us about how Fabius helped develop Rome's response to Hannibal's invasion of Italy?

army into the trap. Once the four legions were in place, Hannibal's hidden soldiers attacked from behind. Minucius' Roman army was surrounded.

Fabius witnessed it all from afar and gave the order to reinforce Minucius' position. Once Fabius joined the battle, Hannibal retreated back to camp. He did not want to risk his troops fighting both consuls. Minucius accepted his mistakes and returned to his position as Master of the Horse until new consuls were elected.

Roman response to Hannibal 216–203 BC

After Cannae, Marcellus helped Rome contain Hannibal in the south of Italy. He was a plebeian **praetor** who rose to prominence during the Second Punic War. He became the first Roman general to succeed against Hannibal, when he protected the town of Nola from capture with the disgraced survivors of Cannae. Rome had discovered a general capable of matching, if not defeating, Hannibal. Marcellus prevented Hannibal from taking control of the Campania region. If Hannibal had seized this area he would have geographically linked most of his allies in the south of Italy.

Rome's consuls also began to target Carthage's allies to counter defeats in Italy. For example, the massacres at Herdonia and Silarus killed 31,000 of 34,000 Roman soldiers who fought there. Such setbacks would have crippled other city states. Not the Romans, they managed to fight in Iberia, siege Hannibal's allies in Capua and Syracuse, and defeat Hanno the Elder in Beneventum, southern Italy.

When Hannibal secured an alliance with Tarentum in 212, it should have given Hannibal tight grip of southern Italy, but by 211 Roman tactics meant he was losing control of that region. Hannibal tried to lift the siege of Capua by attacking Rome. In contrast to the period 218–216, Rome's consuls maintained the siege of Capua rather than rushing to the defence of Rome. Hannibal failed to take Rome and Capua fell. In 209 BC, Marcellus pursued Hannibal around northern Italy, while Fabius Maximus defeated the city of Tarentum.

Hannibal still posed a threat. He killed both of Rome's consuls in 208, including Marcellus. Yet the inconclusive nature of the war continued into 207. Gaius Claudius Nero drew Hannibal into another stalemate at Grumentum, before marching north to destroy Hannibal's brother, Hasdrubal, as he crossed the Alps in the Battle of Metaurus. In 205, Mago Barca, his other brother, landed in Genoa with what remained of his Iberian army. He wanted to reorganise Hannibal's Celtic and Ligurian allies in northern Italy, but was prevented from doing so by the Roman army. Both Hannibal and Mago were recalled to Africa in 203.

FIGURE 2.17
Dedication for Quintus Fabius Maximus (CIL 11.1828).

ACTIVITY

Summarise how Rome responded to Hannibal after Cannae

THE IMPACT OF SCIPIO AFRICANUS ON THE SECOND PUNIC WAR

It is at this point in the war that Hannibal's eventual vanquisher took command. Scipio (son of the defeated general of the same name) belonged to one of the most powerful

KEY INDIVIDUAL

Publius Cornelius Scipio Africanus

Dates: 236–183 BC

Roman general and consul

Brilliant commander famous for defeating Hannibal, for which he was given his last name, Africanus. He had previously fought in Iberia (Spain) to recover the territory for Rome from Carthage.

ACTIVITY

- Summarise how Scipio Africanus conquers Iberia.

Roman patrician families. His early life would have been spent preparing for military and political service. At Ticinus his bravery saved his father's life. He survived Cannae and began searching for political positions in Rome to enhance his reputation.

In 211 BC, his father and uncle were killed fighting Hasdrubal in Iberia. According to Livy (26.18–26.19), no one was brave enough to step forward to replace them, except Scipio. At the age of twenty-five, one year younger than Hannibal, he was put in charge of Rome's Iberian army.

When Scipio arrived in Iberia, Carthage controlled all the country north and south of the Ebro. Scipio, however, had an important advantage over Carthage. Rome could afford to supply reinforcements for Italy and Iberia, and its command of the Mediterranean meant supply routes remained open throughout the conflict.

The conquest of Iberia

Scipio's first military action was significant. Landing his small army at the mouth of the river Ebro, Scipio was able to travel several hundred miles upriver to capture New Carthage. Scipio's tactics allowed him to capture the Carthaginian citadel (**PS** Livy 26.46.8). The capture of the Carthaginian headquarters gave Rome the upper hand. Scipio had seized Carthage's war stores and supplies (**PS** Livy 26.47). He also controlled Carthage's harbour in Iberia. Transporting Iberian silver to Carthage would become increasingly difficult as the war in Iberia progressed.

Livy (26.50) shares a story about a beautiful Iberian woman who was offered to Scipio as a prize for his military achievements. Scipio discovered that the captured woman was promised to an Iberian chieftain named Allucius. Scipio returned the abducted woman to Allucius along with the money her parents had offered to buy her freedom. This act of kindness impressed the local Iberian tribes. They reinforced Scipio's small army and many of them abandoned Carthage to support Rome. It is likely that this is all part of the myth built up around Scipio in later times. Scipio used his base in Tarraco to force Carthage out of Iberia. Battles at Beacula and Ilipa were turning points in Scipio's successful capture of Iberia.

FIGURE 2.18
Iberian soldier on a monument from fourth–second-century Osuna.

At the Battle of Baecula in 209 BC, Scipio feared that if he fought a long battle Mago and Hasdrubal, son of Gisco, would reinforce Hannibal. Scipio therefore ordered his men to attack Hasdrubal's position in the hills. This caused panic and convinced Hasdrubal to assemble as many troops as possible to march to Italy and reinforce his brother. Hasdrubal never made it. At the Battle of Metaurus, Hasdrubal was killed by Gaius Claudius Nero.

After Hasdrubal's death, Carthage sent additional reinforcements to help Mago. When Scipio heard of this he sent his deputy, Silanus, to attack Mago. Silanus surprised the Carthaginian camp and, in the panic which followed, the Carthaginian army broke apart. Mago managed to regroup most of his army and joined Hasdrubal, son of Gisco, at Ilipa. Gisco and Mago had between 54,000 and 70,000 men. Scipio's army was about 43,000, but could have been as high as 55,000 with Iberian troops. Scipio used the element of surprise to defeat the Carthaginians and drive them out of Iberia.

Before sailing back to Rome, Scipio met the Numidian princes Syphax and Masinissa. Syphax had been Rome's ally throughout the Punic War and had attacked Hannibal's ally, King Gala, in eastern Numidia to try to stop Gala from providing Numidian cavalry to Carthage. Syphax abandoned his alliance with Rome after marrying Hasdrubal's (son of Gisco) daughter. He then allied to Carthage.

Masinissa, Gala's son, on the other hand, could see Rome had gained the upper hand. Friendship with Rome was an opportunity to increase his power and influence in the region. He abandoned his father's allies and formed an alliance with Rome.

DEBATE WITH FABIUS MAXIUMS

On his return to Rome in 205 BC, Scipio was elected as consul. He was only thirty-one. Scipio made it clear that he intended to take the war to Africa, while Hannibal was still in Italy.

Fabius Maximus led the opposition to the expedition. Livy (28.40–28.42) tells us that he still feared Hannibal's power. In his opinion, Hannibal still had the potential to destroy Rome. Hannibal was still able to create armies from Italian cities who had defected to Carthage. Fabius urged caution. He recognised that Scipio had achieved a great deal, but feared he was becoming too ambitious. Fabius asked Scipio to attack Hannibal in Italy.
Fabius closed with the words:

> I regret our decision to elect Publius Cornelius Scipio to consul. He feels as if the powers of consul are his to use to pursue his own ambitions. Rather than using these powers to serve and protect Rome.
>
> Livy, *The History of Rome* 28.42

In his reply (Livy 28.43–28.45) Scipio stated:

> for too long Italy has suffered from flame and sword. It is time that the people of Carthage feel the same. For fourteen years we have witnessed the horrors of war, and our farmland has been turned into battlefields.
>
> Livy, *The History of Rome* 28.44

The Senate was reluctant to provide additional troops. Scipio was able to use the men from the Sicilian garrison. Many of the men in the Sicilian garrison were soldiers who had been disgraced at Trebia and Cannae. Scipio used his influence in Sicily to encourage the rich Sicilians to pay for a cavalry force. Scipio also used his allies and supporters in Rome to create a volunteer army of 7,000 men. Anxious to invade Africa, Scipio asked the Senate for permission to sail.

EXPLORE FURTHER

Read Livy 28.39–28.45 for the full discussion between Fabius and Scipio.

- Summarise the reasons Fabius gives for caution.
- Summarise the reasons Scipio provides for attacking Africa.

Invasion of Africa

Scipio sailed to Africa in 204 BC and immediately sieged the city of Utica near Carthage. A large force of Numidians and Carthaginians approached Scipio's position under Syphax and Gisco's command. Scipio managed to organise a small force of Roman

FIGURE 2.19
Map of Carthage and the surrounding area at the time of Scipio's attack.

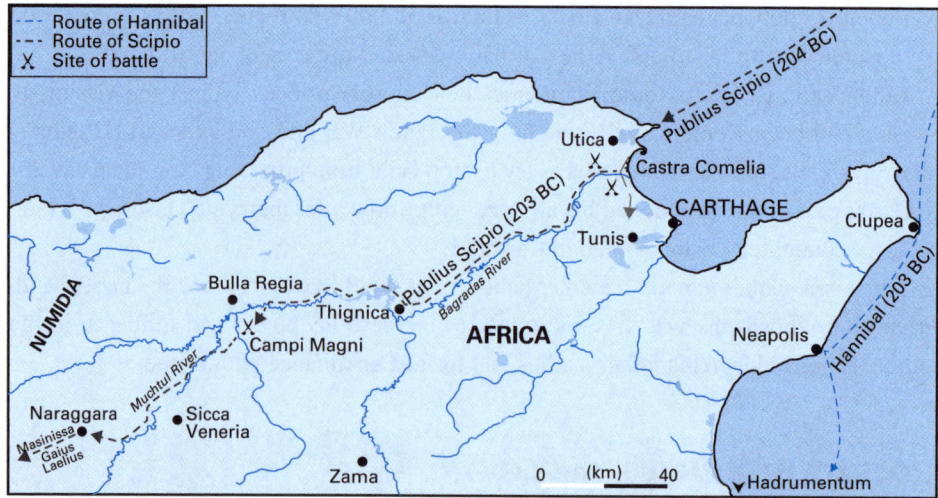

soldiers to set fire to the Carthaginian camp. In the panic which followed, Scipio attacked the fleeing Carthaginians and Numidians. In this way almost 40,000 men died.

Syphax was eventually captured and spent the rest of his life in Italy as a prisoner of the Roman Empire. This helped increase Masinissa's growing control over Numidia. With Syphax removed from Numidia, Carthage had lost an important ally.

After the defeat of Utica, Carthage began to negotiate an end to the war with Rome. It recalled Hannibal and Mago from southern and northern Italy. Scipio responded by offering terms to the Carthaginians. Once Hannibal arrived in Carthage, the Senate ended negotiations and prepared for war.

ACTIVITY

Use your summaries of the Roman response to Hannibal's invasion of Italy to complete this table.

Roman General	Tactics	Outcomes
Publius Cornelius Scipio		
Tiberius Sempronius Longus		
Gaius Flaminius		
Quintus Fabius Maximus		
Marcus Minucius		
Lucius Aemilius Paullus and Gaius Terentius Varro		
Publius Cornelius Scipio Africanus		

2.3 The Changing Nature of Rome's Response to Hannibal

TOPIC REVIEW

Boost your knowledge

Describe:

a. Sempronius', Flaminius', Paullus' and Varro's response to Hannibal
b. Fabius Maximus' response to Hannibal
c. Scipio Africanus' conquest of Iberia
d. Scipio Africanus' invasion of Africa

Stretch your understanding

Explain:

a. why Rome's early response to Hannibal failed
b. the strengths and weaknesses of Fabian tactics
c. the differences between Fabius Maximus and Scipio Africanus' tactics
d. how Scipio Africanus was successful in Iberia and Africa

PRACTICE QUESTIONS

1. a. Who was appointed Master of the Horse in 217 BC? [1]
   b. Give **two** reasons why Fabius Maximus' dictatorship was not renewed in 217 BC. [2]
   c. Give **two** examples of Scipio Africanus' success in Iberia. [2]
2. 'Roman ambition rather than Hannibal's tactics were responsible for the Carthaginian victories.' How far do you agree with this view?
   You must use and analyse the ancient sources you have studied as well as supporting your answer with your own knowledge. [20]

2.4 How Did Rome Defeat Carthage?

TOPIC OVERVIEW

- reasons for Hannibal's withdrawal from Italy, including pressure from the Carthaginian Senate and supply problems
- the significance of the Numidian cavalry supporting Rome and regional unrest caused by the Roman invasion of Africa
- the murder of Hasdrubal
- Hannibal's conference with Scipio before Zama
- the Battle of Zama
- the reasons for Hannibal's defeat
- impact of the defeat on Carthage and Rome

The prescribed source for this topic is:

- Livy, *The History of Rome*, Book 30, sections 20 and 29–36

Scipio Africanus' invasion of Africa panicked the Carthaginian Senate. They sent for Hannibal and his brother, Mago, to return to Carthage, while entering into peace negotiations with Rome. On Hannibal's return the situation had worsened significantly, a Carthaginian force had destroyed a Roman trade vessel to seize its grain and feed Carthage. At the Battle of Zama, Hannibal found himself with an inexperienced army facing Scipio Africanus who had driven Carthage out of Iberia. Although the battle was close fought Scipio Africanus was triumphant and the peace treaty was as crippling as the Treaty of Lutatius. Carthage once again found itself without an empire, but also challenged by Masinissa the prince of Numidia. Masinissa's pressure upon Carthage eventually led to its destruction in the Third Punic War 149–146. Rome, however, used its victory to expand in Africa, Iberia and the Mediterranean.

2.4 How Did Rome Defeat Carthage?

WHY DID HANNIBAL WITHDRAW FROM ITALY?

In the previous two sections we have mentioned some of the reasons for Hannibal's withdrawal from Italy. Some of the most important are listed below:

- the invasion of Africa by Scipio Africanus
- the failure to take advantage of victories at Trasimene and Cannae
- loss of Iberia and the impact on supplies and funding
- Fabian strategy
- Rome's resources
- Rome's ability to fight on multiple fronts

When Hannibal was ordered to leave Italy in 203 BC, he had spent almost fifteen years fighting there. According to Livy (30.20) Hannibal's response to the order from Carthage was pure rage.

> The story goes that he gnashed his teeth, groaned and came close to tears when he heard what the delegates had to say. When they had explained their mandate, he exclaimed: 'The men who tried to push me back by cutting off my supplies of men and money are now calling me back – not by devious means, but plainly and openly! You see, the people who have vanquished Hannibal are not the Romans, who have been cut down and driven away so many times; they are the Carthaginian senate, by means of their disparagement and envy. It is not Scipio who will pride himself and exult over the disgrace of my return, no: it is Hanno, who has destroyed my house beneath the ruins of Carthage, since he could do it no other way.'
>
> Livy, *The History of Rome* 30.20

On his journey home Hannibal began to blame himself for his defeat.

> He said that Scipio, who had never seen a Carthaginian in Italy during his consulship, had dared to go to Africa; whereas he, who had slain 100,000 soldiers at Trasimene and Cannae, had wasted his energy round Casilinum, Cumae, and Nola. Amid these complaints and regrets he was taken from his long occupation of Italy.
>
> Livy, *The History of Rome* 30.20

There is no way of knowing what Hannibal really thought. Livy's account is a Roman interpretation of how the great Carthaginian general must have felt.

Scipio Africanus' invasion of Carthage was a real and present danger. Hannibal must have acknowledged that he was needed to protect his homeland. Even though he had spent very little of his life in Carthage it is very likely that he was a patriot.

While examining Hannibal's leadership of the defence of Carthage it is important to remember a few facts. Hannibal was a stranger in Carthage. There is a real possibility that if, as Livy and Polybius claim, Hannibal had started the war he would have been blamed for the loss of Iberia. Especially as he achieved nothing of lasting value in Italy.

Yet the Roman historians claim that Carthage broke off negotiations when Hannibal returned and his countrymen asked him to lead their defence. Hannibal even went on to lead Carthage's government after defeat. The people of Carthage probably saw him as a

PRESCRIBED SOURCE

The History of Rome **Book 30, sections 20 and 29–36**

Date: late first century BC

Author: Livy (*c.* 64/59 BC–AD 17)

Genre: History

Significance: major source for early Roman history and mythological–historical account of the foundation of Rome

Content of the prescribed sections: the end of the Second Punic War and Hannibal's defeat

Read it here: OCR Source Booklet

ACTIVITY

Read Livy 30.20 and answer the following questions.

- How does Hannibal react to the decision to leave Rome?
- How useful is this extract to a historian examining Hannibal's leadership during his invasion of Rome?
- To what extent do you think Livy's assessment of Hannibal's defeat is accurate?

hero. It is very plausible that Carthage appreciated Hannibal's role in keeping Rome from invading Africa for over fourteen years.

WHY WAS HANNIBAL UNABLE TO DEFEAT ROME?

Livy (PS 30.20) claims that Hannibal was angry with the Carthaginian Senate for not supplying him with sufficient reinforcements. This extract is probably pure fiction, designed to add to Livy's narrative. Hanno the Elder took reinforcements to Italy after Cannae. Furthermore, we can hypothesis that Hannibal knew the importance of Iberia. He himself left the majority of his force there before crossing the Alps.

It is likely that Hannibal would have appreciated the difficulties associated with supplying new men. There were few good harbours under Hannibal's control in southern Italy. After the loss of Capua in 211, Hannibal found it difficult to mobilise reinforcements or supplies from Carthage. Rome also controlled the Mediterranean Sea, which meant supplying troops was very risky. While this was a major cause of Hannibal's failure in Italy, there are other significant factors to consider.

Hannibal always had one eye on Iberia. In 218 BC, he had left New Carthage with 102,000 soldiers. He reduced this to 59,000 after leaving the Pyrenees. A significant portion of his force was, therefore, placed under the command of his brother Hasdrubal to defend Iberia. This force was further reduced to 46,000 at the Rhone. When he arrived in Italy he only had 26,000 men. Hannibal was reliant upon foreign fighters from the beginning of his invasion of Italy. Many overlook this because of Hannibal's successes at Trebia, Trasimene and Cannae.

FIGURE 2.20
Map of Hannibal's invasion. The arrow shows his route (the Alps route is an approximation) and the key battles are marked with [●].

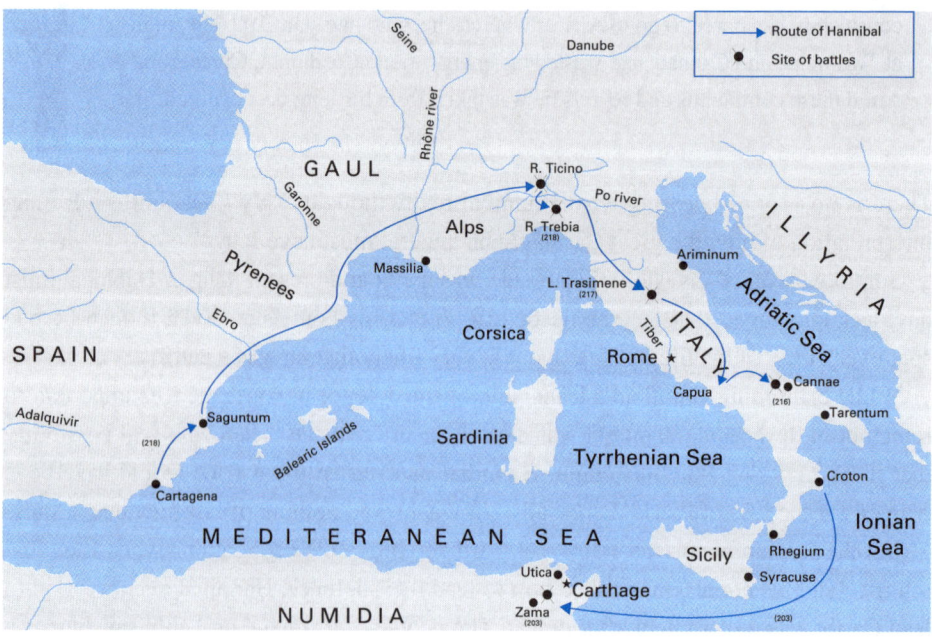

Hannibal had been able to create new units with his Celtic and Italian allies. Samnite and Bruttian troops had also been crucial in the period after Cannae. They had allowed Hannibal to create a second army to pressurise Rome's Italian allies. Unfortunately, attacks upon Capua and Tarentum, and the failed march on Rome in 211 BC, reduced Hannibal's ability to threaten Rome with his Italian and Celtic allies.

Carthage was fighting in Iberia as well. This meant that Hannibal's theatre of war was probably of secondary importance to Carthage. His brother, Mago, did not return to Italy after Cannae. Hasdrubal Barca's defeat at the Battle of the river Ebro had made the defence of Iberia a priority.

After the downfall of Iberia, the Roman generals made sure Hannibal's brothers could not reinforce him. When his brother, Hasdrubal, was killed at the Battle of Metaurus, his decapitated head was thrown into Hannibal's camp. Furthermore, Mago's attempt to join Hannibal after the fall of Iberia in 205 BC was frustrated when he was trapped in northern Italy, while Hannibal was trapped in southern Italy.

The adoption of the Fabian strategy by the Roman Senate was another significant factor. After the fall of Cannae, Hannibal's success in securing alliances with Tarentum and Capua was used against him. The Roman forces besieged these cities and forced Hannibal to come to their aid. His march on Rome in 211 BC was designed to try to relieve the pressure upon Capua. Rome, however, had sufficient military power to defend their city and continue the siege of Capua. Hannibal managed to breach Rome's city walls, but the Senate stood firm and repelled Hannibal from Rome and defeated Capua. Fabius Maximus was correct. Rome's military power was significant. After Cannae, the Roman population was militarised and food supplied by Rome's allies. Hannibal could not make a significant breakthrough.

The appointment of Marcellus as consul was another factor. In 212 BC, Hannibal had captured Tarentum, but could not take control of the harbour. Marcellus modified the Fabian strategy by using **attrition**. Marcellus would follow Hannibal, but would engage in battles designed to reduce Hannibal's armies and weaken his support with his Italian allies. He would follow Hannibal but, unlike Fabius, Marcellus, would meet him in large scale battles.

Marcellus' tactic meant that Hannibal demanded more men from his allies and, as a consequence, damaged his reputation among them. Hannibal's promise to free them from Roman control looked less likely during Marcellus' consulship. These tactics led to Hannibal losing Tarentum in 209 BC. Hannibal eventually defeated Marcellus and killed him in battle. This reminded Rome of the threat Hannibal still posed.

The death of his brother, Hasdrubal, in 207BC caused Hannibal to retreat to Calabria where he awaited reinforcements which never came. By adopting the Fabian strategy, Rome did not face any more disasters like Trasimene or Cannae. Their superior numbers and wealth meant they could survive Hannibal's attacks upon the Roman countryside. Hannibal, however, did not have a large enough army to risk a more aggressive policy and meet Rome's multiple armies.

Part Two Depth Study 1: Hannibal and the Second Punic War

FIGURE 2.21
Bronze bust of Scipio Africanus.

KEY INDIVIDUAL

Masinissa (can be spelled Massena)
Date: 238–148

Numidian prince who became the first king of Numidia

Fought for Carthage, before switching sides and supporting Scipio Africanus against Carthage, notably at the Battle of Zama. With Roman help, he united the eastern and western Numidian tribes to become the first king of a united Numidia. His aggressive actions encouraged Carthage to declare war on Numidia in 149, breaking their treaty with Rome. This started the Third Punic War.

DID HANNIBAL WANT TO FIGHT SCIPIO AFRICANUS AT ZAMA?

By the time Hannibal had returned to Carthage, a truce had been declared between the two cities. Scipio and Carthage had agreed a treaty which would end the Second Punic War. Carthage would surrender its empire and agree to remain in Africa. Rome demanded compensation for damages in the war, and Carthage would have to reduce its fleet.

When Hannibal returned with his Italian army, the Carthaginian Senate broke off the negotiations for two reasons. Hannibal's return had provided hope to Carthage, and they hoped he could defeat Scipio and negotiate a better peace treaty. This new found hope also caused Carthage to break its truce with Rome. The siege placed around Carthage had caused widespread starvation. When a Roman fleet became stranded off the coast of Africa, the Carthaginians attacked. They captured the Roman fleet and seized its supplies to feed the people.

Feeding the people came at a high cost. Scipio prepared for war and Hannibal was placed in charge of an inexperienced Carthaginian army. We are led to believe that many African tribes fought reluctantly. It is possible they saw hope in Scipio's invasion of Africa, especially since Rome had formed an alliance with Masinissa, a Numidian prince. Scipio Africanus now had access to Numidian cavalry.

According to Polybius, and repeated in Livy (30.29–30.36), Hannibal asked Scipio Africanus for a peace conference. The account presents two very different leaders. Hannibal pleads for peace and praises the achievements of Scipio. Livy presents him as a tired man grieving for the men and family he has lost.

> As for myself, time sees me now an old man returning home to the native land he left while still a boy. Success and failure have long since taught me that philosophy is a better guide to action than any reliance upon blind Fortune. You are young and luck has always been on your side. This, I fear, will make you too aggressive when what we need is quiet diplomacy
>
> Livy, *The History of Rome* 30.30

Scipio, on the other hand, is confident and keen to start the battle and force peace upon Carthage.

> As for myself, I am all too aware of human weakness, and there is no need to lecture me on the power of Fortune; I know very well that all our deeds are subject to a thousand strokes of luck. I would be all too willing to admit that my conduct was arrogant and brutal, if of your own free will you had come to me to ask for peace before you abandoned Italy, embarked your army, and withdrew to Africa, and if I had rejected your proposals out of hand. But now I have no such inhibitions, when we are here in Africa, on the eve of battle, and I have dragged you protesting and against your will to these negotiations.
>
> Livy, *The History of Rome* 30.31

FIGURE 2.22

Illustration of the meeting between Hannibal and Scipio Africanus after the Battle of Zama.

ACTIVITY

Read Livy, PS 30.29–30.31 and answer the following questions.

- Why does Livy claim Hannibal wanted to negotiate terms with Scipio before the Battle of Zama?
- Create a list outlining the reasons Hannibal gives for peace.
- Create a list outlining the reasons Scipio gives for war.

The negotiations fail and Hannibal returns to his camp to prepare for the defence of Carthage.

WHY DID HANNIBAL LOSE THE BATTLE OF ZAMA, 202?

The two armies at Zama reflected the changing fortunes of the two cities. Rome had a superior cavalry and a battle hardened infantry. Hannibal had many new recruits which gave him a numerical advantage, but they lacked experience. The Carthaginian army also had eighty war elephants which could give Hannibal an advantage. The main difference between the two armies was their generals. Scipio Africanus was young and confident. Hannibal Barca was feeling the effects of over twenty years of continuous warfare and lacked confidence in his army. During the battle he would rely upon his Italian veterans to try and seize the initiative.

FIGURE 2.23
Coin depicting the Numidian prince Masinissa.

Hannibal had about 36,000 infantry, 4,000 horsemen and eighty war elephants. Scipio Africanus had 29,000 infantry and over 6,000 horsemen.

Hannibal arranged his troops in a traditional line. His elephants were placed at the front. His inexperienced Carthaginian cavalry were on the right and his loyal veteran cavalry on the left. Behind the elephants he placed the mercenaries, Carthaginian citizens and veterans. Hannibal knew Scipio liked to use direct tactics to punch a hole through the infantry. By placing his veterans at the back he would prevent a retreat.

Scipio adopted a similar tactic. He placed his least experienced soldiers, called the hastati, at the front. Then he placed his core force, called the principes, in the centre. Finally, the triarii, the most experienced soldiers were placed at the rear. Scipio placed his Numidian cavalry, commanded by Masinissa, opposite Hannibal's cavalry veterans. He planned to neutralise the threat of Hannibal's experienced horsemen. Scipio placed his veteran Italian cavalry opposite the inexperienced Carthaginian cavalry. Scipio's main worry was the war elephants. They had to potential to smash through his inexperienced troops and cause a retreat.

Scipio's experience of warfare in Iberia had prepared him for war against elephants. The hastati were trained to fight in a new formation. To Hannibal, they would appear to be a continuous line which was vulnerable to elephant attacks. In fact, the hastati were organised into columns with large lanes between each unit. To hide this from Hannibal, Scipio placed **maniples** of **skirmishers** in front of the hastati. When the elephants charged, the maniples would move to the side and allow the elephants to pass through the Roman army. In this way, the elephants would be attacked from the side and be removed from the battle.

Livy's account (PS 30.32–30.36) of the battle is widely criticised for focusing upon Scipio's successes. There is some balance, but as we have seen in Livy's Preface, he is writing his history to celebrate the glory of Rome. The Battle of Zama is definitely an example of this.

> **maniples** a subdivision of a Roman legion
>
> **skirmishers** hand-to-hand combatants with little training

FIGURE 2.24
Carthaginian elephants march towards Roman infantry.

Hannibal started the battle by ordering his elephants to march forward. As they neared the Roman lines, the Roman cavalry blew horns to frighten the elephants. This strategy had some success. A small number of elephants threw off their riders, turned about, and stampeded Hannibal's veteran cavalry. Masinissa took this opportunity to take Hannibal's veteran cavalry off the battlefield. Hannibal, seeing the danger, ordered the Carthaginian cavalry to do the same to the Roman cavalry.

Meanwhile, the remaining elephants had walked into a trap and were massacred between the lanes created by the hastati.

> The javelins of the regular infantry kept up a hail of missiles from every quarter, until the elephants were driven out of the Roman lines and turned against their own troops, putting to flight the Carthaginian cavalry on the right wing also. Laelius, with his cavalry on the Roman left, added to their panic as they fled.
>
> Livy, *The History of Rome* 30.33

Within an hour Hannibal had lost two of his most powerful units, but so had Rome. The first phase had given Scipio an advantage. The second phase was less decisive. After destroying the elephants, Scipio ordered the hastati to march against Hannibal's infantry. Hannibal's first line was pushed back, but the mercenaries were not allowed to retreat. Hannibal forced the mercenaries to disperse into the second line and pushed back against the Roman infantry. Scipio's hastati took heavy losses and had to reinforce his front line with his principes.

Study questions
Read Livy 30.32–30.36 and answer the following questions.

1. How does Livy describe the Roman army?
2. How does Livy describe the Carthaginian army?
3. List the different strategies Scipio Africanus used to defeat Hannibal.
4. Why does Livy believe Hannibal lost the Battle of Zama?

FIGURE 2.25
Scipio Africanus meets Hannibal at the Battle of Zama. For dramatic effect, the artist has used a larger Indian elephant, as opposed to the smaller African elephants. Cornelis Cort, 1567.

The third phase was similar to the second. Scipio pushed forward against Hannibal's second line. Hannibal refused to let the Carthaginian citizens retreat and ordered them to reinforce his veteran third line. Hannibal ordered his men to wait while Scipio reorganised his troops.

The final phase was the bloodiest. Both commanders took heavy casualties. The battle turned in Rome's favour when the Roman cavalry returned and attacked the Carthaginians from behind. The result was a massacre. 20,000 Carthaginian troops were killed, and a further 20,000 captured. Hannibal escaped with many of his veterans. Rome only lost 2,500 men. The Second Punic War was effectively over.

WHAT WAS THE IMPACT OF THE SECOND PUNIC WAR ON CARTHAGE?

Defeat at Zama ended Carthaginian resistance. The Carthaginian Senate sent envoys to Scipio. Scipio was in no mood to meet with them until he had crushed their spirit. Firstly, Scipio rounded up any Carthaginians who had escaped from Zama. Secondly, Scipio wanted to cause widespread fear and starvation, so he continued the blockade. He did this so the Carthaginian embassy would accept his terms.

Scipio stayed true to his word and forced Carthage to sign a treaty so punishing it would not threaten Rome again. Carthage was ordered to pay compensation of 10,000 talents over fifty years. Its navy was reduced to ten warships, and Carthage could not wage war without Roman permission.

The most surprising outcome of the peace negotiations was the appointment of Hannibal as **sufete** of Carthage. He began to reform Carthage's political system. He is credited with limiting the time judges could serve in **the Hundred and Four** to two years. By the Second Punic War, we are led to believe that the Hundred and Four exercised tyrannical powers over Carthage. Under Hannibal's rule, Carthage prospered and by 191 BC was able to pay all the compensation to Rome forty years early. Hannibal's rule, however, was not easy and he was eventually forced into exile and went to Syria. Here he served the Syrian king until his death.

After Hannibal's exile, Masinissa increased his pressure on Carthage. A failed peace conference between Carthage and Numidia resulted in the Third Punic War in 149 BC. Three years later, Numidia and Rome destroyed Carthage. This time the city did not survive. Its 50,000 citizens were sold into slavery and Carthage became a Roman outpost.

> **sufete** a magistrate of Carthage, similar to the consuls of Rome
>
> **Hundred and Four** described in Aristotle's *Politics* as judges who made sure Carthage's generals served the best interests of Carthage

What was the impact of the victory upon Rome?

The Second Punic War had a huge impact upon Rome. Although its impacts upon Roman society and politics were not going to significantly affect Rome until seventy years later.

It took many years for Roman agriculture and farming to recover from Hannibal's and Fabian Maximus' scorched earth tactics. Ordinary people, however, would not have seen much difference. During the war Rome had imported grain and food from abroad to feed its population. This had freed up ordinary Romans from farming and allowed the male population to enlist into the Roman army.

Rome's adoption of an expansionist foreign policy on an unprecedented scale would alter Rome's social structure significantly. For over thirty years, Rome maintained the same military levels as during the Second Punic War. This turned Rome into a highly-militarised society. A large proportion of the Roman population relied upon overseas conflicts for their wages. This created new opportunities for the rich families in Rome. Consuls and officers who led the Roman army had the opportunity to gain the support of ordinary Romans. Furthermore, Roman Imperialism allowed these families to create powerful power-bases outside of Rome. Finally, the shift from a rural society towards a militarised one allowed rich families to purchase large estates across Italy which were maintained by slaves. When the army was demobilised large numbers of poor Romans found themselves without land or jobs.

Italy became more united. Those cities which had harboured resentment towards Rome had been defeated and forced to accept allegiance. It would take over a century for a number of Italian cities to reunite and challenge Roman dominance in the Social War of 90 BC. Although these city-staes failed to gain their independence, the war contributed to the eventual collapse of the Republic.

Rome did, however, gain a great deal from the defeat of Hannibal. It confirmed its domination of the western Mediterranean and added Iberia to its sphere of control. In fact, Rome's victory over Carthage is traditionally seen as the beginning of the Roman Empire. It had stronger links with North Africa with a new Numidian ally. These links would allow Rome to expand into Africa and establish it as the breadbasket of the empire. This in turn allowed Rome to subjugate much of Europe and Asia.

ACTIVITY

- Summarise the impact of the Second Punic War on Carthage and Rome

TOPIC REVIEW

Boost your knowledge

Describe:

a. reasons for Hannibal's defeat in Italy
b. events leading to the Battle of Zama
c. the Battle of Zama
d. Impact of the Second Punic War on Rome and Carthage

Stretch your understanding

Explain:

a. why Hannibal lost in Italy
b. why Carthage and Rome failed to negotiate terms before Zama
c. why Scipio won at the Battle of Zama
d. how far Rome and Carthage were affected by the Second Punic War

Part Two Depth Study 1: Hannibal and the Second Punic War

PRACTICE QUESTIONS

Passage B

Hannibal derived no pleasure from their report. They told him that Masinissa had arrived that very day, with some 6,000 infantry and 4,000 cavalry, though he was particularly struck by his opponent's obvious confidence, which he felt must surely have some basis in reality. He was fully aware that he himself was the reason for the war and that by his arrival he had broken the terms of the armistice and any hope of a permanent peace treaty. But he calculated that he was likely to get rather more generous terms, if he negotiated a peace before he was defeated and while his army was still intact. So he sent an envoy to Scipio to ask for a chance to hold discussions. Whether he did this on his own initiative or on the instructions of his government, I have no way of telling. Valerius Antias records that he was defeated by Scipio in a preliminary encounter, in which he lost 12,000 men and a further 1,700 taken prisoner. It was after this that he went to Scipio's camp as an official envoy with ten other colleagues.

Livy, *The History of Rome* 30.29

1. What can we learn from Passage B about Hannibal's situation before the Battle of Zama? [5]
2. Using details from Passage B, explain how accurate you think Livy's account of these events is. [5]

Further Reading

General texts on the period
Beard, Mary, *SPQR* (London: Profile, 2016), pp. 170–84.
Cary, M. and H.H Scullard, *A History of Rome* (Basingstoke: Palgrave Macmillan, 1980), 3rd ed., pp.124–37.
Hornblower, Simon and Tony Spawforth, *The Oxford Companion to Classical Civilisation* (Oxford: Oxford University Press, 2014).
Southern, Patricia, *Ancient Rome: The Republic 753–30 BC* (Stroud: Amberley Publishing, 2011), pp. 97–116.

Focused texts
Bagnell, Nigel, *The Punic Wars: Rome, Carthage and the Struggle for the Mediterranean* (London: Pimlico 1999).
Bagnall, Nigel, *Essential Histories: The Punic Wars 264–146 BC* (Oxford: Osprey, 2002).
Daly, Gregory, *Cannae: The Experience of Battle in the Second Punic War* (London: Routledge 2003).
Fields, Nic, *The Roman Army of the Punic Wars 264–146 BC* (Oxford: Osprey, 2007).
Fields, Nic, *Carthaginian Warrior 264–246 BC* (Oxford: Osprey, 2010).
Flower, Harriet (ed.) *Cambridge Companions to the Ancient World: The Cambridge Companion to the Roman Republic* (Cambridge: Cambridge University Press, 2004), ch.10.
Goldsworthy, Adrian, *Fall of Carthage: The Punic Wars 265–146 BC* (London: Orion, 2003).
Hoyos, Dexter (ed.), *Blackwell Companions to the Ancient World: A Companion to the Punic Wars* (Oxford: Blackwell, 2015).
Lazenby, J.F., *The Second Punic War* (Warminster: Aris and Phillips, 1978).
Lazenby, J.F., *The First Punic War* (London: University College London, 1996).
Macdonald, Eve, *Hannibal: A Hellenistic* Life (London: Yale 2015).
Mellor, Ronald, *The Roman Historians* (Abingdon: Routledge, 1999).
Sorek, Susan, *Ancient Historians* (London: Bloomsbury, 2012), ch. 11 Polybius; ch. 15 Livy; ch. 22 Plutarch.
Southern, Patricia, *The Roman Army: History 753 BC–AD 476* (Stroud: Amberley Publishing, 2016).

Documentaries
BBC, *Ancient Rome: The Rise and Fall of an Empire*, Hannibal episode (BBC DVD, 2006).

Ancient Sources
Electronic versions can be found online.
Livy, *The War with Hannibal*, trans. Aubrey de Selincourt (London: Penguin 1965).
Livy, *Hannibal's War*, trans. J.C Yardley (Oxford: Oxford University Press, 2009).
Mellor, Ronald, *The Historians of Ancient Rome: An Anthology of the Major Writings* (Abingdon: Routledge, 2012).
Nepos, Cornelius, *Lives of Eminent Commanders*, trans. J.C Rolfe (London: Loeb, 1989).
Polybius, *The Rise of the Roman Empire*, trans. Ian Scott-Kilvert (London: Penguin, 1979).
Polybius, *The Histories*, trans. Robin Waterfield (Oxford: Oxford University Press, 2010).

What to Expect in the Exam: Section B

DEPTH STUDY: HANNIBAL AND THE SECOND PUNIC WAR, 218–201 BC

This chapter aims to show you the types of questions you are likely to get in Section B of the Rome and its Neighbours exam. It offers some advice on how to answer the questions and will help you avoid common errors.

The examination

The Roman depth study is in the same exam paper as the Roman Period Study – The Foundations of Rome 753–440 BC. You can answer Section A and Section B in any order you like. Just remember that the exam lasts 1 hour and 45 minutes. Section B is worth 45 marks, so you need to make sure you organise your time accordingly.

This component of the GCSE examination is designed to test your knowledge, understanding and evaluation of Hannibal and the Second Punic War.

There are three Assessment Objectives in your Ancient History GCSE. Questions will be designed to test these areas. To remind yourself what these are read page 70 in the period study exam chapter.

Be aware that there is some overlap with Ancient History Assessment Objectives. As you will see in the table on the next page, questions 9 and 10 assess multiple assessment objectives. For example, AO2 and AO3 both require you to make 'judgements' on the 'historical events and historical periods'.

In the exam, you should be able to demonstrate:

- a good grasp of the 'Hannibal story' and its key characters
- a basic understanding of the geography of Italy, Spain and Hannibal's (approximate) route from New Carthage to Italy
- an awareness of the political structures of Rome and how this affected Rome's response to Hannibal's invasion of Italy
- a good knowledge of the prescribed sources
- an awareness of the different interpretations about Hannibal's leadership and the Roman response to Hannibal's invasion, and the different conclusions that can be drawn from these

When analysing and evaluating your evidence in order to make judgements, you should be able to:

- analyse and evaluate the causes and consequences of the main events of the Second Punic War
- analyse and evaluate the significance of key individuals and events and how they impacted upon the course of the Second Punic War
- look at change and continuity; including the rate of change and the relative success of different developments. For example, Hannibal's leadership and Rome's response to the Second Punic War
- use your knowledge, evaluation and analysis in combination to produce a logical conclusion.

When evaluating how the portrayal of events by the ancient sources relates to the historical contexts in which they were produced, you should be able to demonstrate:

- an understanding of the approaches used by Polybius, Livy and Plutarch, and how the nature of their work potentially affected its usefulness and accuracy
- a good grasp of the context of each prescribed source, including visual sources, and how far the ancient author creates an accurate portrayal of the event
- an awareness of how other authors have interpreted the events in the prescribed sources

QUESTION TYPES

There are five different types of question. It is important to remember that the Second Punic War questions begin at question 6. The table below shows how they are assessed.

Question	Type of question	AO1 marks	AO2 marks	AO3 marks	Total marks
6	Discrete factual knowledge	5	–	–	5
7	What can we learn from the source	–	–	5	5
8	Evaluate the source	–	–	5	5
9	Second-order concepts	5	5	–	10
10	Essay using ancient source knowledge	5	5	10	20

There are no SPaG marks awarded for the Depth Study questions.

Question 6 will test your knowledge. This question will be divided into a number of sub-questions.

Question 7 and 8 will supply you with a passage or a visual source from the prescribed sources. A list of the prescribed sources can be found at the start of each chapter and on the OCR web-page. Question 7 will ask you to identify key features from the passage. Question 8 will require you to evaluate the accuracy of the passage.

Question 9 will ask you to explore a second-order concept. A second-order concept is a historical skill used to analyse the past, for example, change and continuity, similarity and difference, significance, cause and consequence.

Finally, Question 10 is an essay question which will explore your knowledge and understanding of the topic and relevant prescribed sources. It will also assess your ability to use this information to create a line of substantiated argument.

Question 6 – knowledge questions

There will be 5 marks available for question 6 all testing factual knowledge (AO1). The 5 marks will be broken down into a series of short-answer questions, typically worth 1, 2 or 3 marks.

These questions will usually start with one of the following stems:

- State . . .
- Identify . . .
- Name . . .
- Give **one** example of . . . Give **two** reasons for . . .

For example: *Name the Roman consul who fought at the Battle of Trasimene.* [1]

- **Answer:** Gaius Flaminius [1]

This question has only one answer. You do not have to write in full sentences, and the answer should be brief.

For example: *Give **two** tactics employed by Fabius Maximus during his dictatorship.* [2]

- **Answer:** To follow Hannibal's army and watch his every move. [1] To avoid a large-scale conflict with Hannibal. [1]

This answer is also brief. There is in fact no need to write full sentences if it seems that only a single word or a phrase is needed.

Question 7: source question

Questions 7 and 8 both use the same prescribed source. It could be a passage from one of the ancient historians or a visual source from the archaeological record.

Question 7 will ask you to identify several features from the source and develop what this tells you about the question focus (AO3).

Question 7 will usually start with the following:

7. What can we learn from Passage B about . . .? [5]

What to Expect in the Exam: Section B

Here is an example:

> Passage B
> When Antiochus heard this story, he was convinced that Hannibal was expressing his genuine feelings and speaking the truth, and so put aside all his former mistrust. For our part we should regard this as unmistakable proof of Hamilcar's hostility and of his general attitude towards Rome, and indeed this was confirmed by the facts, for he succeeded in instilling into his son-in-law Hasdrubal and his son Hannibal an enmity towards Rome which it would be impossible to surpass. Hasdrubal in fact died before these intentions could be fully demonstrated, but events gave Hannibal the opportunity to prove only too clearly the hatred of Rome which he had inherited from his father.
>
> Polybius, *Histories* Book 3.12

○ 7. What can we learn from Passage B about Hamilcar's role in causing the Second Punic War? [5]

When answering question 7 you must remember that this question is only worth 5 out of 45 marks and make sure you organise your time accordingly.

- After reading the passage you need to identify several key features or details from the passage – Hasdrubal influenced his family; Antiochus was convinced by Hannibal's story.
- Try to infer what this tells us about the question focus – Hasdrubal was an influential man who made his family desire revenge against Rome; Hannibal felt his father had taught him to hate Rome.
- To summarise: read the passage carefully, identify several key features or details and outline what you can learn from these details.

Answer:
You should be able to develop several points, which might include:

○ Hannibal and Hasdrubal were influenced by Hamilcar.
○ Hasdrubal could not have had much impact upon the Second Punic War because he died ten years before it started. If he hated Rome this much he would have declared war on them himself.
○ Antiochus was convinced by Hannibal's story.

NB. If you are struggling to understand the passage, try to find something from the passage which seems important to the story and explain why it is important.

Question 8 – source question

Question 8 will assess your ability to use, analyse and evaluate a prescribed source within its historical context and then draw a conclusion about how far its portrayal is accurate. For example, you might be asked how its accuracy may have been affected by influences upon its creator (AO3).

NB. Visual sources such as a coin, bust or a relief sculpture could be assessed by exploring the potential purpose of the source. In some cases you may be able to assess whether this is an accurate portrayal of the event or individual. Other examples may be good examples of propaganda used to convey a particular message.

Question 8 will usually be phrased as follows:

8. Using details from Passage B, evaluate how accurate you think x's account of y is? [5]

As in the exam we will be using the same source from question 7.

8. Using details from Passage B, evaluate how accurate you think Polybius' account of this event is? [5]

The following are some of the tests you can use. Remember you are looking for the strengths and weaknesses of the passage.

- What knowledge do you have of this event or other interpretations of this event? Does your wider understanding make this passage accurate or inaccurate?
- What is the historian's method? Is this method a strength, weakness or both when evaluating this passage?
- Is the extract detailed, or is it an overview? Is this typical of this historian?
- Finally, the aims of the historian might affect the reliability. This will not be relevant for all passages. So avoid general comments such as 'Livy was writing 200 years later so he has the benefit of hindsight.' Instead explain how this might affect the accuracy of this particular passage.
- If it is a visual source think about why it was created and when. A dedication or triumphal arch may be designed to celebrate something. Would it, therefore, focus on an individual's failings or weaknesses?
- Remember to identify the key features from the source to support your evaluation, otherwise you will not be meeting the full requirements of the question.

To summarise: identify a few strengths or weaknesses of author's treatment of the topic, or alternatively develop one or two points in detail.

Although you do not need a conclusion it is good practice to make a statement about how accurate you think the passage is.

Answers may include:

You should be able to develop a few of the following points:

- Polybius travelled around the Ancient world speaking to eye-witnesses. This is very useful to the historian because it provides important insights, such as Antiochus' conversation with Hannibal. However, his eyewitnesses may not be truthful. Antiochus may have exaggerated the story for personal reasons.
- Hamilcar and Hasdrubal both agreed to peace treaties with Rome. This implies Polybius' view is inaccurate.
- Polybius is trying to blame Carthage for starting the war and reassure Greeks to accept Roman control.

When looking at a passage you must remember question 8 is only worth 5 out of 45 marks so make sure you use your time accordingly.

Question 9: second-order concepts

In GCSE Ancient History you will need to answer questions on second-order concepts (see p. 74 for more info in the Period Study exam chapter): change and continuity, similarity and difference, significance, cause and consequence. In the Depth Study, these questions will be assessing AO1 and AO2. This means you will be required to demonstrate good knowledge and understanding, alongside analytical and evaluation skills which lead to a supported conclusion.

The questions **may** look something like this:

- **Change and continuity**. These questions may ask you to explore an event or an aspect of the Second Punic War and explain how much change there was between two points.
- *e.g. 9. Explain how far x changed during y.*
- **Similarity and difference.** These questions may ask you to explore an aspect of the Second Punic War and explain if individuals or events responded to it in a similar or different way.
- *e.g. 9. Explain whether x's response was different/similar to y's.*
- **Significance.** These questions may require you to explore the importance of an individual or event upon the whole of the Second Punic War.
- *e.g. 9. Explain the importance of x in the Second Punic War.*
- **Cause.** These questions may ask you to explain how an event happened or why an individual took a particular course of action.
- *e.g. 9. Explain what caused x.*
- **Consequence.** These questions may ask you to explain the impact of an event or individual.
- *e.g. 9. Explain the impact of x.*

Here is an example of how to answer a second-order concept question,

- *9. Explain whether the Roman consuls at Cannae used the same tactics as Sempronius at Trebia.* [10]
- Remember this question asks you to use your knowledge (AO1) to identify, develop and assess key features from the passage to make a judgement about the second-order concept (AO2)
- Identify several possible features. These must be supported by the source and/or your own knowledge
- You must make sure that each of these features is linked back to the question and its importance evaluated.
- Most significantly you must reach a substantiated judgement.

Answers may include:

You might include several examples of similarities and differences such as:

- Similar – Varro and Sempronius were tricked by Hannibal's tactics and underestimated him.

- Similar – Paullus warned Varro not to be rash; Publius Cornelius Scipio warned Sempronius to wait.
- Different – Sempronius had a much smaller force than Varro.
- Different – Sempronius wanted an early victory to contain Hannibal, Varro dropped Fabius Maximus tactics to try and defeat Hannibal in an attempt to secure popular support.

Remember that question 9 is worth 10 out of a possible 45 marks, make sure that you organise your time accordingly.

To summarise: identify several possible answers and use them to create a sustained line of argument.

You do not need to use the ancient historians in this answer. You will be rewarded, however, if you can show the different interpretations in relation to the question focus.

Question 10: essay question

The final question is an essay question which assesses all three assessment objectives in combination. You will need to be able to use factual knowledge and understanding alongside your knowledge of the prescribed sources to provide evidence to support and challenge the question posed. Furthermore, you will need to analyse and explain this evidence in order to make a substantiated judgement about how far you agree with the question posed.

You will also have to evaluate the context of the ancient evidence you have used to judge its accuracy and potential weight. The best students will use this evaluation to inform their judgement.

AO1 and AO2 are both worth 5 marks each. AO3 is allocated ten marks.

As with question 5 in Section A, your essay will be marked according to the best fit with the mark scheme.

Your essay question will be much broader than question 9 and will expect you to draw upon material from across the whole Depth Study. The question will usually present you with a statement and ask you to make a judgement about 'how far' you agree with it.

The following is an example of a possible essay question:

○ 'The Romans won the Second Punic War because they could afford to make mistakes.' How far do you agree with this view? [20]

Answer:

Could afford to make mistakes because:

○ Crippling defeats at Trebia, Trasimene and Cannae did not destroy Rome. Livy 21.54 (Trebia); 22.44–22.48 (Cannae) and Polybius 3.84.
○ Roman resources; such as wealth, man power and naval power; were significantly greater than Carthage's resources. It could fight on many fronts. Polybius 3.89 (Roman resources).

Mistakes could have been costly because:

- Rome was vulnerable after Trebia, Trasimene and Cannae. Fabian tactics were needed to help reorganise Rome's military forces. Polybius 3.85 (Trasimene).
- Hannibal failed to take advantage of Trasimene and Cannae. Livy 22.51 (Aftermath of Cannae). Yet he was very successful in acquiring allies – Macedonia, Tarentum and Capua which threatened Rome's position in Italy.

This is not an exhaustive list – but designed to give you a flavour of what you might choose.

Key points:

Use the same advice from question 5 in Section A (pp. 76–77), but remember:

- You need to use your knowledge of ancient sources to support and challenge the question posed.
- You must evaluate the accuracy and weight of the ancient sources and use this evaluation to develop your line of argument and judgement.
- Avoid general observations about accuracy, such as Livy was writing over 150 years later and so he was not reliable.
- Make sure your analysis of the sources is linked to the question and supported by an example.
- This example should be linked to the question, not just a general comment about the author. For example, you could not use the example from Livy's Preface where he admits to using supernatural reasons to explain the past for a question about Hannibal's victory at Cannae. This would not be a valid criticism.

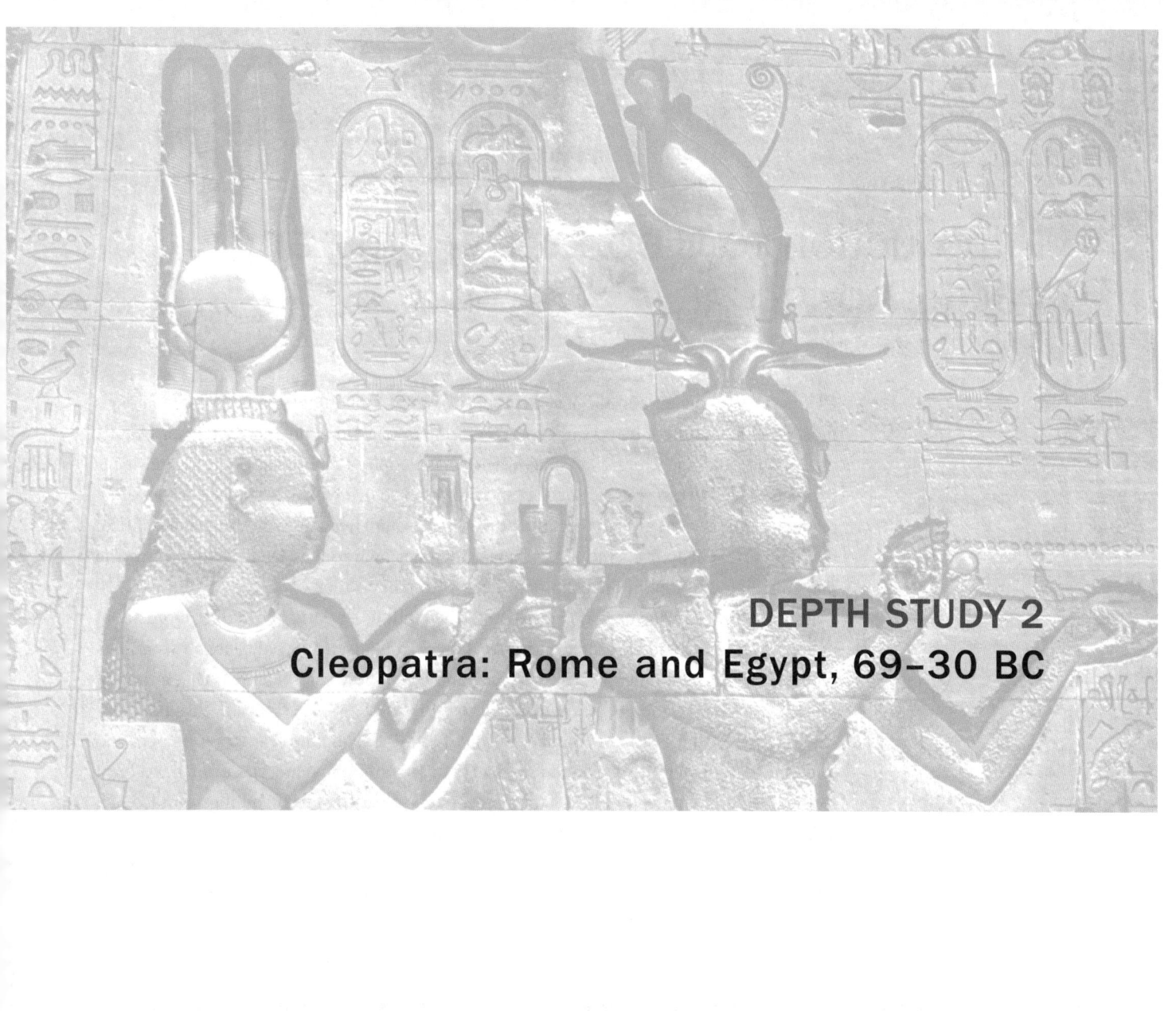

DEPTH STUDY 2
Cleopatra: Rome and Egypt, 69–30 BC

Introduction to Cleopatra: Rome and Egypt, 69–30 BC

Cleopatra VII, queen and the last Pharaoh of Egypt, is without doubt one of history's most colourful and controversial characters. She is renowned nowadays for her beauty, intelligence and sparkling charisma. Yet it was Cleopatra's political courage and independence, and her striving for success and prominence in a world dominated by men that made her truly remarkable in the ancient world. Through her astute thinking and political manoeuvring, Cleopatra's influence transcended her own role as Queen of Egypt as she played an integral role in the changing face of Roman politics.

This depth study has been designed not only to allow learners to discover more about the fascinating life and character of the great queen, but also to reveal Cleopatra's impact on the complex relationship between Rome and Egypt between 69 and 30 BC, a time of tremendous change and political turmoil across the whole Mediterranean. Through close examination of the ancient evidence, this study will also enable learners to understand how and why different interpretations of Cleopatra's actions and character have been formed. With the majority of the unit's prescribed source material coming from Roman sources, learners will also have to consider how the contemporary Roman view of Cleopatra has perhaps shaped our modern interpretations such as Elizabeth's Taylor beguiling queen in the 1963 film *Cleopatra*. This is a unit packed with political scheming, curious anecdotes, wealth and splendour, love and war.

EXAM OVERVIEW

Your examination for Cleopatra will require you to show knowledge and understanding of the material you have studied. This component is worth 45 marks – 15 based on AO1 skills, 10 on AO2, and 20 on AO3.

Question 11 will consist of a number of short factual questions worth a total of five marks.

Questions 12 and 13 will require you to study a passage of text or visual source. Question 12 will be a comprehension question, whereas question 13 will need you to evaluate the source. Each question is worth 5 marks.

Question 14 will ask will ask you use second-order concepts such as continuity, change, cause, consequence, significance and similarity and difference within situations. This question is worth 10 marks.

Finally, question 15 is a longer essay-style question worth 20 marks.

Introduction to Cleopatra: Rome and Egypt, 69–30 BC

The component has been broken down into four sections, which differ very slightly from the specification topics. The first section looks at the context for Cleopatra's rule and Cleopatra as queen, covering spec topic 1 and spec topic 2. The second section looks at Cleopatra's relationship with Caesar, covering the first half of spec topic 3 and the civil war from spec topic 2. The third section covers the remainder of spec topic 3 looking at Antony and Cleopatra's relationship and the fourth section covers spec topic 4 on the Battle of Actium.

TIMELINE OF CLEOPATRA'S LIFE AND REIGN

Date (BC)	
69	Birth of Cleopatra; mother Cleopatra V
57	Ptolemy Auletes expelled from Egypt. Cleopatra VI queen
56	Berenice IV queen
55	Gabinius restores Auletes to the throne. Berenice IV executed
51	Death of Ptolemy Auletes. Cleopatra VII and Ptolemy XIII become rulers. Cleopatra appears alone on coins as queen
49	Cleopatra forced to flee Egypt; she tries to organise an army
48	Ptolemy murders Pompey. Caesar arrives in Egypt. Cleopatra returns to Alexandria. Caesar organizes the joint rule of Cleopatra and Ptolemy; Ptolemy's advisors, Pothinus and Achillas, start the Alexandrine war
47	Ptolemy XIII defeated and drowned. Cleopatra made ruler with Ptolemy XIV co-ruler. Cleopatra's head appears on coins without partner
47	Birth of Caesarion
46–44	Cleopatra in Rome. Statue placed in the temple of Venus Genetrix. Caesar's Egyptian triumph
44	Cleopatra leaves Rome
	Ptolemy XIV dies. Ptolemy XV Caesarion becomes co-ruler
43	Cleopatra sends help to Cassius (which never reaches him); Cleopatra supports the triumvirate, Octavian Antony and Lepidus
41	Antony and Cleopatra meet in Tarsus. Arsinoe is killed in Ephesus
41–40	Antony spends the winter in Alexandria
	Parthian invasion.
40	Alexander Helios and Cleopatra Selene born
	Perusine War. Antony marries Octavia

38	Ventidius defeats the Parthians and forces them to retreat from Syria
	Antony and Octavia celebrate Panathenaic games in Athens
	Antony proclaimed Neos Dionusios in Ephesus
	Settlement of the East. Polemo given Pontus; Amyntas given Galatia; Herod given Judaea; Cleopatra given several old Ptolemaic possessions in the Levant
37	Cleopatra joins Antony at Antioch. Antony marries Cleopatra according to Egyptian rituals
36	Antony invades Parthia and was defeated
35	Cleopatra joins Antony in Syria
34	Armenia invaded and taken over
	Donations of Alexandria
33	The triumvirate ends; Octavian and Antony prepare for war
31	Actium
30	Antony and Cleopatra suicide

> **EXAM TIP: SECOND-ORDER CONCEPTS**
>
> During this Depth Study, you will be required to reflect on second-order historical concepts, just as you were in the period study (see pp. 19, 22, 33, 43, 53 and 60). Remember to think about the following second-order concepts: continuity, change, cause, consequence, significance, similarity and difference.

3.1 Cleopatra as Queen of Egypt

TOPIC OVERVIEW

Cleopatra's life and character:

- Cleopatra's family and Macedonian heritage
- her likely education and upbringing
- her character as depicted in the sources, including her charm, her humour and her courage

Cleopatra as queen of Egypt, including political, domestic and foreign policies

- the death of Ptolemy XII and Cleopatra's first years as Queen
- Cleopatra's relationship with her brothers and Arsinoe
- the expansion of Egyptian territory under Cleopatra
- Cleopatra's relationship with her subjects
- her Graeco-Egyptian public persona and representation in the archaeological sources
- the promotion of Isis as her patron goddess and the rationale for this.

The prescribed sources for this topic are:

- Plutarch, *Life of Mark Antony* 27, 29, 83, 86
- Plutarch, *Life of Julius Caesar* 48–49
- Coin of Ptolemy Auletes, British Museum, wearing a diadem with the Ptolemaic Eagle
- Coin of Cleopatra, with distinctive hairstyle and hooked nose, British Museum
- Head of Cleopatra as a young woman, British Museum
- Relief portraits of Cleopatra and Caesarion from Dendera
- Coin of Cleopatra and Caesarion minted in Cyprus

Cleopatra was born into the Ptolemaic dynasty, which had ruled Egypt since 305 BC. The sources reveal her to be an intelligent and well-educated woman. She is presented as a charismatic woman, whose charm, humour and courage stand out as traits of her character. As the last Pharaoh of Egypt, she ruled over her subjects prosperously. She had a difficult relationship with her siblings and managed to overcome their own advances for power. In Alexandria, she was particularly able at keeping her subjects happy. She used

> **KEY INDIVIDUAL**
> **Cleopatra VII**
> **Dates:** 69–30 BC
> **Date of Reign:** 51–30 BC
> Queen of Egypt for twenty-one years and the final Pharaoh of Egypt

an identification with the goddess Isis to stress her own divinity and promote herself further to her subjects.

CLEOPATRA'S FAMILY AND MACEDONIAN HERITAGE

Cleopatra was born in 69 BC (some sources suggest 70 BC) into the Ptolemaic Dynasty. She was the daughter of Ptolemy XII Auletes but the exact identity of her mother and the location of her birth are unknown. Unfortunately, we have no evidence for Cleopatra's childhood years and so can only make judgements from other evidence presented in the sources. For example, we can estimate her birth date by working back from her age at her death given by Plutarch.

Cleopatra certainly had one older sister, called Berenice, a younger sister, called Arsinoe, and two still younger brothers, Ptolemy XIII and Ptolemy XIV.

Her family had been ruling Egypt since 305 BC. One of Alexander the Great's leading generals, Ptolemy, had taken Egypt for himself as Alexander's empire was divided on his death. He had ruled as **Pharaoh** and set up a prosperous family dynasty, setting up Alexandria as one of the World's most influential cities. However, in the years before Cleopatra's birth, the family's dynastic rule was struggling. Fighting within the family was common and Cleopatra's father, **Ptolemy XII Auletes**, had to rely on Rome for support of his rule. When Cleopatra was born, she entered into a powerful and distinguished family dynasty but at a time of declining prosperity and growing uncertainty for the family. They had grown dependent on external support, particularly from the increasingly dominant superpower of the Mediterranean, Rome. **CW**

> **pharaoh** the common title for the monarchs of Ancient Egypt, holding both political and religious significance

The Ptolemaic Dynasty was hence of Macedonian-Greek heritage and so this formed the base of Cleopatra's cultural identity. Indeed, her name 'Cleopatra, meaning 'honoured in her ancestry' or 'the glory of her father', was a very common Macedonian name, before it was commonly used by the Ptolemies in Egypt. However, by the birth of Cleopatra, the family had been in Egypt for nearly 300 hundred years. While the family's Macedonian heritage was undoubtedly important, the family's connection to Egypt and their new Egyptian heritage and assimilation to the Pharaohs was of growing importance and relevance.

> **KEY INDIVIDUAL**
> **King Ptolemy XII Auletes**
> **Dates:** 115–51 BC
> **Date of reign:** 81–58 BC, 55–51 BC
> The father of Cleopatra, Ptolemy XII, 'The Flute-Player', who ruled over Egypt for twenty-seven years before his death in 51 BC

FIGURE 3.1
Family tree of Cleopatra VII.

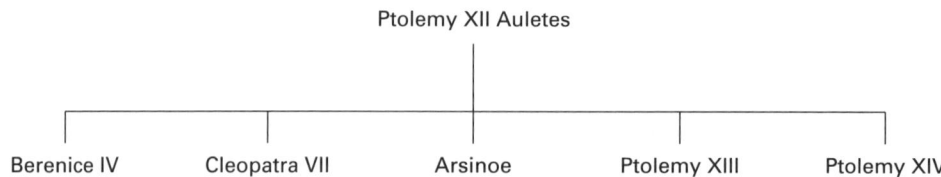

3.1 Cleopatra as Queen of Egypt

> **PRESCRIBED SOURCE**
>
> **Coin believed to be Ptolemy XII Auletes**
>
> **Date:** 69 BC
>
> **Obverse:** head believed to be of Ptolemy XII Auletes wearing a **diadem**, the **Hellenistic** sign of Kingship
>
> **Reverse:** traditional Ptolemaic eagle and inscription: ['of king Ptolemy']
>
> **Significance:** coinage was often used to display a portrait of power, rather than the image of reality. Here, Ptolemy XII links himself to his ancestor Ptolemy I by wearing the diadem
>
> **View it here:** OCR Source Booklet and Figure 3.2

> **diadem** a crown or headband symbolising sovereignty
>
> **Hellenistic** the period of Greek language, history and custom between the death of Alexander the Great and the death of Cleopatra

FIGURE 3.2
Coin believed to be Ptolemy XII Auletes.

CLEOPATRA'S EDUCATION AND UPBRINGING

Little is known about Cleopatra's education but it is likely she was educated in Alexandria by top tutors drawn to the city by its scholarly reputation. As a member of the royal family, she would have received a first-rate education. There is no evidence to suggest it but one could suggest that the wit and intelligence she displayed in her later life might have been formed from her regular interactions with scholars from the Museum of Alexandria.

It is perhaps useful at this stage to consider how Cleopatra's education compared to that of other women across the ancient world. In Greece and Rome, most girls were not educated, learning important skills of the household at home from their mother instead. However, girls in wealthy families would be educated in reading, writing and arithmetic either taught alongside boys or by a tutor at home. As they got older, the majority of wealthier girls would focus on the life lessons taught by their mother, on organising slaves, preparing family dinners and displaying obedience to her husband. However, a more academic education could be pursued. Cleopatra's education would probably have

> **EXAM TIP: REVISING PRESCRIBED TEXTS**
>
> It is always a good idea to read the prescribed texts carefully and write a brief synopsis or overview of each one. It is also useful to write a few sentences evaluating each prescribed source. Is the text/source accurate; where did the author find this information; and finally, does it have a different interpretation to other ancient historians.
>
> It is also a good idea to underline difficult words, or unfamiliar names. You could then create a glossary to help improve your understanding.

EXPLORE FURTHER

For more information on the rule of the Ptolemaic Dynasty, read:

Hölbl, G. *A History of the Ptolemaic Empire* (Abingdon: Routledge, 2000)

Part Two Depth Study 2: Cleopatra: Rome and Egypt

> **Study question**
> Read Plutarch *Life of Antony* 27
>
> What can you learn about Cleopatra's education and intelligence from this passage?

PRESCRIBED SOURCE

Life of Mark Antony

Author: Plutarch (AD 40–120)

Prescribed chapters: 27, 29, 83, 86

Date: AD 75

Genre: biography (biographical lives of famous Greek and Romans told in pairs)

Significance: An anecdotal overview of Antony's initial meeting and interaction with Cleopatra

Read it here: *The Makers of Rome* (London: Penguin, 2004); OCR Source Booklet

been a very similar process, but it is certainly an attractive idea to believe hers was more academic since she was in the academic heart of the ancient world.

Due to the concept of family inter-marriage, Ptolemaic women occasionally became queen and so were heavily involved in the politics and running of the nation. They were strong, independent and wealthy women and so likely had an education to match.

Cleopatra was clearly an intelligent woman. Plutarch *Life of Mark Antony* 27 highlights her ability to speak nine languages (eight mentioned plus Greek) and possibly more. Notably, Latin is not one of those languages so she most probably used Greek to converse with Julius Caesar and Mark Antony. She was the first person of her family line to learn the native Egyptian tongue as the Ptolemies preferred to speak Greek.

When Cleopatra was around twelve years old, in 58 BC, her father, Ptolemy XII, angered the citizens of Alexandria and faced a possible attempted coup. As a consequence, he fled to Rome for safety to gain support. We are unsure if the young Cleopatra followed her father to Rome at this stage or not. Cleopatra's sister, Berenice, seized the throne in her father's absence. Cleopatra's father remained in exile for three years before returning with an armed Roman force. Whether Cleopatra accompanied her father or not, this tumultuous period would have had a huge impact on her life as Cleopatra witnessed events that would mirror her own future – the forced deposition of a King, the rise of a young queen and ultimately, the need for support from Rome to ensure the security of one's position.

THE DEATH OF PTOLEMY XII AND CLEOPATRA'S FIRST YEARS AS QUEEN

The death of Ptolemy XII Auletes

Ptolemy XII returned from Rome in 55 BC with an armed Roman force. He was successful in reclaiming control of Alexandria and Egypt. He ordered the execution of his daughter Berenice IV but although back in power, he remained a very unpopular figure.

Before his death, Ptolemy XII passed his will over to the Romans for safe-keeping to ensure that it was executed upon his death. His will stated that Egypt be left to his eldest daughter, Cleopatra, and his eldest son, Ptolemy XIII, to rule jointly. Ptolemy XIII was only seven or eight years old at this stage and his sister seemed a sensible choice as co-regent until he was of age to rule himself. However, now in her late teens, Cleopatra was already planning to rule by herself. This is a contentious issue among scholars. Some have suggested that Cleopatra may have ruled jointly with her father before his death and used this as a springboard to secure her own sole rule. The evidence for this, however, is inconclusive.

Ptolemy XII ruled until the spring of 51 BC when he died of unknown causes. Up to his death, he remained unpopular with the Egyptian people and, as a consequence, his children took over a struggling and divided kingdom, fully dependent on Roman support.

Cleopatra's first years as queen

Honouring Ptolemy XII's will, Cleopatra, aged eighteen, and her brother, Ptolemy XIII, aged ten, were made co-rulers of Egypt in 51 BC. However, with Ptolemy's young age, he could only rule with the help of **regency advisors**. This meant that Cleopatra could become the dominant ruling force of the two but left her as a target for his ambitious advisors. It is likely that a marriage between Ptolemy and Cleopatra was either planned or may have taken place, but there is no record of such a wedding occurring so we cannot know for sure. The balance of evidence suggests, however, that early in her co-reign Cleopatra made an effort to rule independently of her brother, calling herself the 'father-loving Goddess' (Thea-Philopator).

> **regency advisors** a group of important officials put in place to help rule a kingdom when the heir to the throne is too young to rule

The young king and queen's first political test came in 50 BC. Syria, a Roman province, had been attacked by Parthian forces. The Roman governor of Syria, Marcus Calpurnius Bibulus, sent his two sons to Egypt to ask for support from the **Gabinians** to drive off the Parthian attack. The Gabinians had become accustomed to the luxury of Alexandria. Instead of following the brothers' request, they rebelled and murdered Bibulus' two sons. Cleopatra and Ptolemy were in a difficult position: do they upset Rome by not taking action against the murderers or do they upset the Gabinians, the armed force crucial for ensuring their rule? Cleopatra and Ptolemy arrested the ring-leaders and had them sent to Bibulus, choosing to risk the support of the Gabinians in return for avoiding further punishment or retribution from Rome.

> **Gabinians** Roman soldiers of Aulus Gabinius, who helped reinstall Ptolemy XII Auletes to power and then remained in Alexandria for a number of years after his death

At this stage, Ptolemy XIII was supported by three key advisors – his tutor, Theodotus, the soldier, Achillas and the eunuch, Pothinos. With their support, Ptolemy began to isolate Cleopatra, targeting power for himself. After a poor harvest in 50 BC, tension ran high in Alexandria as the dispute between Cleopatra and Ptolemy continued. In 49 BC, in desperation, it seems Cleopatra began to openly recognise her brother as co-ruler.

Rome declared support for Ptolemy XIII. Cleopatra had been outmanoeuvred by her young brother and his advisors. In the process, she had lost almost all of her important supporters in Alexandria. Concerned for her own safety, in 48 BC, she left Alexandria for Syria with her last supporters to raise an army against her brother. Egypt was about to be rocked by civil war (see p. 170 for more on the Civil War in Alexandria).

> **Study questions**
> 1. Create a spider diagram to show the challenges Cleopatra faced on becoming Queen.
> 2. How useful are the sources in furthering our understanding of Cleopatra's childhood?
> 3. How well do you think Cleopatra ruled Egypt in her first years as Queen?

CLEOPATRA'S RELATIONSHIP WITH HER BROTHERS AND ARSINOE

The Ptolemaic family was both complicated and competitive. Cleopatra was the second eldest child of Ptolemy XII Auletes and felt entitled to her own share of power. This brought her in direct conflict with her younger siblings, Ptolemy XIII and Ptolemy XIV, as well as her rebellious sister, Arsinoe. Her relationship with her brothers and Arsinoe can be summarised as follows:

Ptolemy XIII (63–47 BC) – Cleopatra and her eldest brother ascended to power together in the spring of 51 BC. Cleopatra tried to capitalise on her brother's young age and attempted to rule independently. Ptolemy was killed in the ensuing civil war. There was a difficult relationship between brother and sister as some believe Cleopatra did all she could to rule independently and deny her brother his right to rule. However, the sources are unclear on this and it would seem that Ptolemy's advisors, rather than the young man himself, were responsible for ensuring Cleopatra never got on with her brother.

Arsinoe IV (birth date unknown – 41 BC) – the younger sister of Cleopatra proved very troublesome in Cleopatra's quest for power. During the war between Caesar and Ptolemy XIII, Arsinoe, with her tutor, Ganymede, broke out of custody in the royal palace and joined the Egyptian forces against Caesar. When Caesar won, Arsinoe was taken captive and in 46 BC she appeared in Caesar's triumph in Rome. She was spared death and taken into custody at the Temple of Artemis at Ephesus. However, her lingering presence provided a constant threat to Cleopatra as Arsinoe was a legitimate challenger to her power. Arsinoe was executed on Antony's orders in 41 BC and some sources attribute responsibility for this to Cleopatra.

Ptolemy XIV (60–44 BC) – Cleopatra's brother, and husband, was thirteen when he came to power with Cleopatra in 47 BC, a partnership imposed by Caesar. Cleopatra had learnt from her mistake with Ptolemy XIII and tried to rule co-operatively with Ptolemy XIV. Yet, she still held all influence and left Ptolemy ruling little other than in name. It is likely he travelled with Cleopatra to Rome. However, he died in 44 BC of illness and Cleopatra has been linked by hearsay with his death.

For Cleopatra, her siblings were little more than obstacles in her pursuit of power. Ptolemaic customs preferred a woman to co-rule rather than to rule on her own so her shared rule with her brothers was a necessary problem. Her elder brother, Ptolemy XIII, died in a civil war fighting against her and her sister died at the order of her lover. The grim life of the Ptolemaic family meant that suspicion and rivalry was constantly prevalent.

THE EXPANSION OF EGYPTIAN TERRITORY UNDER CLEOPATRA

One of Cleopatra's great successes as queen was her expansion of Egyptian territory. By cultivating positive relationships with Rome through her affairs with Caesar and Antony, she regained a lot of old Ptolemaic possessions in the Eastern Mediterranean. Her first gain was Cyprus, lost to Rome in the will of Ptolemy X, and returned to Ptolemaic control by Caesar. In 37 BC, when Cleopatra went to Antony's aid in Antioch, she received, according to Plutarch *Life of Mark Antony* 36 **PS** the following territories:

- Phoenicia
- Coele Syria
- Cyprus
- a large part of Cilicia
- the balsam producing part of Judaea
- all that part of Arabia of the Nabataeans which slopes toward the Red Sea

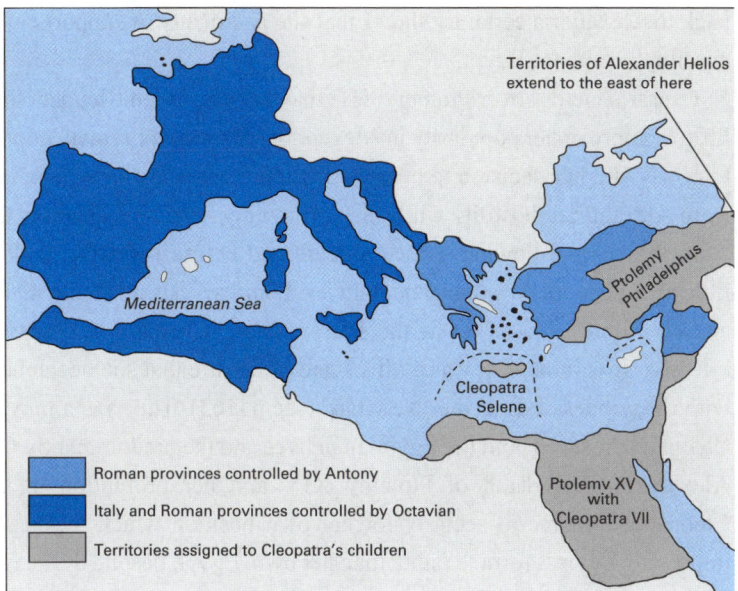

FIGURE 3.3
A map detailing the land handed out in the Donations of Alexandria.

This was a significant addition to Egyptian control and importantly provided additional resources which were scarcely found in Egypt such as timber. She also received coastal control and trading ports with Phoenicia and Cilicia. The additions strengthened Egypt's economy and bolstered Cleopatra's popularity in Alexandria.

In 34 BC, Antony's Donations of Alexandria expanded Egypt's reach even further (see p. 191 for more on the Donations). Here, the addition of the grand empires of the Medians and Parthians, not yet in Antony's control, were added to Egyptian control. Caesarion was named as the heir to this new empire. These were awarded in a grand ceremony in Alexandria and would have represented a significant upturn in their fortune and territory to the Egyptian people. The reality, however, was that the Donations had little practical implication. Antony handed over lands which he had not yet conquered to infant monarchs. Cleopatra would have known that Egypt would not derive any benefit or control of these lands but the very public recognition of their addition to Egyptian control would have pleased the people and furthered Cleopatra's reputation as a ruler.

CLEOPATRA'S RELATIONSHIP WITH HER SUBJECTS

It is difficult for us to truly assess Cleopatra's popularity with her subjects as the source material for the majority of her twenty-one years in power is more focused on her external actions from Roman and Greek sources rather than her day-to-day rule. At the start of her reign, it seems she was unpopular with the Alexandrians who saw her as submitting to Rome. Ptolemy XIII's advisors may have used this to their advantage when Cleopatra was forced out of the city. Her decision in the poor harvest of 50 BC to force all grain to be shipped to Alexandria may have been a desperate ploy to regain the support of the Alexandrian elite. However, the fact that Cleopatra was able to raise an army to march back to Alexandria certainly shows that she had plenty of support outside of the city and possibly outside of Egypt.

Caesar's victory over Ptolemy XIII may have installed Cleopatra into power but it did little to improve her popularity in Alexandria. She was extremely unpopular on her return to power and her decision to process down the Nile may have been taken to remove her from Alexandrian hostility while also promoting herself as queen to the rest of Egypt.

In the years following Caesar's death and before her affair with Antony, we know little about Cleopatra's domestic policies. Poor harvests in 41 and 40 BC brought famine and civil unrest but as far as the sources show, Cleopatra seems to have managed an effective government. It was at this stage of her life that she began her close association with the goddess **Isis** as the 'New Isis' (see p. 163). This was a move designed to draw Cleopatra closer to both the Egyptian natives and the predominantly Greek population of Alexandria. The death of Ptolemy XIV and her promotion of Caesarion allowed Cleopatra a degree of security for her own position which meant she could focus on improving Egypt's fortune rather than her own. Egypt, despite the heavy debts of Ptolemy XII's reign and poor harvest, was run efficiently throughout her rule and the extension of their territory, even if only gained through Roman support, would have brought her further popularity.

> **Isis** the ancient Egyptian goddess of magic, fertility and motherhood

CLEOPATRA'S CHARACTER AS DEPICTED IN THE SOURCES

The biggest challenge in discussing Cleopatra's character is the availability of source material. The little contemporary written evidence we have about Cleopatra's life tends to come from non-Egyptian sources. The main sources for Cleopatra's life are Greek and Roman, written years after the death of the queen by men who would never have met her in person.

However, this does not mean that we cannot take enough away from the sources available to us to form some image of Cleopatra's character. This image may not be the full picture of the historical Cleopatra's unique personality but we are able to, at least, add colour to our own thoughts of how the queen acted and behaved. However, in creating this image, one must remember the limitations of the sources and how we are forced to use possibly hostile Roman sources to form our views.

Cleopatra's charm

From the Roman sources, the fascinating charm of Cleopatra is emphasised. She is presented as having great wit and intelligence, matching that of her male counterparts. Evidence of this charm comes from Plutarch:

> Her beauty, so we are told, was not itself outstanding; it did not immediately strike those who saw her; yet being with her had an inescapable hold
>
> Plutarch, *Life of Mark Antony* 27

However, we must consider that the Romans wanted to justify why two of their great men rejected Roman reason for the love of a foreign woman. By exemplifying Cleopatra's 'inescapable' charm, they could remove any blame from their own statesman as victims of her charm. For Julius Caesar, it was her charm that Plutarch claims struck him first:

> It is said that because of this plan of Cleopatra's, Caesar was first charmed by her and afterwards he liked her more because of her sweet conversation and pleasant entertainment

Plutarch, *Life of Julius Caesar* 49

Her charm was not reserved for powerful men alone. Plutarch *Life of Mark Antony* 27 comments that Dellius, the messenger sent by Antony to call Cleopatra to Tarsus (see p. 184), found her 'cunning and cleverness in conversation' overwhelming.

The queen's education in Alexandria may have helped her become an eloquent and intelligent woman with a vivacious wit and captivating charm. She used her magnetism for her own advantage, to seduce powerful men and create security for herself and her kingdom. Even on her deathbed, Plutarch (*Life of Mark Antony* 83 ) noted that Octavian praised Cleopatra's charm.

Yet, the presentation of her charm could have been exaggerated to highlight the strengths of Cleopatra by pro-Roman sources. She becomes a greater adversary when resolute in defeat and this promotes the strength of Rome in defeating such an enemy. Plutarch, who presents a largely negative view of Antony throughout his work, could have represented Cleopatra in a similarly negative light but repeated allusions to her charm suggest that this was one of the key elements of her character.

Cleopatra's humour

Surprisingly perhaps, one element of Cleopatra's character that Plutarch particularly draws out is her sense of humour. Despite her constantly uncertain political position, we see in her interactions with Antony and others a playful side to the great queen. In court with Antony, Plutarch reveals that she played dice, drank and laughed with Antony.

Antony's boyish sense of humour and immaturity was well known across the Roman world and Plutarch (*Life of Mark Antony* 29) comments that Cleopatra even joined in with one of his more bizarre pastimes of dressing up as common people and wandering the streets of Alexandria making fun of people.

This sort of anecdote may be presented by Plutarch to highlight the depths to which Cleopatra went to indulge Antony, but if true, it does offer an entertaining view of the queen.

Anecdotes were a common occurrence in biography to add colour to the work but the truth of each story is debatable. If we choose to believe them, all these examples provide a refreshingly human view of Cleopatra. They provide an insight into her character away from the isolated image of Cleopatra as royal queen and show us a glimpse of her true personality and nature – an outgoing, charismatic and intelligent queen.

Study question
Read Plutarch, *Life of Mark Antony*, 29

What does the anecdote about Mark Antony and Cleopatra's fishing trip reveal about their personalities? Explain your views.

PRESCRIBED SOURCE

Life of Caesar

Author: Plutarch (AD 40–120)

Prescribed chapters: 48–49

Date: AD 75

Genre: biography (biographical lives of famous Greek and Romans told in pairs)

Significance: Biography of Caesar detailing his initial meeting with Cleopatra and the civil war in Alexandria

Read it here: OCR Source Booklet

> **Study questions**
>
> 1 What picture of Cleopatra is created by Horace in *Odes* 1.37? **PS**
> 2 From your knowledge of the prescribed sources, what are some of Cleopatra's negative personality qualities?

FIGURE 3.4
Coin of Cleopatra, with distinctive hairstyle and hooked nose, British Museum. **PS**

> **PRESCRIBED SOURCE**
>
> **Coin of Cleopatra**
>
> **Minted in:** Ascalon
>
> **Date:** 50/49 BC
>
> **Obverse:** head of Cleopatra with distinctive hairstyle and hooked nose
>
> **Significance:** Material evidence of Cleopatra's appearance from early in her life
>
> **View it here:** British Museum, OCR Source Booklet and Figure 3.4

Cleopatra's courage

Yet, there was an altogether more serious side to the queen. She was raised as a princess during a time of great political instability. To ensure her personal safety at the same time as ruling effectively for twenty-one years required plenty of political and personal courage. She successfully defeated rival factions, earned the trust of influential foreign leaders and peacefully ruled over her own people.

Her bravery is evident from a young age when she first went to meet Caesar (see p. 171). For Cleopatra to take such a risk and meet such a powerful man, when the outcome of the meeting was unknown, highlights how in a dangerous time she took risks to secure her own safety. She was astute and believed her intelligence and charm could secure favour with Caesar.

There are many other stories of Cleopatra's political courage but more notable perhaps was Cleopatra's personal bravery. As we will see, the Romans, who generally vilified the queen after her death, praised her defiant bravery in her final days. Horace's *Ode* 1.37 **PS** praises her for not trembling when death approached. According to Plutarch *Life of Mark Antony* 86 **PS**, Octavian saw the same courage at Cleopatra's death as he 'admired her noble spirit'. It was, of course, important for Octavian to have Cleopatra represented as a worthy enemy so as to magnify his victory.

We will never be able to appreciate fully the character and personality of Cleopatra. The outcome of her struggle with Rome meant that her memory was forever tainted and official records, documents and memories lost. Discoveries to flesh out further her life are few and far between. We have to make do with what we have, anecdotes and stories retold years after her death and consider their validity and reliability to understand who is creating images of Cleopatra and why.

CLEOPATRA'S GRAECO-EGYPTIAN PUBLIC PERSONA AND REPRESENTATION IN THE ARCHAEOLOGICAL SOURCES

When Ptolemy I, a Macedonian-Greek, became Pharaoh of Egypt in 305 BC, he understood the importance of combining cultures and adopting Egyptian imagery and customs. This would warm Egyptians to their new leader, who had resented previous oppressive regimes' ignorance and condemnation of their ancient culture. Cleopatra continued this practice and created her public persona and image to fuse Greek and Egyptian customs. The majority of ancient depictions of Cleopatra portray her in the Hellenistic style of a ruler, wearing a diadem, the jewelled crown and Hellenistic symbol of sovereignty. These Hellenistic depictions present a more realistic yet stylised portrait of the queen.

Cleopatra's Hellenistic appearance

The archaeological sources provide a picture of how the queen presented herself. Identification of busts is often difficult so we cannot always be certain that any image identified as Cleopatra was actually her. However, certain elements of her appearance do appear consistently. In the bust on this page and coin opposite, her hooked nose, a Ptolemaic family trait, can be seen along with her braided hair drawn back in a bun and held down by a diadem.

Her coinage presents the queen in a Hellenistic style. There is a realism to her portrait and it highlights her aged wisdom and gravity. As a coin, the image was designed to show Cleopatra's power, not her beauty. We simply do not know if this is how the real Cleopatra looked, but it does present to us an image of how she may have wanted to have been seen.

In Fig. 3.5 the same hooked nose and hair style can be seen. The lack of a diadem suggests that this is either Cleopatra as a younger woman or another young noble woman resembling Cleopatra from the time when the Ascalon coin was circulated in 50/49 BC. We simply do not know and can only guess.

FIGURE 3.5
Head of Cleopatra as a young woman, British Museum.

Cleopatra's Egyptian presentation

In Egyptian motifs, the depiction of Cleopatra is much grander. One such image believed to be of Cleopatra is a black basalt statue currently stored in the Hermitage in St. Petersburg.

The regal beauty and power of Cleopatra are strongly expressed here. Her figure is highlighted by her well-fitting dress and the grand Egyptian tripartite wig contrasts strongly with her Hellenistic braided bun. Crowning her wig is a triple **uraeus**, the sacred snake a symbol from the Ancient Egyptian kings worn to show their sovereignty. Yet, blended with this most ancient of Egyptian symbol is a Greek symbol, the cornucopia or horn of plenty. This symbolised to the Greeks abundance and prosperity. We can see here the difference in iconographic traditions. Her Hellenistic portrait is of a more realistic stylisation while her Egyptian appearance is grander. The important point when considering the different representations of Cleopatra is why the Ptolemies presented themselves in two different fashions – to appeal to all the cultural and ethnic diversity of their subjects.

uraeus sacred snake used as a symbol of sovereignty and power

THE PROMOTION OF ISIS AS HER PATRON GODDESS AND THE RATIONALE FOR THIS

Around the time of the birth of Caesarion in 47 BC, Cleopatra began closely associating herself with the Egyptian goddess Isis. The cult of Hellenised Isis was wide-reaching across the Mediterranean, particularly popular in Greek ports and Rome. The story of Isis, at least the version we are told by Greek sources, clearly resonated with Cleopatra.

Isis was idealised as the perfect wife and mother. She also represented fertility and re-birth. The connections to Cleopatra are easy to see; Cleopatra as Isis, the lover of a murdered man (Caesar) and single mother ruling and protecting her son (Caesarion). Long before, Ptolemaic royal woman had associated themselves with Isis. Cleopatra, however, saw herself as a 'New Isis' and the birth of Caesarion allowed her to use the image to portray her own position as a semi-divine mother. Her association with Isis would be a more intimate and intense relationship than seen before.

PRESCRIBED SOURCE

Head of Cleopatra as a young woman

Type: Bust

Date: unknown

Material: limestone

Significance: A possible representation of Cleopatra as a young woman but we are unsure of whether it is definitely her

View it here: British Museum, OCR Source Booklet and Figure 3.5

From a Greek viewpoint, she portrayed herself as a creator of culture, stability and abundance.

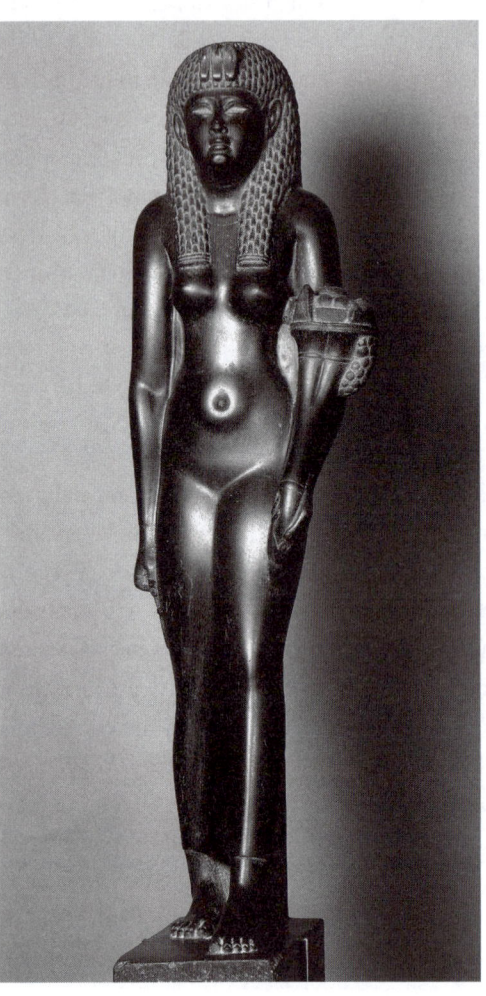

FIGURE 3.6
Statue of Cleopatra.

> **EXPLORE FURTHER**
>
> Watch the BBC's *Cleopatra – A Timewatch Guide* (2015) which explores how views of Cleopatra's appearance have changed over the years.

> **EXPLORE FURTHER**
>
> Research the full back story of Isis to discover how her story was similar to that of Cleopatra

FIGURE 3.7
Coin minted in Cyprus showing Cleopatra as Isis with Caesarion.

PRESCRIBED SOURCE

Coin of Cleopatra and Caesarion minted in Cyprus

Obverse: bust of Cleopatra as the goddess Aphrodite with Caesarion depicted as her son Eros

Reverse: the sacred cone of Aphrodite

Significance: Cyprus had been given back to Ptolemaic possession by Julius Caesar. This coin shows Cleopatra's concerted effort to have her son represented alongside her

View it here: OCR Source Booklet and Figure 3.7

3.1 Cleopatra as Queen of Egypt

In her association, she often dressed as Isis for formal events. A coin, minted on the Ptolemaic island of Cyprus, shows Cleopatra as the mother Isis with Caesarion, barely able to be made out, on her breast as she rears her young son. This was a common scene as the Mother of the Pharaoh was traditionally linked with Isis.

Temple monuments, most famously the reliefs at the Temple of Hathor in Dendera, presented Cleopatra's divine image on a grand scale.

This large relief shows Cleopatra behind her son as they make offerings to the Gods, of which Isis is included. Caesarion has prominence while his dutiful mother follows. Caesarion is dressed in regal pomp as the protective God, Horus in the form of a falcon, hovers above him. Cleopatra is equally regal, holding a sistrum the rattle commonly associated with Isis.

By her death, Cleopatra had created a memorable image of her divinity. The Ptolemies were always seen as divine but Cleopatra went further, exploiting religion for her own political gain not only in Egypt but across the Eastern Mediterranean. In the process, she was able to promote Caesarion into a acclaimed and respected position. The images highlight a politically astute queen who was able to use a common religious figure to strengthen her bond with both her Egyptian and Greek subjects.

> **PRESCRIBED SOURCE**
>
> **Relief of Cleopatra and Caesarion**
>
> **Location:** Temple of Hathor in Dendera
>
> **Date:** *c.* 35 BC
>
> **Description:** Cleopatra stands as Egyptian queen behind her son, the king Caesarion, as they process to present offerings to the Gods
>
> **Significance:** A representation of how Cleopatra displayed the importance of her role as mother
>
> **View it here:** OCR Source Booklet and Figure 3.8

FIGURE 3.8
Cleopatra stands behind her son in a religious procession. The reliefs at the Temple of Hathor in Dendera.

Part Two Depth Study 2: Cleopatra: Rome and Egypt

TOPIC REVIEW

Boost your knowledge

Describe:

- the key events leading to Cleopatra and Ptolemy XII's accession to the throne
- how Cleopatra added territory to Egyptian control
- the way Cleopatra was represented in material sources
- the relationship Cleopatra had with each of her siblings

Stretch your understanding

Explain:

- why Cleopatra's relationship with her brother caused conflict in Egypt
- how Cleopatra's relationship with her subjects changed over her reign
- why Cleopatra's portrayal as Isis was important for the safety of her rule
- how Cleopatra's education and upbringing influenced her character

PRACTICE QUESTIONS

1. **a.** Name **two** territories added to Egypt's control during Cleopatra's reign. [2]
   b. Name **one** of Ptolemy XIII's key advisors. [1]
   c. Give **two** reasons for Cleopatra's promotion of herself as Isis. [2]

Passage A

Once, however, he went fishing, caught nothing and was annoyed especially since Cleopatra was there also. So he ordered some fishermen to dive down and without being seen attach some previously caught fish to his line; he then pulled up two or three of these – but he did not manage to do this without Cleopatra noticing. She told her friends what he had done, and invited them to come and watch the next day. As a result, a large number of friends climbed into the boats. When Antony let down his line, she ordered one of her servants to go down first to his hook and attach a salted Black Sea fish. Antony was convinced that he had caught a fish, so he pulled his line up, and as expected, everyone started laughing. Cleopatra then said to him 'Commander, you had better hand over your fishing-rod to the kings of the Pharos and Canopus; you should be hunting cities, kingdoms, and continents'.

Plutarch, *Life of Mark Antony* 29

2. What can we learn from Passage A about Cleopatra's character? [5]

3.2 Cleopatra's Relationship with Julius Caesar, 48–44 BC

> **TOPIC OVERVIEW**
>
> **Cleopatra as queen of Egypt, including political, domestic and foreign policies**
>
> - Civil war between Cleopatra and Ptolemy XIII
>
> **Cleopatra's relationships with Caesar (48–44 BC) and Mark Antony (41–30 BC) and their political significance**
>
> - Rome's relationship with client states and attitude to foreigners
> - the importance of Egypt for Rome economically and politically
> - Rome's involvement in Egypt in the 60s and 50s BC
> - Cleopatra's initial meeting with Caesar and his decision to support her
> - Cleopatra's personal and political relationship with Caesar and its impact on both Rome and Egypt
> - the birth of Caesarion
> - Cleopatra's visit to Rome and her reception
>
> **The prescribed sources for this topic are:**
>
> - Plutarch, *Life of Julius Caesar* 48–49
> - Cassius Dio, *Roman History* 42.44–45; 43.27
> - Suetonius, *Life of Divine Julius* 52
> - Cicero, *Letter to Atticus* XV.15
> - Coin of Cleopatra and Caesarion minted in Cyprus
> - Relief portraits of Cleopatra and Caesarion from Dendera

Julius Caesar came to Egypt in 48 BC in pursuit of his enemy, Pompey the Great. He found that Pompey had been murdered on the orders of Ptolemy XIII and was outraged. Cleopatra returned from exile to meet with Caesar and the two began an affair. Cleopatra used Caesar's support to return to power in Alexandria and Ptolemy XIII was defeated by Caesar in the subsequent war which followed. The affair between Caesar and Cleopatra was unpopular in Rome. This was particularly evident during Cleopatra's visit to Rome. Cleopatra and Caesar had a son, named Caesarion, and the couple grew ever closer. However, as Caesar sought further power himself, he was assassinated by a group of Senators in 44 BC. Cleopatra was forced to flee Rome for her own safety and return to Egypt to solidify her position as ruler.

ROME'S RELATIONSHIP WITH CLIENT STATES AND ATTITUDE TO FOREIGNERS

Since launching their first offensive against the Carthaginians in 264 BC, Rome's empire and influence had been steadily growing across the Mediterranean. By the time of the reign of Cleopatra's father, Rome was the ancient world's dominant power. Its empire spread from Spain in the west to Asia minor in the east. One key method employed by the Romans to install peace across the Empire was the installation of **client-kings**. This was essentially an extension of the long-standing Roman tradition of the **patron-client** relationship.

Client-kings worked in a similar, albeit more significant, fashion. They were kings or rulers of foreign nations who often relied on the support of Rome to ensure their own position in power. These kings acted as clients to Rome, and the state, rather than an individual, acted as the patron. Client-kings tended to come from nations which bordered or lay between Roman controlled provinces; this allowed Rome to carefully manage its borders as well as further its influence across the Mediterranean. Rome's support came in the form

> **client-king** kings and rulers of non-Roman controlled provinces, who were aided by Roman favour in return for their support of Rome
>
> **patron-client** the mutual relationships common in Roman society where one Roman helps out a less influential or wealthy Roman

FIGURE 3.9
Map of the Roman Republic by the death of Caesar.

of supporting the client-king and ensuring their position in power remained secure. In return, the client-king would provide resources in the form of armed forces, grain or financial aid whenever Rome requested it. These kings were independent rulers in their own nation but found themselves very much dependent on Rome for their own position.

Rome was an extremely diverse city with foreigners coming from Gaul, Hispania, Central and Eastern Europe, Greece, Asia Minor, Syria and beyond. Foreign trade brought a constant traffic of people to the Mediterranean's most dominant city. Many foreigners would have entered the city initially as slaves. However, this did not make foreigners popular in the city. Romans were xenophobic, holding a fear or dislike of foreign nations. They strongly believed that the Roman was superior to all others. Juvenal, a Roman satirist, reflected the over-crowding of foreigners in the city in his Satire, 3 commenting 'I can't stand a Rome full of Greeks!'. Yet the span of empire meant that foreign ideals and customs did pervade Roman society. Foreign religious cults, such as that of Mithras or Isis, offered some Romans an alternative from conventional religion. Such cults were particularly popular with soldiers in the provinces. So, although we generally find a Rome scornful of foreign nations, we do find evidence of cooperation between Rome and her conquered nations.

> **Study question**
> Explain why a client-king relationship was beneficial to:
> - the client-king
> - Rome

> **EXPLORE FURTHER**
> One of the best-known examples of a client-king is King Herod I of Judaea. Research his life to see how his relationship with Rome kept him in power.

THE IMPORTANCE OF EGYPT FOR ROME ECONOMICALLY AND POLITICALLY

- **Natural Resources** – Egypt was a land of excellent natural resources. Each year, the flooding of the Nile created very fertile land next to the river which the Egyptians could farm with great effect.
- **Political Potential** – Ambitious Romans knew they could harness the potential of Egypt for their own political gain.
- **Wealth** – As a result of their ample natural resources and location, Egypt had a thriving economy and was a nation of great wealth.
- **Location** – Egypt's location made it appealing politically and economically for Rome. Its position in the southern Mediterranean along with the Nile provided excellent trade options and resources for Rome.

> **ACTIVITY**
> What was the most important reason for Egypt's importance to Rome? Rank the factors in order of importance.

ROME'S INVOLVEMENT IN EGYPT IN THE 60S AND 50S BC

In 168 BC, a Roman ambassador prevented Antiochus IV of Syria from attacking Alexandria, claiming that such an attack would be an attack on Rome itself. This was Rome's first direct intervention in Egyptian affairs.

Cleopatra's father's, Ptolemy XII, rule began in 81 BC. After some difficult years in power, he lost the support of much of Alexandria and became a very unpopular figure in

> **friend and ally of the Roman people** the official title given to a client-king or ruler as a reward for loyalty or good service, confirming their support from Rome

FIGURE 3.10
A bust of Julius Caesar.

> **KEY INDIVIDUAL**
> **Gaius Julius Caesar**
> **Dates:** 100–44 BC
>
> One of the most famous Romans of all time, Julius Caesar was a Roman politician, general and writer. His assassination in 44 BC is seen as a turning point in Roman history

> **ACTIVITY**
> Create Top Trump cards for each of the historical characters introduced so far

Egypt. He realised that he needed the support of Rome to survive. In 59 BC, **Julius Caesar** was persuaded to pass a law as Consul acknowledging Auletes as a '**friend and ally of the Roman people**', the title commonly given to client-kings. Auletes paid a staggering bribe of 6,000 talents (over half of Egypt's annual total revenue!) for this formal recognition in the belief that it would secure his future as king. It was a bribe he was unable to afford personally and so he had to borrow the amount from many Roman-lenders and Caesar himself. This title and recognition gave Auletes temporary security but hatred of Rome meant that resentment for the king grew intensely. This debt is mentioned in Plutarch *Life of Caesar 48* **PS** and was a key reason for Caesar's involvement in the war between Cleopatra and Ptolemy XIII.

Despite this formal title, Auletes remained unpopular in Alexandria and in 58 BC, he fled the city for Rome. Cleopatra may have accompanied him on this journey but the sources are unclear. In the meantime, his eldest daughter, Berenice, took power in Alexandria. In 57 BC, the Senate agreed to restore Ptolemy to power. Yet, squabbling over which Roman would take the command, meant there was no action for a long time. **CW**

Finally, Ptolemy bribed the Governor of Syria, Aulus Gabinius, in 55 BC with 10,000 talents, to help reinstall him into power. Gabinius led an armed force against Berenice and defeated the queen and her consort, completing Auletes' restoration. The survival of Ptolemy XII's reign in Egypt now rested on Roman support. A number of Roman soldiers remained in Alexandria to enforce Ptolemy's support and in return, Ptolemy had to ensure that these soldiers were looked after adequately. These soldiers became known as the Gabinians and would stay in Egypt for a number of years, building Rome's military presence in Egypt and forcing subsequent Egyptian rulers to be dependent on Roman support. The situation was no different when Cleopatra took power. Locked in civil war with her brother, Ptolemy XIII, she was forced to appeal to Roman help to secure her own position.

CIVIL WAR BETWEEN CLEOPATRA AND PTOLEMY XIII, 48–47 BC

Cleopatra knew from her father's experience that being driven out of her kingdom did not mean she could no longer be queen. But she had to raise an army quickly to capitalise on her remaining support in Egypt. She travelled east perhaps to Ascalon, a city on the coast of Palestine which had won its independence from Judaea through support from the Ptolemies. She was probably well-received and recruited an army. This is all suggested by coinage minted in Ascalon in support of Cleopatra, although we are not certain if she did travel to the city or received their support in another way.

Somehow Cleopatra, by the summer of 48 BC, had raised a significant enough army of mercenaries to return to Egypt and face her brother. Ptolemy XIII was aware of Cleopatra's movements and sent his general Achillas to meet with Cleopatra's forces. It was now that the Roman Civil War would have its first major impact on Egypt and Cleopatra's story. Word reached Achillas that Pompey the Great, in flight after his defeat by Caesar at Pharsalus, was coming their way. Pompey had been a friend of Cleopatra's father, Ptolemy XII Auletes, and had aided the King in his search for legitimacy in Rome. **CW**

The death of Pompey the Great

Ptolemy and his advisors were to be present for Pompey's imminent arrival. They now had to decide what to do with him. After much debate, the advisors recommended that Pompey be killed before he could reach land. This would win favour with Julius Caesar, whose support they would now require. It would also probably speed up the time spent by Caesar in Egypt and thus make him less likely to get involved in their affairs. Pompey was executed on the coast line by one of Ptolemy's men as he was welcomed by the Egyptians.

In October 48, Julius Caesar arrived in Alexandria in pursuit of Pompey. He was met by Ptolemy XIII and his advisors, eager to reveal their murderous actions. However, as Plutarch *Life of Caesar* 48 PS reveals, Caesar was outraged at the murder.

Although Pompey's death was undoubtedly positive news for Caesar, he still felt plenty of remorse for a worthy foe. The murder of a friend and former son-in-law had been futile and treacherous. Caesar had been denied the chance to show off his vaunted clemency. His next move shocked Ptolemy XIII still further. With his armed force leading the way, he processed straight through Alexandria and took up residence in the Royal Palace complex. This angered the fiercely independent citizens of Alexandria, who resented the Roman's arrogance and there were a number of riots.

Caesar announced that he had come to settle the dispute between Ptolemy XIII and Cleopatra. He also demanded that the Ptolemies repay the heavy debt still owed to Rome by their father. This was a blow for Ptolemy who had been in full control of the civil war. He now had to rely on the decision of another. His decision to kill Pompey had not paid off. Pothinus particularly resented Caesar's stay in the city and did all he could to drive the Roman away. As Plutarch *Life of Caesar* 48 PS tells us, the eunuch tried many things to convince Caesar that to raise the money would take time. He gave the Roman soldiers the worse grain to eat, and used only cheap earthenware at dinners in the palace rather than the usual Ptolemaic fancy ware. Pothinus' plan only had a negative effect as Plutarch reveals his actions drove Caesar to recall Cleopatra.

To settle the civil war, Caesar needed to speak to both sides. Without doing so he could not ensure that his decision would be respected. Cleopatra's army still lay east near Pelusium and, with the ambitious advisors of Ptolemy XIII clearly willing to go to murderous lengths to secure control, she had to find a safe but secretive way into Alexandria.

FIGURE 3.11
Pompey the Great.

> **S & C**
> Read the full account of Pompey's death in Plutarch's *Life of Pompey* 77–80.
>
> How does Plutarch's way of writing about the Egyptians suggest his opinion of them?

> **EXPLORE FURTHER**
> Billows, R.A. *Julius Caesar: The Colossus of Rhodes* (Abingdon; Routledge, 2009) is a useful secondary source for the relationship between Caesar and Cleopatra

CLEOPATRA'S INITIAL MEETING WITH CAESAR AND HIS DECISION TO SUPPORT HER

According to Plutarch *Life of Caesar* 49 PS, Cleopatra left her forces at Pelusium and secretly made her way to Alexandria in a small fishing boat with a Sicilian friend, Apollodorus. On disembarking, she needed to find a safe way into the presence of Caesar without being detected by Pothinus' armed guard. The pair waited until nightfall before Cleopatra hid herself in a bundle of sheets or 'bed-sack' which Apollodorus carried into the palace. When Apollodorus reached Caesar, Cleopatra emerged from the sheets.

ACTIVITY

Choose a famous character from history, modern or ancient, and read a biography of their lives.

How does the writing of modern biography compare to the extracts of Plutarch you have read?

S&C Read Plutarch's *Life of Alexander* 1, *Life of Pericles* 2–4 and *Life of Lycrugus* 1 to find out more information about Plutarch's aims in his writing.

KEY INDIVIDUAL

Plutarch
Dates: AD 46–120

Born in Chaeronea in Greece in AD 46, Lucius Mestrius Plutarchus was a Greek historian, biographer and philosopher. His most famous works include his *Parallel Lives* series of biographies and the *Moralia*, a set of philosophical essays and speeches

---

ACTIVITY

Divide into groups and debate:

Do you think Caesar was testing Cleopatra's resourcefulness by demanding to meet her in Alexandria?

EXAM TIP: SOURCE SKILLS

Plutarch

The majority of the prescribed sources for this component are from **Plutarch's** *Life of Mark Antony*. Written *c.* 75 AD, Plutarch wrote a number of biographies, pairing a life of a famous Greek with that of a famous Roman. His *Parallel Lives* were designed to provide moral lessons and examples for future generations. He does not attempt to give readers a full history of a time period or series of events but rather focuses on what is revealed about that character from various stories and anecdotes. It is from his *Life of Mark Antony* that much of what we know about Cleopatra can be found.

When considering the reliability of his work, it is important to consider Plutarch's motive for writing. At the beginning of his *Life of Alexander*, Plutarch stressed that it was 'lives' and not 'history' which he aimed to write. His work is, therefore, filled with anecdotes and tales rather than battle formations or political reports. Some historians believe Plutarch has a tendency to slightly alter the accounts of his sources to allow certain character traits to shine through.

How much, therefore, can we trust Plutarch's writing? Plutarch wrote over one hundred years after Cleopatra's death. His version of Cleopatra may have been shaped by the Roman propaganda and bias spread after her defeat. His sources for his Cleopatra anecdotes are also unclear. He claims his grandfather had a friend who knew Cleopatra's cook and that he had access to a memoir of Cleopatra's physician, Olympus. These are hardly the most reliable sources of information. It does seem unlikely that in the course of writing so many popular biographies Plutarch would deliberately look to deceive his reader. He can be considered as accurate as his sources. He wanted vibrant and interesting characters but is happy to admit where he is unsure of a source or story. He does generally write chronologically and so his history is easy to follow. It is, therefore, perhaps best to treat Plutarch with both trust and caution. We should always question why he decided to include each anecdote, how he might have known about the story, and whether other sources concur or disagree with the history he presents.

This is a fanciful tale, but one which we must question as it only appears in Plutarch's account. This does not automatically mean it is a fabrication but does therefore require a thorough examination. Although the requirement for a stealthy entrance is certainly believable, other elements of the story are harder to believe. Would Apollodorus, carrying a load of laundry, have been able to approach Caesar so easily? Why did Ptolemy's guards not suspect the suspicious character? Plutarch *Life of Caesar* 48 **PS** does mention that Cleopatra and Caesar had already been in some form of communication so perhaps Caesar was expecting Cleopatra to arrive in such a fashion. This dramatic entry does seem to ring true with the queen's courageous and theatrical personality.

Whether we believe Plutarch's story or not on the nature of her arrival, Cleopatra did arrive and meet with Caesar in late 48 BC. The meeting was not without risk as she could not be sure how Caesar would treat her and she was placing herself much closer to her enemies. The twenty-one-year-old queen stood in front of the most powerful man in the world and she intended to do whatever she could to win him over. From that first meeting, it seems Caesar and Cleopatra were captivated with each other. Caesar, in his third marriage at fifty-two years old, had a reputation for his active interest in women and had been involved in plenty of affairs. She was young, intelligent and attractive. However, it is important not to consider their affair as simply a romantic relationship. Caesar may have been seduced, but if he was, then it was done on his terms and because the events suited him. Cleopatra, on the other hand, understood that her charm could be employed for her own personal and political relationship to flourish with Caesar. Cleopatra spent the night with Caesar, but it would be wrong for us to assume that Caesar was simply a victim of Cleopatra's beguiling and predatory nature.

Ptolemy XIII woke the next morning to find Cleopatra in the palace and intimate with Caesar. Shocked and angry, the thirteen-year-old king ran out of the palace, threw off his crown and cried out that he was being betrayed. Caesar had him brought back into the palace and this sparked angry protests in Alexandria. Confident as ever, Caesar called a formal assembly together and, unfurling Ptolemy XII's will, announced that the conditions of the will were to be followed and Ptolemy and Cleopatra were to rule as king and queen. In a surprising move, he also announced Cleopatra's brother and sister, Ptolemy XIV and Arsinoe, as King and Queen of Cyprus, returning the old Ptolemaic land from Roman control back to Egypt.

> **Study questions**
>
> 1 Do you believe Plutarch's story of Cleopatra's arrival? Explain your views.
> 2 What were the risks Cleopatra faced when attempting to meet with Caesar?

FIGURE 3.12
In this seventeenth-century painting by Pietro da Cortona, Caesar gives Cleopatra the throne of Egypt.

Why did Caesar choose to support Cleopatra?

- **Physical attraction** – Caesar was a promiscuous man who had multiple marriages and affairs throughout his life. As Suetonius tells us (*Life of Divine Julius* 52 **PS**), he had plenty of affairs with foreign queens as well. Numerous sources tell us that he was captivated by Cleopatra's charm and beauty. It is unlikely that his physical attraction alone drove him to action, but it certainly could have played a part.
- **Political sense** – By supporting Cleopatra, Caesar could force Ptolemy and his advisors to work harder to earn his trust and support. Caesar needed the wealth and resources of Egypt to ensure his own success in Rome. Cleopatra undoubtedly needed Caesar's support more than he needed hers. Yet, he will have recognised that Cleopatra was likely to be a better friend to Rome and Caesar than Ptolemy XIII.
- **A dislike for Ptolemy and his advisors** – Ever since his angry reaction to his 'gift' of the head of Pompey, Caesar had a poor relationship with Ptolemy and his advisors, particularly Pothinus. As discussed previously, Pothinus resented Caesar's involvement and did all he could to make the Roman's time in Alexandria difficult. Punishing Pompey's murderers would also have been a popular decision in Rome.

> **PRESCRIBED SOURCE**
>
> **Life of Divine Julius**
>
> **Author:** Gaius Suetonius Tranquillus
>
> **Prescribed chapter:** 52
>
> **Genre:** biographical history
>
> **Significance:** A biographical view of the life of Julius Caesar detailing here his relationship with Cleopatra
>
> **Read it here:** OCR Source Booklet

However, Caesar's decision was not a popular one with all parties. Pothinus sent for Achillas to bring their army to Alexandria. Soon, Egypt was once again embroiled in civil war as Alexandria came under a fierce siege. Achillas led the siege and Caesar's small band of men struggled to fight back in four months of difficult guerrilla warfare. At one stage, Caesar listened to the request of the Alexandrian people and allowed Ptolemy XIII to be released from Caesar's custody to try to calm the situation. Ptolemy, however, only incited further revolt and Caesar's forces began to struggle. Soon reinforcements for Caesar came from the East. Ptolemy's forces came to meet the reinforcements and were defeated at the Battle of the Nile in February 47 BC. Ptolemy XIII drowned in the river Nile as Caesar took full control of Egypt. He announced that Cleopatra and her younger brother, Ptolemy XIV, would rule Egypt together. Shortly after, following the Ptolemaic custom, the two were married but Cleopatra intended to rule independently of her 14-year old brother and husband. Historian Cassius Dio wrote of this relationship in your prescribed source:

> In reality Cleopatra was to hold all the power alone, since her husband was still a boy, and because of Caesar's favour she could do anything. So she accepted that she would live with her brother and pretend to share the rule with him but in truth she ruled alone and spent her time with Caesar.
>
> Cassius Dio, *Roman History* 42.44

> **PRESCRIBED SOURCE**
>
> **Roman History**
>
> **Author:** Cassius Dio (AD 155–235)
>
> **Prescribed chapters:** 42.44–45, 43.27
>
> **Date:** AD 200
>
> **Genre:** history – account of Rome from the landing of Aeneas to AD 229
>
> **Significance:** A general history of the rise of Rome
>
> **Read it here:** OCR Source Booklet

This had been an unsuccessful approach in the past and had led to her exile yet with Caesar's support confirmed, Cleopatra was confident in keeping her brother/husband in check.

> **Study questions**
>
> Read Plutarch, *Life of Caesar* 49 **PS** on the Alexandrian war and answer the following questions:
>
> 1. From whom does Caesar receive a rumour that Pothinus was plotting his death?
> 2. What happens to the Library of Alexandria during the fighting?
> 3. How did Caesar save some crucial papers when he was forced into the water and what does this tell us about him?
> 4. Who does Plutarch say Caesar leaves in charge of Egypt?

CLEOPATRA'S PERSONAL AND POLITICAL RELATIONSHIP WITH CAESAR AND ITS IMPACT ON BOTH ROME AND EGYPT

For the duration of the four-month siege of Alexandria, Cleopatra remained in the Royal Palace as Caesar's companion and their relationship blossomed. Immediately, the impact of the affair could be seen in Egypt and Rome. In Alexandria, as we have seen, Caesar had made the decision to not fully annexe Egypt as a Roman province, instead installing Cleopatra and Ptolemy XIV as client-monarchs instead. This may have been for a sensible political reason. To annexe a new province at a time of great instability for the Roman Republic would have been more trouble than good. However, one could be swayed by the more romantic reason of Caesar installing Cleopatra as queen out of affection. This is certainly a possibility but it is most likely that it was a mixture of the two. His affair fostered a closer bond with Cleopatra and by installing someone he was intimate with as queen, it ensured loyalty. Cleopatra, however, would have been in little doubt that the future success of the Ptolemaic dynasty now lay in Caesar's hands.

Public perception was clearly important to Caesar. Cassius Dio *Roman History* 42.44 **PS** reveals that it may have lay at the heart of his decision to install Cleopatra as queen. He was at a pivotal point in his ambitious career. The defeat of Pompey left him poised to increase his hold on power, but he still had plenty of people to convince. Cassius Dio wrote in *Roman History* 42.44 **PS** that Caesar forced Cleopatra to marry her younger brother for the sake of peace in Alexandria.

The negative attitude of Romans towards foreigners may have weighed on Caesar's mind at this stage. His affair with an Eastern queen would undoubtedly would have caused some resentment in Rome but it was important for him to maintain his relationship with Cleopatra to ensure the benefits of the resources of Egypt.

In Alexandria, the reception of the affair and the result of the civil war created a tense atmosphere. Caesar remained unpopular with the Alexandrians, and Cleopatra, whose bulk of support lay outside of the city, had to prove her legitimacy and right to rule.

At this stage, we must not forget that before his journey to Egypt, Caesar had been locked in civil war. Pompey may have been defeated but Caesar still had matters to attend to in Rome, allies of Pompey to defeat and he had to capitalise on his victory at Pharsalus. Yet, for four months, he had been engaged in the siege of Alexandria. Surely he would have been eager to return to Rome? However, rather than speed off after he had installed Cleopatra into power, Caesar remained in Egypt for a few more months. When we ask ourselves why he remained into mid 47 BC, we are forced to consider both Caesar's mind and his heart having an impact on his decision. It made logical sense for him to remain in Alexandria with his forces to make sure that Cleopatra's accession to the throne was not challenged. Yet also, he may have simply wanted to spend some time at leisure with his mistress. He had been worn down by warfare for years and may have wanted some distraction before returning to the complex situation awaiting him in Rome.

The sources certainly suggest that plenty of time was spent at leisure. Plutarch tells us that he went sightseeing, visiting the tomb of Alexander the Great. Suetonius highlights the extent of his leisure:

> But he especially loved Cleopatra. He often kept feasts with her going until dawn and he sailed with her in the state yacht through Egypt almost as far as Ethiopia – or at least would have, if his army had not refused to follow him there.
>
> Suetonius, *Life of Divine Julius* 52

The Ptolemies often sailed on huge ornate barges which they would sail up the Nile as a procession in front of their citizens, who, outside of the major cities, would not have had much contact with their rulers. It was a tremendous show of the wealth and power of the Ptolemaic dynasty. The exact extent of the barge journey is not clear (Plutarch and Dio make no mention of it and it is only mentioned by one secondary source, Appian) but it would have been an extravagant voyage showing off Cleopatra in full pomp and allowing Caesar to explore the land he now controlled.

Alongside their personal relationship, the political relationship between the two began to have an impact in Egypt and Rome. Cleopatra finally had the stability to rule her country as she saw fit. The procession on the barge signalled a new era for Cleopatra as queen. She still needed to gain official support from Rome but her relationship with Caesar made this very likely. For Caesar, his personal relationship with Cleopatra was unpopular in Rome but the political association was very beneficial for the city. Egypt's resources could be put to good use and ensured that Rome had a consistent grain supply

ACTIVITY

Divide into groups and debate:
Was the relationship between Caesar and Cleopatra more beneficial to Rome or Egypt?

FIGURE 3.13
Barges similar to the ones that might have carried the Ptolemies are shown on Egyptian temple walls, such as this procession of pharaoh and seven gods.

and extended access to further trade opportunities. He had punished the murderers of Pompey and successfully solved the family struggle of the Ptolemies for the benefit of Rome. For both parties, the relationship, soon to be cemented by a son, was politically and personally mutually beneficial.

THE BIRTH OF CAESARION

Around July or August 47 BC, Caesar left for Asia Minor to campaign further into the East. It was around the same time that Cleopatra had her first child. She called the boy Ptolemy Caesar and the Alexandrians quickly gave the boy the nickname **Caesarion**. There was little doubt in their mind as to the boy's father.

The sources, however, do cast some doubt about the boy's paternity. Suetonius does not provide any definitive answers:

> He allowed her to call her son by him by his own name. Certain Greek writers have reported that he was similar to Caesar in appearance and in his way of walking. Indeed M. Antonius confirmed to the senate that he had been acknowledged by him and that C. Matius and C. Oppius knew this along with the rest of Caesar's friends. Of them Oppius, on the grounds that this matter needed some explanation and defence, published a book saying that he was not Caesar's son as Cleopatra claimed.
>
> Suetonius, *Life of Divine Julius* 52

The focus of these comments lies in hearsay and speculation. We must question who these 'certain Greek writers' were and whether **Mark Antony** and 'other friends of Caesar' are impartial observers. For Mark Antony, it would be beneficial for Caesar to be the boy's father as it would raise doubts as to the legitimacy of Octavian as Caesar's heir. The comment regarding Gaius Oppius' written denial is particularly interesting. Would such a written denial be required if there was not a common belief that Caesar was the boy's father? Oppius was also a friend of Caesar's and so may have been looking to defend his friend.

Plutarch *Life of Caesar* 49 adds little, simply commenting 'she had a son by him whom the Alexandrians called Caesarion'. It seems Caesar himself did little to acknowledge or reject the boy. As a non-Roman, Caesarion could not inherit anything from Caesar. It would have been of little political advantage for Caesar to recognise the boy.

For Cleopatra, however, the importance of Caesarion cannot be understated. It strengthened her relationship with Caesar and Rome. When Ptolemy XIV died in 44 BC, Caesarion, only three years old, was made co-ruler with Cleopatra. With his mistress and son on the throne, Caesar had full security in Egypt and could benefit fully from its resources. In return, Cleopatra had complete control of her homeland in the safety of Rome's full support.

To remind the native Egyptians of her son (and the link to Rome he provided), Cleopatra prominently promoted Caesarion. This was done on coinage (see Fig. 3.7) but most notably, this can be seen in the reliefs at the Temple of Hathor at Dendera (Fig. 3.8, see p. 165 for full comment on the reliefs). The temple, which had begun to be redesigned by Ptolemy XII Auletes, shows Caesarion as king leading an offering to the Gods. Cleopatra, as dutiful mother and Queen, stands behind her son.

KEY INDIVIDUAL
Mark Antony
Dates: 83–30 BC

A Roman politician and general who played an important role in the aftermath of Julius Caesar's death. He attempted to claim power in Rome for himself with Cleopatra but was defeated by Octavian and committed suicide in 30 BC

Study questions

1 How do you think the people of Alexandria reacted to Caesarion's birth? Explain your views.

2 How useful is the coin of Cleopatra and Caesarion as evidence of their relationship?

CLEOPATRA'S VISIT TO ROME AND HER RECEPTION

A year after Caesar's departure from Egypt, in the late summer of 46 BC, Cleopatra visited Rome with a royal party, including her husband, Ptolemy XIV, and her son, Caesarion. Around the same time in Rome, Caesar celebrated a quadruple **triumph**, celebrating his victories in Gaul, Egypt, Pontus and Africa. Arsinoe, Cleopatra's rebel sister, was included in the procession of defeated enemies but was not executed as often customary. Instead, she was sent into custody at the Temple of Artemis in Ephesus. At the festivities, Cassius Dio comments that Caesar's soldiers sang songs mocking Caesar's affair with Cleopatra. It is unclear if Cleopatra was present for the triumphs or heard such jeering but her presence seems unlikely.

Cleopatra and her party were hosted in Caesar's villa across the river Tiber and stayed for some time. Although she undoubtedly wanted to see her lover and introduce her son to his father, the purpose of the visit was primarily political. Her rule was still fully dependent on both Roman support and the Roman forces based in Alexandria. Her affair brought her the full support of Caesar but she needed a more concrete and official recognition of her power. Cleopatra and Ptolemy XIV sought this formal recognition through the courting of influential Romans. She would probably have met with Mark Antony and certainly met with Cicero who writes in *Letter to Atticus* XV.15 **PS**, to whom she promised, but failed to deliver, a gift of books. Cleopatra's appeals, combined with Caesar's influence, had the desired effect as the Senate formally recognised her and Ptolemy XIV's position as rulers and as 'friends and allies of the people of Rome', the same title her father had received in 59 BC. This meant Cleopatra's position was no longer totally dependent on her relationship with Caesar. She may have sensed the growing discontent for Caesar in Rome and so will have felt much more secure with formal recognition.

FIGURE 3.14
The Temple of Hathor at Dendera.

3.2 Cleopatra's Relationship with Julius Caesar, 48–44 BC

Despite Cleopatra's success in gaining recognition, her reception in Rome was frosty. As we have previously seen, the Romans had a number of pre-conceived ideas about foreigners and women. In the minds of most Romans, Cleopatra's visit simply confirmed these concerns. Of her stay, Cicero wrote in his *Letter to Atticus* XV.15:

> I hate the Queen. Ammonius (the one who is meant to keep her promises) knows that I have a good reason for it. What she promised, indeed, were all things of a logical type and suitable to my position…the arrogance of the Queen herself, when she was at the pleasure gardens across the river Tiber. So I won't have anything to do with that lot.
>
> Cicero, *Letters to Atticus* XV.15

One must be wary of simply accepting Cicero's account of Cleopatra's general unpopularity since he so personally disliked her. Caesar, however, was unmoved by the criticism and showered Cleopatra with gifts and honours during her visit. Suetonius *Life of Divine Julius* 52 says he 'called her to Rome and did not let her leave until he had ladened her with high honours and rich gifts'.

Her negative reception had a direct impact on Caesar himself as his association with the Queen provided further ammunition for his critics. Cassius Dio *Roman History* 43.27 discusses Caesar's growing unpopularity in Rome.

The suggestions that the greatest cause of resentment towards Caesar at this time was Cleopatra seems unlikely. Cassius Dio was writing almost 200 years after the events and so would struggle to be able to comment accurately on public opinion at the time. However, this 'censure' does agree with Cicero's own comments on the queen's unpopularity.

PRESCRIBED SOURCE

Letters to Atticus XV.15

Author: Cicero

Genre: letters – letters sent between Marcus Tullius Cicero and his friend, Atticus

Significance: A letter between prominent Romans discussing contemporary views of Cleopatra in Rome

Read it here: OCR Source Booklet

THE ASSASSINATION OF CAESAR AND ITS CONSEQUENCES FOR CLEOPATRA

Caesar left Rome in the winter of 46 BC to campaign in Spain. On his return to Rome in the autumn of 45 BC after another successful campaign, he received further public honours, including being made **dictator** for life. For the republicans of Rome, where the political system had been introduced to prevent one man from becoming too powerful, Caesar's constant rise was of grave concern. Consequently, a group of Senators, led by Marcus Junius Brutus and Gaius Cassius Longinus, assassinated Caesar on March 15 44 BC in the Theatre of Pompey.

This was a seminal moment in Rome's history. Cleopatra, who was in Rome at the time, quickly recognised that the death of her Roman guardian made her position very difficult. Cleopatra fled Rome shortly after Caesar's death. She would probably have feared for her own safety and would have understood that political turmoil and war would follow Caesar's death.

Cleopatra's visit to Rome had been of mixed success. She had received the formal recognition she required to continue to rule but had lost in Caesar her closest ally and connection to Rome. On a much more personal level, she had lost a man she loved, the father of her child. Rome would now be thrown into political chaos and Cleopatra quickly had to work out how she could best survive.

> **dictator** a magistrate appointed for six months to deal with a national emergency or crisis and in full control of the army and government during that time

179

Part Two Depth Study 2: Cleopatra: Rome and Egypt

TOPIC REVIEW

Boost your knowledge

Describe

a. how a relationship with a client-king worked
b. how Rome aided Ptolemy XII in the 50s BC
c. the key events of the civil war between Cleopatra and Ptolemy XIII
d. the first meeting between Julius Caesar and Cleopatra as told by Plutarch

Stretch your understanding

Explain:

a. why Egypt was of political and economic importance to Rome
b. how Roman viewed foreigners and why
c. how Caesar and Cleopatra's relationship had an impact on Rome and Egypt
d. why Julius Caesar chose to support Cleopatra over Ptolemy XIII

PRACTICE QUESTIONS

Passage B

But he especially loved Cleopatra. He often kept feasts with her going until dawn and he sailed with her in the state yacht through Egypt almost as far as Ethiopia – or at least would have, if his army had not refused to follow him there. He finally summoned her to the city of Rome and sent her back only when she had received the greatest honours and rewards. He allowed her to call her son by him by his own name. Certain Greek writers have reported that he was similar to Caesar in appearance and in his way of walking. Indeed M. Antonius confirmed to the senate that he had been acknowledged by him and that C. Matius and C. Oppius knew this along with the rest of Caesar's friends. Of them Oppius, on the grounds that this matter needed some explanation and defence, published a book saying that he was not Caesar's son as Cleopatra claimed. Helvius Cinna a tribune of the people admitted to several others that he had written and prepared a proposal, which Caesar had ordered to be made law while he was away.

Suetonius, *Life of Divine Julius* 52

1. Using details from Passage B, explain how accurate you think Suetonius' account of these events is? [5]
2. Explain why a relationship with Julius Caesar was beneficial for Cleopatra and Egypt. [10]

3.3 Cleopatra's Relationship with Mark Antony, 41–30 BC

> **TOPIC OVERVIEW**
>
> - Mark Antony's position in Roman politics after Caesar's death
> - Cleopatra's meeting with Mark Antony at Tarsus
> - the development of the political and personal relationship between Cleopatra and Mark Antony and its significance for both Egypt and Rome
> - the role played by Cleopatra in the breakdown of Mark Antony and Octavian's relationship, including the donations of Alexandria
>
> **The prescribed sources for this topic are:**
>
> - Plutarch, *Life of Mark Antony* 24–33, 36–37, 51, 53
> - Silver denarius of Antony and Cleopatra minted in 32, declaring Antony's conquest of Armenia and giving Cleopatra's title as 'queen of kings and of her sons who are kings'

Mark Antony and Cleopatra had a significant relationship over the years 41–30 BC. Following Caesar's death, Antony's efforts to gain power led him to seek support from allies in the East. He met with Cleopatra and the two began an affair. It was an affair advantageous for both sides. Cleopatra received the support of a hugely influential Roman while Antony could rely on the resources and wealth of Egypt for his campaigns in the East. Set alongside this was the rise of Octavian, Caesar's great-nephew and rightful heir, in Rome. Antony and Octavian came into constant conflict to the point where war became inevitable. This was particularly clear when Antony spurned his wife, Octavia, the sister of Octavian, for Cleopatra. Antony was made out to have betrayed Rome for his Egyptian family and Octavian declared war on Cleopatra.

Part Two Depth Study 2: Cleopatra: Rome and Egypt

MARK ANTONY'S POSITION IN ROMAN POLITICS AFTER CAESAR'S DEATH

Who was Mark Antony?

Caesar's death brought further chaos to Rome. On one side stood the conspirators, led by Brutus and Cassius, who believed they had restored the Republic and prevented tyranny. On the other side were Caesar's supporters and friends, shocked by the conspirators' actions and eager for revenge. The **Caesarian** supporters were led by Marcus Antonius, known in English as Mark Antony (see p. 177, Key Individual box).

Using his power as **consul**, Antony held an emotive funeral for Caesar and harnessed the late man's support from the people of Rome. The conspirators were soon forced to flee from Rome. Antony now held a very prominent position in Rome. As Consul, he was Rome's leading politician. As Caesar's deputy, he could benefit from Caesar's popular support and use his treasury to fund his own campaign and pay off his own debts.

However, Caesar's will revealed a troubling issue for Antony. Gaius Octavius, Caesar's eighteen-year-old great-nephew, was to be adopted as Caesar's son and heir. Antony's claim to be Caesar's rightful successor was now in jeopardy

Mark Antony and Octavian

With the arrival of Octavian in Rome, Antony found himself in a difficult position. Octavian demanded access to Caesar's treasury so he could pay the people of Rome the amount ordered in Caesar's will. Antony denied this as he had probably already spent the money to pay off his own debts. Octavian was young and politically inexperienced but had the name of Caesar behind him. This meant a number of soldiers, previously loyal to Julius Caesar, quickly supported Octavian. The Senate, who feared Antony's ambition, felt they could manipulate the young Octavian and so supported him. Feeling the tide turning in Rome, Antony, with his year term up as consul, went north to govern Gaul.

In Gaul, Antony waged an illegal attack on the current governor, Decimus Brutus. Octavian was sent with an army and two consuls to support Brutus. Antony was defeated at the Battle of Mutina and forced to retreat further into Gaul. Both consuls died in the battle and extraordinarily, since a consul had to be forty-two years old before he could

Caesarian supporters of Julius Caesar

FIGURE 3.15
Bust of Mark Antony, currently in the Vatican Museum.

Study questions

1 What problems did Antony face in the days after Caesar's death?
2 How do you think Cleopatra would have viewed the activity in Rome after Caesar's death? Explain your views.

KEY INDIVIDUAL

Gaius Octavius 'Octavian'
Dates: 63 BC–AD 14

Octavian was the great-nephew and heir of Julius Caesar. After defeating Caesar's assassins, Octavian shared power with Antony and Lepidus until 31 BC when he defeated Antony and Cleopatra's at the Battle of Actium. He later received the name of 'Augustus' from the Senate and ruled Rome in the position we now know as 'Emperor' be elected, the empty consulship was granted to the nineteen-year-old Octavian in August 43 BC.

It was at this stage that Octavian met with Antony and Marcus Lepidus, who controlled an army in Trans-Alpine Gaul, agreed to share power as the **Second Triumvirate**. Unlike the first triumvirate, which was an unofficial pact between three powerful men, Julius Caesar, Marcus Crassus and Pompey this Great, this was a constitutionally formed agreement which gave the three men official power over all others, including the Senate and consuls. The powers would last for five years. Antony, who had been at the brink of failure, had managed to secure power for himself again.

The triumvirs could now set out to avenge Caesar's death. By October 42 BC, the conspirators had been defeated in Greece in two battles at Philippi. Brutus and Cassius had both committed suicide. Now in full control, the triumvirate reorganised their control. Lepidus, who was rapidly losing power, was given Africa, while Antony received the Eastern provinces and Octavian the West. Antony marched through Greece to reorganise the east and begin planning his next moves. There was undoubtedly still tension between Octavian and Antony but, with the defeat of Caesar's assassins and the separation of the two men, peace reigned for a while. Antony had not achieved all he had wanted but he had recovered from his defeat at Mutina. He now had an excellent opportunity to strengthen his political position through a series of successful and lucrative campaigns in the East.

> **Second Triumvirate** the political alliance of Antony, Octavian and Lepidus in 43 BC

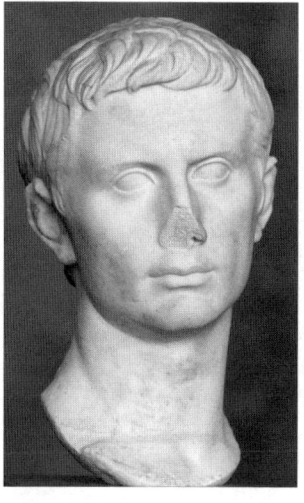

FIGURE 3.16
A youthful portrait bust of Octavian/Augustus.

Cleopatra 44–41 BC

The uncertainty of Rome's political situation left Cleopatra in a difficult position. She left Rome shortly after Caesar's death. She understood that she needed to stabilise and affirm her own power in Egypt. In the summer of 44 BC, Ptolemy XIV died of unknown causes. Cleopatra has been linked with playing a part in the boy's death but there is no evidence to confirm this. Caesarion, aged only three, was proclaimed co-ruler as Ptolemy XV soon after (see p. 177 for birth of Caesarion). This gave Cleopatra full dynastic control. Her only family opposition was now her sister, Arsinoe, alive but in custody at the Temple of Ephesus. Little is known about Cleopatra's next few years but poor harvests from 43–41 BC meant she had to work hard to keep the people happy. It was important she maintained good trade links and ensured that the agricultural system was efficiently managed. At this point, she particularly promoted her association with the goddess Isis (see p. 163).

Cleopatra kept one eye on the situation in Rome. She sent soldiers to the aid of Caesar's supporters. She even led a squadron of warships in person to meet the triumvirs but bad weather forced a retreat home. Cassius, one of the conspirators, had tried to gain her support and requested grain and money from Cleopatra. She had managed to hold off from meeting his demands. The victory of Octavian and Antony vindicated Cleopatra's decision not to help the conspirators. This put her in a good position to continue to gain support from Rome. She now had to choose whether to approach Octavian or Antony in order to ensure her own security.

> **ACTIVITY**
>
> Create a flow chart comparing the different fortunes of Antony and Octavian after the assassination of Julius Caesar.

> **Study questions**
>
> 1 How do you think would Cleopatra have viewed these events in Rome? Explain your views.
> 2 Do you think Antony's political position was stronger or weaker in 42 BC than in 44 BC?

FIGURE 3.17
Cleopatra presents offerings to Isis on this stela.

EXPLORE FURTHER

For an entertaining, accessible but thorough overview of this period, read Tom Holland's *Rubicon: The Triumph and Tragedy of the Roman Republic* (London: Abacus, 2004)

CLEOPATRA'S MEETING WITH MARK ANTONY AT TARSUS

Antony spent the winter of 42 BC in Athens, enjoying himself and preparing for his excursion further east. He quickly endeared himself to the Athenian people as he took part in Athenian religious customs and adopted Greek styles of dress. Antony had a playful personality and enjoyed the finer things in life. This would be an element of his character which would draw him to the wealth of Egypt but was also scorned by more-traditional Romans.

As mentioned earlier, Plutarch's *Parallel Lives* series of biographies sought to compare a famous Greek with a famous Roman. Plutarch's *Life of Mark Antony*, the longest of our prescribed sources, was paired with the *Life of Demetrius*, the former King of Macedonia, who was of a similar temperament to Antony and both brought down by their love for luxury. This moralising by Plutarch is important for readers to be aware of when assessing how accurate a portrait of Antony and Cleopatra we can find in his work. Plutarch tries to create a character in Antony who gives into vice and temptation too easily. It acts as an example not to follow for anyone in power. This is particularly clear in Plutarch *Life of Mark Antony* 24 (PS) as Plutarch contrasts the position of Antony and Octavian in the winter of 42 BC where Octavian has been worn down by trouble in Rome whereas Antony has enjoyed his winter at leisure.

We must be wary here of Plutarch's efforts to paint a negative picture of Antony. This direct comparison of the two men, emphasised by how the coverage of Antony is twice the length as that of Octavian, was designed to vilify Antony.

Antony moved to Ephesus in the spring of 41 BC and stories abound of his grand entry into the city, dressed as a great Hellenistic king. The people of the area readily accepted Antony as a god. This was common practice in Hellenistic areas (see Stretch and Challenge box). However, it was a practice abhorred in Rome. Antony's luxury and extravagance is a constant feature of the pro-Roman sources designed to tarnish his reputation.

To find further revenue for his campaigns, Antony turned to the wealth of Egypt. He would have been well-aware of Cleopatra's history with Caesar and would have met her numerous times. A positive relationship would be beneficial for both sides. Antony, now based in Tarsus in Cilicia, sent a messenger, Dellius, to summon Cleopatra to him. According to Plutarch *Life of Mark Antony* 25 (PS), Dellius quickly 'understood her cunning and cleverness in conversation' and believed she would be able to influence Antony easily. Cleopatra agreed to travel and Plutarch believes her intention to win over Antony were clear from that moment.

> **S&C** Praising men as gods was common practice in Hellenistic nations. An example from the Bible highlights this. In Acts 14.12, the apostles Paul and Barnabas are proclaimed as Hermes and Zeus by the Ephesians.

PRESCRIBED SOURCE

Life of Mark Antony

Author: Plutarch (AD 40–120)

Prescribed chapters: 24–33, 36–37, 51, 53

Date: AD 75

Genre: biography (biographical lives of famous Greeks and Romans told in pairs)

Significance: A biographical view of how the relationship between Antony and Cleopatra developed

Read it here: OCR Source Booklet

FIGURE 3.18
Mark Antony enters Ephesus dressed as a Hellenistic king in this eighteenth-century painting by Natoire.

Part Two Depth Study 2: Cleopatra: Rome and Egypt

> **Study questions**
>
> 1 How reliable is the account of Cleopatra's preparations for visiting Antony in *Life of Mark Antony* 25?
> 2 What can you learn about Egypt from this passage?
> 3 What can you learn about Cleopatra's qualities as a leader from these events?

> **ACTIVITY**
>
> Read Plutarch *Life of Mark Antony* 24 (PS) and:
>
> - Find examples of Antony's treatment of provincial leaders. What can you conclude as to how Antony manged client-kings?
> - If you were a Roman citizen in Rome and heard such stories, what would you think of:
>   ○ Antony
>   ○ Octavian

> **ACTIVITY**
>
> Read Plutarch *Life of Mark Antony* 26 (PS) and from the details given, draw Cleopatra's boat and label it appropriately

The description of Cleopatra's arrival to Tarsus in Plutarch's *Life of Mark Antony* 26 (PS) is magnificent. It rivalled Antony's own grand entry into Ephesus. Cleopatra arrived on one of her huge boats, a pleasure boat of the grandest proportions. Plutarch tells us that she was dressed to look like Aphrodite. Her arrival quickly drew large crowds away from the city and to the shores of the river Cydnus. In a rather amusing tale, we are even told that Antony, who was in the market receiving guests, was soon the only person left there as all others had gone to see the queen's arrival. Antony sent an invitation to the queen to join him for dinner, but she declined. Instead, she invited Antony to her boat for a show of Alexandrian wealth at its finest. Antony accepted and was hosted to a magnificent spectacle.

Antony and Cleopatra spent time together in Tarsus. Plutarch's *Life of Mark Antony* 27 (PS) discusses Cleopatra's charm and it is clear from Plutarch's description that he believed Cleopatra was seducing Antony. In *Life of Mark Antony* 28 (PS), Plutarch comments how Cleopatra's charm won him over. Antony was taken aback, not so much by the queen's beauty, but her beauty combined with her wit and intellect. The pair soon became lovers. However, business was also achieved as Cleopatra successfully persuaded Antony to remove her final obstacle to total power – her sister, Arsinoe. Antony had Arsinoe executed and supported Cleopatra in power in return for her resources and financial support for his Parthian expedition. For the triumvir and the Queen, it was a mutually beneficial affair.

EXAM TIP: SOURCE ANALYSIS

We must be aware that Plutarch's narrative here fits the typically negative Roman view of Cleopatra and Antony. Cleopatra as a glamorous and charismatic temptress flaunting great luxury while the naïve Antony easily succumbs to her charms and his pursuit of luxury. Her arrival was undoubtedly splendid, but the representation of Antony as so naïve and weak to instantly fall in love and blindly pursue Cleopatra is an unfair representation of such an accomplished man. On the other side, it is unfair to view Cleopatra as using her wealth simply for seductive means. Grand arrivals and extravagant shows of wealth were a very common form of Ptolemaic display.

THE DEVELOPMENT OF THE POLITICAL AND PERSONAL RELATIONSHIP BETWEEN CLEOPATRA AND MARK ANTONY AND ITS SIGNIFICANCE FOR BOTH EGYPT AND ROME

Winter in Alexandria 41–40 BC

Antony spent the winter of 41–40 BC in Alexandria with Cleopatra. Plutarch in *Life of Mark Antony* 28 PS, continuing his negative and moralising view of Antony, claims that Antony 'let himself be carried off by [Cleopatra] to Alexandria'. He continues his negativity to say that Antony and Cleopatra spent that winter at grand leisure. In this section, Plutarch reveals one of his sources, Philotas, a doctor who knew one of Cleopatra's cooks and had passed on stories to Plutarch's grandfather. Sections 28 and 29 are filled with anecdotes of Cleopatra and Antony's enjoyable winter, playing amusing games among the citizens of Alexandria. They provide very human portraits of the two characters but we must question how Plutarch knew the ins and outs of their intimate lives and whether these stories were simply added from rumour to aid his desired characterisation.

Perusine War

While Antony was in Alexandria, the Parthians had made serious advances in the East and forced Antony to leave Alexandria. Antony found out that Octavian's support had grown in Rome. However, he was not yet universally popular. He had allowed Sextus Pompeius, the son of Pompey the Great, to take control of the Mediterranean Sea. Many living in the country were angry at the loss of their land to Caesar's resettled veterans. Lucius Antonius, Antony's brother and **consul** for 40 BC, moved on this unpopularity to try to unseat Octavian. With the help of Antony's wife, Fulvia, Lucius raised a substantial army but was soon blockaded in the town of Perusia and forced to surrender. Lucius' life was spared and Fulvia fled to meet with Antony but died of illness on the way. Antony was forced to turn away from the East and head back to Italy to sort out the situation. The impact of the relationship between Cleopatra and Antony may have forced Fulvia to act in an effort to regain the affection of her husband. This was significant for Rome as it highlighted the growing tension between Antony and Octavian and the wedge Cleopatra was driving between Antony and Rome.

The triumvirs met in Brundisium in autumn of 40 BC to adjust their agreement. Plutarch writes of the events which followed:

> Instead they made peace between them and divided up the leadership of the Empire, drawing a boundary with the Ionian Sea and giving to Antony the East, and to Octavian the West; Lepidus was allowed to have Africa.
>
> Plutarch, *Life of Mark Antony* 30

To create an even stronger bond between Octavian and Antony, it was decided that Antony marry Octavian's recently widowed sister, Octavia. She was a noble and respected woman in Rome and had formerly been married to the consul, Marcellus. It was a

Study questions

1. Why did Octavian not blame Antony for the Perusine War? Explain your views.
2. Why did Antony marry Octavia and not Cleopatra?
3. What would Cleopatra have thought of Antony's marriage? Explain your views.

political marriage but Antony was still expected to treat his wife with respect. Meanwhile, in Alexandria, Cleopatra had just given birth to twins, a son and a daughter. As we will come to see, Antony's marriage to Octavia was a pivotal moment. It made the bonds between Antony and Octavian no longer just political but personal. Mistreatment of Octavia would be a serious personal affront to Octavian. The impact of Cleopatra and Antony's relationship could now have significant consequences for Rome and Egypt. Plutarch in *Life of Mark Antony* 31 **PS** gives an account of the marriage. He paints a very positive picture of Octavia. This is designed to make the reader feel more sympathy for her when she is abandoned and display Antony as once again ignoring reason for lust.

The marriage signalled a new peace for Rome. Octavian and Antony's relationship had been temporarily reconciled. The two men now looked to sort out the lingering issue of Sextus Pompey's control of the Mediterranean. They met with Sextus at Misenum in the spring of 39 BC and agreed to allow Sextus to hold Sardinia and Sicily, in return for keeping the sea free of pirates and sending a certain amount of grain to Rome. Plutarch *Life of Mark Antony* 32 **PS** outlines the deal and their meeting.

In the summer of 37 BC, Antony, Octavia and Octavian met at Tarentum to discuss their next moves. Sextus had quickly broken the agreement made at Misenum and Octavian required further forces to attack him. After long negotiations, the Treaty of Tarentum was put into place.

Study question

Read Plutarch *Life of Mark Antony* 33 **PS**

What does this passage reveal about Antony's character? Explain your views.

The terms of this treaty were as follows:

- extended the power of the triumvirs for a further five years
- Antony's son was to be married to Octavian's daughter
- Antony was to receive a significant number of additional soldiers for his Parthian campaign
- Octavian would receive 120 ships from Antony to help him finally defeat Sextus Pompey.

ACTIVITY

Create a timeline charting the key events from the creation of the Second Triumvirate in 43 BC to the Treaty of Tarentum in 37

Antony promptly handed over the ships but the legions owed to him were delayed. This treaty, which according to Plutarch was all brought together by Octavia's efforts, again tied the two men closer but also gave each other the resources to win their respective wars. Antony sailed back East as he proceeded to Antioch to await the arrival of Octavian's troops over the winter.

With the backing of Antony and Rome, Cleopatra had been ruling over Egypt from 41 BC to 37 BC. Her relationship with Antony provided security for her rule. This allowed her to focus on running her country and promoting herself as queen.

Antony now summoned Cleopatra to Antioch to winter with him. This was not an act simply driven by his desire to see his lover but also had a political motive. She could provide grain, money and a fleet for his campaign into Parthia. Once again, Plutarch's account of his summoning of Cleopatra is tarnished by his negative view of Antony:

> Now the disastrous flaw in his character, asleep for so long, – his passion for Cleopatra – flared up again all the greater as he approached Syria; they had imagined it had been charmed away and lulled to rest by common sense and good reasons.
>
> Plutarch, *Life of Mark Antony* 36

In return for her help, Cleopatra asked for old Ptolemaic kingdoms to be returned to her power. Antony agreed and so a number of Eastern kingdoms were added to Egyptian power. Plutarch *Life of Mark Antony* 36 **PS** outlines the full list of additions. This was a hugely significant increase in land and useful resources not found in abundance in Egypt.

These gifts were consistent with Mark Antony's other acts of generosity and reorganisation in the East. Cleopatra was a loyal ally to Rome and may have been rewarded for her loyalty. She was also seen as a competent ruler and so it was to Rome's benefit to have her ruling over extra lands. However, her relationship with Antony would have had an impact on the amount of land she was rewarded. The two became lovers once again and Antony officially recognised his two children with Cleopatra, Alexander Helios (of the Sun) and Cleopatra Selene II (of the Moon), as his own, an act which annoyed most Romans more than the gift of land. Antony had no reason to acknowledge these children since they were born to a foreigner and so we are to left wonder what he had to gain from doing so. Cleopatra, on the other hand, returned to Egypt in triumph, proclaiming it as a new era for Egypt, even adjusting the calendar to reflect this and taking new titles.

The relationship between Cleopatra and Antony had far-reaching significance for both Egypt and Rome. For Rome, it was significant because:

- **Resources of Egypt** – Antony's relationship with Cleopatra maintained Rome's control over the rich resources of Egypt. He could not only line his own pocket with Egypt's wealth but also maintain a good supply of grain to Rome ensuring the support of the Roman population.
- **Impact on Antony's reputation** – The relationship had a negative impact on Antony's reputation in Rome and caused resentment with more traditional Romans. Since Octavian was based in the city, he could manipulate public perception of their relationship as he wished.
- **Octavia** – Antony's marriage with Octavia presented a dangerous obstacle for his relationship with Cleopatra. If he treated Octavia poorly by continuing his affair, Antony would run the risk of personally embarrassing Octavian. This could create a trigger for war.
- **Loss of land** – Antony's generosity towards Cleopatra and Egypt had resulted in more land being placed in her possession. This could potentially backfire if Cleopatra were to use these lands to strengthen her own position at the expense of Rome.

For Egypt, it was significant because:

- **Dynastic security** – Just as with Julius Caesar, Antony's relationship with Cleopatra provided the queen with security and support for her rule. She was able to use Antony to ensure the execution of her only possibly dynastic threat, her sister Arsinoe. By elevating Caesarion to power alongside her, Cleopatra could now rule without fear of opposition.
- **Support to rule** – Through the security gained from her relationship with Antony, Cleopatra could spend the years when Antony was absent on ruling her

> **ACTIVITY**
>
> Divide into groups and debate:
>   Was the relationship of Antony and Cleopatra more significant to Egypt or to Rome?

own country and ensuring its prosperity. For a number of years, it had been rare for a Ptolemaic leader to be able to rule without fear of opposition. Cleopatra could use this security to better her nation and win the support of her subjects.

- **No interference from Rome** – Cleopatra's relationship with Antony created a level of trust between Rome and Egypt. For the first time in a long time, Egypt could operate without Roman interference. It still had to offer its resources to Rome but there was no political meddling.
- **Expansion** – The additional land gained in 37 BC from Antony extended Egypt's powerbase. It was a boost for Egypt as it returned to its former strength.

THE ROLE PLAYED BY CLEOPATRA IN THE BREAKDOWN OF MARK ANTONY AND OCTAVIAN'S RELATIONSHIP, INCLUDING THE DONATIONS OF ALEXANDRIA

Antony headed into Parthia in 36 BC and was initially successful with his joint-Roman and Egyptian army. However, the campaign soon turned into a disaster and Antony lost up to 30,000 men. This was hugely damaging for his reputation. Leaving his army in Armenia, he returned to Syria in the winter of 36 BC to await help and resources from Cleopatra. In the town of Leuke Come, 'the White Village', he desperately awaited Cleopatra's arrival. Plutarch's depiction of Antony now takes a particularly negative turn. He portrays the general turning to drink to relieve the pain of defeat and his desperate longing for Cleopatra in Plutarch *Life of Mark Antony* 51 **PS**.

Antony had now been away from Octavia for well over a year and it appears that by this stage she was but an afterthought. Antony needed Cleopatra, not simply for her resources but also for her company. It had been a disastrous campaign for Antony, emotionally and physically. Cleopatra, who had recently had her third child with Antony, Ptolemy Philadelphus, provided a distraction from this disappointment. Her security lay in the support of Antony and so she needed him to rebound, and quickly.

> **EXPLORE FURTHER**
>
> Find out more about Rome, Parthia and Crassus' lost Eagles by researching the Battle of Carrhae

Meanwhile, Octavian had successfully defeated Sextus Pompey. He also pushed Lepidus out of the triumvirate. His victory, though an easier undertaking than Antony's, stood in stark contrast to Antony's defeat. Octavian continued to manoeuvre himself into a strong position.

In the spring of 35 BC, Octavia travelled to Athens with an armed force and a substantial amount of resources to try to aid her husband. Plutarch claims Octavian only allowed her to go so that if she was ignored or mistreated by Antony, it would give Octavian the excuse for war he was looking for. If one considers the level of Octavian's political manoeuvring, Plutarch's assumption seems a fair one but we do not know for sure. Antony wrote to Octavia to tell her to remain in Athens and Octavia, although upset, offered to send her reinforcements to him.

To prevent Antony from leaving her, Cleopatra is said to have pretended to love Antony, ignore food, constantly embrace him when he was nearby and burst into tears in his absence. At the same time, her attendants shamed Octavia and promoted Cleopatra's love. The level of truth in all of this is for the reader to decide. It is likely that after bearing three children Cleopatra did love Antony. However, the theatrical side of Cleopatra's character, first seen in her meeting with Julius Caesar, would make such a display likely. She had identified Octavia as a threat to her power and so did all she could to ensure Antony would stay with her and neglect his wife. Her toying with Antony had the desired effect:

> At last they melted and unmanned Antony so much that he was afraid that Cleopatra would kill herself, and so went back to Alexandria.
>
> Plutarch, *Life of Mark Antony* 53

The use of 'unmanned' here is particularly strong as Plutarch continues to build the image of the weak Antony overcome by feminine charm and guile. In reality, in Egypt, he could regroup, enjoy himself and consider his next steps. Octavia returned to Rome, where her brother suggested she divorce her husband. Octavia, always depicted in sources as a loyal wife, refused and continued to support Antony from Rome.

Study question

From 35 BC, how do the sources present Cleopatra and Antony's relationship turning negative and self-destructive? Explain your view

The Donations of Alexandria 34 BC

Antony proceeded to Alexandria with Cleopatra, breaking off all relations with Octavia. At the start of 34 BC, Antony had success in Armenia and returned to Alexandria to celebrate. Antony entered the city in great pomp dressed as the god Dionysus in a grand procession. It mirrored closely a Roman **triumph** and many Romans considered it to be a disrespectful imitation. A triumph could only take place in the city of Rome as celebration of a victory for Rome and as a sacrifice to Jupiter Optimus Maximus. Whether Antony meant this disrespect is up for debate, but one must remember that he had made very similar grand and festive entries into cities before.

FIGURE 3.19
Silver denarius of Antony and Cleopatra minted in 32, declaring Antony's conquest of Armenia and giving Cleopatra's title as 'queen of kings and of her sons who are kings' (British Museum).

PRESCRIBED SOURCE

Coin (denarius) of Antony and Cleopatra

Minted by: Antony

Obverse: Cleopatra in diadem with her title as 'queen of kings and of her sons who are Kings'

Reverse: Antony with inscription 'For Antony, Armenia vanquished'

Significance: we can see here that by 32 BC Antony wished to be viewed as ruling in tandem with Cleopatra. Her title gained at the Donations of Alexandria is used on the coin and Antony celebrates his only major campaign victory

View it here: OCR Source Booklet and Figure 3.19

> **Study questions**
>
> 1 Why do you think Antony chose the support of Cleopatra over Octavia? Explain your views.
> 2 What did Antony hope to achieve with the Donations of Alexandria?

A few days later, an important event occurred which became known as the Donations of Alexandria (see Fig. 3.3). Antony called together a great crowd in the gymnasium of Alexandria. Cleopatra, dressed as the goddess Isis, sat alongside Antony on golden thrones, with their children on thrones as well. Plutarch reveals what Antony did next:

> First he announced that Cleopatra was Queen of Egypt, Cyprus, Libya, and Coele Syria, and that Caesarion was to rule with her. Caesarion was considered to be a son of Julius Caesar, who had made Cleopatra pregnant. Secondly he said that his sons by Cleopatra were to be named Kings of Kings, and to Alexander he gave Armenia, Media and Parthia (once it was conquered); to Ptolemy he gave Phoenicia, Syria, and Cilicia.
>
> Plutarch, *Life of Mark Antony* 54

It was a big move by Antony, splitting up an empire and refiguring the Ptolemaic empire with Roman land for his future heirs to run. It was all a great show and it infuriated Octavian. Threatened by the legitimisation of Caesarion, Octavian now began to speak out publicly against Antony. It is important to remember that the basis of Antony's power was his Roman triumviral power, yet he now acted like a foreign conqueror and king. The Donations of Alexandria signalled the change of Antony's attitude, no longer content to share power but eager to establish himself and his descendants as the basis for a new Ptolemaic order in the East.

TOPIC REVIEW

Boost your knowledge

Describe:

- Mark Antony's position in Roman politics following the assassination of Julius Caesar
- how Octavian became involved in the aftermath of Julius Caesar's death
- the meeting of Antony and Cleopatra at Tarsus
- the events now known as the Donations of Alexandria

Stretch your understanding

Explain:

- why Mark Antony met with Cleopatra in Tarsus
- how the relationship of Antony and Cleopatra was significant for Egypt
- why the marriage between Antony and Octavian was significant in the breakdown of relations between Antony and Octavian
- why the Donations of Alexandria were viewed poorly in Rome

PRACTICE QUESTIONS

1. a. Name **two** of the three men who formed the Second Triumvirate. [2]
   b. Where did Cleopatra go to meet Antony in 37 BC? [1]
   c. Name **two** territories awarded by Mark Antony in the Donations of Alexandria. [2]
2. 'Antony's relationship with Cleopatra was driven solely by ambition, not love.' To what extent do you agree with this view?

   You must use and analyse the ancient sources you have studied as well as supporting your answer with your own knowledge. [20]

3.4 The Battle of Actium and its Significance for Egypt and Rome

> **TOPIC OVERVIEW**
>
> - causes of the war between Octavian and Antony/Cleopatra
> - preparations for the battle
> - key events of the battle, including the roles of Octavian, Agrippa, Mark Antony and Cleopatra
> - different views of the battle in the sources
> - the outcome and the reasons for it as described by the sources
> - impact of the battle on Cleopatra's and Antony's careers
> - Mark Antony's suicide
> - the method of Cleopatra's suicide and reasons for her actions
> - the significance of the suicides for Octavian
>
> **The prescribed sources for this topic are:**
>
> - Plutarch *Life of Mark Antony* 55–69; 72–79; 81–86
> - Velleius Paterculus, The Roman History, 2.82–87
> - Horace, Odes, 1.37
> - Virgil, *Aeneid*, 8.675–731

The Battle of Actium was the critical battle between Mark Antony alongside Cleopatra and Octavian. It was a naval battle that took place on the western coast of Greece. The battle was closely fought until Cleopatra and her sixty Egyptian warships fled from the battle. Mark Antony immediately followed leaving his army and reputation in tatters. Octavian pursued Antony and Cleopatra to Alexandria. Mark Antony and Cleopatra, in the face of certain defeat, both committed suicide. This left Octavian to become the most powerful man in the world as the first Roman emperor, Augustus. In Rome, the Battle of Actium became a central part of Augustus' propaganda and Roman poets presented the battle in a variety of ways.

CAUSES OF THE WAR BETWEEN OCTAVIAN AND ANTONY/CLEOPATRA

1. **Antony's treatment of Octavia** – Antony snubbed Octavia's attempt to bring him aid and resumed his affair with Cleopatra. This insulted Octavian and effectively positioned Egypt against Rome. According to Plutarch, *Life of Mark Antony* 57 (PS), Antony evicted Octavia and her children from her house in Athens. Octavia wept as she left, fearing she would be the cause of war.

2. **The Donations of Alexandria** (see p. 191) – Octavian wasted no time in capitalising on Antony's acts in 34 BC. The donations were explained in Rome as a weak Antony betraying his Roman roots, giving away Roman land to his foreign family at Cleopatra's command.

3. **Political slander and propaganda** (Plutarch, *Life of Mark Antony* 55–56; 58–59 (PS)) Octavian and Antony constantly accused each other of wrong-doing and insulted one another with lies. The propaganda war was fierce. Plutarch reveals his opinion in *Life of Mark Antony* 59 (PS) that most of the charges were generally believed to be made up.

4. **Antony's will, 32 BC** (Plutarch, *Life of Mark Antony* 58–59 (PS)) – Concerned about the rate Antony and Cleopatra were amassing their forces, Octavian had to act quickly. Two of Antony's supporters deserted him and revealed to Octavian the supposed contents of Antony's will which had been left in Rome. Octavian seized the will and read its contents. Many Romans regarded this illegal act as a disgrace. According to the will, Antony was to be buried in Alexandria and Caesarion recognised as Caesar's heir. The terms of the will outraged many in Rome.

5. **Cleopatra's image in Rome** (Plutarch, *Life of Mark Antony* 58 (PS)) – Octavian made Cleopatra the focus of his propaganda campaign. He convinced the people that she was to blame for Antony's downfall. She came to be seen as a sorceress who ruled Antony with magic and sexual desire. We do not know of the exact impact of these rumours so must judge for ourselves how much they may have been believed. Octavian could now declare war on a foreign queen rather than a fellow Roman.

6. **Political ambition of Antony and Octavian** – Was war between Antony and Octavian inevitable? Both men strived for absolute power. They were not going to be content to share it. From the moment of Octavian's arrival in Rome after Caesar's death, the two men were rivals. It was simply a matter of time before the rivalry between them had to be resolved through war.

> **ACTIVITY**
>
> What do you think was the most important cause in the start of war between Octavian and Antony/Cleopatra? Rank the causes in order of importance.

In 32 BC, the Roman Senate branded Cleopatra a public enemy and declared war on Egypt. Antony was not named but was implicated in the war because of his continued support of Cleopatra. Octavian's propaganda had worked. He now had to prepare for the decisive conflict publicised as Octavian and Rome versus Cleopatra and Egypt.

Part Two Depth Study 2: Cleopatra: Rome and Egypt

> **Study questions**
> Read Plutarch, *Life of Mark Antony* 60 **PS** and answer the following questions:
> 1 Why does Plutarch include the stories of the omen in his account?
> 2 What effect does the inclusion of omens in his account have on our judgement of Plutarch as an historian?

EXAM TIP: ASSESSING THE SOURCES FOR THE BATTLE OF ACTIUM

There are a range of sources available for the preparations and events of the Battle of Actium, the key battle in the war between Antony and Octavian. However, a number of sources written by authors alive at the time need to be approached with caution. As the famous adage goes, 'history is written by the victors' and so authors writing under Octavian's rule presented Octavian in a favourable light. It should also be noted that in 27 BC, three years after his victory, Octavian was given the name 'Augustus' as the first Emperor of Rome. Any reference to Augustus is referring to Octavian. In these sources, the portraits of Antony and Cleopatra fit Octavian's propaganda campaign. Cleopatra is depicted as the enchanting, foreign temptress controlling the weak Antony. We must, therefore, use these sources carefully and they will be examined in the section 'Different views of the battle in the sources'.

PREPARATIONS FOR THE BATTLE

> **PRESCRIBED SOURCE**
>
> **Life of Mark Antony**
>
> **Author:** Plutarch (AD 40–120)
>
> **Prescribed chapters:** 55–69
>
> **Date:** 75 AD
>
> **Genre:** biography (biographical lives of famous Greek and Romans told in pairs)
>
> **Significance:** These sections cover in some detail pre-battle manoeuvres and actions of the Battle of Actium
>
> **Read it here:** OCR Source Booklet

The two sides quickly assembled their armies. Plutarch *Life of Mark Antony* 61 **PS** suggests Antony and Cleopatra had a force of 500,000 ships, 100,000 infantrymen and 12,000 cavalrymen. Octavian had mustered 250 warships, 80,000 infantrymen and a similar amount of cavalrymen to Antony. Military numbers are often inflated and inaccurate in ancient sources, but it is clear from the composition of these armies that war at both land and sea was expected.

Plutarch wrote of Antony's chosen tactic:

> Antony now had become so controlled by Cleopatra that, although he was far stronger on land, he wanted to win his victory at sea, all for the sake of Cleopatra
>
> Plutarch, *Life of Mark Antony* 62

Octavian's forces, ably led by his close friend and able admiral Marcus Agrippa, left their base on the Italian coast in early 31 BC and took the southern Greek coastal town of Methone. From this point, they advanced north and took several towns on the coast line, surprising Antony by striking from the south rather than the north as he expected. In response to this movement, Antony readied his fleet in the mouth of the gulf at Actium. Agrippa continued to have success. He captured a number of key towns and cut off supplies to Antony's camp. Antony was blockaded and Octavian now had the upper hand.

In Antony's camp, food went short, illness spread and morale rapidly dropped as the rate of desertion increased. There were a number of small attempts to break out on land with minimal success for both sides. Some kings now deserted Antony for Octavian (Plutarch *Life of Mark Antony* 63 **PS**) and the leader of Antony's land army pleaded with his commander to retreat and move the fight to land, not sea. His argument, if we are to believe Plutarch, was persuasive.

3.4 The Battle of Actium and its Significance for Egypt and Rome

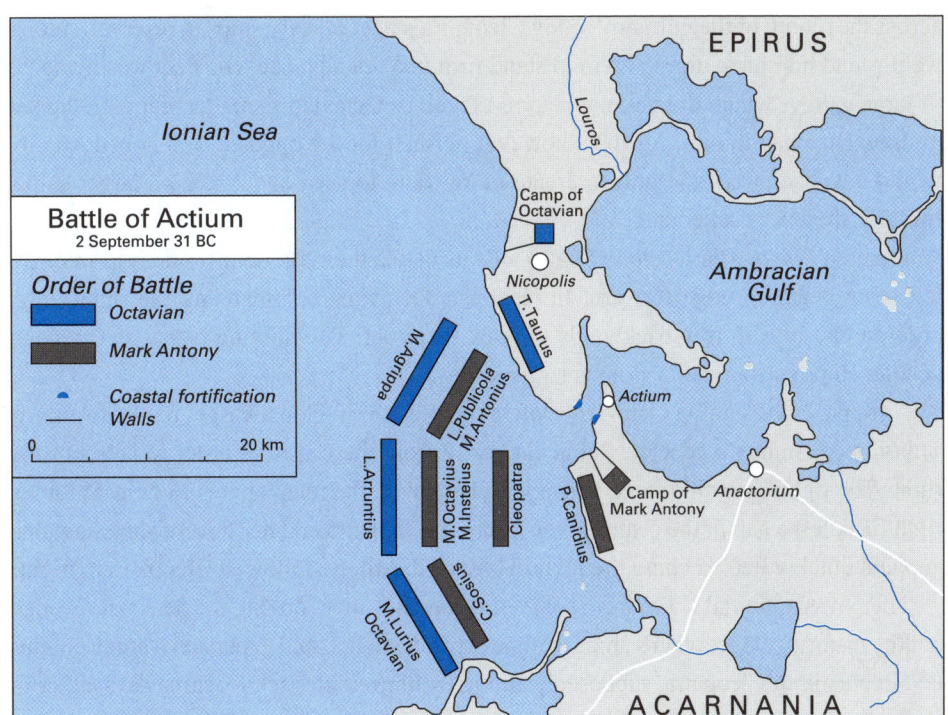

FIGURE 3.20
Initial deployment of troops at Actium.

However, Cleopatra, who Plutarch claims was already planning her retreat from battle, won the argument and Antony was resolved to fight his way out of the blockade by sea. Antony probably now realised that his best bet was to cut his losses, retreat to Alexandria, regroup and then bring a fresh attack to Octavian. In a tactical but desperate move, he burnt all the ships he could no longer crew and prepared his forces for battle. Plutarch *Life of Mark Antony* 64 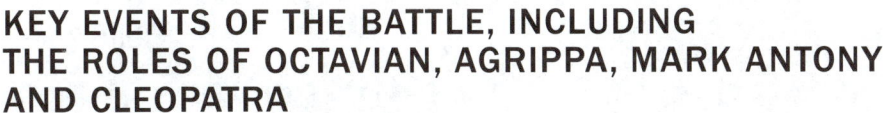 highlights Antony's prospects heading into battle:

> That he had little hope himself is shown by the fact that, when his captain wanted to leave their sails behind, he forced them to put them on the ships and take them with them, saying that they must not give any fugitive from the enemy a chance to escape.
>
> Plutarch, *Life of Mark Antony* 64

The sails had been removed as the ships in battle would be propelled by oarsmen; they would only need the sails hoisting if a longer journey, such as a retreat to Alexandria, was planned! This story, which also appears in Cassius Dio's account, reveals Antony may have gone into the battle with one eye always on his retreat. This is important as it highlights how the corrupted view of Antony's cowardice may simply be a Roman invention.

KEY EVENTS OF THE BATTLE, INCLUDING THE ROLES OF OCTAVIAN, AGRIPPA, MARK ANTONY AND CLEOPATRA

On the 2 September 31 BC, the battle took place. Antony led his ships out of the gulf and formed his navy up opposite Octavian's. Antony's forces were spread in three sections across the mouth of the gulf, protecting Cleopatra's fleet of sixty ships in reserve. Antony went round his ships, urging them to stand firm and not advance. His fleet was made up of large galleys which did not manoeuvre as well as Octavian's smaller ships. He hoped to draw Octavian to him. Agrippa, however, wished for the opposite and hoped Antony would advance out of the gulf to create more room to surround Antony's larger ships. Initially, there was stalemate.

Plutarch *Life of Mark Antony* 66 **PS** tells us that at the sixth hour (midday), Antony's left wing began to edge forward. In response, Octavian, commanding the right wing, ordered his ships to row backwards to draw them out. The fighting began as Octavian smaller ships surrounded Antony's larger galleys.

Agrippa, commanding Octavian's left, attempted to envelop the right flank of Antony. This forced Antony's general, Publicola, away from the centre in order to help out the right. The fighting at this stage was equal. However, the manoeuvres to help Antony's right flank left a gap in the centre of the fighting. Cleopatra and her fleet of ships saw this gap and quickly fled catching the favourable wind. Antony followed Cleopatra in flight.

There was an initial chase from some of Octavian's men looking for personal revenge but the majority of Octavian's ships, without sails, were not able to pursue. Antony continued in pursuit of Cleopatra, supposedly sitting by himself on deck for three days either in shame or anger. A number of ships escaped with Antony but the majority of his fleet were left fighting. The remaining fleet, leaderless and faced with a now high sea and high wind, surrendered at 4 p.m. and Plutarch, *Life of Mark Antony* 68 **PS** reveals no more than 5,000 were dead (although he does not mention if that is a total number of one side) and 300 ships were captured. Octavian burnt the remainder of Antony's fleet. Antony's land army of nineteen legions was shocked by their leader's flight and soon deserted.

ACTIVITY
Write a report in the style of a newspaper article reporting the events of the Battle of Actium

Study questions
Read Plutarch *Life of Mark Antony* 66–67 **PS**

1. In *Life of Mark Antony* 66, how does Plutarch present Antony's character?
2. Outline the details of Antony's pursuit of Cleopatra

FIGURE 3.21
This nineteenth-century engraving depicts an imagined Roman naval battle.

DIFFERENT VIEWS OF THE BATTLE IN THE SOURCES

The Roman narrative of the Battle of Actium is consistently presented across the sources. We must decide ourselves whether the amount of different evidence for the nature of the battle outweighs the pro-Roman bias of the sources. The sources present the following picture: Antony and Cleopatra met Octavian and Agrippa, fighting was tightly contested in the open water before Cleopatra fled with her forces and Antony followed leaving the battle to be won by Octavian. Yet in a number of sources the glory of the battle and the role of certain characters and their actions have been exaggerated. We are left only to judge each source on its accuracy to determine its usefulness in helping us understand what actually that day at Actium.

> **Study questions**
> Read Velleius Paterculus *The Roman History* 2.82–86 **PS** and answer the following:
> 1 How does Velleius highlight the importance of the Battle of Actium?
> 2 In what ways is Augustus presented in Velleius' account?

Velleius Paterculus *The Roman History* 2.82–86

Velleius Paterculus was a Roman historian who wrote a history of Rome from the end of the Trojan War through to AD 29. He wrote with a heavily **rhetorical** and **hyperbolic** style. He was writing during the reign of Tiberius, Augustus' successor, and so flatters Augustus and Tiberius. This is clearly reflected in his account of Actium. His account in the prescribed sources starts before Actium but the tone remains the same throughout. In section 82, he discusses how Antony got himself into 'the greatest difficulties' in Parthia and the East. Section 83 notes how a number of key figures left Antony to join Octavian. In section 84, his account of the battle begins. His whole account is based in praise of Octavian. He notes that before the battle the outcome was a 'certainty' (84). He refers to the battle as the 'greatest' and it is portrayed as a key turning point in Roman history. Although there may be some subjective truth in that, the battle itself was neither a great feat of military brilliance nor particularly decisive.

> **rhetorical** a form of writing focused on effect more than content
>
> **hyperbole** a deliberate over-exaggeration

Velleius puts little focus on the early engagements but immediately jumps to Cleopatra's flight and Antony's cowardly reaction to follow her. He contrasts Antony's actions with the bravery of his soldiers to further blemish Antony's character.

This is a heavily biased account but that does not mean it is of no use. We must not simply trust Velleius' word at face value. Instead, it allows an insight into the pro-Augustan message which was spread following the battle and was still believed even after Augustus' death.

> **PRESCRIBED SOURCE**
>
> **Roman History**
>
> **Author:** Velleius Paterculus (*c.* AD 19–*c.* 31)
>
> **Prescribed chapters:** 2.82–87
>
> **Date:** AD 30
>
> **Genre:** history (history of Rome from the fall of Troy up to AD 29)
>
> **Significance:** A history of Rome told from a pro-Augustan viewpoint, focusing here on the moments before and after the Battle of Actium
>
> **Read it here:** OCR Source Booklet

Virgil, *Aeneid* 8.675–731, The Shield of Aeneas

Publius Vergilius Maro, known as Virgil, was one of Rome's greatest poets. Writing between 42 and 19 BC, he was one of a number of poets supported by Octavian's cultural advisor, Maecenas. His most famous work, the epic poem the *Aeneid*, tells the story of the Trojan prince Aeneas' efforts to fulfil his destiny to find a city and begin a great civilisation in Italy. It was a Roman foundation epic poem and is considered one of the most important poems in Western literature. Indirectly, the poem was meant to be a celebration of a new golden age in Rome which was to be ushered in by Augustus. His account of the Battle of Actium comes in the poem when the hero, Aeneas, receives a shield, made by

Part Two Depth Study 2: Cleopatra: Rome and Egypt

> **PRESCRIBED SOURCE**
>
> **Aeneid**
>
> **Author:** Virgil (70–19 BC)
>
> **Prescribed lines:** 8.675–731
>
> **Date:** 19 BC
>
> **Genre:** poetry (epic poem on the story of Aeneas)
>
> **Significance:** An epic poem of the efforts of the Trojan prince Aeneid to found the Roman race. In this section, Aeneas receives a new shield made by the God, Vulcan, which depicts the Battle of Actium at its centre
>
> **Read it here:** OCR Source Booklet **CW**

the god Vulcan, from his mother the goddess Venus. On the shield, some of the future great achievements of Rome are depicted as decoration. Crucially, in the centre of the shield, at pride of place among all of Rome's achievements, comes a depiction of the Battle of Actium. Virgil, similarly to Velleius, places great emphasis on the significance of Octavian's victory.

In Virgil's discussion of the battle formation in lines 679–83 **PS**, Octavian is grandly depicted leading his men, the gods and Rome into battle. The universal support for his role in the war, from both men and gods, is important in legitimising Octavian's attack. The political importance of Octavian's deified father, Julius Caesar, watching over him and supporting him cannot be understated.

On the other side, Antony is depicted as leading a horde of barbarian tribes and joined by his 'greatest outrage of all, his Egyptian wife'. It was common in the propaganda which followed Octavian's victory for Cleopatra to not even be named in texts, such was the disgust that Romans were meant to feel for her. Virgil's account is full of poetic invention, for instance Antony's vast galleys are likened to islands. The Roman gods play an integral role in the victory, emphasising again Octavian's divine support.

Very little detail of the actual battle is given but once again the battle is over when Cleopatra flees. Yet Virgil's depiction does not stop there, he writes about the aftermath of the victory for Octavian and the **triple triumph** he would eventually receive in Rome. When reading Virgil's account, we must remember that the poet was supported by Augustus and, although Virgil does not always stick his pro-Augustan script, the scene on Aeneas' shield is clearly designed to highlight the glory of Augustus and the significance of his victory.

> **KEY EVENT**
>
> **triple triumph** in 29 BC, Octavian celebrated a triple triumph in Rome for his victories in Illyria, Actium and Alexandria

THE OUTCOME AND THE REASONS FOR IT AS DESCRIBED BY THE SOURCES

Why did Antony lose the Battle of Actium?

1. **Poor timing** – Plutarch *Life of Mark Antony* 58 **PS** calls Antony's inability to start the war earlier his 'greatest mistake'. Antony's position in the East and support from Cleopatra allowed him to rally a vast and experienced army quickly. Octavian was distracted by matters in Rome and did not have Antony's reputation as a general to rely on. If Antony had begun the war earlier and pushed towards Italy quicker, he could have avoided being trapped in Actium and fought the war on his own terms.

2. **Underestimating Octavian and Agrippa** – Antony was struck with surprise when Octavian's forces struck from south of his position, not the north as he expected. He had underestimated the ability of Agrippa and allowed himself to be outflanked.

3. **Poor preparations** – Antony's army was a shadow of its former self when fighting at Actium begun. His force had been blockaded for months by Octavian and his men were weakened by a food shortage and disease. Antony should not have allowed himself to be blockaded. His inability to break the siege meant he entered the battle weak and thus had to consider flight as an option.

> **ACTIVITY**
>
> Read Virgil's account of the Battle of Actium in *Aeneid* 8.675–731 **PS**. Find three examples of the following and explain why each might have benefitted Octavian:
>
> - description of Antony's character
> - negative portrayal of Cleopatra
> - supporters of Octavian

3.4 The Battle of Actium and its Significance for Egypt and Rome

IMPACT OF THE BATTLE ON CLEOPATRA'S AND ANTONY'S CAREERS

In the aftermath of the battle, Octavian gained the majority of Antony's fighting force and destroyed most of his navy. Antony was left reeling from the defeat. The flight of Antony and Cleopatra, as told in Plutarch *Life of Mark Antony* 67 **PS**, had ensured that Cleopatra's treasury was still intact and that both remained alive. The sources represent Antony's reputation as now lying in tatters. Plutarch *Life of Mark Antony* 69 **PS** describes how Antony attempted to kill himself when he found out that a key general had defected. When he eventually made it to Alexandria, the sources tell us that he locked himself away depressed. If we believe, however, that Antony's intentions were always to flee, then we can perhaps imagine Antony behaving differently in the days and months after the battle.

Cleopatra made a grand entry into Alexandria to prevent news of the loss reaching her citizens and creating civil unrest. She now feared her own position. Caesarion and Antyllus, Antony's son, both came of age and were promoted in public life. This showed the public that her family was still strong and in power. She now had to ensure her reputation could survive the defeat and prepare her forces for the inevitable arrival of Octavian and Agrippa.

Following Actium, Octavian had generously rewarded the cities of Greece before he was forced to return to Italy to deal with some disgruntled veterans. He and Agrippa now prepared to take Alexandria. This is notably unlike the presentation given in the sources of a swift and relentless pursuit. The pursuit was not only important to remove the threat of Antony and Cleopatra but also to gain the treasury of Alexandria to help pay off his soldiers.

> **DEBATE**
>
> Split into groups and debate the following:
>
> 'Antony's defeat at Actium was due more to his mistakes than Octavian's successes.' To what extent do the sources agree with this view?

MARK ANTONY'S SUICIDE

Antony and Cleopatra now made separate appeals to Octavian. Antony requested to be allowed to live as a private citizen in Athens, while Cleopatra requested that her children be allowed to rule Egypt. Octavian rejected Antony's plea but supposedly told Cleopatra that he might listen to her demands if she killed or exiled Antony.

In the spring of 30 BC, Octavian advanced on Egypt. In response, Cleopatra built a pyre in her **mausoleum** ready to burn herself and her riches should Octavian take the city. With Octavian moving closer, Antony won a small cavalry skirmish and marched back to Alexandria in triumph. However, Plutarch *Life of Mark Antony* 74 **PS** tells us the soldier rewarded by Cleopatra for fighting the best in the skirmish deserted Antony's forces that night. Antony challenged Octavian to single combat but was refused. At this point, Antony decided to attack Octavian but that night Plutarch *Life of Mark Antony* 75 **PS** informs us that at this stage even the gods deserted Antony, a supposed sign of his upcoming defeat.

Antony drew up his forces and watched as his navy sailed out to meet Octavian's. Rather than engaging the enemy, Antony's men raised their oars in salute to Octavian and deserted their leader. Antony's cavalry and infantry did the same. Plutarch *Life of Mark Antony* 76 **PS** reveals Antony was distraught and believed he had been betrayed by

> **mausoleum** a grand burial chamber, usually reserved for one family or dynasty

201

> **PRESCRIBED SOURCE**
>
> **Life of Mark Antony**
>
> **Author:** Plutarch (AD 40–120)
>
> **Prescribed chapters:** 72–79; 81–86
>
> **Date:** AD 75
>
> **Genre:** biography (biographical lives of famous Greek and Romans told in pairs)
>
> **Significance:** These sections detail the suicide of Antony as Octavian arrives in Alexandria and the dramatic story of Cleopatra's suicide
>
> **Read it here:** OCR Source Booklet

Cleopatra. She feared his anger and hid away, sending messengers to announce her own death. Antony believed these messages and decided to kill himself. He asked a slave to commit the deed for him, but the slave killed himself first. Antony then plunged his sword into his belly and fell to the floor.

However, the blow was not fatal and rather than carry out a final blow, he was taken to Cleopatra. Cleopatra did not open the doors to allow him in. Instead, Antony was raised up to the queen through a window. She reacted in grief at the sight of her dying lover and he finally died in her embrace. Antony's death is certainly dramatic and suicide was the honourable end. Velleius Paterculus notes the honour of Antony's end stating that he 'answered the accusations of cowardice by his death' (Velleius Paterculus *Roman History* 87 **PS**) Yet, it was a death full of confusion and misfortune. It was an inglorious end for one of Rome's most accomplished men.

THE METHOD OF CLEOPATRA'S SUICIDE AND REASONS FOR HER ACTIONS

Octavian entered Alexandria in great pomp and spoke to the citizens before attempting to negotiate with Cleopatra. The queen was still locked in her mausoleum and the Roman envoys could only speak to her through a window. Plutarch *Life of Mark Antony* 79 **PS** describes how one Roman kept Cleopatra talking in the window while another took a ladder and entered through a different window. He managed to wrestle Cleopatra to the ground and stop her from wounding herself. She was taken as prisoner to the Royal Palace. At some point Antyllus was necessarily killed but Cleopatra's other children were treated well, except Caesarion, who was too much of a threat to Octavian. He was killed after Cleopatra's death, fleeing for India and betrayed by his tutor. His death was necessary since, as Areius reports in Plutarch's account 'It is not a good thing to have many Caesars' (Plutarch *Life of Mark Antony* 81 **PS**).

Octavian allowed Antony a splendid royal funeral and Cleopatra buried the body in deep grief. Soon afterwards, she fell ill through grief and her own self-inflicted wounds from her grieving.

Octavian went to meet Cleopatra and there are differing accounts of their meeting in the sources. Plutarch presents a favourable picture of Cleopatra, weak and scruffy yet still beautiful. She appealed to Octavian, blaming Antony for her actions and pleaded for pity. However, Plutarch's account of this meeting is very different to the account given by the historian, Cassius Dio, so the truthfulness of Plutarch's report can be questioned.

Cleopatra then discovered that she was destined to be sent to Rome with her children to be paraded in triumph as Caesar's conquest. Whether she actually received this information or not, it is likely that Cleopatra knew that this was potentially her fate. She would have been marched with her children in chains through Rome, a defeated and embarrassed queen. At this stage, she resolved her mind to suicide. Plutarch *Life of Mark Antony* 84 **PS** presents Cleopatra with a great final speech at Antony's tomb. She is presented as emotional but resolute in the salvation of her honour. The reliability of this scene should be questioned as it was likely an invention by Plutarch.

> **EXPLORE FURTHER**
>
> Read Cassius Dio *Roman History* 51.13 for his account of Cleopatra's meeting with Octavian and compare it with Plutarch *Life of Mark Antony* 83 **PS** – what judgements can you make on the two sources?

3.4 The Battle of Actium and its Significance for Egypt and Rome

The exact events of her suicide are unclear in the sources. Plutarch *Life of Mark Antony* 85 **PS** reveals she managed to smuggle an **asp** into her prison chamber, hidden beneath the leaves in a delivery of figs. She sent a written tablet to Octavian, who on realising what the message meant, sent men to enter her chamber. They found Cleopatra, dressed as the Queen of Egypt, dead as her attendants lay dying around her. Plutarch himself reveals the lack of precision in his recounting of these events where he even comments 'No one really knows the truth' (Plutarch *Life of Mark Antony* 86 **PS**) and gives alternative methods of her death.

Cleopatra was admired for her death by Octavian and many Romans as she displayed her noble spirit. She died at the age of thirty-nine and was given a royal burial next to Antony. This respect for Cleopatra even passed into propaganda as Octavian presented her as a worthy opponent. Horace, a Roman poet supported by Augustus, wrote of the queen:

> Determined to die, she became even more fierce; she had no intention, although no longer a queen, to be brought in ships to Rome, and led in a proud triumph, for she was not some obscure, ordinary woman.
>
> Horace, *Ode* 1.37

This depiction of Cleopatra may seem strange considering the negativity with which she was generally viewed in Rome. In highlighting her bravery in death, the greatness of Octavian in overcoming her is emphasised.

Horace's account also helps us to understand the reasons for Cleopatra's actions. She was too honourable to allow herself to be paraded through Rome. Her honour and the honour of her family demanded that she not allow this to happen. Heartbroken and unable to stomach the dishonour of defeat, Cleopatra grandly ended her life, dressed as a queen and on her own terms.

> **PRESCRIBED SOURCE**
>
> ***Odes***
>
> **Author:** Horace (65–8 BC)
>
> **Prescribed poem:** 1.37
>
> **Date:** 23 BC
>
> **Genre:** poetry (poetry covering a range of themes)
>
> **Significance:** Roman poetry celebrating Octavian's victory at Actium and his subsequent victory in Alexandria. The poet also praises Cleopatra for her bravery in suicide.
>
> **Read it here:** OCR Source Booklet **CW**

FIGURE 3.22
Seventeenth-century basin showing scenes from the life of Cleopatra. What can you identify?

THE SIGNIFICANCE OF THE SUICIDES FOR OCTAVIAN

The suicide of Antony was significant for Octavian for the following reasons:

1. **Elimination of a rival** – The victory at Actium had been a huge step forward for Octavian in defeating Antony and gaining complete control in Rome, but with Antony still alive, and supported by Cleopatra's wealth, his old enemy still posed a threat. His suicide left Octavian without doubt as the most powerful Roman in the world.
2. **PR success** – After the desertion of his men, Antony had no chance of defeating Octavian. It had become an unfair fight which Octavian could only win. However, he still had to eliminate Antony to ensure fully his own power. Antony's death in battle would have been acceptable in Roman eyes since he was fighting on behalf of a foreign enemy. But, the execution which Octavian may have had to have ordered would not have been seen favourably by Romans nor any of Antony's former supporters who sympathised with his downfall. His suicide, therefore, came as a relief. It saved Octavian from damaging his own reputation at a critical time.

Cleopatra's suicide was significant for Octavian for the following reasons:

1. **Control of Egypt and its resources** – Cleopatra's death left Egypt at Octavian's full disposal, particularly its abundance of wealth and resources. Octavian was desperately in need of a cash surge to pay off his soldiers, plus those of Antony's men he had bribed, for their service at Actium and Alexandria. Control of Egypt also meant that Rome would now have a steady supply of grain, keeping civil unrest over grain shortages at a minimum. Egypt would now remain in Rome's hands and be a key part of the Empire.
2. **Elimination of a rival in Caesarion** – Cleopatra's son, Caesarion, still posed something of a threat to Octavian's legitimacy as Julius Caesar's rightful successor. With Cleopatra's death, Octavian was free to take action and, although the details are shady, he executed Caesarion, removing the final possible threat to his position. Caesarion also stood as an embarrassing reminder of Julius Caesar' affair with Cleopatra.
3. **PR success** – If you remember, Arsinoe, Cleopatra's sister, had been led through Rome in triumph by Julius Caesar. Rather than executing her as customary, the crowd had pitied her and she was sent into guarded exile. Octavian could not risk the same happening with Cleopatra. Her suicide, although potentially lost him the glory of parading her through the city, did prevent the awkward possibility that the Roman crowd could pity her.

3.4 The Battle of Actium and its Significance for Egypt and Rome

TOPIC REVIEW

Boost your knowledge:

Describe:

- the key causes of the war between Antony and Cleopatra and Octavian
- how the war between Cleopatra and Octavian was presented to the people of Rome
- the events of the Battle of Actium
- the suicides of Antony and Cleopatra

Stretch your understanding

Explain:

- why war was inevitable between Octavian and Antony
- why the pre-battle manoeuvres greatly harmed Antony's chances of winning the Battle of Actium
- how the sources differ in their portrayals of the Battle of Actium
- why the suicide of Cleopatra was significant for Octavian

PRACTICE QUESTIONS

1. Explain the significance of the suicides of Antony and Cleopatra to Octavian and Rome. [10]
2. 'The sources over-exaggerate the importance of the Battle of Actium'. How far do you agree with this view?
   You must use and analyse the ancient sources you have studied as well as supporting your answer with your own knowledge. [20]

Further Reading

Focused texts on Cleopatra, Caesar and Antony:
Abbott, J., *Cleopatra* (Texas: Simon, 2001).
Burnstein, S., *The Reign of Cleopatra* (Oklahoma: Oklahoma University Press, 2007).
Goldsworthy, A., *Antony and Cleopatra* (London: Weidenfield & Nicolson, 2010)
Grant, M., *Cleopatra* (London 1972)
Hughes-Hallet, L. *Cleopatra: Histories, Dreams and Distortions* (London: Bloomsbury, 1990).
Meier, C., *Caesar* (trans. D. McLintock) (London, 1995).
Rice, E.E. *Cleopatra* (Stroud: Sutton, 1999).
Roberts, A., *Mark Antony: His Life and Times* (Worcester; Malvern Publishing, 1988).
Southern, P., *Mark Antony: A Life* (Stroud; Amberley, 2012).
Southern, P., *Antony and Cleopatra* (Stroud; Amberley, 2009).
Tyldesley, J. *Cleopatra: Last Queen of Egypt* (New York; Basic Books, 2008).
Walker, S and P. Higgs, *Cleopatra of Egypt: From History to Myth* (London: British Museum Press, 2001).

General period texts on Rome and Egypt
Crawford, M.H., *The Roman Republic* (Glasgow; Fontana, 1978).
Chauveau, M., *Egypt in the Age of Cleopatra* (trans. D. Lorton), (Ithaca; Cornell University Press, 2000).
Gabba, E., *Republican Rome, the Army and the Allies* (trans. Cuff, P.J), (Oxford; Blackwell, 1976).
Green, P. *Alexander to Actium: The Historical Evolution of the Hellenistic Age* (Berkeley; University of California Press, 1990).
Hölbl, G., *A History of the Ptolemaic Empire* (Abingdon; Routledge, 2000).
Holland, T., *Rubicon: The Triumph and Tragedy of the Roman Republic* (London; Abacus 2004).
Scullard, H.H., *From the Gracchi to Nero* (London; Methuen, 1959).
Seager, R., *Pompey: A Political Biography* (Oxford; Blackwell, 1979).
Syme, R. *The Roman Revolution* (Oxford; Oxford University Press, 1939).

Film and TV
Caesar and Cleopatra (starring Vivian Leigh, dir. Gabriel Pascal, 1945).
Cleopatra (starring Elizabeth Taylor, dir. Joseph L. Mankiewicz, 1963).
Cleopatra (TV series, starring Leonor Varela, 1999).
Rome (HBO TV series, 2002).
Cleopatra: A Timewatch Guide (BBC documentary, 2015).

Preparing for the Exam: Section C

DEPTH STUDY: CLEOPATRA: ROME AND EGYPT, 69–30 BC

This chapter aims to show you the types of questions you are likely to get in Section C of the Rome and its Neighbours exam. It offers some advice on how to answer the questions and will help you avoid common errors.

The examination

The Roman depth study is in the same exam paper as the Roman Period Study – The Foundations of Rome 753–440 BC. You can answer Section A and Section C in any order you like. Just remember that the exam lasts 1 hour and 45 minutes. Section C is worth 45 marks, so you need to make sure you organise your time accordingly.

This component of the GCSE examination is designed to test your knowledge, understanding and evaluation of Cleopatra and her Impact on Roman Politics.

There are three Assessment Objectives in your Ancient History GCSE. Questions will be designed to test these areas. To remind yourself what these are read p. 70 in the period study exam chapter.

Be aware that there is some overlap with Ancient History Assessment Objectives. As you will see in the table on the next page, questions 14 and 15 assess multiple assessment objectives. For example, AO2 and AO3 both require you to make 'judgements' on the "historical events and historical periods."

In the exam, you should be able to demonstrate:

- a good grasp of the 'Cleopatra story' and its key characters.
- A basic understanding of the events from the death of Ptolemy XII Auletes to the death of Cleopatra
- an awareness of the relationships between Cleopatra and Julius Caesar and Mark Antony
- a good knowledge of the prescribed sources
- different interpretations about Cleopatra's life and character and the different conclusions that can be drawn from these.

When analysing and evaluating your evidence in order to make judgements, you should be able to:

- analyse and evaluate the causes and consequences of the war between Cleopatra, Mark Antony and Octavian
- analyse and evaluate the significance of key individuals and events and how they impacted upon the course of Cleopatra's life.
- look at change and continuity; including the rate of change and the relative success of different developments. For example, Mark Antony's change of character and Cleopatra's response to the rise of Octavian.
- use your knowledge, evaluation and analysis in combination to produce a logical conclusion.

When evaluating how the portrayal of events by the ancient sources relates to the historical contexts in which they were produced, you should be able to demonstrate:

- an understanding of the approaches used by all the authors, especially Plutarch, and how the nature of their work potentially affected its usefulness and accuracy
- a good grasp of the context of each prescribed source, including visual sources, and how far the ancient author creates an accurate portrayal of the event
- an awareness of how other authors have interpreted the events in the prescribed sources

QUESTION TYPES

There are five different types of question. It is important to remember that the Second Punic War questions begin at question 11. The table below shows how they are assessed.

Question	Type of question	AO1 marks	AO2 marks	AO3 marks	Total marks
11	Discrete factual knowledge	5	–	–	**5**
12	What can we learn from the source	–	–	5	**5**
13	Evaluate the source	–	–	5	**5**
14	Second-order concepts	5	5	–	**10**
15	Essay using ancient source knowledge	5	5	10	**20**

There are no SPaG marks awarded for the Depth Study questions.

Question 11 will test your knowledge. This question will be divided into a number of sub-questions.

Question 12 and 13 will supply you with a passage or a visual source from the prescribed sources. A list of the prescribed sources can be found at the start of each chapter and on the OCR web-page. Question 12 will ask you to identify key features from the passage.

Question 13 will require you to evaluate the accuracy of the passage.

Question 14 will ask you to explore a second-order concept. A second-order concept is a historical skill used to analyse the past, for example, change and continuity, similarity and difference, significance, cause and consequence.

Finally, Question 15 is an essay question which will explore your knowledge and understanding of the topic and relevant prescribed sources. It will also assess your ability to use this information to create a line of substantiated argument.

Question 11 – knowledge questions

There will be 5 marks available for question 6 all testing factual knowledge (AO1). The 5 marks will be broken down into a series of short-answer questions, typically worth 1, 2 or 3 marks.

These questions will usually start with one of the following stems:

- State . . .
- Identify . . .
- Name . . .
- Give **one** example of . . . Give **two** reasons for . . .

For example: *Name the naval battle fought between Antony, Cleopatra and Octavian in September 31 BC.* [1]

- **Answer:** Battle of Actium [1]

This question has only one answer. You do not have to write in full sentences, and the answer should be brief.

For example: *Give **two** reasons why Cleopatra committed suicide.* [2]

- **Answer:** To prevent being led in triumph through the city of Rome. [1] To save her personal and family honour [1]

This answer is also brief. There is in fact no need to write full sentences if it seems that only a single word or a phrase is needed.

Question 12 – source question

Questions 12 and 13 both use the same prescribed source. It could be a passage from one of the ancient historians or a visual source from the archaeological record.

Question 12 will ask you to identify several features from the source and develop what this tells you about the question focus (AO3)

Question 12 will usually start with the following:
   12. What can we learn from Passage C about. . . .? [5]

Here is an example:

Passage C

Now Cleopatra displayed her flattery, not like Plato says in four sorts; while Antony was spending his time either in some amusement or some serious matter, she was always bringing some new pleasurable diversion or charming activity, and so keeping him well- trained and under control day and night. She played dice with him, drank with him, hunted with him, and when he exercised himself in full armour she watched him; when at night he liked to stand outside the doors or windows of the ordinary people to make fun of those inside, she used to put on the clothes of a servant-girl and join him in his games. Antony also would dress up like some slave. He often returned home driven by abuse and sometimes blows. In fact most people knew it was him. The Alexandrians enjoyed this sort of silly behaviour and played along with their usual good taste, saying with affection that Antony put on his tragic face for the Romans and his comic one for them.

Plutarch, *Life of Mark Antony* 29

- 12. What can we learn from Passage C about the relationship of Antony and Cleopatra? [5]

When answering question 12 you must remember that this question is only worth 5 out of 45 marks and make sure you organise your time accordingly.

- After reading the passage you need to identify several key features or details from the passage – Cleopatra flattered Antony and brought him pleasure as a distraction; often, the two joked and played games together in Alexandria.
- Try to infer what this tells us about the question focus – Cleopatra and Antony had a strong bond and were very close; there was a a lighter side to their relationship.
- To summarise: read the passage carefully, identify several key features or details and outline what you can learn from these details.

Answer:

You should be able to develop several points, which might include:

○ Cleopatra often cheered Antony up when he was in a serious mood
○ Cleopatra used her playfulness with Antony to keep herself in control of Antony which suggests a level of manipulation in their relationship
○ Antony's playful manner in front of Alexandrians, which was different to his serious manner with the Romans, shows his comfort and happiness in his relationship with Cleopatra

NB. If you are struggling to understand the passage, try to find something from the passage which seems important to the story and explain why it is important.

Question 13 – source question

Question 13 will assess your ability to use, analyse and evaluate a prescribed source within its historical context and then draw a conclusion about how far its portrayal is accurate. For example, you might be asked how its accuracy may have been affected by influences upon its creator (AO3).

NB. Visual sources such as a coin, bust or a relief sculpture could be assessed by exploring the potential purpose of the source. In some cases you may be able to assess whether this is an accurate portrayal of the event or individual. Other examples may be good examples of propaganda used to convey a particular message.

Question 13 will usually be phrased as follows:

13. Using details from Passage C, evaluate how accurate you think **x's** account of **y** is? [5]

As in the exam we will be using the same source from question 12 on the previous page.

13. Using details from Passage C, explain how accurate you think Plutarch's account of these events is? [5]

The following are some of the tests you can use. Remember you are looking for the strengths and weaknesses of the passage.

- What knowledge do you have of this event or other interpretations of this event? Does your wider understanding make this passage accurate or inaccurate?
- What is the historian's method? Is this method a strength, weakness or both when evaluating this passage?
- Is the extract detailed, or is it an overview? Is this typical of this historian?
- Finally, the aims of the historian might affect the reliability. This will not be relevant for all passages. So avoid general comments such as 'Plutarch was writing 150 years later so he has the benefit of hindsight.' Instead explain how this effects the accuracy of this particular passage.
- If it is a visual source think about why it was created and when. A dedication or triumphal arch may be designed to celebrate something. Would it, therefore, focus on an individual's failings or weaknesses?
- Remember to identify the key features from the source to support your evaluation, otherwise you will not be meeting the full requirements of the question.

To summarise: identify a few strengths or weaknesses of author's treatment of the topic, or alternatively develop one or two points in detail.

Although you do not need a conclusion it is good practice to make a statement about how accurate you think the passage is.

Answers may include:

You should be able to develop a few of the following points:

- Plutarch often added anecdotes on character into his work, but does not state his source for such information. This is particularly troubling given the strange nature of the story.

- Cleopatra's dramatic fake affection and starvation to keep Antony with her are mentioned later in Plutarch when Octavia is trying to join up with Antony. This suggests that her manipulation of Antony in the story was likely.
- Plutarch was writing a biography of Antony designed to highlight how his desire for luxury and wealth led to his downfall. This anecdote would fit that agenda.

When looking at a passage you must remember question 13 is only worth 5 out of 45 marks so make sure you use your time accordingly.

Question 14 – second-order concepts

In GCSE Ancient History you will need to answer questions on second-order concepts (see p. 74 for more info in the Period Study exam chapter): change and continuity, similarity and difference, significance, cause and consequence. In the Depth Study, these questions will be assessing AO1 and AO2. This means you will be required to demonstrate good knowledge and understanding, alongside analytical and evaluation skills which lead to a supported conclusion.

The questions **may** look something like this:

- **Change and continuity**. These questions may ask you to explore an event or an aspect of Cleopatra's life and explain how much change there was between two points.
- *e.g.14. Explain how far x changed during y.*
- **Similarity and difference.** These questions may ask you to explore an aspect or event in Cleopatra's life and explain if individuals or events responded to it in a similar or different way.
- *e.g. 14. Explain whether x's response was different/similar to y's.*
- **Significance.** These questions may require you to explore the importance of an individual or event upon the whole of the Cleopatra's life and her influence in Roman politics.
- *e.g. 14. Explain the importance of Antony's relationship with Cleopatra for Rome.*
- **Cause.** These questions may ask you to explain how an event happened or why an individual took a particular course of action.
- *e.g. 14. Explain what caused x.*
- **Consequence.** These questions may ask you to explain the impact of an event or individual.
- *e.g.14. Explain the impact of x.*

Here is an example of how to answer a second-order concept question,

- *14. Explain the events which caused the Battle of Actium.* [10]
- Remember this question asks you to use your knowledge (AO1) to identify, develop and assess key features from the passage to make a judgement about the second-order concept (AO2)
- Identify several possible features. These must be supported by the source and/or your own knowledge

- You must make sure that each of these features is linked back to the question and its importance evaluated.
- Most significantly you must reach a substantiated judgement.

Answers may include:

You might include several examples of different possible causes such as:

- Antony's rejection and divorce of Octavia in favour of Cleopatra was a personal insult to Octavian and highlighted his favour of Egypt over Rome.
- Octavian's reading of Antony's will in Rome turned all popular opinion of Antony in Rome against him
- The creation of Cleopatra's negative representation in Rome made it easy for Octavian to declare war on her instead of Antony
- Octavian's own pursuit of power made war inevitable

Remember that question 14 is worth 10 out of a possible 45 marks, make sure that you organise your time accordingly.

To summarise: identify several possible answers and use them to create a sustained line of argument.

You do not need to use the ancient historians in this answer. You will be rewarded, however, if you can show the different interpretations in relation to the question focus.

Question 15 – essay question

The final question is an essay question which assesses all three assessment objectives in combination. You will need to be able to use factual knowledge and understanding alongside your knowledge of the prescribed sources to provide evidence to support and challenge the question posed. Furthermore, you will need to analyse and explain this evidence to make a substantiated judgement about how far you agree with the question posed.

You will also have to evaluate the context of the ancient evidence you have used to judge its accuracy and potential weight. The best students will use this evaluation to inform their judgement.

AO1 and AO2 are both worth 5 marks each. AO3 is allocated ten marks.

As with question 5 your essay will be marked according to the best fit with the mark scheme.

Your essay question will be much broader than question and will expect you to draw upon material from across the whole Depth Study. The question will usually present you with a statement and ask you to make a judgement about 'how far' you agree with it.

The following is an example of a possible essay question:

○ 'Antony's downfall was solely due to the charm of Cleopatra'. To what extent do you agree with this view? [20]

Answer

Downfall caused by charm because:

- Plutarch *Life of Antony* 66 claims Antony's flight from Actium was driven by his lust for Cleopatra. This was seen as cowardice and lost him the respect of his followers.
- Rejection of Octavia, which caused a costly rift between Antony and Octavian, was driven by desire to see Cleopatra again – Plutarch *Life of Antony* 53
- The Donations of Alexandria in 34 BC were a disastrous move and lost him his remaining support in Rome.

Other causes for Antony's downfall not reliant on his relationship with Cleopatra:

- His failure in his campaign in the East was through his own failings as a general and contributed greatly to his downfall – Velleius Paterculus 2.82
- Failure to start the war with Octavian earlier when Octavian was still to rally enough troops was a tactical blunder – Plutarch *Life of Antony* 58
- He underestimated Octavian and Agrippa before Actium, allowing himself to be surrounded.

This is not an exhaustive list – but designed to give you a flavour of what you might choose.

Key points:

Use the same advice from Section A (pp. 76–77) but remember:

- You need to use your knowledge of ancient sources to support and challenge the question posed.
- You must evaluate the accuracy and weight of the ancient sources and use this evaluation to develop your line of argument and judgement.
- Avoid general observations about accuracy, such as Plutarch was writing over 150 years later and so he was not reliable.
- Make sure your analysis of the sources is linked to the question and supported by an example.
- This example should be linked to the question, not just a general comment about the author.

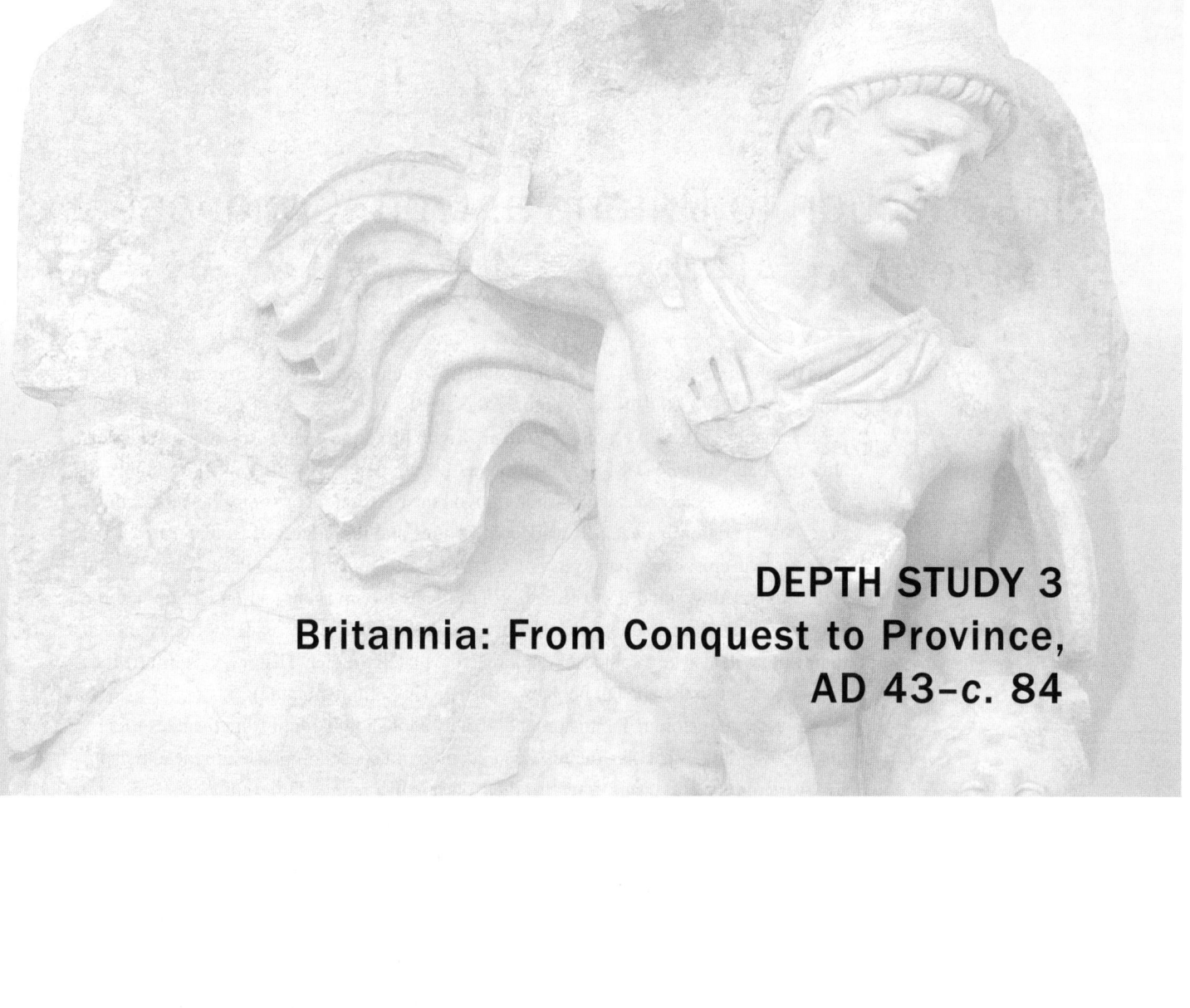

DEPTH STUDY 3
Britannia: From Conquest to Province, AD 43–c. 84

Introduction to Britannia: From Conquest to Province, AD 43–c. 84

This depth study explores the complex factors which lie behind the Roman invasion of Britain in AD 43, and it also explores the stages of the conquest of Britain and the achievements of the governors of Roman Britain up to the end of Agricola's governorship (probably in *c*. AD 84). In addition, as we go along, we will look at a number of places, events and sources which shed light on the two other Key topics in the specification – co-operation between Romans and Britons and the effects of Roman rule on the Britons, and episodes when some of the Britons (Caratacus, Boudicca, Venutius and Calgacus) tried to stand up to Rome. What effects the invasion had on Britain and the ways in which Romans viewed the Britons (and particularly the leaders of resistance to their rule) will also be a subject to explore. Note that, in Ancient History, the term Britons is used to refer to the ancient peoples of Britain (in Latin, Britannia).

The Roman historian Tacitus probably knew a lot about Britain from the tales told by his father-in-law, Agricola. Tacitus wrote a eulogy (a speech in praise of a dead person) for Agricola several years after he died during the reign of the emperor Domitian. According to Tacitus, during Domitian's reign it had not been safe to praise anyone but the emperor himself! A good deal of information about what happened in Britain under the Romans comes from this source, known as the *Agricola*. However, it has to be interpreted with care, because it was intended to praise Agricola and to enhance his reputation

EXAM OVERVIEW

Your examination for Britannia: from Conquest to Province will require you to show knowledge and understanding of the material you have studied. This component is worth 45 marks – 15 based on AO1 skills, 10 on AO2, and 20 on AO3.

Question 16 will consist of a number of short factual questions worth a total of 5 marks.

Questions 17 and 18 will require you to study a passage of text or a visual source. Question 17 will be a comprehension question, whereas question 18 will need you to evaluate the source. Each question is worth 5 marks.

Question 19 will ask will ask you use second-order concepts such as continuity, change, cause, consequence, significance and similarity and difference within situations. This question is worth 10 marks.

Finally, question 20 is a longer essay-style question worth 20 marks.

after his death. Nevertheless, because of this work, we know more about the career and activities of Agricola, and especially his time as governor of Britain (*c. 77–c.84*) than we do about any other individual.

How this section matches the specification

There are four sections in the specification:

- **Claudius' invasion of Britain**
- **The changing policies of the various Roman governors. The significance and success of these governors**
- **Cooperation between Romans and Britons and the effects of Roman rule**
- **Resistance after the invasion**

Clearly, if the subject is tackled in the order of these headings, much has to be dealt with twice. What is covered in the last two topics is actually the gist of what is involved in the first two, but considered thematically! So to make it easier to understand, the different elements of the last two, 'cooperations between Romans and the effects of Roman rule' and 'resistance after the invasion', are handled as we go along – the ways in which the Britons resisted Rome had a massive influence in shaping the 'changing policies of the various Roman governors', after all.

As a result, this component is divided into three topics, the second and third of which take elements from each of the specification's sections 2, 3 and 4. The second topic here looks particularly at the aftermath of the Roman invasion and the rebellions of Caratacus in 47–51, Boudicca in 60/61 and Venutius in 69; the third topic considers elements of Romanisation and the later rebellion of Calgacus in 81–83. The Topic Overview boxes detail the specification elements covered in each topic so that it is clear what material may be found where. As the Romans themselves found, Roman Britain was sometimes hard to categorise!

Each Topic Overview also contains a list of the Prescribed Sources. Remember that many of the prescribed sources shed light on more than one section of the specification or issue: Camulodunum (Colchester) can be used to explore 'The submission of the tribes to Claudius at Camulodunum', 'the effects of Roman rule and the extent of change' and 'urbanisation', and 'cultural, religious and lifestyle changes' – all from the third section of the specification; but it was also a focus for 'the resistance campaign of Boudicca' in the fourth section.

The conquest of Roman Britain in a nutshell

Tacitus provides a neat summary of the Roman conquest of Britain in *Agricola*, chapter 13, which serves as a good overview of its early period (Tacitus is writing in *c.* 97/98):

The Britons themselves actively submit to the levy, tributes, and the other obligations of government, provided that they are not treated unfairly. They bitterly resent unfair treatment, their subjection only extending to obedience, not to slavery. Accordingly, Julius Caesar, the first of all Romans who entered Britain with an army, although he terrified the inhabitants by a successful engagement and gained control of the shore, may be considered to have made posterity aware of it rather than handed the country to

> posterity. Soon came our civil wars; the arms of the generals were turned against the Republic; and Britain was neglected long even after the establishment of peace. The divine Augustus called this 'policy' and Tiberius 'precedent'. It is certainly agreed that an expedition into Britain had entered Caligula's thoughts, natural fickleness making him swift to change his mind, together with the mighty attempts against Germany meant it came to nothing. The deified Claudius was the man who carried out such a great task: legions and auxiliary units were conveyed across the Channel and Vespasian* was given a share in the command: this was the start of the good fortune which was soon to follow him. Tribes were crushed, kings were captured, and Vespasian's greatness was revealed by the fates.
>
> Tacitus, *Agricola* 13

(The Romans referred to dead emperors – and before them, Julius Caesar – as 'deified' – a term used to mean that the Romans thought that they had become gods.)

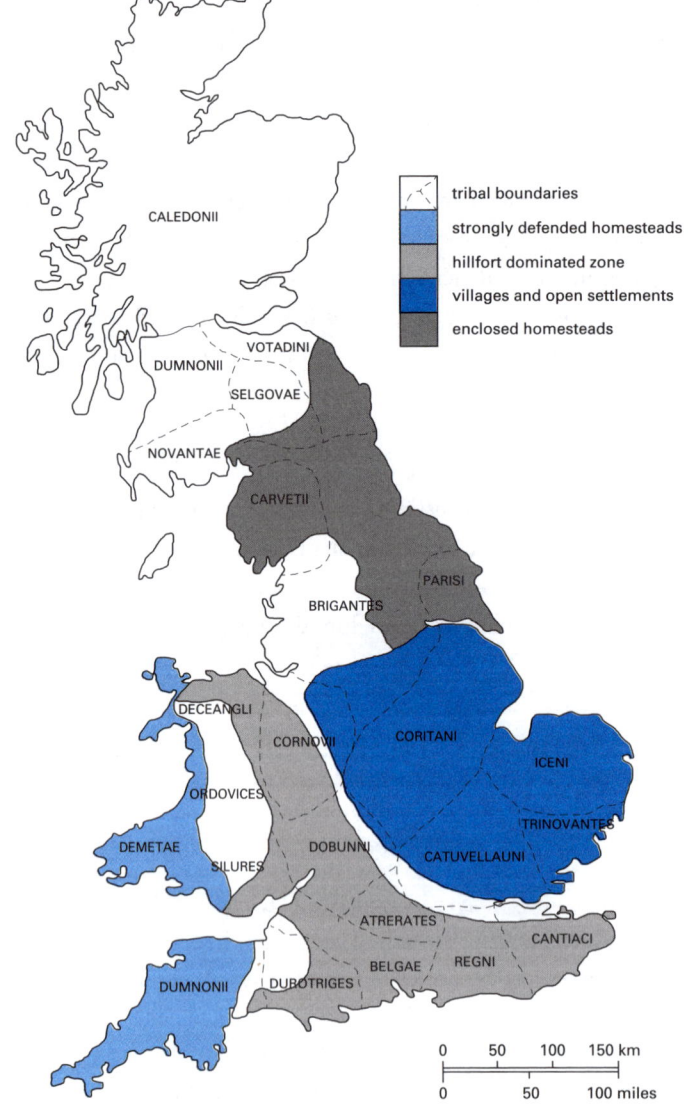

FIGURE 4.1
Map showing the tribes or civitates of Roman Britain and their varied types of settlement.

Study questions

First, read *carefully* what Tacitus says in *Agricola* 13 **PS**.

1. What opinion does he have of the Britons? Do you think he admires them or looks down on them? Use the text to support your answer.
2. Which Roman leader does Tacitus admire the most in this passage and why? Again, cite from the text to support your answer.

One other point to bear in mind as you embark on this study: the Romans called all the people who lived in the island of Britain 'Britons'; but, as we shall see, the locals may not have thought of themselves as that at all. They show much more interest in their identities as members of different tribes, as the evidence of coins and other objects shows. They seem to have differed quite a lot in the kind of social organisations they had, and even in the pottery designs they used. Even more important, they seem to have been rivals and fought each other for land and power.

TIMELINE OF THE INVASION OF BRITANNIA

This timeline provides the key dates of the most important events in our study of Britannia (remember the dates BC go *down* and dates AD go *up*):

Before Claudius' invasion:

c. 100 BC	Portland and Hengistbury Head (both located in Dorset, on the south coast of Britain) in use as ports trading with the continent first coinage may be in use by this time
58–51 BC	Julius Caesar conquers Gaul (modern France and Belgium)
55 BC	Caesar's first expedition to Britain
54 BC	Caesar's second expedition to Britain
49–44 BC	Caesar dictator in Rome; assassinated in 44 BC
44–31 BC	civil wars in Rome
31–23 BC	Octavian (later Augustus) becomes princeps (sole ruler)
37, 27, 26 BC	? expeditions to Britain planned by Augustus
by *c.* 15 BC	named coins appear: the Catuvellauni (a British tribe – see map on p. 218) start to extend their influence and their borders
AD 9	loss of three legions in Germany; Augustus changes his policy from expansion to holding on to what Rome already controls
by AD 14	British kings Tincomarus and Dubnovellaunus come to Rome asking for Roman help – they have been driven out of their lands
	British rulers make offerings to the gods at Rome
AD 39/40	Adminius (king of the Atrebates tribe) driven out of Britain by Cunobelinus, a rival British king, who dies by AD 43
AD 40	Caligula's expedition to Britain planned and abandoned
AD 41/2	Verica, king of the Atrebates, flees from Britain and asks Claudius for help

After Claudius' invasion (governors and their dates are shown in **bold**)

AD 43	Claudius' invasion, with four legions and about 20,000 auxiliaries (40,000 in total). He comes to Britain in person to accept the surrender of British tribes at Camulodunum (Colchester) and even brings a regiment of elephants to impress the native Britons
AD 43–47	**Aulus Plautius**
AD 43–47	Vespasian campaigns to the west; conquest of southern and eastern Britain complete; Aulus Plautius received an ovation in Rome
AD 47–52	**Publius Ostorius Scapula**
AD 47	First rebellion of the Iceni (a tribe in modern East Anglia/Lincolnshire)
AD 47–52	Ostorius Scapula campaigns against Caratacus (a British chief who led the resistance against Rome) on what are now the borders of Wales
AD 49	Camulodunum (Colchester) is established as a colonia
	Londinium (London) emerges as a trading centre at about this time
AD 51	Defeat and capture of Caratacus; he is taken to Rome and pardoned by Claudius
AD 52–57	**Aulus Didius Gallus**
AD 52–58	parts of Wales conquered; in the territory of the Brigantes (roughly modern Lancashire and Yorkshire) Rome supports Queen Cartimandua against King Venutius
AD 57–?58	**Quintus Veranius**
AD ?58–61	**Gaius Suetonius Paulinus**
AD 60	Paulinus attacks Mona (Anglesey), a Druid stronghold
AD 60/61	Boudicca leads a revolt of Iceni and Trinobantes; destruction of Camulodunum (Colchester), Londinium (London) and Verulamium (St Albans)
AD 61/2–63	**Publius Petronius Turpilianus**
AD 63–69	**Marcus Trebellius Maximus**
AD 69	civil war in Rome: Year of the Four Emperors
	Venutius starts a major internal civil war in Brigantian territory against his queen, Cartimandua – Rome assists Cartimandua; Venutius defeated AD 71

AD 69/70	Vespasian becomes emperor; empire-wide policy sees end of client states as a means of rule
AD 69–71	**Marcus Vettius Bolanus**
AD 71–73/4	**Quintus Petillius Cerealis**
AD 71	Venutius defeated; conquest of north Wales and northern Britain begins
AD 73/4-77	**Sextus Julius Frontinus**
	southern Wales (Silures) conquered
	major works in British cities begins
c. AD 75	Fishbourne Palace (near modern Chichester) begun; ?work on the first temple at Bath begun by this time
AD 77–83/84	**Gnaeus Julius Agricola**
	Roman expansion north continues into the territory of the 'Caledonii'
AD 83 (or 84)	Battle of Mons Graupius – Calgacus and the Caledonii are defeated
	Agricola replaced by Sallustius Lucullus (governor from AD 83–84 until 96)

4.1 Claudius' Invasion of Britain, AD 43

TOPIC OVERVIEW

Claudius' invasion of Britain

- the reasons for the invasion: Caesar's earlier attempts to invade, the political situation in southern Britain, including tensions within and between the Catuvellauni and Atrebates
- the political situation in Rome, including the considerations of Claudius in the context of his own position and the preparations of Caligula
- the main events of the invasion including Roman preparations, crossing the Channel, and the encounters at the Medway and Thames
- Claudius' role in the invasion and its propaganda value to him
- the second phase, including Vespasian's campaign and the Fosse Way

The prescribed sources for this topic are:

- Cassius Dio, *History of Rome* 60.19.1–60.22.2; 60.23.1–60.23.6; 60.30.2
- Josephus, *Jewish War*, 3.1.2
- Suetonius, *Caligula*, 44.2; 46.1
- Suetonius, *Claudius*, 13.2; 17.1–17.3; 21.6; 24.3
- Suetonius, *Vespasian*, 4.1–4.2
- Tacitus *Annals* 12.23

- Gold stater of Verica
- Gold stater of Cunobelinus
- Bronze coin of Cunobelinus
- Aureus of Claudius (BM 1863,0501.1)
- Silver didrachma of Claudius (RIC 122)
- Arch of Claudius (ILS 216) (LACTOR 4.22)
- Tombstone of Sex. Valerius Genialis
- Tombstone of Rufus Sita

A NOTE ON THE SOURCES

As you can see from the list of sources on the previous page, some are written records composed by Romans and Greeks which mention Roman activity in Britain, and some are archaeological remains such as coins and tombstones. All need to be handled *critically* – which does not mean that they are automatically dismissed or regarded as untrustworthy – but when we examine them we need to ask what point of view their author might have had, what message they are trying to communicate, and hence how useful they are as evidence. For example, the inscription from Claudius' arch is original, and genuine – but it *is* propaganda. Claudius would have been foolish to include downright lies on his arch, but he might have been selecting information to improve his reputation, just as modern politicians might do when writing their memoirs. We also have to remember that original sources can be interpreted in different ways because of the values *we* apply to them.

> **KEY INDIVIDUAL**
> **Claudius**
> **Dates:** AD 10–54
> Emperor of Rome AD 41–54

CLAUDIUS' INVASION OF BRITAIN, AD 43

There are three basic points to consider when we ask why Claudius invaded Britain in AD 43 – we will look at them in detail below. They are:

1. because of his own political situation in Rome, Claudius desperately needed to establish himself and to strengthen his reputation so that he could claim to be seen as a leader;
2. earlier efforts at invading or preparing to invade Britain made it the 'obvious choice' for a Roman emperor wishing to make his name;
3. the tribal regimes in southern Britain were unstable and some British kings had begun to look to Rome for help.

We will now look at each point in detail.

> **KEY EVENT**
> Claudius' invasion of Britain, AD 43

1. Claudius' position at Rome

Claudius succeeded his nephew Gaius, better known as Caligula, when Caligula was murdered by his own bodyguards, the Praetorian Guard. They found Claudius hiding behind a curtain and took him to their camp just outside Rome. Claudius had been kept

---

EXAM TIP: SECOND-ORDER CONCEPTS

During this Depth Study, you will be required to reflect on second-order historical concepts, just as you were in the period study (see pp. 19, 22, 33, 43, 53 and 60). Remember to think about the following second-order concepts: continuity, change, cause, consequence, significance, similarity and difference.

in the shadows by the imperial family on account of his disabilities: he had a limp, spoke with a stammer, and tended to dribble from the corner of his mouth. According to Suetonius, even his mother Antonia had called him 'a monster of a man'. Even so, he was now chosen to be the next emperor. This how the Jewish historian Josephus described the events:

> [After the murder of Gaius, Claudius hid in the palace] . . . Gratus, one of the palace guard . . . recognised Claudius and said to his companions 'Here is a Germanicus, let us make him emperor'. Claudius . . . was afraid that they would kill him . . . and besought them to spare him. [They carried him off and saluted him as emperor.] The soldiers crowded round Claudius, glad to see his face, approving the choice of him as emperor, out of regard for Germanicus, who was his brother and had left behind a vast reputation among all that knew him.
>
> Josephus, *Antiquities* 19.3.1–2

Claudius was not only Caligula's uncle but (as Josephus stresses) was also the brother of the now-dead Germanicus. He had been a very fine soldier and had been extremely popular with the Roman army.

Despite the support of the Praetorian Guard, Claudius did not fit the bill as an ideal Roman emperor. He was a scholar rather than a soldier, and therefore did not match the stereotypical idea of a great leader for the Romans. As a result, there were several attempts to replace him, as this passage from his *Life* written by Suetonius tells us:

> **PS**
>
> Asinius Gallus and Statilius Corvinus, grandsons of the orators Pollio and Messala, plotted a revolution, bringing along with them several of Claudius' freedmen and slaves. Furius Camillus Scribonianus, his governor in Dalmatia, started the rebellion, but it was quashed in the space of five days by the legions who had changed their allegiance. For when orders were given them to march to meet their new emperor, the eagles could not be decorated, nor the standards pulled out of the ground, whether it was by accident, or divine intervention.
>
> Suetonius, *Claudius*, 13.2

PRESCRIBED SOURCE

Claudius

Author: Suetonius

Date: AD 121

Genre: biography

Significance: important source for the lives of the emperors despite being written some time after the events it describes

Prescribed sections: 13.2; 17.1–17.3; 21.6; 24.3

Read it here: OCR Source Booklet

4.1 Claudius' Invasion of Britain, AD 43

> **EXAM TIP – REVISING PRESCRIBED TEXTS**
>
> It is always a good idea to read the prescribed texts carefully and write a brief synopsis or overview of each one. It is also useful to write a few sentences evaluating each prescribed source. Is the text/source accurate; where did the author find this information; and finally, does it have a different interpretation to other ancient historians?
>
> It is also a good idea to underline difficult words, or unfamiliar names. You could then create a glossary to help improve your understanding.

ACTIVITY

- Why would many Romans think that Claudius was not a suitable man to be emperor? Read over the last section and write a short summary in your own words.
- In what ways do you think that invading Britain would have made Romans take Claudius more seriously as emperor?

S & C

How serious were the different attempts that were made on Claudius' life? Read the passage from Suetonius carefully and think about the detail he includes.

- Using the internet, can you find out more detail of these events? (If you find this a challenge what does it tell you about the nature of studying Ancient History?)

2. Julius Caesar's earlier attempts to invade

Caesar's two expeditions to Britain in 55 and 54 BC are generally regarded as unsuccessful. They probably established closer links between Britain and continental Europe, but in terms of military conquest they did not achieve very much (see the passage from Tacitus' *Agricola* 13 PS on pp. 217–218). However, Caesar made the most of his achievements in his *Commentaries* written at the time, and probably read out loud back at Rome, to the delight of his supporters.

The maps in Fig. 4.2 give an idea of the kind of world which the Romans thought they lived in They are based on descriptions given by the ancient writers Eratosthenes and Strabo. Try to identify Britain!

Caesar's first expedition of 55 BC lasted little more than a couple of weeks. It consisted of two legions and some cavalry (who were blown off course, and only thirty cavalry troops made it across with their horses). T.W. Potter has commented that

> Caesar presents the Romans' military achievement in the best possible light; but despite a subsequent victory, and a tally of hostages, the return to Gaul in jerry-rigged boats (i.e they were patched together in a hurry) before the winter set in can hardly have been an unqualified success.
>
> Potter, 'The Transformation of Britain', in P. Salway, *The Roman Era*, p. 14

As the following extracts show, Caesar himself tried to make the best of what happened – to make sure that he kept and even improved his reputation as a great general. He wrote his

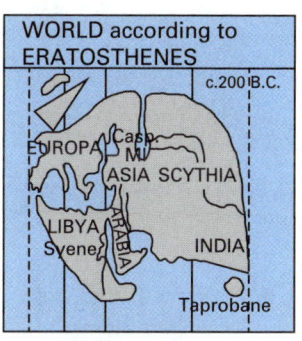

FIGURE 4.2
From *Muir's Historical Atlas Ancient and Modern.*

> **MODERN PARALLEL**
>
> Caesar's invasion of Britain has been likened to landing a man on the moon. Romans thought that Ocean was a divine being, so crossing it could be seen as taunting the gods. And as for Britain, it lay right on the edge of the world, so who could say what horrors were to be found there?

> **Study questions**
>
> 1 Read the passage Caesar, *Gallic War* 4.33.1.1 (LACTOR 11 A4) carefully and summarise the reasons why Caesar wanted to visit Britain and the problems he identified.
> 2 What reasons might the merchants have had for not wanting to help Caesar?

> **S&C**
>
> Summarise the tactics used by the Britons.
> - How did their tactics differ from Roman ways of fighting?
> - Read the two passages on the right carefully. Do you think that Caesar was impressed by the Britons?

Commentaries in the third person – he refers to himself as 'he' – so that a later historian could use them as the basis for a more developed work of history, but Roman writers considered that they were perfectly good as they were. First, his justification for making the expedition:

> Only a little of the summer remained; as the whole of Gaul tends northwards, winter comes early in these regions. Despite this, Caesar decided to travel to Britain, as he was aware that in almost all of the Gallic Wars, our enemy had received assistance from there. Even if there was not enough time to mount a full campaign, it would still be of great benefit just to go to the island and gain some understanding of the nature of its people, places, ports and approaches, all of which were largely unknown to the Gauls.
>
> Caesar, *Gallic War* 4.20.1 (LACTOR 11 A1).

Caesar also had some interesting comments about the military tactics used by the Britons:

> This is how they fight with chariots. First they ride around on all sides and throw weapons, and by the very dread of the horses and clattering of the wheels they throw a large part of the ranks into confusion; and when they have penetrated the cavalry troops, they jump down from the chariots and engage on foot. Meanwhile the charioteers withdraw from the battle little by little and then arrange their chariots so that if their men are closely pursued by the enemy horde, they have a means of retreat available to them. So they display in battle the mobility of cavalry and the stability of infantry, and through intense daily use and practice are so well-trained that they are accustomed to hold back their galloping horses on a precipitous slope, to control and turn them in a short time, and to run along the pole, stand on the yoke and then very quickly regain the chariot.
>
> Caesar, *Gallic War* 4.33.1.1 (LACTOR 11 A4)

Caesar was prevented from getting back to the continent by storms in the Channel, and had to fight off raiding parties of Britons for several days, until he met them head-on, defeated them and took hostages (prisoners of war). The Britons sent messengers to Caesar seeking peace. Caesar says he doubled the number of hostages – he clearly did not trust the Britons – and then 'because the equinox was approaching' (i.e. it was coming up to 21 September) he sailed back to Gaul.

Caesar's Second Expedition in 54 BC was much more determined. He took five legions, making up an army approaching 30,000 strong, and spent several months engaging the Britons in combat, finally defeating them in a battle north of London, possibly at Wheathampstead, though the location is not certain. The Senate in Rome had awarded him a twenty-day thanksgiving for the first expedition, but Caesar did not seem to believe his own propaganda and a real victory over the Britons was needed. This is his own account of some of the preparations he made:

> Caesar . . . ordered the legates (officers) who commanded the legions to build as many ships as they could during the winter, and to repair the old ones. He showed what designs to use: for ease of loading them and hauling them up on land he made them a little shallower than those which we tend to use on our sea – this the more so

since he had discovered that because of the frequent changes of the tides, the waves there were less great; for transporting freight and a great number of beasts of burden he made them wider than those we use on other seas. He ordered all of them to be built swift-sailing, in regard to which issue their lowness helped very much. He commanded that that which was of use for arming the ships be brought from Spain.

Caesar, *Gallic War* 5.1.1 (LACTOR 11 A5)

Caesar's forces still found it hard to combat the Britons with their unusual and effective tactics, but they successfully crossed the Thames in a surprise attack. Finally, Caesar forced the British tribes into an allegiance. Their leader, Cassivellaunus of the Catuvellauni tribe (see the map on p. 218) tried to cut off Caesar's supply-route and destroy his ships, but when this failed, he was forced to submit. Caesar also notes in passing that the Britons did not work together:

> Cassivellaunus enlisted the help of four kings who ruled in Kent – their names were Cingetorix, Carvilius, Taximagulus and Segovax – but their assault was countered by a surprise attack by the Romans. So Cassivellaunus used Commius, of the Atrebates tribe, as a go-between and negotiated a surrender. Once again Caesar demanded hostages and decided what taxes Britain should pay each year to the people of Rome. He also ordered Cassivellaunus not to harm Mandubracius or the Trinobantes, and then returned to the continent with all his forces

Caesar, *Gallic War* 5.22–5.23 (LACTOR 11 A10)

Caesar's achievement almost certainly acted as an inspiration for Claudius. Anyone who finished what Caesar had started would be seen as even greater. Something like this seems to have happened in the sculpture from Aphrodisias (modern Turkey) shown in Fig. 4.3, in which Claudius appears depicted as a triumphant soldier. It was produced over one hundred years later, as part of a series of sculptures commemorating great Roman conquerors.

Study questions:
Read Caesar, *Gallic War* 5.1.1 and 5.22–23.
1. How does Caesar try to show that he is an effective leader in these passages?
2. What points does Caesar make in his account to stress his success in this expedition?
3. What evidence is there in these passages that British tribes were hostile to one another?

3. The political situation in southern Britain

Caesar had noted a lack of co-operation between British tribes, and as he left the island in 54 BC he laid down conditions for their behaviour: 'He ordered Cassivellaunus (of the

Explore Further

Read Caesar's own accounts of his expeditions to Britain in the *Gallic Wars*, Books 4 and 5, in full. They are included in the LACTOR volume Literary Sources for Roman Britain, and there is also a readable Penguin translation of them.

- How successful was Caesar, according to Caesar? See especially Book 5 chapters 18–22.
- How does this compare with what Tacitus says in his summary of Roman dealings with Britain in Agricola 13 (PS), included in the Introduction to this section, pp. 217–218?

Part Two Depth Study 3: Britannia: From Conquest

FIGURE 4.4
Gold stater of Verica, from the Atrebates c. AD 10–40). Part of the Alresford Hoard, found in Hampshire in 1880.

FIGURE 4.3
Fragment of the frieze from the temple of Venus at Aphrodisias, showing the emperor Claudius.

PRESCRIBED SOURCE

Gold stater of Verica

Date: AD 10–40

Obverse: vine leaf; text 'VIRI'

Reverse: horseman; text 'CO FI'

Text reads: Verica/son of Commius

Current location: British Museum

Significance: original, independent evidence for the existence of Verica, and emphasises the importance for British kings of belonging to a 'dynasty'

Catuvellauni tribe) not to harm Mandubracius or the Trinobantes (this tribe was located north of the Thames, and their prince Mandubracius had come to Caesar to ask for help).' As we noted earlier, there was probably no such concept as Britons for the native tribes, whose cultures and allegiances were distinct and conflicting. There is some other evidence for tensions between the tribes, too: this may be reflected by the ways in which the kings of tribes in the southern parts of Britain began to copy Roman practice by issuing coins with their names on them.

Here are some coins issued by British kings: both are said to date from the period c. AD 10–40.

The face or 'heads' side of the coin in Fig. 4.4 has an abbreviated form (think text-messaging for the ancient world!) of the name 'Virica' with a vine-leaf in the centre. The reverse ('tails') shows a horseman, with the wording CO(MMI) F(ILIVS) or 'son of Commius' around it (LACTOR 4 no. 7). Verica, the third southern ruler to style himself 'son of Commius', probably succeeded Eppillus as the ruler of Calleva (Silchester, capital of the Atrebates) sometime in the early first century AD.

This coin may be the work of a Roman-trained engraver, and the vine-leaf on the obverse (face) may suggest a pro-Roman outlook.

'Virica' or 'Verica' is almost certainly the 'Berikos' mentioned by the historian Cassius Dio as asking Claudius for help: 'a certain Berikos, who had been driven out of the island as a result of civil war, persuaded Claudius to send a force there'.

4.1 Claudius' Invasion of Britain, AD 43

> ### PRESCRIBED SOURCE
>
> **Gold stater of Cunobelinus**
>
> **Date:** AD 10–40
>
> **Obverse:** ear of wheat; text 'CAMV'
>
> **Reverse:** horse; text 'CVN'
>
> **Text reads:** Camulodunum/Cunobelinus
>
> **Current location:** British Museum
>
> **Significance:** original, independent evidence for the existence of Cunobelinus and for the importance of Colchester

FIGURE 4.5
Gold stater of Cunobelinus, c. AD 10–40 (BM 1977,0434.11).

The coin in Fig 4.5, also a gold stater, was issued by Cunobelinus, who ruled over much of south-east Britain, north and south of the Thames, between c. AD 10 and 40, whose capital was at Camulodunum, the British predecessor of Roman Colchester, where this coin was apparently minted. The obverse (front) reads CAMV, while an abbreviation for Cunobelinus, CVN, appears with a horse on the reverse. Some fifteen other gold staters issued by Cunobelin are available to view on the British Museum website.

The ear of unimproved wheat (probably a kind of wheat called spelt, which is bearded, and accounts for its earlier misidentification as barley) on the obverse of Cunobelinus' gold coin is evidently a counterpart to the vine-leaf on Verica's issues. Although the precise significance of this emblem is unclear, wheat was one of the principal exports from Britain at this time according to Strabo 4.5.2 (LACTOR 11 B3.2) and it may therefore be a symbol of the kingdom's wealth and indicate its trading links with the continent.

Both these coins are gold – a precious metal – and they may therefore be symbolic as much as practical. The copper-alloy coins shown in Figure x.x may have been in regular use, and indicate a Roman or Mediterranean practice springing up in southern Britain before the Roman invasion in AD 43.

British kings already saw Rome as a source of support in their political difficulties: Augustus notes in his *Achievements of the Divine Augustus* or *Res Gestae Divi Augusti* that

> There fled to me as suppliants various kings: from the Parthians Tiridates and later Phraates son of King Phraates; Artavasdes king of the Medes and Artaxares king of the Adiabeni; from the Britons Dumnobellaunus and Tincommius.
>
> Augustus, *Res Gestae* 32. 1: LACTOR 11 32. 1

This must be before AD 14 (when Augustus died). A suppliant is someone who approaches another person hoping for help. It seems that these two British kings had been driven out of their territories and thought that the Romans would put them back on their thrones. It also suggests that they regard the Romans as 'allies', even if they were

KEY PLACE

Camulodunum
(Colchester) tribal capital of the Trinobantes – possibly under the control of the Catuvellauni at the time of the Roman invasion in AD 43; first capital of the province of Britannia, and a colony for veterans after AD 49

Study questions

1. What images did these British Kings put on their coins?
2. What do these images symbolize or represent?

Part Two Depth Study 3: Britannia: From Conquest

FIGURE 4.6
A bronze coin of Cunobelinus showing a boar and a face, c. AD 10–40.

PRESCRIBED SOURCE

Bronze coin of Cunobelinus

Date: AD 10–40

Obverse: head, facing right; text CVNOBELINVS REX

Reverse: image of a bull, head down; text TASC(IOVANI FILIVS)

Text reads: King Cunobelinus, son of Tasciovanus

Current location: British Museum

Significance: made of bronze, this is lower value, and may indicate that the coinage was becoming a real means of exchange and not just status symbols or means of exchanging precious metal

---

The bronze coin in Fig. 4.7 may illustrates Cunobelinus' desire to stress his dynastic claims by appealing to the fact that he was a descendant of Tascovianus, king of the Trinobantes from c. 25–10 BC, and thus a legitimate ruler of the tribe.

Obverse: Pegasus, facing to the right; inscribed CVNO (i.e. CVNOBELINVS)
Reverse: The goddess Victory sacrificing a bull, both facing right; inscribed TASCI (i.e. (son) of TASCOVIANVS)

FIGURE 4.7
A bronze coin of Cunobelinus showing Pegasus and the goddess Victory.

Explore Further

- Use the internet to look up more British gold coins on the British Museum website at https://www.britishmuseum.org/research/collection_online/search.aspx and use terms like 'British gold stater' or 'pre-Roman British coins'. See how much has been found! Note that Cunobelinus is called Cunobelin on the British Museum site.
- Use the internet to research other evidence for the way that British tribes were taking to Roman or Continental products and goods: look these up:
  - Stanway Burial
  - Lexden tumulus
  - Hengistbury Head

4.1 Claudius' Invasion of Britain, AD 43

> **PRESCRIBED SOURCE**
>
> ***History of Rome***
>
> **Author:** Cassius Dio
>
> **Date:** c. AD 150–235
>
> **Genre:** history
>
> **Significance:** a distinguished politician, born in Nicaea in Bithynia (modern Turkey) and later became a consul at Rome. He also spent twenty-two years writing his *Roman History*, in eighty books. Cassius Dio made careful and extensive use of earlier historians, which makes him a valuable and useful source on this period, despite the fact that he was writing about 180 years after the events he describes
>
> **Prescribed sections:** 60.19.1–60.22.2; 60.23.1–60.23.6; 60.30.2
>
> **Read it here:** OCR Source Booklet

not 'friends'. As we shall see, another king came to help for Claudius and provided him with a reason to invade. According to the historian Cassius Dio:

> a certain Berikos, who had been driven out of the island due to a war between tribes, persuaded Claudius to send a force there.
>
> Cassius Dio, *Roman History* 60.19.1

This Berikos is almost certainly the same Verica whose name appears on coins from the early first century AD such as the example on the previous page, which is just one of many which have been found.

CALIGULA'S PREPARATIONS FOR AN INVASION – AD 40

In addition we should note that Claudius did not have to start entirely from scratch, because Caligula had made plans for an invasion of Britain himself, as Suetonius tells us.

> He [Caligula] did nothing more than receive the submission of Adminius, the son of Cunobellinus, a king of the Britons, who had been exiled by his father and came over to the Romans with a small band of men. Yet, as if the whole island had been surrendered to him, Caligula dispatched elaborate letters to Rome ordering the imperial messengers to proceed by carriage right into the forum and to the senate-house, and only to deliver the letters to the consuls in the temple of Mars, and at a fully assembled senate.
>
> Finally, as if he were about to undertake a war, with his battle line drawn up on the edge of the Channel, with his *ballistas* and other artillery deployed and with nobody

knowing or guessing what on earth he was about to do, suddenly Caligula ordered them to collect seashells and to fill their helmets and laps of their tunics, calling these 'spoils of the Ocean' 'owed to the Capitoline and Palatine'. As a mark of his victory, he erected a very tall tower from which – as at Pharos in Alexandria – fires would shine out at night to guide the passage of ships. Caligula then announced to the soldiers a bounty of a hundred denarii per man, as if he had outshone every example of generosity. He said 'Go away happy: Go away rich'.

Suetonius, *Caligula* 44.2; 46.1

ACTIVITY

Read through the two paragraphs above from Suetonius' biography of Caligula. Then think about these questions:

- How serious do Caligula's plans appear to be?
- What effect do you think his actions had on his army?

PRESCRIBED SOURCE

Caligula

Author: Suetonius

Date: AD 121

Genre: Biography

Significance: important source for the lives of the emperors despite being written some time after the events it describes

Prescribed sections: 44.2; 46.1

Read it here: OCR Source Booklet

Further Study

Read this passage by the historian Cassius Dio, and as you go through it, compare it to what Suetonius tells us in the passages *Caligula*, 44.2 and 46.1.

- How similar are they?
- What does this tell us about the ways in which ancient historians used earlier work in their own writing?

When Caligula reached the Ocean, as if he were about to advance into Britain, he drew up his soldiers on the beach. He then embarked on a trireme, putting out from the shore and then sailing back again. Then he took his seat on a lofty platform, and gave the soldiers the signal as for battle, ordering the trumpeters to urge them on. Then suddenly he ordered them to pick up sea-shells. Having secured these spoils, for it was evident that he needed plunder for his triumphal procession, he became greatly elated, as if he had subdued the Ocean itself. He gave many presents to his soldiers. He took back the shells to Rome, in order to exhibit his plunder there as well.

Cassius Dio, *Roman History* 59.25.1 (LACTOR 11 D2.2n), (adapted)

THE MAIN EVENTS OF CLAUDIUS' INVASION

As we have seen, Claudius inherited a challenge to live up to his late brother Germanicus as a soldier and needed to establish his reputation as a genuine Roman leader. According to Cassius Dio, he had an invitation from Verica, prince of the Atrebates tribe, to get directly involved in Britain.

In addition, we should not discount the work that the Roman army must have done in AD 40 when Caligula planned his aborted invasion. The emperor may not have been serious, and he may have been distracted by events in Germany (though later ancient writers tend to focus more on the erratic aspects of his behaviour), but the army almost certainly prepared thoroughly. When they were called upon again to prepare an invasion three years later, they probably had a good idea of how to carry it out.

Claudius assembled a very large force made up of four legions and a number of auxiliary units, many of which were cavalry troops with specialist skills which were able to perform specific tasks. This army was even bigger than the one Caesar took on his second expedition and probably numbered about 40,000 in total. The written sources do not tell us who they were but the composition of the invading army can be identified from inscriptions and particularly tombstones, some of which are included on the previous page. Others can be identified from LACTOR 4.1–22, particularly the legions, which were Legio II Augusta, Legio IX, Legio XIV Gemina, and Legio XX.

We have to rely on Cassius Dio for information about the events of the invasion of AD 43. Other Roman writers such as Tacitus almost certainly described it (and Cassius Dio would have had access to them) but the parts of Tacitus' *Annals* which would have contained it have not survived. As we shall see, Suetonius only briefly mentions some events about the invasion in his biography of the emperor Vespasian (see p. 111).

Preparation for the invasion and crossing the channel

This is what Cassius Dio tells us about the start of the invasion:

> ... Aulus Plautius, a senator and a man of great reputation, led a campaign against Britain ... Plautius took charge of the campaign, but he had some difficulty in getting his army to leave Gaul, because they were angry at the idea of campaigning outside the boundaries of the Roman world. They would not obey Plautius, until Narcissus, who had been sent out by Claudius, went up onto the tribunal of Plautius and tried to speak to them. [3] At that point they became much angrier at this attempt by Narcissus and would not allow him even to say anything. Then suddenly altogether they started shouting the familiar chant 'Io Saturnalia'. [At the Saturnalia the slaves put on the clothes of the master and hold a festival.] Straightaway they willingly obeyed Plautius. But all this had delayed their leaving late in the season.
>
> Cassius Dio, *Roman History* 60.19.1–3

Study questions

1 According to Cassius Dio, why did the Roman troops object to crossing to Britain?
2 How does what happened here compare to the account of the earlier 'invasion' planned in AD 40?

Study questions

Read the passage Cassius Dio, *Roman History* 60.19.4–5 .

1 What encouraged the Roman soldiers as they crossed the Channel?
2 What does this tell us about how the Romans interpreted natural phenomena?
3 How similar were the British tactics to their ways of fighting against Julius Caesar?

KEY INDIVIDUAL

Aulus Plautius
Dates: first century AD
Commander-in-chief of the invasion forces in AD 43, and first governor of Britain. He had a successful political career and was a senator (member of the Roman Senate)

Cassius Dio also provides us with some details about the actual invasion, though his words can be interpreted in different ways:

> They were sent over in three divisions, so that they would not be prevented from landing, as might have happened if they had happened to be a single force. While crossing, they became disheartened when driven back, but then were encouraged when a flash of light coming from the east shot towards the west in the direction they were sailing. They landed on the island with no one to oppose them.
>
> For the Britons did not expect them to arrive because of the information they had received, and they had not gathered together a force. Even then, they did not come to close quarters, but fled into the swamps and forests, hoping instead to wear down the Romans and force them to sail away again empty handed, just as had happened at the time of Julius Caesar.
>
> Cassius Dio, *Roman History* 60.19.4–5

The first encounters with the Britons

Cassius Dio describes how the Romans surprised the British tribes opposing them by crossing two rivers using a tactic developed by German auxiliaries who dismounted and then held on to their horses' saddles to cross deep water. Dio does not name the first river, but it is usually thought to be the River Medway (assuming that the landing only took place in Kent): but note that the tribe he mentions is the Bodounni, which is thought to be a mispronunciation of the Dobunni, whose capital was at Corinium (Cirencester), though it may be a tribe whose only mention comes here: many of the tribal names given by Caesar do not appear after AD 43. If it is assumed that the Romans landed at three

S&C Compare this account with summaries of the Allied invasion of Normandy in 1944, during the Second World War. How much planning went into this?

DEBATE

Different modern writers have interpreted what Cassius Dio meant by 'sent over in three divisions' in different ways.

One popular school of thought is that the forces were taken across the Channel in successive waves. No one knows where the landing-site was but somewhere on the south coast of Kent seems most likely. The first wave would have established a beachhead or secure landing-ground so that the following troops could land safely. We have already seen that Caesar used this approach on his withdrawal from Britain after his second expedition.

An alternative view is that the Romans landed simultaneously at three different places – perhaps one in Kent, and at other places further west such as Fishbourne, near to Chichester harbour. If they were claiming to restore Verica to his throne it would make sense to land in what might well have been friendly territory where he might have had local support to help the Romans. It would also explain how Vespasian was able to campaign against British tribes in the west of Britain so very quickly – Chichester is quite a way to the west of Kent.

- Which makes most sense to you? (Hint: there is no right answer, but think about the significance of there being 'three divisions.')

MODERN PARALLEL

Similar tactics for crossing rivers were used by more recent cavalry units until they were replaced by tanks in the twentieth century.

places at the same time it must be a different river, and Vespasian is mentioned as leading this attack. The second passage names the River Thames. Dio may be talking about two different parts of the campaign, not one consecutive series of events. His account is not as clear as we might wish but it is the only one we have!

Crossing the ?Medway:

> Therefore Plautius had great difficulty in finding them; when he finally did find them he first defeated Caractacus, and then Togodumnus, the sons of Cunobelinus, who had died recently. The Britons at that time were not independent but different kings ruled each tribe.
>
> These two kings fled and Plautius gained the surrender of part of the Bodunni tribe, whom the Catuvellauni controlled. He then left behind a garrison, and advanced further into the island. When he reached a certain river, the Barbarians thought the Romans would be unable to cross without a bridge. Because of this, they took less care in camping on the opposite bank of the river. Plautius sent across some German auxiliaries, who were used to crossing the strongest currents in their armour.
>
> When they unexpectedly fell upon the enemy, they did not attack any of the men but the horses which drew their chariots. In the subsequent confusion not even the Britons' mounted men were able to get to safety. Next Plautius sent across Flavius Vespasianus, who later became emperor, and his brother Sabinus, who was his second-in-command.
>
> So they also got across the river and, surprising the barbarians, killed many of them. The rest did not flee, but on the next day they joined battle again. The outcome of the battle was uncertain until Gaius Hosidius Geta, after just avoiding being captured, at last overcame the enemy so effectively that he was awarded the honours of a triumph, even though he had not been a consul.
>
> Cassius Dio, *History of Rome* 60.20.1–4

Crossing the Thames:

> At this point the Britons retreated back to the River Thames, at a place where it enters the sea and forms a pool at high tide. They crossed this easily, since they knew where there were places of solid ground and easy passages.
>
> However, the Romans, in pursuing them, failed in their efforts to cross. So again the Germans swam across, and others went a little way upstream and crossed by a bridge. Then they attacked the enemy from different sides at the same time, and massacred many of them. They pursued the survivors without thinking and fell into swamps that were hard to get out of, and many were lost
>
> Cassius Dio, *History of Rome* 60.20. 5–6

At this point, Aulus Plautius halted his advance. According to Dio, it was because the British tribes had rallied to avenge their dead leader, Togodumnus (not to be confused with the Togidumnus or Cogidumnus we will encounter later on! Think how many English kings were called Henry, or French kings Louis). It may have been 'political' so that Claudius could cross over to Britain in person and claim the credit for finishing the campaign, rather like the ceremonial cutting of a ribbon to open a building or the laying of a dedication stone. This is what Cassius Dio says:

Study question
Did the Romans find it easy to defeat the Britons? (Read the passages above very carefully and do not jump to conclusions!)

> Because of this and also because Togodumnus had died, the Britons, far from surrendering, united all the more to avenge him. Plautius being afraid did not advance further, but secured what he had gained at present and sent for Claudius. This he had been ordered to do, if there was some stronger resistance; and besides, a lot of other equipment had already been put together for the expedition, including elephants. On the arrival of the message, Claudius placed other matters in Rome and command of the army in the hands of Lucius Vitellius . . . Then he set out for the army in Britain. He sailed down the river Tiber to Ostia, and next sailed by the coastal route to Massilia (Marseilles).
>
> From there he travelled both by road and river until he reached the Ocean. He crossed over to Britain and joined the army which was waiting for him at the River Thames. Taking command of the legions, he crossed the river, and attacked the barbarians who had gathered to oppose his arrival; he defeated them in battle and took Camulodunum (Colchester), the capital of Cunobelinus. As a result of this, he won over several tribes some through mutual agreement, others by force, and was saluted as Imperator a number of times contrary to normal practice (for it is the custom for no one to be given this title more than once from the same war). He took away the weapons from those who surrendered and put these tribes under the command of Plautius. He ordered him to subdue the remainder of the island. He himself hurried back to Rome, sending ahead the announcement of his victory by his sons-in-law Magnus and Silanus.
>
> Cassius Dio, *History of Rome* 60.21. 1–5

FIGURE 4.8
A map of Claudius' invasion.

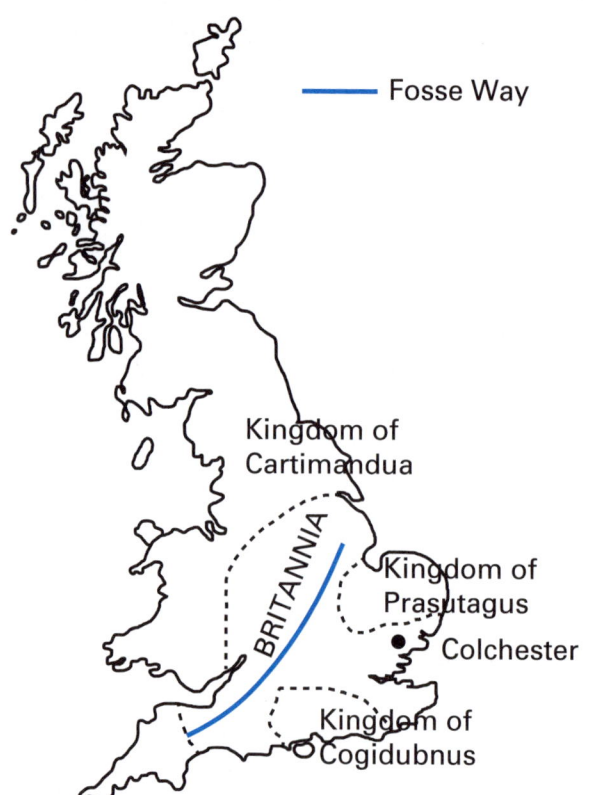

KEY INDIVIDUAL

Vespasian
Dates: AD 9–79

A Roman general involved in the conquest of AD 43 (but not in overall command – he was legate or commanding officer of the Second Legion Augusta). Later, he was emperor AD 69/70–79. Tacitus thought he was a 'good' emperor, unlike Vespasian's younger son Domitian

4.1 Claudius' Invasion of Britain, AD 43

THE INVASION CONTINUES

The second phase of the invasion saw a consolidation of Roman control of Britain up as far as a line approximately from Cirencester to Lincoln; this was a communication road which was once thought to be a limes, a boundary marking the limit of Roman territory, but is not now considered to have been regarded as a firm frontier by the Romans. However, it roughly marks the approximate edge of the first expansion of Roman control in Britain. It is now called the Fosse Way, though it was not known by that name in Roman times. It takes its name from the fossa or ditch which ran alongside it.

By about AD 49, the 'conquest' seems to have been regarded as complete, and the Romans used their normal practice of letting local rulers or client kings who were regarded as friendly allies to Rome get on with the business of governing the locals, while they established a capital for the territory they ruled directly at Camulodunum (Colchester), Cunobelinus' old tribal capital. We will look at this in more detail later (p. 247).

The campaign in the West was led by Vespasian, as the following extracts from ancient sources show. He was extremely successful in his command of the Second Legion Augusta and extended Roman control to the southwest of Britain very quickly.

> [Nero] only found Vespasian capable of doing what was necessary and able to take on a war of such a size as this one. Having been a soldier from his youth he had grown old in the army. Previously he had brought peace back to the Romans in the west when it had been thrown into disorder by the Germans. With his men he had won over Britain which was not known up until that time. By this victory there he provided [Nero's] father Claudius with the opportunity to lead a triumph at no personal effort.
>
> Josephus, *Jewish War*, 3.1.2

PRESCRIBED SOURCE

Jewish War

Author: Josephus

Date: first century AD

Genre: history

Significance: an independent account of the way in which Claudius came to be emperor, supporting other sources such as Suetonius

Prescribed sections: 3.1.2

Read it here: OCR Source Booklet

> In the reign of Claudius, thanks to Narcissus, Vespasian was sent to Germany in command of a legion. Being transferred from there to Britain, he engaged with the enemy thirty times. He conquered two very powerful tribes, captured more than twenty towns (*oppida*), and the Isle of Wight, which is very close to Britain; partly under the command of Aulus Plautius, a commander of consular rank and partly under Claudius himself. As a result, he received triumphal decorations, and within a short time, two priesthoods, besides the consulship, which he held during the last two months of the year [in AD 51].
>
> Suetonius, *Vespasian* 4.1–4.2

Evidence from tombstones also helps us to see how far the Roman advance progressed: there are two examples in the prescribed texts.

The tombstone of Sextus Valerius Genialis was found in 1836 and is now in the Corinium Museum, Cirencester. It is dated to the Claudian-early Flavian period. Its *Roman Inscriptions of Britain* number is *RIB* 109.

Its inscription reads as follows:

> Sextus Valerius Genialis, trooper of the Cavalry Regiment of Thracians, a Frisiavone tribesman, from the troop of Genialis, aged 40, of 20 years' service, lies buried here. His heir had this set up.

PRESCRIBED SOURCE

Vespasian

Author: Suetonius

Date: AD 121

Genre: biography

Significance: important source for the lives of the emperors despite being written some time after the events it describes

Prescribed sections: 4.1–4.2

Read it here: OCR Source Booklet

237

Study question
According to Josephus and Suetonius, how much of the conquest of Britain was actually due to Vespasian? Make a list of points – highlight the text to help you (ask your teacher first!)

EXPLORE FURTHER
Both prescribed tombstones can be seen on the *Roman Inscriptions of Britain* website at http://romaninscriptionsofbritain.org/

PRESCRIBED SOURCE

Tombstone of Rufus Sita

Date: mid-first century AD

Current location: Gloucester City Museum

Significance: contemporary evidence for the presence of specific Roman military units in Gloucestershire; note the stylised, 'triumphalist' portrayal of the deceased riding over a defeated enemy

EXPLORE FURTHER
Fuller details of these tombstones can also be found in the LACTOR volume *Roman Inscriptions of Britain*, nos. 13 and 14.

His tombstone shows a cavalryman brandishing his lance above a fallen enemy. He carries a shield and probably a standard (a banner or other regimental insignia mounted on a pole). The Frisiavones lived in the area of the lower Rhine, close to its mouth, so it is probable that Genialis was recruited to the Cavalry Regiment of Thracians when it was serving in Lower Germany, its base before it came to Britain. If that is so, Genialis, with twenty years' service, can have died no later than AD 62. He has the tria nomina or three names of a Roman citizen: *Sextus* is his praenomen or first name, *Valerius* is his nomen, his tribe or clan name, and *Genialis* (which means kind), is a 'cognomen' which may have originated as a nickname and could be inherited. Romans often referred to one another by their cognomen.

Rufus Sita, of the cohors VI Thracum (*RIB* 121), has a similar tombstone, dated to the mid-first century AD. He was buried at Kingsholm, near Gloucester (Glevum) His tombstone, found in 1824, is now in Gloucester City Museum. His inscription reads as follows:

> Here lies Rufus Sita, cavalryman in the sixth cohort of Thracians. He lived for 40 years and served for 22 years. His heirs had this set up, according to his will.

His tombstone depicts a cavalryman with a shield in his left hand and a long sword or spatha at his right side, brandishing a spear over his fallen enemy. Above this scene is a sphinx, guardian of the tomb, with lions on either side. The cohors VI Thracum was made up of both infantry and cavalry and was probably part of the garrison of Kingsholm, a military base founded in the 40s and evacuated in the late 60s AD. It was replaced by the fortress and later colony at Gloucester fortress. See Fig. 4.9.

S & C Use the internet to research the archaeology at Maiden Castle, Dorset, where some gruesome evidence may support what the ancient writers say about Vespasian's activities against the Durotriges (a British tribe located in modern Hampshire and Dorset).

Study questions
Read the two inscriptions and look carefully at the images of the tombstones.

1. How did their comrades want these men to be remembered? What were they proud of?
2. If you were a Briton how would *you* react to these images appearing in your country?

4.1 Claudius' Invasion of Britain, AD 43

FIGURE 4.9
Tombstones of Sextus Valerius Genialis (left) and Rufus Sita (right).

PRESCRIBED SOURCE

Tombstone of Sex. Valerius Genialis

Date: mid-first century AD

Current location: Corinium Museum, Cirencester

Significance: contemporary evidence of the presence of specific Roman military units near Cirencester; note the stylised, 'triumphalist' portrayal of the deceased riding over a defeated enemy

CLAUDIUS' ROLE IN THE INVASION AND ITS PROPAGANDA VALUE TO HIM

Thus the evidence from written sources and archaeology indicates that the Roman invasion of Britain proceeded fairly quickly, and Roman military control spread from the south coast of Britain as far as the west, to the Bristol Channel, and to the east in Colchester. As we have seen, Claudius does not seem to have played a large role in the invasion in person. However, its success was something for which he could claim great credit, and he could regard it as a major achievement: there are a number of sources which illustrate exactly how important it was (or perhaps, how well it could be manipulated for him). The prescribed sources are all included here in this section. Think too about the sculpture from Aphrodisias, p. 228.

> When the Senate learned of these successes, they gave him [Claudius] the title of Britannicus and awarded him permission to hold a triumph. They also voted that there should be an annual festival in celebration of the event and that two triumphal arches should be set up, one in Rome and one in Gaul, because it was from there that he had set sail and crossed to Britain. They also granted the same title of Britannicus to his son, with the result that eventually the boy came to be called Britannicus normally. They also granted Messalina the right of using a front seat at the theatre, just as Livia had enjoyed, and the right of using the *carpentum* (a covered carriage).
>
> Cassius Dio, *History of Rome* 60.22.1–2

Students might also like to explore the German *Epigraphischen Datenbank Clauss-Selby* at http://db.edcs.eu/epigr/epi_en.php which also has pictures of these and several others mentioned in LACTOR 4. Its search engine is very user-friendly! Just type in the Latin names (or even part of them).

Fragments of the triumphal arch from Rome survive, supporting what Dio had to say (it was still surviving in his own day, and stood until the fifteenth century). Fragments of it are on display in the courtyard of the Palazzo dei Conservatori, Capitoline Museum.

> To Tiberius Claudius Caesar Augustus Germanicus, the son of Drusus, pontifex maximus, holding the tribunician power for the 11th time, consul for the 5th time, imperator for the 22nd (?) time, censor, the father of the fatherland, from the senate and Roman people because he has conquered eleven Britain kings in few days without any losses and have been the first to transfer their kingdoms and the barbarous peoples situated beyond the Ocean into the power of the Roman people.
>
> Arch of Claudius (ILS 216)

In his biography of Claudius, Suetonius explicitly states that British kings surrendered to him (*Claudius* 21.6).

Cassius Dio describes Claudius' return to Rome in fulsome terms:

> In this way, parts of Britain were taken into the Empire at this time. After this, in the year when Gaius Crispus (for the second time) and Titus Statilius were consuls [AD 44], Claudius returned having been away from Rome for six months; of these he spent only sixteen days in Britain. He then celebrated his triumph. He did everything else according to custom, ascending the steps of the Capitol on his knees, supported by his sons-in-law on either side.
>
> He granted to the senators, who had campaigned with him the triumphal ornaments, and not just to those who had been consuls . . . After dealing with these matters, he held his triumph . . . This was all done because of the events in Britain; so that others might more easily be persuaded to come to an agreement with the Romans, it was decreed that all agreements, which either Claudius or his legates had made, should have the same authority as if made by the Senate and the Roman People.
>
> Plautius, after his excellent handling of the war in Britain and the success of his achievements, was both praised by Claudius and awarded a triumph.
>
> Cassius Dio, *History of Rome* 60.23.1–6, 30.2

Note that Cassius Dio here says that Aulus Plautius was granted a 'triumph' just like the emperor, but he is probably wrong; according to Suetonius, this is what the emperor did for Aulus Plautius:

> . . . He decreed to Aulus Plautius the honour of an ovation, going to meet him as he entered the city, and walked with him to the Capitol, and on the way back, Claudius took the left side, giving him the post of honour.
>
> Suetonius, *Claudius* 24.3

An ovation was a specific acclamation made by an army to its general, like giving him three cheers: they called out loud the word 'imperator' or 'general'. We might

4.1 Claudius' Invasion of Britain, AD 43

FIGURE 4.10
This photograph shows part of the fragmentary remains of the inscription from the Arch of Claudius.

PRESCRIBED SOURCE

Inscription from the Arch of Claudius

Date: arch dedicated AD 51

Significance: celebrates Claudius' invasion of Britain

Reference no.: ILS 216

Ancient location: central Rome

Modern location: fragments in Capitoline Museum

Read it here: LACTOR 4, 22 and OCR Source Booklet

compare the way that crowds shout the names of their heroes at football matches or other sporting events. We have also seen how Suetonius records that Vespasian received a triumph (see p. 237). Dio has probably confused his sources about the different generals.

Claudius also took advantage of his success to stage a (quite obscure) religious ceremony, as Tacitus notes:

> The emperor Claudius widened the city boundary (*pomerium*) of Rome, in accordance with the ancient custom, according to which, those who had enlarged the empire were permitted also to extend the boundaries of Rome. But Roman generals, even after the conquest of great nations, had never exercised this right, except Lucius Sulla and the Divine Augustus.
>
> Tacitus, *Annals* 12.23

Lucius Sulla had been a very famous Roman general, and the deified Augustus was the first emperor: by undertaking this action, Claudius was equating himself with them.

Finally, Claudius made use of coinage as propaganda to emphasise his achievement. This was a common way for Roman leaders to promote themselves, but Claudius makes specific use of his victory over the British tribes, and the coin on the next page, an aureus, mirrors the evidence for the arches erected to celebrate the victory (it was minted at Rome, not in Britain, incidentally):

Another coin issued by Claudius is this silver didrachma (Fig. 4.12), minted at Caesarea in Cappadocia *c*. AD 46–48, with the legend DE BRITANNIS, which show

PRESCRIBED SOURCE

Annals

Author: Tacitus

Date: early second century AD

Genre: history

Significance: one of the principal written sources for our period, though Tacitus is well known for being hostile to the emperors and to the imperial form of government

Prescribed sections: 12.23

Read it here: OCR Source Booklet

Part Two Depth Study 3: Britannia: From Conquest

FIGURE 4.11
Aureus of Claudius.

PRESCRIBED SOURCE

Aureus of Claudius

Date: AD 46–47

Obverse: head of Claudius wearing laurel wreath, facing right; text TI(BERIVS) CLAVD(IVS) CAESAR AVG(VSTVS) P(ONTIFEX) M(AXIMVS) TR(IBVNICIA) P(OTESTATE) VI IMP(ERATOR) XI

Reverse: triumphal arch with an equestrian statue on top, with two trophies, one either side; text DE BRITANN(IS).

Text reads: 'Tiberius Claudius Caesar Augustus, chief priest, in his sixth year of tribunician power, hailed *imperator* eleven times.'/'(*Erected in commemoration of victory*) over the Britons.'

Current location: British Museum

Significance: contemporary evidence of the value to Claudius of conquering Britain, thus allowing him to present himself as a victorious military leader

FIGURE 4.12
Silver didrachma of Claudius (RIC 122).

PRESCRIBED SOURCE

Silver didrachma of Claudius (RIC 122)

Date: AD 46–48

Obverse: Head of Claudius with laurel wreath; text TI CLAVDIVS CAESAR AVG GERM P M TR P:

Reverse: Claudius in a four-horse chariot holding eagle sceptre; text: DE BRITANNIS

Text reads: 'Tiberius Claudius Caesar Augustus Germanicus Pontifex Maximus of the Plebs'

Minted in: Cappadocia

Significance: contemporary evidence of the value to Claudius of conquering Britain, thus allowing him to present himself as a victorious military leader

Claudius in his triumphal chariot celebrating the conquest of Britain. The coins provide evidence which supports what Suetonius tells us about Claudius' ambitions and the ways in which he exploited his victories in Britain:

He undertook only one expedition, and that a modest one. The Senate had (earlier) decreed him triumphal ornaments, but he regarded this as beneath his dignity as emperor. He sought the honour of a real triumph, and chose Britain as the best field in which to seek this, for no one had attempted an invasion since the time of Julius Caesar and the island at this time was in a turmoil because certain refugees had not been returned to the island . . .

He returned to Rome in the sixth month from the time of his departure, and celebrated a triumph in the most splendid manner. To witness the show, he not only gave leave to governors of provinces to come to Rome, but even certain exiles. From among the enemy spoils he fixed on the gable end of his house on the Palatine, a naval crown next to the civic one, as a commemoration of his having travelled over and as it were 'conquered' the Ocean. Messalina, his wife, followed his triumphal chariot in a covered carriage. Those who had gained triumphal decorations in the same war, followed behind, on foot, in robes with broad stripes. Marcus Crassus Frugi was on a horse with ceremonial regalia and in a robe embroidered with palm leaves, because this was the second time that he had obtained the honour.

Suetonius, *Claudius* 17.2–3

Study questions

Look carefully about all the sources in this section – the texts, the coins, and Claudius' arch.

1. In your own words, list all the ways in which Claudius exploited the military success over the Britons.
2. What impression do you think this had on the people of Rome?

TOPIC REVIEW

Boost your knowledge

Describe:

1. The earlier attempts the Romans had made at invading Britain
2. The advantages of invading Britain rather than any other territory
3. The different stages of the invasion
4. The reaction of different groups of Britons to the invasion

Stretch your understanding

Explain:

1. The amount of contact Britons had with the Roman Empire before the invasion
2. Claudius' urgent need of a military triumph
3. The success of Claudius' invasion in its early stages
4. How Claudius benefitted from the invasion

Part Two Depth Study 3: Britannia: From Conquest

PRACTICE QUESTIONS

1. a. Name the commander-in-chief of the invasion of Britain in AD 43 who then became the first governor of Britain. [1]
   b. Name the **two** rivers which have been identified as holding up the Roman advance. [2]
   c. Give **two** reasons why invading Britain was important for Claudius. [2]

Passage A

Plautius being afraid did not advance further, but secured what he had gained at present and sent for Claudius. This he had been ordered to do, if there was some stronger resistance; and besides, a lot of other equipment had already been put together for the expedition, including elephants. On the arrival of the message, Claudius placed other matters in Rome and command of the army in the hands of Lucius Vitellius, his fellow consul (for he had made him remain as consul for the full half-year like himself). Then he set out for the army in Britain. He sailed down the River Tiber to Ostia, and next sailed by the coastal route to Massilia (Marseilles). From there he travelled both by road and river until he reached the Ocean. He crossed over to Britain and joined the army which was waiting for him at the River Thames. Taking command of the legions, he crossed the river, and attacked the barbarians who had gathered to oppose his arrival; he defeated them in battle and took Camulodunum (Colchester), the capital of Cunobelinus.

Cassius Dio, *History of Rome* 60.21. 1–4

2. Using details from Passage A, explain how accurate you think Dio's description is. [5]

4.2 The Romans in Britain

TOPIC OVERVIEW

The changing policies of the various Roman governors. The significance and success of these governors

- Ostorius Scapula's campaigns including his motives, preparations and tactics
- Didius Gallus' policies towards the Silures and Brigantes
- the significance of the appointments of Quintus Veranius, Suetonius Paulinus and Trebellius Maximus.
- campaigns and achievements of Bolanus, Cerialis and Frontinus including the reasons for their policies
- the influence of different emperors

Cooperation between Romans and Britons and the effects of Roman rule

- the submission of the tribes to Claudius at Camulodunum
- creation of client states: the Atrebates, the Iceni, and the Brigantes
- client states and their relations with Romans

Resistance after the invasion

The resistance campaigns of Caratacus, Boudicca and Venutius:

- the reasons for their resistance and the extent of their success
- the nature of the Roman response to resistance
- the sources' portrayal of the Britons, particularly those who resisted Roman rule

The prescribed sources for this topic are:

- Cassius Dio, History of Rome 62.1.1–62.3.4; 62.7.1–62.9.2; 62.12.1–62.12.6
- Tacitus, *Agricola*, 10–27; 29–37
- Tacitus, *Annals* 12. 31–40; 14.29–39
- Tacitus, *Histories* 3.44–45

COOPERATION BETWEEN ROMANS AND BRITONS AND THE EFFECTS OF ROMAN RULE

KEY INDIVIDUAL

Publius Ostorius Scapula governor of Britain AD 47–52

KEY PEOPLE

The Brigantes a tribe located in the north of Britain, roughly in modern Lancashire and Yorkshire

The first stage of Rome's conquest of Britain was not immediate: Tacitus tells us that the new governor appointed in AD 47, Publius Ostorius Scapula, 'was faced with a chaotic situation' and had to put down hostile tribes to the West and the North of the area under Roman control. He also imposed the Roman law called the lex Iulia de vi publica which forbade any private citizens from carrying weapons in public: Tacitus tells us that 'he disarmed those whose loyalty was suspect and prepared to consolidate the whole area to the south of the Trent and the Severn' (refer to the map on p. 218 for details). This was in contradiction to the warrior-code of the British tribes and it provoked a rebellion among the Iceni which had to be put down by force: direct control was established over a central area, with a provincial capital based at Camulodunum (Colchester); areas to the north and south were left in the control of 'client kings' ruling over 'client states.' The one to the south was even known as the people of the *regni* or 'kingdom'; this had been the area occupied by the Atrebates tribe, and they may have been given this status as a reward for being co-operators with Rome. In what is now Norfolk and Lincolnshire, the tribe left in control was the Iceni, under King Prasutagus; he has also issued coins in his own name and seems to have had a pro-Roman outlook, culturally if not politically (see map on p. 218). The northern border was left in the control of third client king, Venutius of the Brigantes.

This is all spelled out by Tacitus in his *Annals*, who stresses the threats posed by rebellious Britons. Note the distinctions he makes between 'the enemy' and 'our allies' territory' and the positive attitude which he shows towards Publius Ostorius' swift and decisive action:

> Meanwhile, in Britain the pro-praetor Publius Ostorius had a troubled reception, as the enemy had poured into the territory of our allies with a violence that was all the greater because they thought that a new commander would not engage with an unfamiliar army and with winter begun. Ostorius, aware that the first events are those which produce fear or confidence, swept his cohorts forward at speed, cut down those who had resisted, and chased those in disarray. He wanted to prevent them from regrouping so that a bitter and disloyal peace would not follow which would allow no rest to either the commander or to his troops. He disarmed all suspects and suppressed the whole area on this side of the rivers Trent and Severn using garrisons.
>
> The first to revolt against this were the Iceni, a powerful tribe not yet broken in battle, as they had voluntarily become allies. At their suggestion, the surrounding tribes selected a position for battle which was protected by a rustic earthwork with an approach too narrow to allow access to the cavalry. The Roman commander prepared to break through this defence, though he was leading an auxiliary force without the strength of the legions, and distributing the cohorts in appropriate positions, turned even his dismounted cavalry to infantry work. Then, on the signal, they broke through the earthwork. They threw the enemy into confusion, imprisoned by their own defences. With the rebellion on their mind, and every exit barred, the Britons

performed many heroic feats; and during the engagement the legate's son, Marcus Ostorius, earned the decoration for saving the life of a Roman citizen.

Tacitus, *Annals* 12.31

This is how Tacitus described the settlement made by the Romans:

> After the Iceni defeat, all those who were wavering between war and peace settled down, and the army moved against the Decangi. The fields were devastated, booty collected everywhere, while the enemy declined to risk an open battle, or, if they made a stealthy attempt to ambush the column, found their trickery punished. And now Ostorius was not far from the sea facing Ireland, when an outbreak of rebellion among the Brigantes summoned him back. He was determined to attempt new conquests only when he had secured the old. The Brigantes uprising, indeed, was quashed with the execution of a handful of men, who had started the hostilities, and with the pardon of the others. However, neither severity nor mercy converted the Silurian tribe, which continued the struggle and had to be repressed by the setting up of a legionary garrison. In order to achieve that, a colony [**colonia**] was settled on conquered lands at Camulodunum [Colchester]. This was a strong detachment of veterans and they were to serve as a defence against revolt and to get the natives to have a positive attitude towards observing the laws.

Tacitus, *Annals* 12.32

As we shall see, the Iceni ceased to be a client kingdom after the rebellion of Boudicca, in AD 60/61, and the Brigantes were overrun after an internal civil war and a rebellion against Rome by Venutius in AD 69. The southern kingdom seems to have stayed loyal to Rome under a king called Togidubnus or Cogibudnus (the spelling is not known for certain – just do not confuse him with the Togodubnus who died in battle in the initial stages of the invasion – see p. 235). Tacitus tells us in *Agricola* 14 that 'Certain tribal areas were presented to King Cogidubnus (and he continued in utter loyalty within our

Study question
What effects did the actions which Ostorius Scapula took against the Britons have on the British tribes? Refer closely to the two passages from Tacitus on the left to support your answer.

colonia a settlement of veterans (ex-soldiers) made up of land taken from native tribes. Ex-legionaries received a farmstead as part of their pension settlement

DISCUSSION AND DEBATE
Read the passages of Tacitus *Annals* 12.31 and 12.32 and debate this question:

- Were the Romans friendly or hostile to the British tribes?

PRESCRIBED SOURCE

Annals

Author: Tacitus

Date: early second century AD

Genre: history

Significance: one of the principal written sources for our period, though Tacitus is well known for being hostile to the emperors and to the imperial form of government

Prescribed sections: 12.31–40; 14.29–39

Read it here: OCR Source Booklet

> **PRESCRIBED SOURCE**
>
> ### Agricola
>
> **Author:** Tacitus
>
> **Date:** c. AD 98
>
> **Genre:** biography
>
> **Significance:** Tacitus wrote this eulogy or work in praise of his late father-in-law when it seemed safe to do so after the death of the vindictive and oppressive emperor Domitian in AD 96. He evidently knew the man well, and had first-hand knowledge of stories of Agricola's three tours of duty in the province of Britannia. However, because Tacitus wrote it in praise of Agricola, and clearly admired Agricola's military victories – a mark of greatness in Roman eyes – he tends to be very dismissive of other governors, even though they may have been obedient to the express wishes of emperors in the way they acted in Britain
>
> **Prescribed sections:** 12.31–40; 14.29–39
>
> **Read it here:** OCR Source Booklet

own memory)', though in a caustic style typical of his writing, Tacitus adds the comment that 'by an ancient and long accepted habit of the Roman people, kings have been the means of imposing slavery.'

Jumping ahead chronologically, we should note that after Vespasian became emperor in AD 69/70 he seems to have preferred not to use client kings or client states in Britain; although Cartimandua of the Brigantes appealed to the Romans for help (see pp. 256–257), she was not restored to power, and there is no mention of Togidubnus acting as a king after this time; in fact, there are no kings at all acting as collaborators with the Romans in Britain (and Vespasian's son, Titus, brought the dynasty of the kings called Herod to an end in Jerusalem at about the same time, in AD 70). If there was a change in policy, it is possible that Togidubnus would have been made redundant. At about the same time, work began on the construction of a massive palace (it is also known as a villa) at Fishbourne (near Chichester, on the Sussex coast), which is right in the centre of Atrebates territory and may even have been one of the landing-places of the invasion. Was it a reward for Togidubnus' loyalty, as is sometimes suggested? We can never prove it, and we do not know who built it, but the chronology fits very nicely. We can't know who did build it, though it's much more likely to be a (powerful) individual than a state or official project. Whoever they were, they were certainly wealthy and very aware of what a Roman elite residence should look like. If it was built by Togidubnus or his descendants – not unlikely – then they were almost certainly building it from their own resources, rather than being given it as a reward. Another theory, given that is was clearly a luxury dwelling, is that it may have served for visiting Roman dignitaries as well.

FIGURE 4.13
Fishbourne Roman Palace.

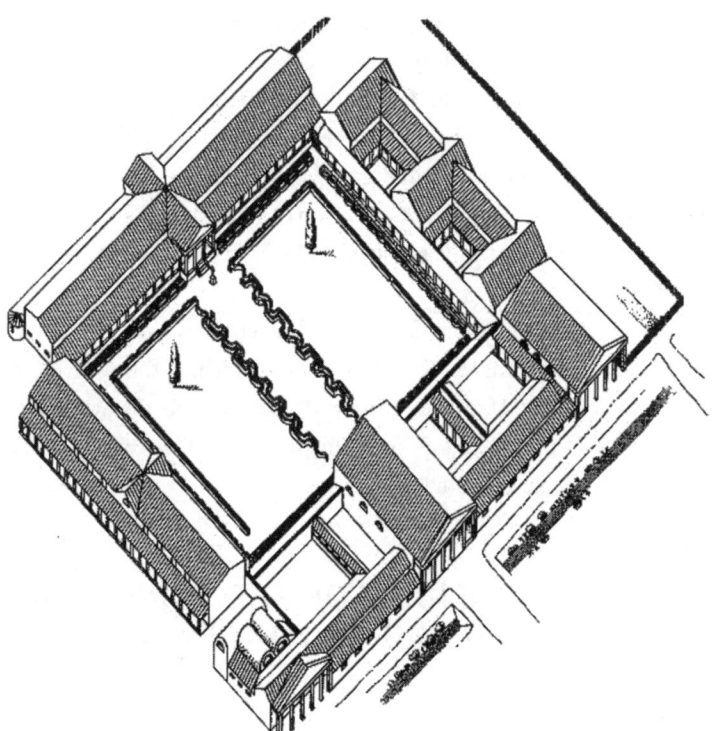

Fig. 4.13 is a drawing of what the villa might have looked like *c*. AD 80: there was nothing similar built in Britain in the same period, and the golden age of villa building in Britain did not occur until the fourth century AD, though there were certainly lavish town-houses with decoration as magnificent as Fishbourne built before then. Nevertheless, Fishbourne remains in many ways one of a kind.

We will look at Fishbourne Roman Palace in more detail in a later Thematic Study section, pp. 262–265.

Despite the significance of Fishbourne, the client state of the Atrebates was not based here, but had a major capital at Calleva Atrebatum (Silchester), near to modern-day Basingstoke. There was also a prominent Roman town at Noviomagus (modern Chichester) which has evidence of early development.

THE CAMPAIGN OF CARATACUS AND THE SILURES

Unlike Togodumnus (see Cassius Dio, p. 236), the British leader, Caratacus, escaped with his life and continued to resist the Romans after other tribes had submitted. He used what is now South Wales, the territory of the Silures, as his base. When he led an attack on the tribe called the Ordovices, the Roman response was determined, if slow. The governor, Ostorius Scapula, was apparently taken by surprise by the challenges he had to face, and he died while in office. It took until AD 51 for Caratacus to be defeated. He clearly did not want to be ruled by the Romans or be counted as one of their allies like

EXPLORE FURTHER
You can find out about Fishbourne Roman Palace at the excellent website provided by the Sussex Archaeological Trust, at https://sussexpast.co.uk/properties-to-discover/fishbourne-roman-palace (or just search for 'Fishbourne Roman Palace').

KEY INDIVIDUAL
Caratacus British tribal chieftain and leader of resistance till AD 49/51

KEY PEOPLE
The Silures a British tribe located in what is now South Wales

Part Two Depth Study 3: Britannia: From Conquest

> **Study questions**
> Read the passages from Tacitus, *Annals* 12.31–40 **PS**.
>
> Summarise the main events of what happened; make a list, or use bullet-points – keep it simple
>
> 1 Look over the passage again. Does Tacitus admire Caratacus or look down on him? Highlight the passage or write quotes out so support your argument.
> 2 For discussion or debate: why do you think Claudius spared Caratacus?
> 3 Imagine that you are one of Claudius' advisory team and prepare an argument to persuade him to have Caratacus spared, or have him executed!

Togidubnus, and despite some early successes holding the Romans back, his efforts to defeat them seem to have been futile.

The story of his resistance to Rome is told in great detail by Tacitus in *Annals* 12.31–40 **PS**. We should note that this is the *only* source which records the resistance of Caratacus and the Roman response to him. There is a lot of archaeo-logical evidence for Roman military camps in Wales, but the efforts to conquer Wales continued for a good twenty years after the defeat of Caratacus, and it is not possible to identify camps from this very early period.

So the way to tackle this topic is to read the account which Tacitus provides, noting the main details, and then answer the study questions which follow. Note particularly the nature of the Romans' response to British resistance, and the ways in which Tacitus portrays the Britons in his account – is he dismissive of them as 'barbarians' or does he admire them – or does he do both?

THE CHANGING POLICIES OF THE VARIOUS ROMAN GOVERNORS; THEIR SIGNIFICANCE AND SUCCESS

We know the names of more governors of Britain from the whole period of the Roman occupation than we do from any other Roman province. From the time line at the beginning of this module, we can identify the first governors of Britain and their years in office; these are listed on p. 252. Simply listing their names, which is what the specification does, might suggest that we know a lot about all of them: we don't. They receive a very uneven treatment in the sources and some of them barely get a walk-on part. Tacitus provides a list of all the governors up to and including his own father-in-law Agricola in *Agricola* 14–17 **PS**. Some governors get a lot more coverage because they appear in other sources too.

The word 'policy' used in the specification about the Roman governors just means 'what did they intend to do?' or 'what were they told to do?' Their 'significance' means 'how important were they' and 'what did they achieve?' Their 'success' might be measured in purely military terms (if their job was to defeat the enemy) or in terms of development and reconciliation (if they wanted the province to grow, pay more in taxes, and stop rebelling!).

Overall policy was dictated from Rome, and this might depend on the whim or ambition of the emperor (we have seen how much a military success meant to Claudius). Other parts of the empire might need attention as well. However, there is one quote from the poet Virgil, from his epic the *Aeneid*, which might help us understand Roman attitudes to the British tribes in general. The eventual founder-to-be of Rome, Aeneas, is told that one of Rome's functions in the world is going to be this: *parcere subiectis et debellare superbos*. We can paraphrase this as 'to spare those who are subject to you, and wear down the proud who resist'. It provides some help as we try to understand why the Romans reacted to different events as they did.

The specification makes this look like a lot of material: but there is very limited coverage of some parts, and we will look at other parts – like Boudicca's rebellion

> **ACTIVITY**
>
> One of the most useful tasks you can do in this module is to create your own summary of the governors using the list of their names and dates on p. 252, which is extracted from the time-line above. We have already seen what the first two governors did: you can add more detail as you go but don't put too much in at this stage (as you will see, you will find it hard to do that with Veranius, for example). Use Tacitus *Agricola* 14–17 (PS) as your starting-point: where some governors are mentioned by other sources there are notes in the list on the next page. You may find it useful to add a short quote or two from the sources to remind you what Tacitus or another author thought of this particular governor. Don't add very much on the last of these governors, Agricola, for the time being – we will look at his career in detail later.
>
> You could make it into a poster with lots of space, filling it in by hand or typing it up (I suggest you use landscape format). Keep adding to the list as the course progresses. Doing this will help you to remember who did what where (mastering the unfamiliar names can be a challenge!) and when you have finished, guard your creation: you will find it one of the best tools for helping you to revise that you can have!

in AD 60/61, and the problems in Brigantian territory in AD 69 – in more detail later. And of course, the most detailed accounts of all in *Agricola* describe the man himself, governor from AD 77 to 83. He actually had three tours of duty in Britain; he had been an officer (military tribune) with a legion in the late 50s to early 60s, appointed by Suetonius Paulinus himself, and he had commanded the Twentieth Legion in 70–73, when Rome was extending control northwards into the territory of the Brigantes.

Agricola was not the only example of a governor being chosen on the basis of prior experience: when Rome was attempting to bring Wales under control, a task which involved a lot of fighting in mountainous areas and involving guerrilla warfare, the choice of Didius Gallus, Veranus, and Suetonius Paulinus must have taken into account their experience of mountain warfare in the Balkans, southern Asia Minor, and the Atlas mountains of north Africa respectively.

You should also note that just because Tacitus is very dismissive of the achievements of some governors (or the lack of them, as far as he is concerned), this does not mean that they were failures or that they were not doing just what the emperor at the time actually wanted them to do! Tacitus took his father-in-law Agricola as an ideal, and any governor who did not get involved in military conquest was regarded as falling short of that ideal. Working carefully through what Tacitus tells us – and it is fairly easy to understand – helps to identify what the policy of each governor was – whether to focus on managing what Rome already controlled in a peaceful way, to resist rebellion in areas already controlled by Rome, or to embark of deliberate expansion into new territory (as Agricola eventually did, according to Tacitus).

Here is the list of the names and dates of the governors: (*Ag.* = Tacitus *Agricola* i.e. the work, not the man; *Ann.* = Tacitus' *Annals*).

Part Two Depth Study 3: Britannia: From Conquest

KEY INDIVIDUALS

Dates (AD) and Name	Sources	Policy/ Success	Quotes
43–47 Aulus Plautius	Dio 60. 19–21, Ag. 14	initial conquest success – got an ovation	'outstanding soldier' 'outstanding soldier'
47–52 Ostorius Scapula	Ann. 12, Ag. 14	defeated Caratacus	'outstanding soldier'
52–57 Didius Gallus	Ag. 14		
57–?58 Quintus Veranius	Ag. 14 (barely)		
58–61 Suetonius Paulinus	Ag 14; Ann. 14; Dio 62.1–4, 7–9, 12	Mona; Boudicca's rebellion	
61/2–63 Petronius Turpilianus	Ag. 16; Ann. 14		
63–69 Trebellius Maximus	Ag. 16;		
69–71 Vettius Bolanus	Ag. 16		
71–73/4 Petillius Cerealis	Ag. 17; Tacitus Histories 3.45		
73/4–77 Julius Frontinus	Ag. 17		
77/83 or 84 Agricola	Agricola		

KEY INDIVIDUAL

Boudicca widow of King Prasutagus and Queen of the Iceni who led a major rebellion against Roman control of Britain AD 60/61

RESISTANCE AFTER THE INVASION: BOUDICCA, AD 60–61

EXAM TIP

There are two fairly lengthy prescribed sources for the rebellion of Boudicca, which we need to read through. They are:

- Tacitus, *Annals* 14.29–37
- Cassius Dio, *History of Rome* 62.1.1–62.3.4; 62.7.1–62.9.2; 62.12.1–62.12.6

PRESCRIBED SOURCE

History of Rome

Author: Cassius Dio

Date: *c.* AD 150–235

Genre: history

Significance: a distinguished politician, born in Niceae in Bithynia (modern Turkey) and later became a consul at Rome. He also spent twenty-two years writing his *Roman History*, in eighty books. Cassius Dio made careful and extensive use of earlier historians, which makes him a valuable and useful source on this period, despite the fact that he was writing about 180 years after the events he describes

Prescribed sections: 62.1.1–62.3.4; 62.7.1–62.9.2; 62.12.1–62.12.6

Read it here: OCR Source Booklet

Tacitus' account was probably written in the years after AD 120 – sixty years after the events he describes. Cassius Dio was writing from the end of the second century – so another sixty or seventy years later than Tacitus. Remember there is also a shorter account in *Agricola* 16 (PS).

In short, Boudicca's rebellion was caused by the mistreatment of her tribe and of the Iceni royal family, though as you can see from the Prescribed Sources, Tacitus and Dio disagree about the reasons for the rebellion: Dio says it was caused by heavy-handed Roman action trying to get enormous loans made by Claudius repaid in a hurry (Dio 62.2.1 (PS)). This is entirely plausible since Nero's government of the empire had caused more to be spent than was coming in from taxes – a balance of payments problem. Tacitus gives more detail about the recovery of money but does not mention the loans; instead (*Annals* 14.31 (PS)) he says that when King Prasutagus died, he tried to leave half of his kingdom to the Emperor Nero, and half to his daughters. The Britons did not seem to have trouble about having women as rulers, or giving them the right to own property (Prasutagus seems not to have had any sons), but they were not allowed in Roman custom (Roman women played no official part in government and were not legally allowed to own any property). In addition, when the Romans moved in, they treated the Britons with no respect at all (Tacitus says in *Annals* 14.31 (PS) that they even physically assaulted Boudicca and sexually assaulted her daughters).

Boudicca led her rebellious Iceni tribesmen south and joined forces with another tribe, the Trinobantes, whose capital Camulodunum (Colchester) had been turned into the Roman provincial capital and a colony (see p. 248). here, the veterans (retired legionary soldiers) had treated the local Britons very badly, 'calling them prisoners and slaves', and the nobility of the tribe had been enrolled at great cost into the priesthood which now organised worship of the deified Claudius, conqueror of Britain! These were all reasons why the Britons here were angry. The rebels burned down Camulodunum (the foundations of the temple still survive, see p. 261) and then turned their attention to London.

The timing of the rebellion may have been deliberate, for the governor Suetonius Paulinus was leading a major attack on the heart of Druidism, Mona (Anglesey – this is described in good detail *Annals* 14.29–30 (PS)) and he hurried south as quickly as he could. The commander of the Ninth Legion, based at Lincoln, sent troops to help, but some 2,000 of these were massacred in an ambush; its commander Petilis Cerealis took refuge in his camp after escaping with the cavalry. Suetonius Paulinus could only evacuate London and leave those too frail to escape to their fate. Then the rebels headed north, and according to Tacitus *Annals* 14.33 (PS) they destroyed Verulamium (St Albans), though Dio only mentions 'two Roman cities' being destroyed. It is possible that London was not regarded only as a trading-place and not a city in some quarters.

Dio, *Roman History* 62.7.1 (PS), has particularly gruesome descriptions of the Britons' killing spree (and we should remember that the dead were not just Romans but probably also traders from Gaul, and Britons who had colluded with the Romans were almost certainly among the dead). It is even possible that the Trinobantes, crushed by the Romans, were taking it out on Britons who had not opposed the Roman invasion and had done rather well from the Roman presence. We should also remember that according to the available sources, the Iceni and the Trinobantes were the only tribes who rebelled with Boudicca.

Both Tacitus and Dio agree that after ransacking Verulamium, Boudicca's forces headed north-west, and met the advancing Roman army somewhere in the Midlands. Both also agree that the result was a complete massacre by the Romans and the Iceni royal line – and the rebellion – came to an abrupt end. The Roman response was to try to stop the rebels, and the Nineth Legion was sent south from Lincoln, but it was ambushed on the way and only the cavalry escaped. The commander of the Second Legion Augusta, by this point based in Exeter, failed to respond to the governor's orders to come and help. When Boudicca's forces had been defeated he committed suicide in shame. But in the end, Suetonius Paulinus' forces (and the careful tactics in a location which suited the Romans' military tactics, as Tacitus makes clear (*Annals* 14.37 PS)) were enough to defeat the Britons. According to Dio, *Roman History* 62.12.5 PS, Boudicca escaped

Study questions

1 What provoked Boudicca's rebellion, according to Tacitus and Dio?
2 How hostile had the Iceni tribe been to Rome before this rebellion?
3 How did the Romans manage to win against such an enormous army of rebels?
4 Read through the two accounts of Tacitus and Dio. How would you explain the differences in the accounts?
5 To what extent do you think Dio used Tacitus as a source?

ACTIVITY

The first task is to read through these texts, and note the main points of the story. Once you have got these securely fixed, here are some issues to consider:

- Both Tacitus and Dio include speeches made by the leaders of both sides. Now obviously no one took down notes or recorded either speech at the time: so what is the effect of including them?

Here are some issues you might consider:

○ History writing in the ancient world always included speeches, right from the time of Herodotus;
○ giving speeches was a common form of communication or persuasion in the ancient world, where there was no broadcast or social media;
○ history writing was a genre of literature whose aim was to entertain as much as it was to record facts – it was designed to be read out loud to an individual or an audience;
○ speeches were a usual way of exploring a character's aims or feelings, and explaining the context (instead of writing a paragraph explaining all this in a less entertaining way);
○ ancient historians often used speeches to put across their own interpretations of events and people, and especially to highlight what the writer felt the most important issues were. In many ways they are the "set pieces" of ancient historiography.

- There is quite a lot of archaeological evidence supporting the destruction of the Roman centres at Camulodunum (Colchester), and Londinium (London); there is some less clear evidence about Verulamium (St Albans). The most clear evidence for the destruction horizon left behind comes from Colchester; the most clear recent evidence from London is from a site called No. 1 Poultry, in the City of London (see Stretch and Challenge: Explore Further).

> **Explore Further**
>
> Research the three places which Boudicca's forces destroyed:
>
> - Camulodunum (Colchester) use 'Camulodunum destruction horizon Boudicca' to search the web
> - No. 1 Poultry, London: visit the Museum of London Archaeology Service (MOLAS) website at http://archaeologydataservice.ac.uk/archives/view/no1poultry_molas_2007/ or use 'No. 1 Poultry Roman archaeology' to search the web compare more recent finds at the Bloomberg site in London, at http://www.mola.org.uk/blog/archaeological-research-britain%E2%80%99s-oldest-hand-written-documents-released or use 'Bloomberg Roman site London' to search the web
> - Verulamium (St Albans) use 'Verulamium Roman town' to search the web; note that the archaeology now on display is all part of the later phases of rebuilding the town.

DEBATE OR DISCUSSION

- Do you think that the province of 'Britain would have been lost' without Suetonius Paulinus' quick intervention? (The quote is from Tacitus, *Agricola* 16 **PS**.)

from the battlefield with a large force and would have carried on with her attacks on the Romans, but she fell ill and died. Tacitus (*Annals* 14.37 **PS**) says she poisoned herself.

AFTER BOUDICCA

Tacitus describes at the end of his account in *Annals* 14.38 and 39 **PS** how Suetonius Paulinus was withdrawn from Britain and replaced by Petronius Turpilianus, who Tacitus says 'neither aggravated the enemy, nor was he himself provoked', and dignified this lazy inactivity with the honourable name of peace' (*Annals* 14. 39), and then Trebellius Maximus, who was 'even less active. He never inspected the camps and governed the province as an affable administrator' (*Agricola* 16 **PS**). Rome's policy at this time seems to have been one of placating and encouraging the British tribes.

The death of Nero towards the end of AD 68 was followed by a violent struggle for control of the empire in the Year of the Four Emperors, AD 69, a struggle in which Vespasian emerged as the winner. According to Tacitus in *Agricola* 16 **PS**, Trebellius Maximus was faced with a mutiny and was forced to flee the province; Tacitus tells us that he went to the side of one of the losing contenders for being emperor, Vitellius. His replacement, Vettius Bolanus, was also appointed by Vitellius. However, this may not have been popular with the troops in Britain, for as Tacitus tells us in his *Histories* 3.44, they preferred Vespasian:

> In Britain, the troops generally favoured Vespasian, because he had been put in command of the Second Legion there by Claudius and had distinguished himself in battle. He secured Britain but not without some resistance on the part of the other legions, in which there were many centurions and soldiers who owed their promotions to Vitellius, and were anxious about changing their allegiance from an emperor of whom they had already had some experience.
>
> Tacitus, *Histories* 3.44

Part Two Depth Study 3: Britannia: From Conquest

> **PRESCRIBED SOURCE**
>
> **Histories**
>
> **Author:** Tacitus
>
> **Date:** early second century AD
>
> **Genre:** history
>
> **Significance:** one of the principal written sources for our period, though Tacitus is well known for being hostile to the emperors and to the imperial form of government
>
> **Prescribed sections:** 3.44–45
>
> **Read it here:** OCR Source Booklet

RESISTANCE AFTER THE INVASION: VENUTIUS AND THE BRIGANTES, AD 69

The dissension among the Romans may also have provided a reason why, apparently in the same year AD 69, there was a second major rebellion against Roman interference in the affairs of a native British tribe. This time it was the turn of the Brigantes to rebel, as Tacitus informs us: the rebellion seems to have been due not only for reasons of politics, but a love-affair as well. Cartimandua had already shown herself to be pro-Rome, when she handed over the rebel Caratacus, who had turned to the Brigantes – whose territory lay outside the areas to the south which the Romans controlled through their armies. But from what Tacitus tells us, Cartimandua's political views about Rome were not shared by her husband Venutius, and matters were made worse when Queen Cartimandua tried to depose Venutius and replace him with his own armour-bearer. This seems to indicate just how much power a woman could hold in native British societies – Boudicca being the other well-known example of a woman in a position of power, and Tacitus in *Agricola* 16 tells us that the Britons did 'not distinguish between the sexes when choosing commanders'.

This then provides us with an explanation of the causes of the rebellion. The Roman response in the passage below was to intervene: Tacitus' terse comment is 'we were left with a war to fight'. However, in *Agricola* 16 , Tacitus says that there was a mutiny in the army, that the governor Trebellius Maximus had to go into hiding, afraid of the soldiers under his theoretical command, and his successor Vettius Bolanus was guilty of the 'same lack of action against the enemy'. This takes us to AD 71 (see the time-line on p. 219–220), and only with the arrival of Petilius Cerealis in AD 71 was the territory of the Brigantes invaded (*Agricola* 17). There is no evidence that any attempt was made to restore a royal family to the Brigantes; instead, a policy of expansion was launched which continued right up to the end of our period of study in this module. At any rate, Venutius seems to have been deposed, and in Britain, the policy of employing client kings and queens came to an end. Here is what Tacitus has to tell us about it (he is the only source for this rebellion):

> Inspired by the disagreement of the legions and by the many rumours of civil war that reached them, the Britons plucked up courage under the leadership of Venutius who, in addition to his feisty spirit and hatred of the mention of 'Roman', was fired by his personal resentment toward Queen Cartimandua. Cartimandua ruled the Brigantes, securely through her high birth. She had later strengthened her power when she was credited with having captured King Caratacus by treachery and so provided a fancy addition for the triumph of Claudius. From this came the wealth and the self-indulgence associated with success. Despising Venutius (he was her husband), she took his armour-bearer Vellocatus as her husband and consort. The power of her house was at once shaken by this scandalous act. The people of the tribe supported Venutius, only the passion and her savage spirit of the queen supported the adulterer. So Venutius, calling in aid from outside and at the same time assisted by a revolt of the Brigantes themselves, put Cartimandua into an extremely dangerous position. Then she asked the Romans for protection, and in fact some infantry cohorts and cavalry, after a number of different engagements, finally succeeded in rescuing the queen from danger. The throne was left to Venutius; we were left with a war to fight.

Tacitus, *Histories* 3.45

THE ROMANS MOVE NORTH

The campaigns and achievements of Petilius Cerialis and Julius Frontinus are briefly described by Tacitus in *Agricola* 17 PS. There was a new period of expansion, which may well reflect a deliberate policy of Vespasian. As the new emperor, he wanted to establish himself as the deserved leader of the Roman empire (he was not related by blood to previous emperors in any way). A major triumph such as this would have helped secure his position, as it did earlier for Claudius.

Cerealis expanded Roman control to the north: 'he struck terror by an attack on the Brigantes tribe who are reputed to be the most populous tribe of the whole province. Many battles were fought, sometimes not blood free; and he subjugated the greater part of the Brigantes' territory either in victory or ongoing conflict' (Tacitus *Agricola* 17 PS.). Older accounts of the history of the Romans in Britain suggest that he moved his old legion, the ninth, from a base at Lincoln (on the Fosse Way) up to York. We now know

Study questions

1 In your own words, explain why Venutius disliked being an ally of Rome.

2 Read Tacitus *Agricola* 16 and 17 PS again. What aspect of Roman rule does Tacitus admire most in his descriptions of the activities of the different governors?

KEY INDIVIDUALS

Petilius Cerialis
Governor of Britain AD 71–73/4

Julius Frontinus
Governor of Britain AD 73/4–77

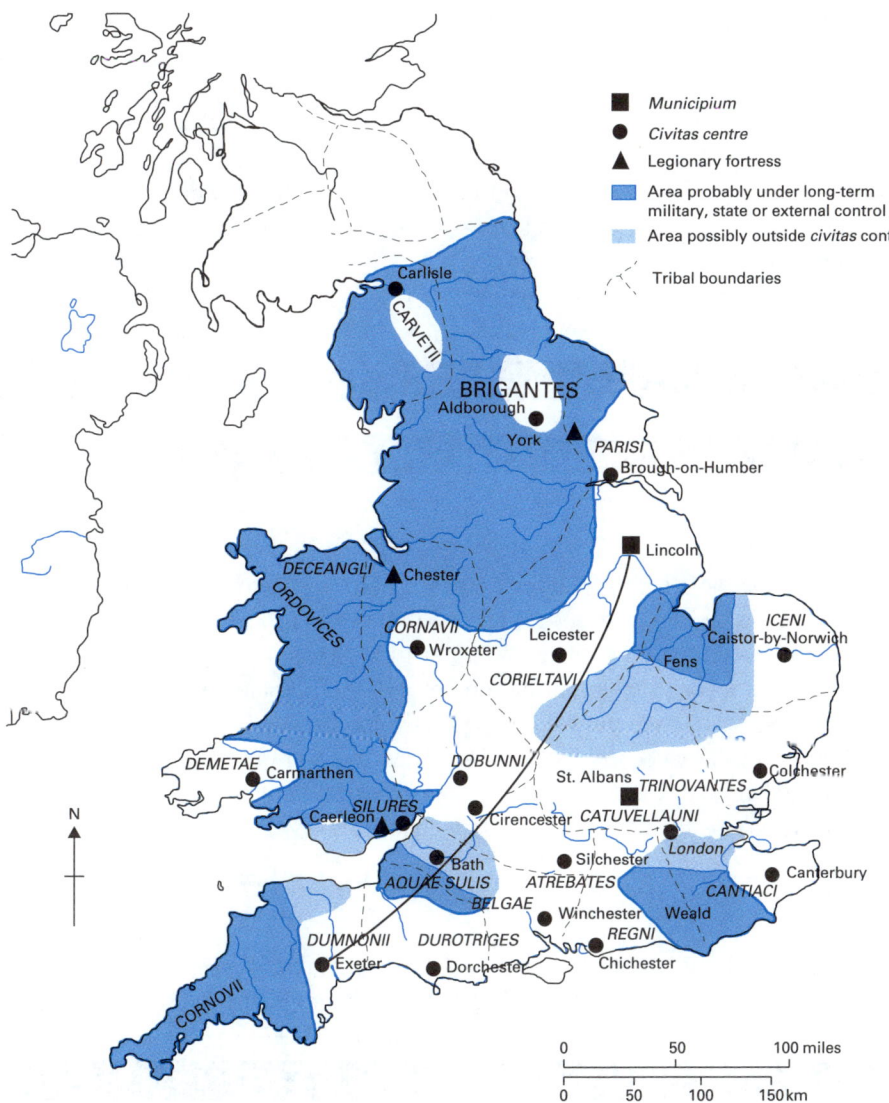

FIGURE 4.14
Map showing the areas which the Romans were now occupying. The 'Fosse Way' ceased to be a frontier and was just a useful communications road.

Part Two Depth Study 3: Britannia: From Conquest

Study question
Why did the Romans move north and west under the governors Petilius Cerialis and Julius Frontinus?

from dendrochronlogy (dating wood through the sequence of tree-rings) that the Romans also reached Carlisle, on the west coast of Britain, during his campaigns: the first Roman fort there was built from timbers felled in AD 72/ 73.

There appears to have been unfinished business in south Wales, too. The north had been subjugated in AD 60 by Suetonius Paulinus, attacking the Druid stronghold at Mona (Anglesey). Now it fell to the next governor, Julius Frontinus, to conquer the Silures. Frontinus was another distinguished Roman, who held the consulship three times and left a written legacy with two little books on *Military Tactics* (or *Stratagems*) and *Aqueducts*.

TOPIC REVIEW

Boost your knowledge

Describe:

1. The actions different governors took towards the Britons
2. The development of the colony at Camulodunum and of tribal centres in the south of Briton
3. Benefits and disadvantages of Roman rule felt by different tribes in Britain
4. The rebellions of Caratacus, Boudicca and Venutius

Stretch your understanding

Explain:

1. Why some governors pursued a policy of military conquest while others are said to have done very little
2. Why the Romans established and encouraged key centres such as Camulodunum and Silchester
3. Why some Britons organized armed resistance against Rome
4. Why the attempts at resisting Rome all ended in failure

PRACTICE QUESTIONS

Passage B

Aulus Plautius, the first man of consular rank to be appointed governor, and his successor Ostorius Scapula were both outstanding in warfare. Little by little, the closest part of Britain was reduced into the form of a province, and moreover a colony of veterans was settled. Certain tribal areas were presented to King Cogidubnus (and he continued in utter loyalty within our own memory), there being an ancient and long established practice of the Roman people to have the kings responsible for slavery. Didius Gallus, the next governor, consolidated the gains of his predecessors, and added a few fortified garrisons in the remoter parts through which he could claim that he had increased size of the province. Veranius succeeded Didius, but died within the year. Suetonius Paulinus then commanded with success for two years, subduing various tribes, and establishing garrisons.

Tacitus, *Agricola* 14

1. What can we learn from Passage B about the qualities and achievements of different governors? [5]
2. Explain why the settlement at Camulodunum (Colchester) was significant during the period. [10]

4.3 Romanisation and Further Resistance

TOPIC OVERVIEW

The changing policies of the various Roman governors. The significance and success of these governors.

- Agricola's campaigns and achievements including his motives, preparations and tactics
- the influence of different emperors

Cooperation between Romans and Britons and the effects of Roman rule

- Romanisation: the effects of Roman rule and the extent of change, including urbanisation and cultural, religious and lifestyle changes
- the economic impact of the Roman army and traders
- Early development in Camulodunum, Fishbourne, Aquae Sulis as examples of the effects of Roman influence

Resistance after the invasion

- the resistance campaign of Calgacus
- the reasons for his resistance and the extent of his success
- the nature of the Roman response to resistance
- the sources' portrayal of the Britons, particularly those who resisted Roman rule

The prescribed sources for this topic are:

- Tacitus, *Agricola*, 18–29, 30–37;
- Tacitus, *Annals* 12.32, 14:31
- Vindolanda tablet 'concerning supplies' (Tab. 343)
- Vindolanda tablet detailing the procurement of materials for the fort (Tab. 309)
- Vindolanda tablet requesting to know if there is an inn to lodge at (Tab. 632)

Romanisation the effects of Roman rule and the extent of change: urbanisation; cultural, religious and lifestyle changes

The term Romanisation is generally used to sum up the social, political and religious changes which happened in areas which the Romans came to dominate – like Britain. In recent times, many scholars have expressed a dislike of the term, arguing that it implicitly makes Roman culture seem more important than native cultures or superior to them, sometimes assumes that pure Roman-ness was obtainable, and does not really acknowledge that provincial society was inevitably a mixture of cultures. Other scholars dislike the idea of the Romans imposing a cultural imperialism, as the British and other European countries did with their more recent empires. At the end of *Agricola* 21 **PS**, Tacitus talks about the Britons adopting Roman culture in the form of 'colonades and warm baths and elegant banquets', and goes on to say that 'The Britons, who had no experience of this, called it "civilization", although it was a part of their enslavement'.

PRESCRIBED SOURCE

Agricola

Author: Tacitus

Date: *c.* AD 98

Genre: biography

Significance: Tacitus write this eulogy or work in praise of his late father-in-law when it seemed safe to do so after the death of the vindictive and oppressive emperor Domitian in AD 96. He evidently knew the man well, and had first-hand knowledge of stories of Agricola's three tours of duty in the province of Britannia. However, because Tacitus wrote it in praise of Agricola, and clearly admired Agricola's military victories – a mark of greatness in Roman eyes – he tends to be very dismissive of other governors, even though they may have been obedient to the express wishes of emperors in the way they acted in Britain

Prescribed sections: 18–29, 30–37

Read it here: OCR Source Booklet

DEBATE

The Latin word Tacitus uses for civilisation in *Agricola* 21 is *humanitas*, and other Roman writers saw it as part of Rome's mission to bring this *humanitas* to the non-Roman or 'barbarian' world (see the quotation from Virgil's *Aeneid* on p. 250). Other recent scholars, such as Greg Woolf, have distinguished between a 'push' by Rome – 'making other peoples into Romans,' if you like – and a 'pull' exerted by peoples outside Rome who saw many aspects of Roman culture as something worth having and deliberately wanted to have a share in them (while not necessarily wanting Rome to rule them!) The debate is a lively one and goes on . . .

We have already seen in our study of Boudicca's rebellion that the first place her forces attacked was Camulodunum (Colchester). Here the Temple of the Deified Claudius was a focal point of Roman power, the symbol of Roman rule in what then made up the 'province'. Remember what Tacitus had to say about its foundation:

a colony (*colonia*) was settled on conquered lands at Camulodunum (Colchester). This was a strong detachment of veterans and they were to serve as a defence against revolt and to get the natives to have a positive attitude towards observing the laws.

Tacitus, *Annals* 12.32

However, the first ex-soldiers to occupy it did not live up to these high ideals:

> The Trinobantes ... hated the veterans most of all, because the new colonists at *Camulodunum* (Colchester) had driven them from their homes, emptied their lands, and called them captives and slaves. The soldiers encouraged the veterans: their way of life was the same, and they hoped for similar freedom. More than this, the temple of divine Claudius was considered to be the fortress of eternal Roman domination, while those who served as his priests poured away their wealth for the sake of religion. Destroying the colony seemed an easy job: it had no defences, because our commanders had been concerned more with what was pleasant to look at rather than with what the town actually needed.
>
> Tacitus, *Annals* 14.31

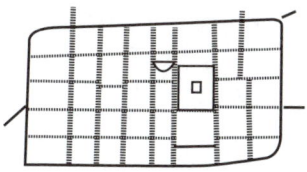

FIGURE 4.15
A reconstructed town plan of Colchester.

Note, however, that the archaeology from Colchester is actually very limited and the location of the forum, for example, has never been found. A small theatre and the site of the temple of Claudius are shown. The base of the temple of Claudius survives – the Normans used it as the foundation for their castle in Colchester after they invaded England in 1066! You can find more information about it at http://www.cimuseums.org.uk/castle.

One feature not shown on this plan is the circus or racetrack, discovered in 2004 outside the town; so far it is the only town in Britain known to have been furnished with one, though most large towns had either a theatre or an amphitheatre.

From what Tacitus tells us, there were obvious effects of Roman rule at this stage in terms of taxation, and involvement of some of the native population in what is known as the imperial cult or the worship of deified emperors. Claudius, now dead, was assumed to have become a god, and his numen or spirit joined with that of the other deified emperors and gods and acted as a protector of the Romans so long as proper respectful worship of him took place. The imperial cult was based on the idea that the success and indeed the survival of the Roman state depended on the goodwill of the gods, and particularly the numen or spirit of the emperors. Offering thanks and prayers to this numen was a way of making sure that the balance of the universe was maintained, and Roman interests protected. The religious aspects were combined with an oath of loyalty to the Roman state and to the living emperor which was undertaken on an annual basis at least by all members of the Roman army and Roman officials. Thus, to show their loyalty to Rome, Britons would be expected to participate in this religious observance.

In fact this was the only imposition of a new religion which the Romans insisted on in Britain. In other instances, they were happy to allow native Britons to continue to practice the worship of their own gods, and they often combined these with Classical deities (as we shall see, this happened at Aquae Sulis, and it was common both among soldiers and civilians), with one exception: Druidism, as we saw earlier (see p. 253), was the one religion practice which the Romans would not tolerate, and both in Gaul and in Britain they took every step to stamp it out completely.

After the rebellion of Boudicca, Camulodunum remained in force as a colony (and by the end of the century, it had been joined by Lindum (Lincoln) and Glevum (Gloucester)), but the provincial capital was moved to Londinium (London). How far Britons were

> **Study questions**
>
> 1 Find all these towns on a map. What does this tell you about how much of Britain the Romans felt confident controlling?
> 2 How did the Romans involve the native British tribes in governing the province?

encouraged to imitate the town life as presented by Camulodunum itself is hard to gauge, and there may have been no change at all in rural areas where life went on just as before; but we should note that Camulodunum was only one of a number of towns which existed in Britain by AD 85. Each had a distinctive grid pattern of streets, a central forum/basilica for trade and local government, a theatre or amphitheatre, and Mediterranean-styled housing, and each is assumed to have been a centre for local government based on the old tribal areas. These were:

- Cantium/Canterbury
- Caesaromagus/Chelmsford
- Verulamium/St Albans
- Venta Icenorum/Caistor-by Norwich
- Novomagus Regnorum/Chichester
- Calleva Atrebatum/Silchester
- Venta Belgarum/Winchester
- Corinum Dobunnorum/Cirencester
- Durnovaria/Dorchester
- Isca Dumnoniorum/Exeter
- Ratae Coreltavorum/Leicester
- Viroconium Cornoviorum/Wroxeter

In addition, the largest of all Roman towns in Britain had grown up as a trading centre:

- Londinium/London

Other civitas capitals or tribal centres further to the north and west were to follow, but these probably date to after AD 85.

So there several ways in which Roman rule had an impact on Britain and the Britons:

- the establishment of a provincial capital and magistrates using Roman law, replacing a British king;
- payment of taxes and dues to the Roman state;
- the introduction of the imperial cult as a part of civic life as well as military life;
- the development of urban life in towns and cities.

> **Study question**
>
> Summarise in short paragraphs what we can learn from the example of Camulodunum (Colchester) about the effects of Roman rule on the Britons

We should note, however, that the introduction of city life probably affected only a very small number of Britons – Prof. David Mattingly has estimated that as few as 3 per cent of the overall population directly experienced what we often think of as the typical changes associated with living in towns, such as buildings built in brick and stone, bathing, and fine dining (in *Imperialism, Power and Identity*, 2011).

FISHBOURNE

> **Further Study**
>
> Use the internet to do some research on one or more of the Roman towns in the list above – or if you live near to one or in one, go and see what your local museum has to offer!

Fishbourne has been looked at already on pp. 248–249. It is an example of Romanisation which we have to use with very great care, because it is a one-off – there is no building like it in terms of magnificence or decoration for several centuries in Britain (the vast majority of luxurious Roman villas known in Roman Britain date from the fourth century AD).

However, its effects on the native population must have been extraordinary – no native Briton had even seen a building like this in his own country! If it was built for King Togidumnus, as is often thought, then it showed the kind of rewards which were available for those who stayed loyal to the Romans.

At some time during or just after the Roman invasion in AD 43, timber buildings (some were probably granaries) were constructed at Fishbourne and it may have acted as a supply-base for Vespasian's campaigns in the south and west (more recent excavations have suggested the possibility that this first phase at Fishbourne might actually be a pre-invasion site, constructed by a local leader importing Roman-style buildings from across the channel in the same way that coins came into use before the invasion).

There was some development of the site after this in *c.* AD 50–60, but it still seems to have had a military function.

Then in *c.* AD 65–70, all the timber buildings were removed and the site was levelled in places. This allowed the building of an enormous building which is known nowadays as the proto-palace. Instead of using timber it was built in stone, including a type of limestone quarried in Britain, in Dorset, known as Purbeck marble. Its floors and walls were

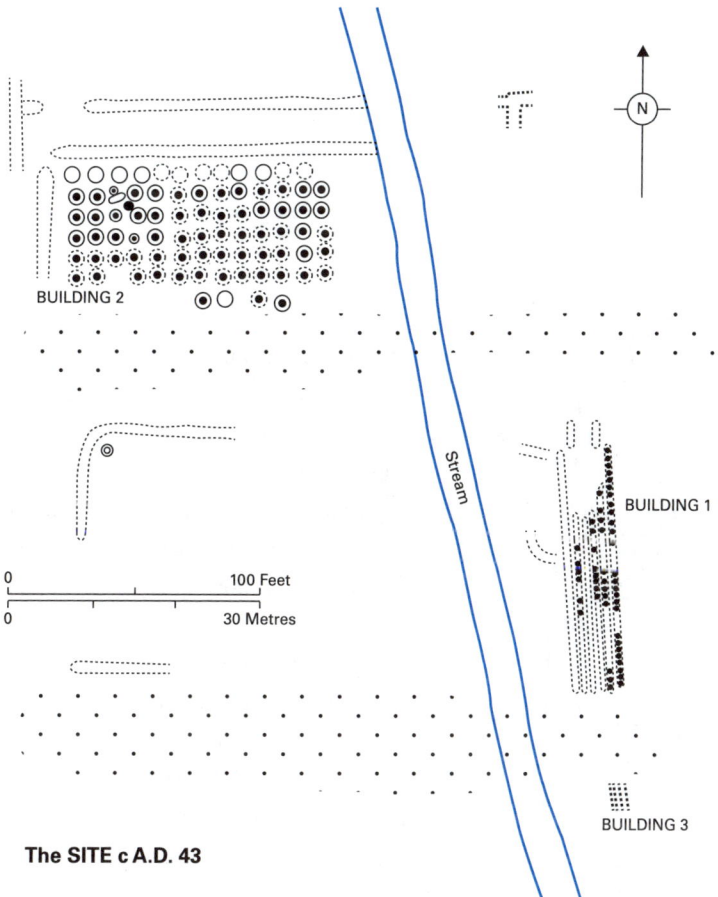

FIGURE 4.16
Drawing of Fishbourne showing the layout of the site at the time of the Roman invasion.

FIGURE 4.17
Diagram of Fishbourne showing the scale of the building.

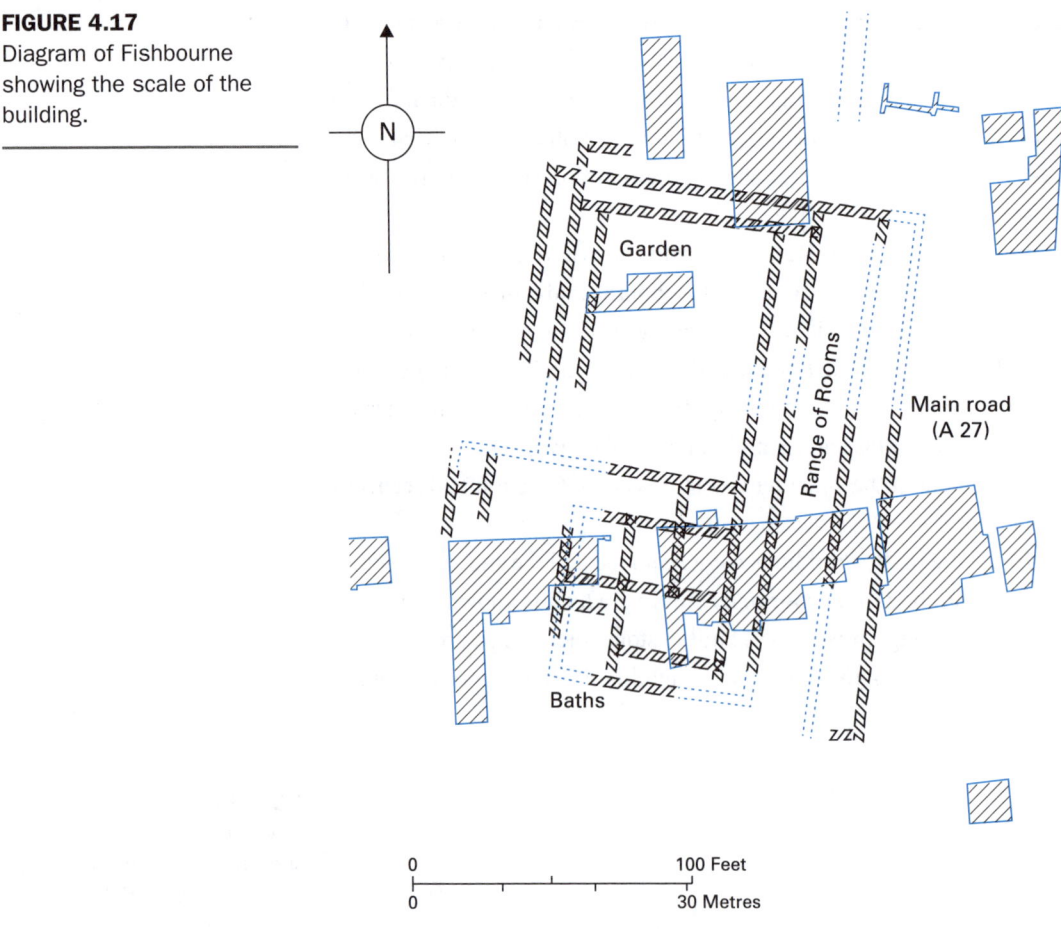

FIGURE 4.18
Plan of Fishbourne c. AD 75.

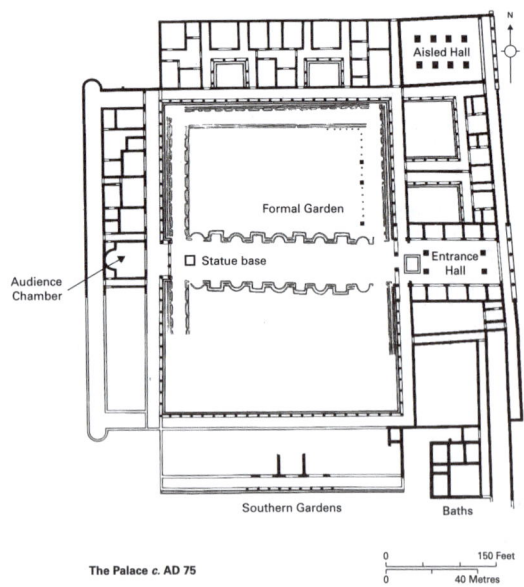

decorated with expensive imported stone (it has been identified in many instances from the waste material left by the workmen). It also had an enormous bath-house at the south end.

At Fishbourne, the proto-palace had black-and-white geometric mosaics on many of the floors (note that the coloured mosaics currently to be seen at Fishbourne are replacements made in the following centuries). The walls were painted in bright colours – red, blue, and yellow – and were decorated with Purbeck marble.

It is interesting to note that a palatial complex of about the same size has been identified in recent excavations conducted by Prof. Michael Fulford from the University of Reading at Calleva Atrebatum (Silchester). It dates from about the same time and with evidence of similar materials being used (M. Fulford, 'Nero and Britain: the Client King's Palace at *Calleva* and Imperial Policy after Boudica', *Britannia* xxxix (2008) pp. 1–14). You can find out more about this site by searching for 'Calleva Atrebatum' on the internet.

This would be astonishing enough by itself: but within about ten years the whole complex of buildings was replaced by a slightly smaller, more compact building – but still an enormous one! – which is known as the Flavian palace (Flavian because the emperors Vespasian, Titus and Domitian were from the Flavian clan).

The site was levelled again, thousands of cubic metres of clay and gravel being moved to create a platform for the building on two levels. The west wing was built on the upper level, and led to an audience chamber (see Fig. 4.18). All the floors had black and white geometric mosaics – with some four exceptions where mortar or opus signinum was employed – and there were numerous rooms leading off each side, probably arranged as three separate suites. It allowed easy movement inside and there was much to impress visitors and even overwhelm them! Inside, walls and ceilings were painted, often designed to make the rooms look as if they were clad entirely in marble, but some paintings included flowers, and a fragment of one panel depicts the corner of a building with the sea behind – you can find examples of this style from Italian towns such as Stabiae or Pompeii. Actual marble, some imported from Asia Minor, was also used. No expense was spared.

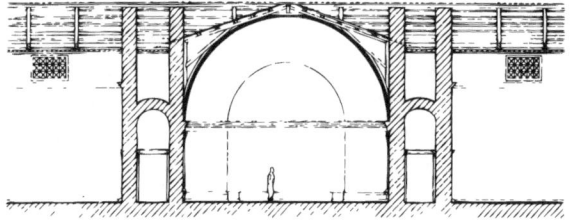
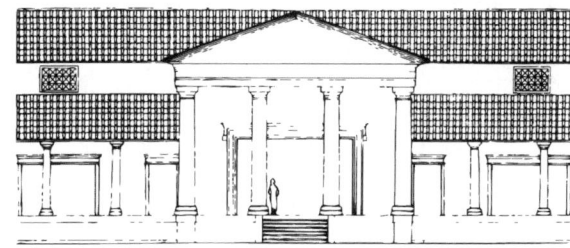

FIGURE 4.19
Architectural reconstruction of the audience chamber at Fishbourne.

While this building was in a class of its own, the techniques employed were mirrored in other parts of the country on a much smaller scale, and native Britons may have been led to adopt a more Mediterranean cultural practice, with square masonry houses in towns replacing the older round timber structures which are typical of native British practice. Even when imitated in timber, these may have had plastered walls with Roman-style decoration.

AQUAE SULIS (BATH)

The third example mentioned in the specification may have been a part of the overall reconstruction programme which the Romans encouraged in Britain after the rebellion of Boudicca. At this location – the modern town of Bath – natural hot springs produce a phenomenal supply of hot water which in pre-Roman times probably produced an area of marsh, and which almost certainly would have had significant religious meaning for the native tribes.

Here the site was Romanised in more ways than one. First, a temple was built at the centre of a complex of buildings in Roman style. Second, the dedication of the temple illustrates the syncretism or combining of worship of gods which modern scholars often give the Latin term interpretatio Romana. The native god Sulis, perhaps a goddess associated with the hot springs, was associated with the Roman goddess Minerva, whose powers may have been seen as overlapping with those of the native goddess. The result

FIGURE 4.20
Reconstruction of the façade of the temple at Aquae Sulis.

FIGURE 4.21
Drawing showing what the layout of Aquae Sulis might have looked like in the late first century AD.

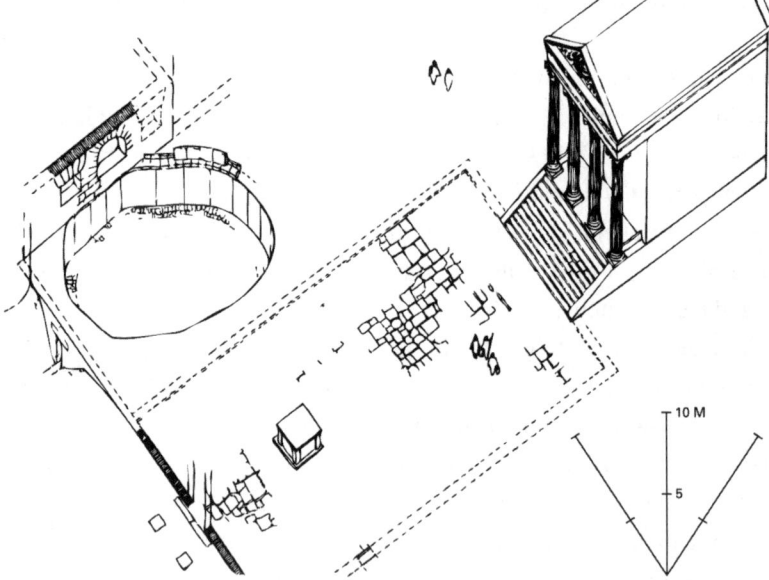

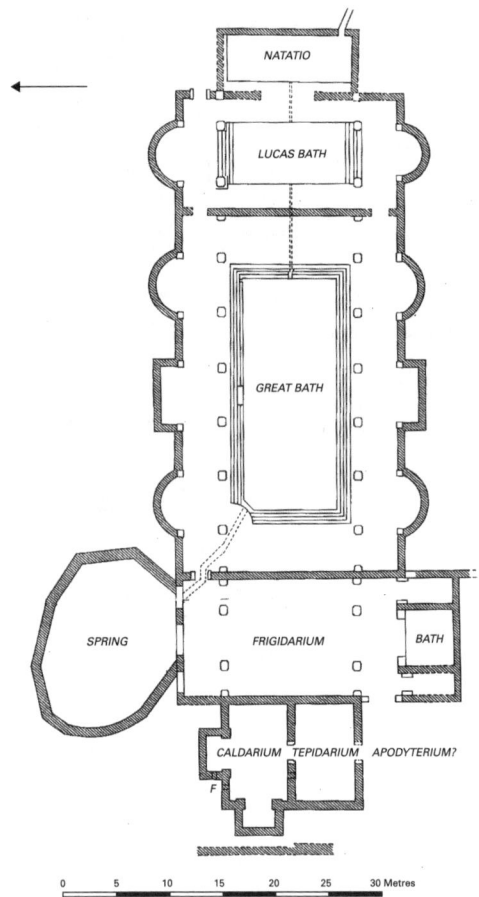

FIGURE 4.22
Drawing showing the layout of the baths complex in the late first century AD.

is a classical temple with classical statuary of the goddess, but dedicated to a hybrid British and Roman deity.

The most obvious part of the Roman impact on the native site at Aquae Sulis was of course the bathing complex, which is perhaps the most Roman aspect of the site and occupies a huge part of it. The Romans did not only make use of the natural hot springs to supply a bath-house of typical Mediterranean design, but also put a reservoir around the spring, which allowed them to get rid of the marsh and build on the surrounding area. This would have made an enormous change in the landscape from the pre-Roman to the Roman periods.

Figs. 4.21 and 4.22 show the layout of the temple area and the ways in which the Romans exploited this natural feature, as well as a reconstruction of what the façade or front view of the temple might have looked like.

The gilded head of the statue of Sulis Minerva has been found, and there are numerous inscriptions from Bath recording the details of the people – mostly soldiers – who went there in order to worship her and to venerate the waters.

> **DEBATE** Who Did *Aquae Sulis* Belong To?
>
> Prof. Michael Fulford has noted that 'although we have no firm evidence for the boundaries of Cogidubnus' kingdom, there is no reason why it could not have included Bath'. Other scholars point out that the flipside of this claim is also true: there is no (or rather very little and rather controversial) evidence that his kingdom *did* include Bath – it's pretty far from Chichester. The issue arises because of the temptation to assign things to Togidubnus simply because we know his name. It just goes to show how thin our written sources for the period really are!

> **Study questions**
>
> 1 Summarise the different ways in which each of these three sites (Camulodunum, Fishbourne and Aquae Sulis) might have affected the native Britons.
> 2 What evidence is there from these three sites for changes in:
>   - culture and lifestyle
>   - religion

> **EXPLORE FURTHER**
>
> A website with good pictures is provided by the Roman Bath museum at http://www.romanbaths.co.uk/ and you can find an excellent description of how Roman baths worked at http://www.historylearningsite.co.uk/ancient-rome/roman-baths/

AGRICOLA'S CAMPAIGNS AND ACHIEVEMENTS, INCLUDING HIS MOTIVES, PREPARATIONS AND TACTICS

This is a further exercise in reading through a fairly detailed text and noting key points in it. It is interesting to see that Agricola served – unusually – for seven years as governor of Britain. Given this very long tenure it seems that Agricola acted in line with the policies of Vespasian (who ruled till AD 79) and Vespasian's elder son Titus (AD 79–81) but as Tacitus says in the *Agricola*, Domitian may have had other ideas, though Tacitus interprets the change in policy in personal terms: 'Other talents could more easily be ignored; good generalship belonged to the emperor' (*Agricola* 39: 'the emperor' must refer to Domitian, Titus' younger brother, emperor from AD 81 onwards).

The has been a massive effort to identify marching camps and forts which may be associated with Agricola's campaigns, but for this course the main focus has to be the lengthy account which Tacitus supplies about Agricola, his father-in-law. There is no substitute for reading it! We can divide it up, so that we address this part of the module using chapters 18–27 and 29, here, and then using the remainder of the Prescribed Source to examine the resistance offered by the chieftain Calgacus, Agricola's principal opponent in the final campaign against the Caledonii.

FIGURE 4.23
Map of North Britain under Agricola.

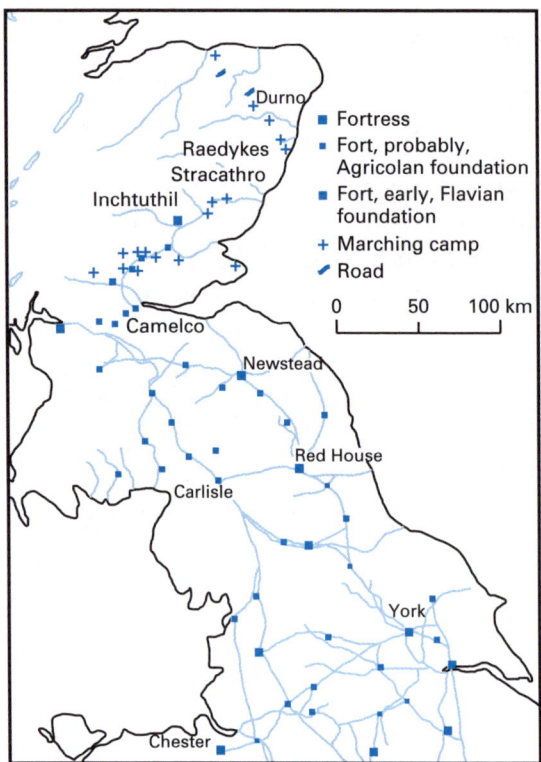

ACTIVITY/STUDY QUESTIONS

It's time to read some more textual source material!

Look at Tacitus *Agricola* 18–27 and 29 **PS** (chapter 28 is not a Prescribed Source). The chapters are not long and they cover the whole period of Agricola's time as governor of Britain: note that Tacitus tends to start the events of each year with the phrase 'at the start of the next summer' – warfare in the ancient world usually ground to a halt during the winter months!

For each year of his governorship, note in brief (just a few words, or a short quote from the text) what he did (= his achievements) and why he did it (= his policy). The chapters can be divided up chronologically as shown below: you can turn this into another poster or a single sheet which will help you with revision.

PS

Year	Chapters
77	18, 19, start of 20 – first actions to make his mark on the province; re-conquers Wales
78	20, 21 – chapter 21 is very interesting for changes in culture and society among the Britons!
79	22 – advance into the area of the River Tay
80	23 – securing new territory
81	24 – further expansion – Ireland considered for invasion
82	25, 26, 27 – conflict with the Caledonii
83	29 – introduction to the final showdown at Mons Graupius

4.3 Romanisation and Further Resistance

We can leave chapters 30–7 of *Agricola* for the next section on Calgacus.

Now summarise the following points:

1. What were Agricola's main achievements?
2. From the text of Tacitus *Agricola* what can we learn about aspects of leadership which Romans (or at least Tacitus) admired the most?
3. How carefully did Agricola prepare to extend Roman control in Britain?

S&C
- Why do you think that Tacitus regards these policies as a form of enslavement? What does he think that the Britons had lost? Think about other parts of the course we have studied.

This is a chance to explore Tacitus's own attitudes as an author. He repeatedly stresses freedom as a motif in his narratives – but what sort of freedom do you think he is referring to? Did he really hope that the Romans would lose, or is he thinking of his own situation back in Rome?

Study questions

Read this passage, taken from Tacitus *Agricola* 21, and answer the questions at the end:

> The following winter passed without disturbance, and was spent in worthwhile activities. Agricola had to deal with a population scattered and uncivilised and therefore inclined to war. His desire was to accustom the people to rest and to be quite through the appeal of amenities/charms of luxuries. Agricola gave private encouragement and public aid to the building of temples, public squares and private houses, praising the keen and reprimanding the slack. And so, a rivalry for honour took the place of forcing them. He likewise provided an education for the sons of the chiefs in the liberal arts, and showed such a preference for the natural abilities of the Britons over the trained skill of the Gauls that they who lately despised the Latin language now desired to speak eloquently in it. Hence, too, a liking sprang up for our style of dress, and the 'toga' was everywhere. Step by step they went astray to things which lead to vice: porticoes, baths, elegant banquets. All this in their ignorance they called civilisation, when it was just a part of their enslavement.
>
> Tacitus, *Agricola* 21 **PS**

1. What does this passage tell us about the ways in which Agricola tried to encourage the Britons to be good Romans?
2. What evidence have you seen from your study so far which supports what Tacitus is saying in this passage?

RESISTANCE AFTER THE INVASION: THE CAMPAIGN OF CALGACUS

This is the climax of the story Tacitus gives us in the *Agricola*. It is constructed in a very formal manner – the two leaders on each side are given speeches (Calgacus the Caledonian is given a very lengthy one, summarising Roman achievements!) before the battle itself is described, with the Roman tactics swiftly overwhelming their British opposition. The same considerations need to be given to these speeches as to the ones given to Boudicca and to Suetonius Paulinus – see pp. 252–255. Tacitus uses a very formulaic structure to

KEY INDIVIDUALS

Calgacus Chief of the Caledonii tribe

> **ACTIVITY** PS
>
> Summarise the course of the Battle of Mons Graupius from the text of the *Agricola*:
>
> - Calgacus' rallying speech: chapters 30, 31, 32, start of 33
> - Agricola's response: chapters 33, 34
> - the battle itself: 35, 36, 37

> **Study questions**
>
> 1 What does Tacitus' account of the Battle of Mons Graupius tell us about how the Romans viewed the Britons?
> 2 What tactics did Agricola use to achieve his victory?
> 3 How similar are Agricola's tactics to those used by Suetonius Paulinus when he defeated the armies led by Boudicca (see pp. 000–000)?

> **Explore Further** S&C
>
> Read the final chapters of Tacitus' *Agricola* (i.e. the chapters after the Prescribed Source, to the end of the work) and think about this question:
>
> - 'Agricola really was the greatest of the governors of Britain up to this time.' How far do you agree with this view?

describe this battle, and the speeches are longer than the account of the battle itself! It is also interesting that Tacitus gives over more space to Calgacus than he does to Agricola. On a first reading we might even suspect Tacitus of sympathising more with Rome's enemy than with Rome's general – but we need to remember that it was the regular practice of Roman historians to 'imagine' the motives of rebel leaders and to express them by means of a speech, and when we read the *Agricola* as a whole, it is quite clear than Tacitus was writing in order to stress the positive achievements of his father-in-law *against* rebels such as Calgacus.

So as you read the final parts of the Prescribed Source – *Agricola* chapters 30–7 – bear in mind the following ways in which they help us to address what we are asked to think about in the specification:

- the speech given to Calgacus tells us about the reasons for his resistance
- the speech given to Agricola tells us about the nature of the Roman response to resistance
- the narrative of the battle itself (and preparations in *Agricola* 25) gives a very good explanation of the extent of Calgacus' success; but note that although he eventually lost, there is evidence in *Agricola* 26 that the Britons had the capability to surprise the Romans and to cause them serious trouble!

THE ECONOMIC IMPACT OF THE ROMAN ARMY AND TRADERS

The last of the Prescribed Sources are an extraordinary source of evidence about the impact the Roman army had on the economy of Britain. These are the Vindolanda tablets, a collection of original documents produced by auxiliary units of the Roman army which illustrate just how important administration and record-keeping was to that organisation. Only two other places in the whole empire – Dura-Eutropos, in the East, and Egypt, where papyri provide a wealth of documentary evidence for civil and military administration – have seen so much material preserved. Strictly speaking, the information which the Vindolanda tablets provide comes from a slightly later period than that covered by the specification but they almost certainly reflect the practice of (at least) auxiliary Roman army units in Britain since the invasion of AD 43.

The tablets survive at Vindolanda because the very acidic peaty soil there has resulted in archaeological conditions which have preserved the wood – it's not that Vindolanda itself was a particularly important fort in the Roman period, it's just the luck of survival. This brings up an important point about the randomness of our sources, particularly archaeological but also textual, for the Roman period – it is as though we have just a few pieces of a much larger jigsaw, which are sometimes very hard to interpret securely!

PRESCRIBED SOURCES

Vindolanda tablets

Date: first and second centuries AD

Significance: rare documentary evidence of daily life in the Roman army

Location: Tabs. 309 and 343 are in the British Museum, London; Tab. 632 is on show at the Vindolanda Museum, Northumbria

Prescribed tablets: Tab. 343 concerning supplies; Tab. 309 detailing the procurement of materials for the fort; Tab. 632 requesting to know if there is an inn at which to lodge

EXPLORE FURTHER

In addition, the tablets are all easily accessible on the website dedicated to them, at http://vto2.classics.ox.ac.uk/. This contains tablets 1–532, and the texts of the first two examples below are taken from this source: detailed commentaries on the tablets are also available on this website.

Vindolanda tablet 343, concerning supplies:

> Octavius to his brother Candidus, greetings. The hundred pounds of sinew from Marinus – I will settle up. From the time when you wrote about this matter, he has not even mentioned it to me. I have several times written to you that I have bought about five thousand *modii* of ears of grain, on account of which I need cash. Unless you send me some cash, at least five hundred *denarii*, the result will be that I shall lose what I have laid out as a deposit, about three hundred *denarii*, and I shall be embarrassed. So, I ask you, send me some cash as soon as possible. The hides which you write are at Cataractonium – write that they be given to me and the wagon about which you write. And write to me what is with that wagon. I would have already been to collect them except that I did not care to injure the animals while the roads are bad. See with Tertius about the 8 *denarii* which he received from Fatalis. He has not credited them to my account. Know that I have completed the 170 hides and I have 119 *modii* of threshed *bracis*. Make sure that you send me cash so that I may have ears of grain on the threshing-floor. Moreover, I have already finished threshing all that I had. A messmate of our friend Frontius has been here. He was wanting me to allocate (?) him hides and that being so, was ready to give cash. I told him I would give him the hides by 1 March. He decided that he would come on 13 January. He did not turn up nor did he take any trouble to obtain them since he had hides. If he had given the cash, I would have given him them. I hear that Frontinius Iulius has for sale at a high price the leather ware (?) which he bought here for five *denarii* apiece. Greet Spectatus and . . . and Firmus. I have received letters from Gleuco. Farewell. (Back) (Deliver) at Vindolanda.

This is a business letter: the commentary at http://vindolanda.csad.ox.ac.uk (tablet 343) notes that 'Octavius uses a variety of financial idioms and a few technical terms', and that:

PS The whole letter is replete with signs of entrepreneurial initiative. The sums of money and goods involved are very considerable: Candidus is asked for 500 *denarii* and Octavius has laid out 300 (a year's pay for a *miles gregarius* (legionary soldier) in this period). The natural conclusion is that Octavius and Candidus are involved in the supply of goods in a military context on a large scale. 5000 *modii* of cereal and hides numbering in the hundreds can hardly be intended for any other market. Octavius (wherever he was) presumably purchased the cereal from local sources. The hides will have come from the military sector since it is surely inconceivable that tanneries operating on this scale can have existed outside it. The reference to the presence of hides at *Cataractonium* (Catterick, lines ii.15–6) is of great interest and well fits the archaeological evidence for a large tannery there in the period between *c.* AD 85 and 120.

One other curious point about this letter is that it was written in two columns, as Roman letters usually were, but starting with the right-hand one and moving to the left: this may be due to the writer being left-handed and wanting to read what he had written as he continued the text. The document is also evidence for the widespread use of cash in the economy – there was no choice but to adapt to Roman currency (and literacy, too) if local traders wanted to deal with the Roman army!

Vindolanda tablet 309, detailing the procurement of materials for a fort

PS Metto (?) to his Advectus (?)
very many greetings.
I have sent you wooden materials through the agency of Saco:
hubs, number, 34
axles for carts, number, 38
therein an axle turned on the lathe, number, 1
spokes, number, 300
planks (?) for a bed, number, 26
seats, number, 8 (?)
knots (?), number, 2 (?)
boards (?), number, 20+
. . ., number, 29
benches (?), number, 6
I have sent you goat-skins, number, 6
I pray that you are in good health, brother.

This very fragmented tablet is a list of material supplied to the army. The majority are items from a carpenter – axles, planks, and so on – described as 'wooden materials'. Both the man who sent it and the man receiving it seem to have been civilian contractors supplying the army. The numbers of the items would suggest that it is quite a significant contract, and it further indicates the demands placed on the British economy by the Roman army – and the opportunities which it provided for civilians running businesses supplying it. It is possible, but not certain, that these civilians could have included native Britons, but there is no specific evidence to support this view.

4.3 Romanisation and Further Resistance

> **S&C**
> - Use a library or the internet to find out more about the Vindolanda tablets.
> - How were they found, and why are they so well preserved?
> - Look up the similar range of material but from civilian source in London, at the Bloomberg site: http://www.mola.org.uk/blog/archaeological-research-britain%E2%80%99s-oldest-hand-written-documents-released or use 'Bloomberg Roman site London' to search the web.

Vindolanda tablet 632, requesting to know if there is an inn to lodge at:

order (accommodation?) to be given to . . .; accommodation moreover where the horses are well housed. Farewell, my dearest brother.

This is the right-hand column of a letter to Flavius Cerealis, the prefect or officer-in-charge of the Ninth Cohort of Batavians at Vindolanda. He is perhaps best known from a birthday party invitation which Claudia Severa wrote to her friend Sulpicia Lepidina, who was the wife of Flavius Cerialis (Vindolanda tablet 291). Flavius Cerialis' name is written in large letters known as 'address script' on the back. It seems to be an order in writing to him from another soldier. The message seems to be less of a request than an instruction to sort accommodation out – for the horses as much as the humans!

THE INFLUENCE OF DIFFERENT EMPERORS

There are two final tasks which we need to complete so that all of the points in the specification are covered. They can be used as part of revision as we look back over material we have already studied. They are:

- the influence of different emperors.
- the sources' portrayal of the Britons, particularly those who resisted Roman rule.

Identifying this is fairly straightforward when we think about what different governors were encouraged or allowed to do in the province and how far Roman control expanded at different times. Compare the dating of governors which we prepared earlier with the dates in which each emperor was in power:

AD 41–54	Claudius	Claudius and Nero are known as Julio-Claudians
AD 54–68	Nero	
AD 69	Galba, Otho, Vitellus	This is known as the year of the four emperors
AD 69–79	Vespasian	Vespasian, Titus and Domitian are known as Flavians
AD 79–81	Titus	
AD 81–96	Domitian	

The influence of these emperors is clear enough apart from Nero. Claudius needed a triumph and encouraged invasion to support a client state, according to the account in Cassius Dio. Nero appears to have encouraged his allies by consolidating Roman support

> **Study questions**
> 1. Read through these passages and note what kind of supplies the Roman army needed.
> 2. What impact might the presence of the Roman army have made on the local economy around a military base such as Vindolanda? Make a list of points based on these passages from the Vindolanda tablets.
> 3. What new skills might the local contractors need to learn in order to trade with the Romans?

for them – the Fishbourne proto-palace dates from the end of his reign – though according to Suetonius:

> He was never at any time moved by any desire or hope of expanding the empire. He even contemplated withdrawing the army from Britain, and only desisted from his purpose because he did not wish to appear to belittle the glory of his father . . .
>
> Suetonius, *Nero* 18

Presumably Suetonius is referring to the time after Boudicca's rebellion, though the other sources, including Tacitus (who had no cause to praise Nero at any time!) show that care was taken to replace a warlike and vindictive governor, Suetonius Paulinus, with governors whose aim was to nurture the province and make sure that there was as little ill-will towards Rome as possible (Tacitus thinks they are fairly useless, you may recall).

Of subsequent emperors, we can discount Galba, Otho and Vitellius on account of the brevity of their reigns (though the last of these made a lot of appointments to positions of authority in Britain). Vespasian's reign sees major expansion in Britain. After he comes to power there is no more reference to any client kings or client states, and as we have seen the start of his reign coincided with trouble in the territory of the Brigantes and led to a further period of expansion. He may have wanted to demonstrate his worth by winning a series of victories (and keeping the army busy!), given that he had no family connections to justify his taking power as emperor. Agricola's tenure as governor started under Vespasian, continued under Titus (who probably continued the expansionist policy of his father) and then reached its end during the start of Domitian's reign; this sequence of changes of emperor in Rome may be another reason why Agricola held the post of governor for seven years when the average was just three. Tacitus in the *Agricola* hints that Domitian was hostile to him personally, and later in *Histories* 1.2 he complains that 'Britain was conquered, then allowed to slip from our grasp', but this is wild exaggeration: in the years following Agricola's moves north into what is now Scotland, the Romans settled on controlling the south of the island, and established a frontier along the line where Hadrian was later to command a wall to be constructed; this remained the northern extremity of the province for the next 350 years, with the exception of the move to the Antonine Wall along the line of the Forth and Clyde (more or less between Glasgow and Edinburgh) from the 140s to the 160s.

ACTIVITY/STUDY QUESTION/DEBATE

- 'Claudius started the Roman occupation of Britain, but later emperors gained much more from it'. Discuss this view.
- 'The Britons gained as much from the Roman occupation of Britain as the Romans did'. How far do you agree with this view?

THE SOURCES' PORTRAYAL OF THE BRITONS, PARTICULARLY THOSE WHO RESISTED ROMAN RULE

This issue involves looking again at the ways in which Tacitus and Dio depict Caratacus, Boudicca, and Calgacus.

In addition, we should look at Tacitus, *Agricola*, 10–12, the section of his work often described as ethnography (the study of different peoples), where he describes the island of Britain as it was then understood, and described the customs and qualities of the inhabitants. Remember that all this was written for a Roman audience, not for GCSE students to get a clear grasp of the detail of Britain and the Britons!

> **S&C** Compare the evidence in the sources you have studied with what other ancient writers have to say about the Britons: try Caesar's ethnographical section in *Gallic Wars* v. 12–15 (LACTOR 11 A16), and the comments of the geographer Strabo, 2.5.8 and 4.5 (LACTOR B3).

Study questions

Look over the different portrayals of Britons in the sources you have studied.

1. What similarities and differences can you find in the sources' portrayal of Britons?
2. How far do you agree that the authors of the sources admired the Britons, even though they were enemies?

TOPIC REVIEW

Boost your knowledge

Describe:

1. the different stages of Agricola's campaigns during his time as governor
2. the resistance and defeat of Calgacus and the Caledonii
3. the effects of Roman rule and the extent of change, including urbanisation and cultural, religious and lifestyle changes
4. the ways in which the different sources portray the Britons

Stretch your understanding

Explain:

1. why Tacitus admires Agricola so much in his work of the same name, and why we need to read it carefully as a result.
2. why Calgacus led his campaign of resistance, according to Tacitus
3. why the Romans encouraged the development of towns, and possible reasons why Fishbourne Palace was constructed
4. how useful the evidence from the Vindolanda tablets is in showing the impact of the Roman army on the Britons and their economic activity

Part Two Depth Study 3: Britannia: From Conquest

PRACTICE QUESTIONS

1. a. Name the place where Agricola's final battle against Calgacus took place, according to Tacitus. [1]
    b. Name **two** of the Roman emperors under whom Agricola served as governor of Britain. [2]
    c. Name **two** other British leaders who led resistance against the Romans. [2]

Source C

Source D

2. Using details from Sources C and D, explain how useful archaeological evidence is in helping us to understand Roman Britain. [5]
3. 'The Britons gained nothing from being invaded by the Romans.' How far do you agree with this view? You must use and analyse the ancient sources you have studied as well as supporting your answer with your own knowledge. [20]

Further Reading

There are masses of books on Roman Britain, large and small, many good, some far-fetched! Here is a list of some useful texts:

de la Bedoyère, Guy, *Roman Britain: a New History* (London: Thames & Hudson, 2013), revised ed. Nice presentation and features, but tends to lack in-depth analysis.

Birley, Anthony, *The People of Roman Britain* (London: Batsford, 1979).

Birley, Anthony, *The Roman Government of Britain* (Oxford: Oxford University Press, 2005). This gives very detailed coverage of the topic but is prohibitively expensive!

Bowman, Alan K., *Life and Letters on the Roman Frontier: Vindolanda and its People* (London: British Museum Press, 1994).

Cunliffe, Barry, *Fishbourne: A Roman Palace and its Garden* (London: Thames & Hudson, 1971).

Cunliffe, Barry, *Roman Bath Discovered* (Stroud: Tempus, 2000).

Frere, Sheppard, *Britannia: A History of Roman Britain* (Abingdon: Routledge & Kegan Paul, 1987), 3rd ed. Extensively revised but still valuable, if the archaeology is now sadly dated in places.

Grainge, Gerald, *The Roman Invasions of Britain* (Stroud: Tempus, 2005).

Hingley Richard and Christina Unwin, *Boudica: Iron Age Warrior Queen* (London: Hambledon Continuum, 2005).

Mattingly, David, *An Imperial Possession: Britain in the Roman Empire* (London: Penguin, 2006).

Salway, Peter (ed.), *The Roman Era* (Oxford: Oxford University Press, 2002). Very interesting chapters on the invasion with an analytical approach.

Southern, Patricia, *Roman Britain: A New History, 55 BC–AD 450* (Stroud: Amberley Publishing, 2011).

Webster, Graham, *Rome Against Caratacus: The Roman Campaigns in Britain AD 48–58* (Abingdon: Routledge, 1983), rev. ed.

Webster, Graham *Boudica: The British Revolt Against Rome AD 60* (Abingdon: Routledge, 1993), rev. ed.

Sources are published in the OCR Source Booklet, but alternative translations and images are available in two volumes published by LACTOR:

Grocock, Christopher (ed.), *Roman Inscriptions of Britain* (LACTOR 4, forthcoming 2017).

Rathbone, Yvette and D. W. Rathbone (eds), *Literary Sources for Roman Britain* (LACTOR 11, 2012).

What to Expect in the Exam: Section D

DEPTH STUDY: BRITANNIA: FROM CONQUEST TO PROVINCE, AD 43–c. 84

This chapter aims to show you the types of questions you are likely to get in Section D of the Rome and its Neighbours exam. It offers some advice on how to answer the questions and will help you avoid common errors.

The examination

The Roman depth study is in the same exam paper as the Roman Period Study – The Foundations of Rome 753–440 BC. You can answer Section A and Section D in any order you like. Just remember that the exam lasts 1 hour and 45 minutes. Section D is worth 45 marks, so you need to make sure you organise your time accordingly.

This component of the GCSE examination is designed to test your knowledge, understanding and evaluation of Britannia: from Conquest to Province.

There are three Assessment Objectives in your Ancient History GCSE. Questions will be designed to test these areas. To remind yourself what these are read page 70 in the period study exam chapter.

Be aware that there is some overlap with Ancient History Assessment Objectives. As you will see in the table on the next page, questions 19 and 20 assess multiple assessment objectives. For example, AO2 and AO3 both require you to make 'judgements' on the 'historical events and historical periods'.

In the exam, you should be able to demonstrate:

- a good grasp of the conquest of Britannia and its key characters
- an understanding of why Britain was invaded by the Romans
- an awareness of different reactions to the invasion by various Britons
- a good knowledge of the various stages or phases of the invasion
- an understanding of the different ways that source-material and archaeological evidence can be interpreted, and the different conclusions that can be drawn about the ways in which Britons may have reacted to the invasion by Rome

When analysing and evaluating your evidence in order to make judgements, you should be able to:

- analyse and evaluate the causes and consequences of the main events of the conquest of Britannia.

- analyse and evaluate the significance of key individuals and events and how they impacted upon the course of the conquest of Britannia.
- look at change and continuity; including the rate of change and the relative success of different developments. For example, the causes and consequences of the different revolts and resistance against Rome, or the development of 'Roman' culture in Britainna such as the growth of towns.
- use your knowledge, evaluation and analysis in combination to produce a logical conclusion.

When evaluating how the portrayal of events by the ancient sources relates to the historical contexts in which they were produced, you should be able to demonstrate:

- an understanding of the approaches used by Cassius Dio, Josephus, Suetonius and Tacitus, and how the nature of their work potentially affected its usefulness and accuracy
- a good grasp of the context of each prescribed source and how far the ancient author creates an accurate portrayal of the event. In the case of archaeological sources, students should be aware of their dates, the context in which they were found, and their value as evidence
- an awareness of how other authors have interpreted the events in the prescribed sources

QUESTION TYPES

There are five different types of question. It is important to remember that the Britannia: from Conquest to Province questions begin at question 16. The table below shows how they are assessed.

Question	Type of question	AO1 marks	AO2 marks	AO3 marks	Total marks
16	Discrete factual knowledge	5	–	–	5
17	What can we learn from the source	–	–	5	5
18	Evaluate the source	–	–	5	5
19	Second-order concepts	5	5	–	10
20	Essay using ancient source knowledge	5	5	10	20

There are no SPaG marks awarded for the Depth Study questions.

Question 16 will test your knowledge. This question will be divided into a number of sub-questions.

Question 17 and 18 will supply you with a passage or a visual source from the prescribed sources. A list of the prescribed sources can be found at the start of each chapter and on the OCR web-page. Question 17 will ask you to identify key features from the passage. Question 18 will require you to evaluate the accuracy of the passage.

Question 19 will ask you to explore a second-order concept. A second-order concept is a historical skill used to analyse the past, for example, change and continuity, similarity and difference, significance, cause and consequence.

Finally, Question 20 is an essay question which will explore your knowledge and understanding of the topic and relevant prescribed sources. It will also assess your ability to use this information to create a line of substantiated argument.

Question 16 – knowledge questions

There will be 5 marks available for question 16 all testing factual knowledge (AO1). The 5 marks will be broken down into a series of short-answer questions, typically worth 1, 2 or 3 marks.

These questions will usually start with one of the following stems:

- State...
- Identify...
- Name...
- Give **one** example of... Give **two** reasons for...

For example: *Name the goddess who was worshipped at the site of Aquae Sulis (Bath).* [1]

- **Answer:** Minerva. [1]

This question has only one answer. You do not have to write in full sentences, and the answer should be brief.

For example: *Name **two** British leaders who were friendly to Rome after the conquest of AD 43.* [2]

- **Answer**: Togidubnus (or Cogidubnus) [1] and Cartimandua. [1]

This answer is also brief. There is in fact no need to write full sentences if it seems that only a single word or a phrase is needed.

Question 17 – source question

Questions 17 and 18 both use the same prescribed source. It could be a passage from one of the ancient historians or a visual source from the archaeological record.

Question 17 will ask you to identify several features from the source and develop what this tells you about the question focus (AO3)

Question 17 will usually start with the following:
17. What can we learn from Passage D about.....? [5]

Here is an example:

Passage D

> Or do you suppose that the Romans will be as brave in war as they are lustful in peace? No, it is to our disagreements and disharmony that they owe their reputation, and they turn the errors of an enemy to the fame of their own army, an army which, composed as it is of every variety of nations. Just as its success holds it together so disaster will break it up. Or do you really think the Gauls and Germans, and, I am ashamed to say, several Britons are bound by loyalty and affection? They may be lending their lives to support a stranger's rule, but they have been its enemies longer than its slaves. Fear and terror are feeble bonds of attachment; if you remove them, those who have ceased to fear will begin to hate. All the incentives to victory are on our side.
>
> Tacitus, *Agricola* 32

○ 17. What can we learn from Passage D about how Calgacus encouraged his followers to fight against the Romans on this occasion? [5]

When answering question 17 you must remember that this question is only worth 5 out of 45 marks and make sure you organise your time accordingly.

- After reading the passage you need to identify several key features or details from the passage – e.g. 'It is to our disagreements and disharmony that they owe their reputation' – showing that the lack of unity among British tribes has enabled the Romans to defeat them; or 'They turn the errors of an enemy to the fame of their own army' – they have depended on British tactical weakness to gain victory over the Britons.
- Try to infer what this tells us about the question's focus – Calgacus is trying to give his soldiers reasons to hope that defeat against the Romans is not inevitable, and he stresses that the Roman army is made up of many different tribal units, which may be a weakness when the Romans come up against a determined enemy.
- To summarise: read the passage carefully, identify several key features or details and outline what you can learn from these details.

Answer:

You should be able to develop several points, which might include:

○ 'do you suppose that the Romans will be as brave in war as they are lustful in peace?' – the Romans are not really all that brave!
○ 'Or do you really think the Gauls and Germans, and, I am ashamed to say, several Britons are bound by loyalty and affection?' – the Romans' allies will fall away – or even change sides (ref. to 'many Britons' fighting alongside the Romans).
○ 'Fear and terror are feeble bonds of attachment' – the Romans inspire no real loyalty, but only rule by fear.

NB. If you are struggling to understand the passage, try to find something from the passage which seems important to the story and explain why it is important.

Question 18 – source question

Question 18 will assess your ability to use, analyse and evaluate a prescribed source within its historical context and then draw a conclusion about how far its portrayal is accurate. For example, you might be asked how its accuracy may have been affected by influences upon its creator (AO3).

NB. Visual sources such as a coin, bust or a relief sculpture could be assessed by exploring the potential purpose of the source. What image were British kings presenting on their coinage? How might the tombstones in the prescribed sources have been regarded by the Roman soldiers – or the local Britons? In some cases you may be able to assess whether this is an accurate portrayal of the event or individual. Other examples may be good examples of propaganda used to convey a particular message.

Question 18 will usually be phrased as follows:

18. Using details from Passage D, evaluate how accurate you think x's account of y is? [5]

As in the exam we will be using the same source from question 17.

18. Using details from Passage D, evaluate how accurate you think Tacitus' account of Calgacus' speech is? [5]

The following are some of the tests you can use. Remember you are looking for the strengths and weaknesses of the passage.

- What knowledge do you have of this event or other interpretations of this event? Does your wider understanding make this passage accurate or inaccurate?
- What is the historian's method? Is this method a strength, weakness or both when evaluating this passage?
- Is the extract detailed, or is it an overview? Is this typical of this historian?
- Finally, the aims of the historian might affect the reliability. This will not be relevant for all passages. So avoid general comments such as 'Tacitus was writing only a decade after the event.' Instead, explain how this might affect the accuracy of this particular passage.
- If it is a visual source think about why it was created and when. A dedication or triumphal arch may be designed to celebrate something. Would it, therefore, focus on an individual's failings or weaknesses?
- Remember to identify the key features from the source to support your evaluation, otherwise you will not be meeting the full requirements of the question.

To summarise: identify a few strengths or weaknesses of author's treatment of the topic, or alternatively develop one or two points in detail.

Although you do not need a conclusion it is good practice to make a statement about how accurate you think the passage is.

Answers may include:

You should be able to develop a few of the following points:

- Tacitus is using a standard technique for an ancient historian – he creates a speech to explain *why* Calgacus might have been resisting Rome

- Tacitus had close access to his father-in-law Agricola, who led the Roman army – and he may have picked up some stories from him which may have included details about why the Britons were resisting Rome, perhaps from prisoners-of-war
- It is unlikely that the speech is anything like exactly what Calgacus said – for a start he would have spoken a local language, not Latin, and it is structured in a very careful, 'classical' way
- Tacitus uses events like this to explore themes of freedom and slavery which he felt were a symptom of the political situation in Rome under the emperors
- When looking at a passage you must remember question 18 is only worth 5 out of 45 marks so make sure you use your time accordingly.

Question 19 – second-order concepts

In GCSE Ancient History you will need to answer questions on second-order concepts (see p 74 for more info in the Period Study exam chapter): change and continuity, similarity and difference, significance, cause and consequence. In the Depth Study, these questions will be assessing AO1 and AO2. This means you will be required to demonstrate good knowledge and understanding, alongside analytical and evaluation skills which lead to a supported conclusion.

The questions **may** look something like this:

- **Change and continuity.** These questions may ask you to explore an event or an aspect of the conquest of Britannia and explain how much change there was between two points
- *e.g. 19. Explain the extent to which x changed when y happened during the period you have studied*
- **Similarity and difference.** These questions may ask you to explore an aspect of the conquest of Britannia and explain if individuals or events responded to it in a similar or different way
- *e.g. 19. Explain whether x and y had similar causes and results*
- **Significance.** These questions may require you to explore the importance of an individual or event upon the whole of the conquest of Britannia
- *e.g. 19. Explain the importance of x*
- **Cause.** These questions may ask you to explain how an event happened or why an individual took a particular course of action
- *e.g. 19. Explain what caused x*
- **Consequence.** These questions may ask you to explain the impact of an event or individual
- *e.g. 19. Explain the impact x had on y*

Here is an example of how to answer a second-order concept question,

- *19. Explain whether the rebellions against Rome led by Caratacus and Boudicca had similar causes and results* [10]

- Remember this question asks you to use your knowledge (AO1) to identify, develop and assess key features from the passage to make a judgement about the second-order concept (AO2)
- Identify several possible features. These must be supported by the source and/or your own knowledge
- You must make sure that each of these features is linked back to the question and its importance evaluated
- Most significantly you must reach a substantiated judgement

Answers may include:

You might include several examples of similarities and differences such as:

- Similar – both leaders tried to unite a number of tribes against the Romans
- Similar – in both Tacitus and Dio, both leaders are given speeches which explain the need to preserve freedom and not suffer slavery at the hands of the Romans
- Different – Caratacus led resistance to Rome from the outset, and withdrew to Wales to continue it; Boudicca and her husband Prasutagus seem to have accepted 'client kingdom' status at first, and the rebellion only began after mistreatment by the Romans when Prasutagus died
- Different – Caratacus' resistance was confined to Wales and did not do very much damage to areas controlled by Rome, whereas Boudicca and her forces destroyed three important places – Camulodonum, Londinium and Verulamium – and were only defeated after harming the province very seriously

Remember that question 19 is worth 10 out of a possible 45 marks, make sure that you organise your time accordingly.

To summarise: identify several possible answers and use them to create a sustained line of argument.

You do not need to use the ancient historians in this answer. You will be rewarded, however, if you can show the different interpretations in relation to the question focus.

Question 20 – essay question

The final question is an essay question which assesses all three assessment objectives in combination. You will need to be able to use factual knowledge and understanding alongside your knowledge of the prescribed sources to provide evidence to support and challenge the question posed. Furthermore, you will need to analyse and explain this evidence in order to make a substantiated judgement about how far you agree with the question posed.

You will also have to evaluate the context of the ancient evidence you have used to judge its accuracy and potential weight. The best students will use this evaluation to inform their judgement.

AO1 and AO2 are both worth 5 marks each. AO3 is allocated ten marks.

As with question 5 in Section A your essay will be marked according to the best fit with the mark scheme.

Your essay question will be much broader than question 19 and will expect you to draw upon material from across the whole Depth Study. The question will usually present you with a statement and ask you to make a judgement about 'how far' you agree with it.

The following is an example of a possible essay question:

- 'The British tribes were totally hostile to the Romans.' How far do you agree with this view? [20]

Answer:

Some were hostile because:

- They were opposed to the idea of losing their freedom to rule themselves – shown in numerous speeches in Tacitus and Dio
- They were already hostile to other British tribes who had called on Rome for help – particularly the Atrebates, whose prince Commius appealed to Claudius
- Some tribes may have appreciated what Roman culture offered but did not want to lose their independence
- They were badly treated by the Romans, even after they had co-operated with them (Boudicca and the Iceni is the obvious example)

Some were not hostile because:

- Rome offered them protection against other British tribes who were threatening them – the example of Verica is the most obvious example to use
- Roman control offered them security – even during Boudicca's rebellion most tribes did NOT rebel against Rome
- There were cultural benefits to be gained from co-operation with Rome, including trade and economic development (this is the 'What have the Romans ever done for us?' topic). Towns, Bath and Fishbourne Roman Palace could be used to support this point
- The presence of the Roman army provided some economic stimulus for locals to become involved in supplying it – this is one way of interporeting the detail in the Vindolanda letters

This is not an exhaustive list – but designed to give you a flavour of what you might choose.

Key points:

Use the same advice from question 5 in Section A (pp. 76–77), but remember:

- You need to use your knowledge of ancient sources to support and challenge the question posed
- You must evaluate the accuracy and weight of the ancient sources and use this evaluation to develop your line of argument and judgement
- Avoid general observations about accuracy, such as 'Cassius Dio was writing over 150 years later and so he is not reliable' – he may have had access to Tacitus and other earlier sources now lost to us

- Make sure your analysis of the sources is linked to the question and supported by an example
- This example should be linked to the question, not just a general comment about the author. For example, you could not use the example that 'Tacitus uses his accounts of the conquest of Britain *just* to complain about the political situation in Rome so nothing he says abut Britain has any value'. This criticism needs to be balanced with the evidence from other authors and from archaeology and tombstones – it is clear that the Roman invasion *did* happen, and Tacitus' accounts would have been looked on with ridicule if he had contradicted what was well known to many other Romans who might have taken part in the campaigns in Britain! It is fair to assess what Tacitus says critically, but the core detail seems to be accurate.

GLOSSARY

agrarian law a redistribution of land or change of the way land is farmed

anachronistic a description of an event which uses features or people who are not alive or available at that time

Apennine culture central European and Italian culture from the late Bronze Age (fifteenth to fourteenth century)

aquifer a rock formation which can be used to supply water

attrition warfare designed to reduce the number of men in the opposing army little by little, employed by Fabius and later Marcellus against Hannibal

augury the Roman tradition of using birds to read the future, or seek divine support for a decision

Caesarian supporters of Julius Caesar

Camenae in Roman mythology they were the goddesses of childbirth, fountains with the ability to tell the future. Vestal Virgins were involved in festivals to celebrate them

Carthage a powerful city in Africa which controlled trade across the Mediterranean until the third century and lost control of the western Mediterranean to Rome after the Punic Wars

celeres a Roman cavalry unit believed to have developed from Romulus' bodyguard

Celtic the culture which dominated the area known as Gaul during this period

censor the administrator of Rome which kept an eye on finances and the people and would also decide membership of the different classes

census a survey to determine the wealth, and consequently the class, of each Roman citizen; used to determine military service

centurion a commander of a century

century a unit in the Roman army. It is unlikely that this system was in place until the Republic

client-king kings and rulers of non-Roman controlled provinces, who were aided by Roman favour in return for their support of Rome

colonia a settlement of veterans (ex-soldiers) made up of land taken from native tribes. Ex-legionaries received a farmstead as part of their pension settlement

Comitia an assembly of Roman citizens which discussed important matters such as war and peace

Comitia Curiata a political assembly divided into thirty groups or curiae who were split among the three tribes of the period of the first king, Romulus. Modern historians are unclear if this council ever existed

comitium the open-air space where Roman citizens would meet to discuss important matters

Conflict of the Orders the dispute between the patricians and the plebeians

consul one of two annually elected magistrates who shared leadership of the Roman army and influenced political decisions in Rome

creditor a person lending money

diadem a crown or headband symbolising sovereignty

dictator a magistrate appointed for six months to deal with a national emergency or crisis and in full control of the army and government during that time

divine intervention the interference (good and bad) of gods in human affairs

envoys representatives sent between cities or countries to improve relationships or prevent conflict

eques, equites (pl.) a social class named because they were men who received a horse from the Roman state and formed the Roman cavalry

flamen a Roman priest who performed rituals for a particular god

flanked on both sides (of an army)

foundation chronology a popular theory that the Roman writer Fabius Pictor created a foundation timeline to organise the history of Rome, by mixing together the different sources he had found with his own narrative

friend and ally of the Roman people the official title given to a client-king or ruler as a reward for loyalty or good service, confirming their support from Rome

Gabinians Roman soldiers of Aulus Gabinius, who helped reinstall Ptolemy XII Auletes to power and then remained in Alexandria for a number of years after his death

Hellenistic the period of Greek language, history and custom between the death of Alexander the Great and the death of Cleopatra

hoplite citizen-soldiers of Ancient Greek city states, and probably the system adopted by Rome in the fifth century

Hundred and Four described in Aristotle's *Politics* as judges who made sure Carthage's generals served the best interests of Carthage

Glossary

hyperbole a deliberate over-exaggeration

Iliad epic Greek poem which describes the 'legendary' war between Greece and the Trojans

imperium in Ancient Rome this gave kings the power to rule or govern. In the Republic, it gave consuls the power to control the army

incite to encourage people to use violence

indict formal accusation that someone has committed a crime

interpretations the different ways historians have viewed the past

interregnum a period of time between two reigns when the normal government is suspended

inviolability legal protection from violence or harm

Isis the ancient Egyptian goddess of magic, fertility and motherhood

land reform governmental policy to distribute land among the poor

largesse giving gifts or money to people

legion unit of the Roman army (used to describe early Roman armies by ancient historians even though there is no evidence for this unit until the fourth and third centuries BC)

lictors Roman bodyguards who protected the king or consul and carried fasces, which symbolised power

literary tradition accounts of Rome's foundation by ancient historians such as Dionysius and Livy; very little of older sources such as Cato and Pictor survives

magistrate an elected office-holder who had responsibility in the Roman state

maniples a subdivision of a Roman legion

Mars the Roman god of warfare and conflict

Master of the Horse dictator's deputy appointed to keep a check on his power and to ensure it was not used to create a tyranny

mausoleum a grand burial chamber, usually reserved for one family or dynasty

mercenary hired soldier who will fight in return for payment

military tribune men organised for military service (not to be confused with the plebeian tribunes of later Roman history)

narrative used by all authors to help readers follow their story and ancient historians similarly used story-lines to help explain the changes and developments introduced in Rome

oral history historical information which is not recorded in writing, but passed down in folk tales, stories, poems or songs, and often mixing fact with fiction to make the event more interesting

orientalising culture during the late eighth century, art and technology from places like Syria in the Near East influenced Greek culture, as can be seen in the pottery and metalwork of the period

outflank move round the side of an enemy force to outmanoeuvre them

patricians a difficult group to define accurately, Livy and Dionysius refer to them as men belonging to Rome's oldest families, many being rich landowners

patron-client the mutual relationships common in Roman society where one Roman helps out a less influential or wealthy Roman

pharaoh the common title for the monarchs of Ancient Egypt, holding both political and religious significance

plebeian tribune powerful tribunes who represented the plebeian class and shared their concerns with the Senate, holding the Senate and consuls to account after the First Secession

plebeians Roman citizens who did not belong to the patrician families

plunder to loot or steal at a time of war

piety being religious

pontiff a Roman high priest who regulated religious practices

praetor Roman magistrate who supported the consuls – usually as an army commander

principes the main Roman infantry: heavily armoured legionaries who formed the core of any Roman army

quorum the number of people from a group needed to make a meeting official – without a quorum, a group like the Senate could not make a decision or recommendation

regency advisors a group of important officials put in place to help rule a kingdom when the heir to the throne is too young to rule

repossess taking the possessions of a person by force when they cannot afford to pay their debt

republic a country without a king; the word derives from the Latin – res publica – the 'public matter' or the people's government

rhetorical a form of writing focused on effect more than content

Roman Forum the oldest market place in Rome

Romanisation the effects of Roman rule and the extent of change: urbanisation; cultural, religious and lifestyle changes

rule by decree passing laws and judgements without listening to others or to previous laws, which suggests a leader or king has total power

scapegoat a person or group of people blamed for something that has happened

secession name given to plebeian protests in the Republic when plebeians left the city to create a new settlement on the Aventine hill or other location

Second Punic War war between Rome and Carthage, from 218 to 203

Second Triumvirate the political alliance of Antony, Octavian and Lepidus in 43 BC

sedition encouraging others to challenge the government

seditious keen to start or participate in an uprising

Senate a council or assembly of Rome's 'best men', during the time of the kings; became a council of retired magistrates who advised consuls from 509, and from 27 advised emperors. Controlled Rome's finances during the Republic

skirmishers hand-to-hand combatants with little training

slingers Carthaginian troops from the Balearic Islands who used small slings to propel small projectiles at their enemy

stele/stela (pl. stelae) an upright stone or wooden column bearing an inscription or design. Usually used as a gravestone

Stoicism an Ancient Greek school of philosophy that believed that virtue is based upon knowledge

subsistence farming when communities make just enough food to feed themselves and their families

sufete a magistrate of Carthage, similar to the consuls of Rome

triumph the ceremonial entry of a victorious Roman general into the city of Rome awarded after a successful campaign or victory

Troy ancient civilisation at the heart of the mythical Trojan Wars, around the end of the thirteenth or early twelfth century

tyrant king or leader who abuses their powers to rule unfairly (the original meaning was not negative, however, and simply meant a ruler with sole power)

uraeus sacred snake used as a symbol of sovereignty and power

urbanisation development of a town as people move from the countryside to take up crafts and trades

urnfield culture a culture that spread from central Europe into Italy before the ninth century; its name comes from the custom of cremating the dead and placing their ashes in urns

velites Roman light infantry, recruited from the poorest plebeians, and given limited training to use javelins and in hand-to-hand fighting (used to describe early plebeian armies by ancient historians even though there is no evidence for this unit until the fourth and third centuries BC)

Vestal Virgin celibate female priestesses who played an important role in Roman society by protecting Rome's sacred flame

Villanovan civilisation an early Iron Age culture of the tenth–sixth centuries BC, which cremated their dead and were skilled in metal work, and which were destroyed by the Etruscan civilisation

war veteran a retired soldier

weight the historical value of a source

SOURCES OF QUOTATIONS

Numbers in **bold** refer to page numbers.

Period Study: The Foundations of Rome

6 'The accounts of . . .' Livy, *History of Rome,* Preface, trans. T.J. Luce (adapted), *Livy: The History of Rome, Books 1–5* (Oxford: Oxford University Press, 2008)); **9** 'In my opinion . . .' Livy 1.4 trans. Luce (adapted); **10** 'At this point . . .' Livy 1.6–1.7 trans. Luce (adapted); **13** 'Romulus decreed that . . .' Dionysius, *Roman Antiquities* 2.9, trans. E. Cary, *Dionysius of Halicarnassus Vol. I: Roman Antiquities Books 1–2* (Cambridge MA: Harvard University Press, 1937) (adapted); **14** 'Under Romulus . . .' Livy 1.43 trans. Luce; **15** 'Whenever the king . . .' Dionysius 2.14 trans. Cary (adapted); **17** 'If you cannot . . .' Livy 1.13 trans. Luce (adapted); **17** 'By introducing . . .' Livy 1.21 trans. Luce; **18** 'There was a . . .' Livy 1.21 trans. Luce; **26–27** 'Lucumo was overjoyed . . .' Dionysius, *Roman Antiquities* 3.48, trans. Earnest Cary, *Dionysius of Halicarnassus Vol. II: Roman Antiquities Books 3–4* (Cambridge MA: Harvard University Press, 1939) (adapted); **30** 'Take the throne . . .' Livy 1.41 trans. Luce (adapted); **31** 'Men whose possessions . . .' Livy 1.43 trans. Luce; **32** 'In establishing this . . .' Dionysius 4.21 trans. Cary; **34** 'Superbus approached . . .' Livy 1.47–1.48 trans. Luce (adapted); **38** 'Sextus had managed . . .' Dionysius 4.46 trans. Cary; **42** 'Seizing the knife . . .' Livy 1.59 trans. Luce (adapted); **44** 'Time is short . . .' Dionysius 4.73 trans. Cary (adapted); **52** 'There are so . . .' Livy 2.21 trans. Luce; **54** 'While they [the . . .' Livy 2.23 trans. Luce (adapted); **58** 'Once upon a . . .' Livy 2.32 trans. Luce (adapted); **58** 'Lucius Furius and . . .' Livy 2.54 trans. Luce (adapted); **63** 'Taking his daughter . . .' Livy 3.47 trans. Luce (adapted); **64** 'Verginius turned to . . .' Livy 3.50 trans. Luce (adapted); **67** 'The battle was on . . .' Livy 4.2 trans. Luce; **73** 'There Verginius created . . .' Livy 3.50 trans. Luce.

Depth Study 1: Hannibal and the Second Punic War

86 'For since many . . .' Polybius, *Histories* 12.4c, trans. I. Scott Kilvert, *Polybius: The Rise of the Roman Empire* (Harmondsworth: Penguin, 1979); **86** 'But once a . . .' Polybius 1.14 trans. I. Scott Kilvert; **96** 'The Carthaginians bitterly . . .' Polybius 3.13 trans I. Scott Kilvert; **97** 'To the Spanish . . .' Livy 21.19 trans. Luce; **101** 'Then After the Celts . . .' Polybius 3.44 trans. OCR; **112** 'Maharbal, his cavalry . . .' Livy 22.51 trans. Luce; **113** 'The Romans persistence . . .' Livy 26.12 trans. Luce; **115** 'Between the armies . . .' Livy 21.54 trans. OCR; **121** 'They made Fabius . . .' Plutarch, *Life of Fabius Maximus* 5 trans. OCR; **125** 'I regret our . . .' Livy 28.42 trans. Luce; **125** 'for too long . . .' Livy 28.44 trans. Luce; **129** 'The story goes . . .' Livy 30.20 trans. OCR; **129** 'He said that . . .' Livy 30.20 trans. OCR; **132** 'As for myself, . . .' Livy 30.30 trans. OCR; **132** 'As for myself, . . .' Livy 30.31 trans. OCR; **135** 'The javelins of . . .' Livy 30.33 trans. OCR; **138** 'Hannibal derived no . . .' Livy 30.29 trans. OCR; **143** 'When Antiochus heard . . .' Polybius 3.12 trans. OCR.

Depth Study 2: Cleopatra

All translations are from the OCR source booklet.

160 'Her beauty, so . . .' Plutarch, *Life of Mark Antony* 27; **161** 'It is said . . .' Plutarch, *Life of Julius Caesar* 49; **166** 'Once, however, . . .' Plutarch, *Life of Mark Antony* 29; **174** 'In reality Cleopatra . . .' Cassius Dio, *Roman History* 42.44; **176** 'But he especially . . .' Suetonius, *Life of Divine Julius* 52; **177** 'He allowed her . . .' Suetonius, *Life of Divine Julius* 52; **179** 'I hate the . . .' Cicero, *Letters to Atticus* XV.15; **180** 'But he especially . . .' Suetonius, *Life of Divine Julius* 52; **187** 'Instead they made . . .' Plutarch, *Life of Mark Antony* 30; **188** 'Now the disastrous . . .' Plutarch, *Life of Mark Antony* 36; **191** 'At last they . . .' Plutarch, *Life of Mark Antony* 53; **192** 'First he announced . . .' Plutarch, *Life of Mark Antony* 54; **196** 'Antony now had . . .' Plutarch, *Life of Mark Antony* 62; **197** 'That he had . . .' Plutarch, *Life of Mark Antony* 64; **203** 'Determined to die, . . .' Horace, *Ode* 1.37; **210** 'Now Cleopatra displayed . . .' Plutarch, *Life of Mark Antony* 29.

Depth Study 3: Britannia

217–218 'The Britons themselves . . .' Tacitus, *Agricola* 13 trans. OCR and C. Grocock; **224** '[After the murder . . .' Josephus, *Antiquities* 19.3.1–2 trans. C. Grocock; **224** 'Asinius Gallus and . . .' Suetonius, *Claudius,* 13.2; **225** 'Caesar presents the . . .' Potter, 'The Transformation of Britain' in P. Salway, *The Roman Era* (Oxford: Oxford University Press, 2002) p. 14; **226** 'Only a little . . .' Caesar, *Gallic War* 4.20.1, trans. Y. & D.W. Rathbone, *LACTOR 11: Literary Sources for Roman Britain* (London: KCL, 2012); **226** 'This is how . . .' Caesar 4.33.1.1 trans. Y. & D.W. Rathbone; **226–227** 'Caesar . . . ordered the . . .' Caesar 5.1.1 trans. Y. & D.W. Rathbone; **227** 'Cassivellaunus enlisted the . . .' Caesar 5.22–5.2 trans. Y. & D.W. Rathbone; **229** 'There fled to . . .' Augustus, *Res Gestae* 32.1, trans. Y. & D.W. Rathbone; **231** 'a certain Berikos, . . .' Cassius Dio, *Roman History* 60.19.1 trans. OCR; **231–232** 'He [Caligula] did . . .' Suetonius, *Caligula* 44.2; 46.1 trans. OCR; **232** 'When Caligula reached . . .' Cassius Dio 59.25.1, trans. Y. & D.W. Rathbone (adapted C. Grocock); **233** '. . . Aulus Plautius, . . .' Cassius Dio 60.19.1–3; **234** 'They were sent . . .' Cassius Dio 60.19.4–5 trans. OCR; **235** 'Therefore Plautius had . . .' Cassius Dio 60.20.1–4, trans. OCR; **235** 'At this point . . .' Cassius Dio 60.20.5–6, trans. OCR; **236** 'Because of this . . .' Cassius Dio 60.21.1–5, trans. OCR; **237** '[Nero] only found . . .' Josephus, *Jewish War* 3.1.2 trans. OCR; **237** 'In the reign . . .' Suetonius, *Vespasian* 4.1–4.2 trans. OCR; **237** 'Sextus Valerius Genialis, . . .' RIB 109, trans. C. Grocock; **238** 'Here lies Rufus . . .' RIB 121, trans. C. Grocock; **239** 'When the Senate . . .' Cassius Dio 60.22.1–2, trans. OCR; **240** 'To Tiberius Claudius . . .' ILS 216, trans. C. Grocock; **240** 'In this way, . . .' Cassius Dio 60.23.1–6, 30.2, trans. OCR; **240** '. . . He decreed to . . .' Suetonius, *Claudius* 24.3, trans. OCR; **241** 'The emperor Claudius . . .' Tacitus, *Annals* 12.23, trans. OCR; **243** 'He undertook only . . .' Suetonius, *Claudius* 17.2–3, trans. OCR; **244** 'Plautius being afraid . . .' Cassius Dio 60.21.1–4, trans. OCR; **246–247** 'Meanwhile, in Britain . . .' Tacitus, *Annals* 12.31, trans. OCR; **247** 'After the Iceni . . .' Tacitus, *Annals* 12.32, trans. OCR; **255** 'In Britain, the . . .' Tacitus, *Histories* 3.44, trans. OCR; **256** 'Inspired by the . . .' Tacitus, *Histories* 3.45, trans. OCR; **258** 'Aulus Plautius, the . . .' Tacitus, *Agricola* 14, trans. OCR; **260** 'a colony (colonia) . . .' Tacitus, *Annals* 12.32, trans. OCR; **261** 'The Trinobantes . . . hated . . .' Tacitus, *Annals* 14.31, trans. OCR; **269** 'The following winter . . .' Tacitus, *Agricola* 21, trans. OCR; **271** 'Octavius to his . . .' Vindolanda tablet 343, trans. C. Grocock; **272** 'The whole letter . . .' Vindolanda tablet 343, trans. C. Grocock; **272** 'Metto (?) to his . . .' Vindolanda tablet 309, trans. C. Grocock; **273** 'order (accommodation?) to . . .' Vindolanda tablet 632, trans. C. Grocock; **274** 'He was never . . .' Suetonius, *Nero* 18, trans. OCR; **281** 'Or do you . . .' Tacitus, *Agricola* 32, trans. OCR.

SOURCES OF ILLUSTRATIONS

1.1 Bibi Saint-Pol/Wikimedia; **1.2** Bloomsbury Academic; **1.3** Robin Iversen Rönnlund/Wikimedia; **1.4** mountainpix/shutterstock.com; **1.5** Bloomsbury Academic; **1.6** Lanmas/Alamy Stock Photo; **1.7** Bloomsbury Academic; **1.8** Walters Art Museum, 1971, by purchase; **1.9** Popperfoto/Contributor/Getty images; **1.10** Bloomsbury Academic; **1.11** Print Collector/Contributor/Getty images; **1.12** Bloomsbury Academic; **1.13** Georges Jansoone/Wikimedia; **1.14** Ptyx/Wikimedia; **1.15** Bloomsbury Academic; **1.16** Woodcut from Giovanni Boccaccio's *De mulieribus claris* (c. 1474); **1.17** Daderot/Wikimedia; **1.18** Jastrow/Wikimedia; **1.19** Universal History Archive/Contributor/Getty images; **1.20** Marta Muscariello/Wikimedia; **1.21** Mary Stansbury Ruiz Bequest; **1.22** engraving by unknown artist; **1.23** from Ellis, *The story of the greatest nations* (1900); **1.24** Woodcut from Giovanni Boccaccio's *De mulieribus claris* (c. 1474); **2.1** Norbert Schnitzler/Flickr; **2.2** Bloomsbury Academic; **2.3** Goldberg Coins; **2.4** Chronicle/Alamy Stock Photo; **2.5** Bloomsbury Academic; **2.6** Bloomsbury Academic; **2.7** Henri Motte 1878; **2.8** Engraving from *The illustrated history of the world for the English people* (1881–84); **2.9** Bloomsbury Academic; **2.10** Bloomsbury Academic; **2.11** Bloomsbury Academic; **2.12** John Trumbull 1773; **2.13** CNG; **2.14** Jastrow/Wikimedia; **2.15** Schurl50/Wikimedia; **2.16** Ohio State University/Gift of Andrew J. Heisserer; **2.17** Granger Historical Picture Archive/Alamy Stock Photo; **2.18** Bloomsbury Academic; **2.19** Bloomsbury Academic; **2.20** Miguel Hermoso Cuesta/Wikimedia; **2.21** Bettmann/Contributor/Getty images; **2.22** Numidix/Wikimedia; **2.23** H. P. Motte 1890; **2.24** Cornelis Cort 1567; **3.1** Bloomsbury Academic; **3.2** WildWinds Ltd; **3.3** Bloomsbury Academic; **3.4** Trustees of the British Museum; **3.5** Trustees of the British Museum; **3.6** De Agostini/S. Vannini/Getty images; **3.7** CNG (www.cngcoins.com); **3.8** Everett Historical/shutterstock.com; **3.9** Bloomsbury Academic; **3.10** 360b/shutterstock.com; **3.11** DEA/A. DAGLI ORTI/Getty images; **3.12** Rama/Wikimedia; **3.13** BasPhoto/shutterstock.com; **3.14** Irina Zholudeva/shutterstock.com; **3.15** Juan Aunion/shutterstock.com; **3.16** Jastrow/Wikimedia; **3.17** Jastrow/Wikimedia; **3.18** Peter Horree/Alamy Stock Photo; **3.19** CNG; **3.20** Bloomsbury Academic; **3.21** Shippen, *Naval battles, ancient and modern* (1883); **3.22** Digital image courtesy of the Getty's Open Content Program; **4.1** Bloomsbury Academic; **4.2** Bloomsbury Academic; **4.3** David J. Lull, Professor Emeritus of New Testament, Wartburg Theological Seminary, Dubuque, Iowa; **4.4** Trustees of the British Museum; **4.5** Trustees of the British Museum; **4.6** Trustees of the British Museum; **4.7** Trustees of the British Museum; **4.8** Bloomsbury Academic; **4.9l** W. Dennis Moss; **4.9r** Gloucester City Museum; **4.10** O. Lyubimova; **4.11** Trustees of the British Museum; **4.12** CNG; **4.13** Bloomsbury Academic after Salway; **4.14** Bloomsbury Academic; **4.15** Bloomsbury Academic after Cunliffe; **4.16** Bloomsbury Academic after Cunliffe; **4.17** Bloomsbury Academic after Cunliffe; **4.18** Bloomsbury Academic after Cunliffe; **4.19** Bloomsbury Academic after Cunliffe; **4.20** Bloomsbury Academic after Cunliffe; **4.21** Bloomsbury Academic; **4.22** Bloomsbury Academic after Cunliffe; **4.23** Bloomsbury Academic.

INDEX

Titles of works are in *italic*. Page numbers in *italic* refer to figures.

A

Actium, battle, 194, 196–200, *197, 198,* 204
Aeneas, *7,* 7–8, 199–200
Africa, Scipio Africanus' invasion, 125–6, 128, 129, 132–6
Ager Falernus, battle, 120–2
Agricola (governor), 216–17, 251, 252, 267–9, *268,* 274
Agrippa, Marcus, 196, 198, 200
Alba Longa, 7, 8, 9, 20
Allobrogian tribes, 101–3
ambitus (ambitio), 27, 34
ancient historians, literary tradition, 3
Ancus Marcius, 6, 20, 21–2, 26, 27
Antony, Mark, 177, 181–92, *182, 185*
    Battle of Actium, 197–8, 200, 201
    relationship with Cleopatra, 161, 187–91
    relationship with Octavian, 182–3, 187–8, 192, 195
    suicide, 201–2, 204
Appius Claudius Crassus, 56, 61, 62, 63, 64, 65
Appius Claudius Regillensis, 53, 55–6, 57, 58
Appius Claudius Regillensis (the younger), 56, 60
Aquae Sulis (Bath), *265,* 265–7, *266*
archaeological evidence, *see* historical evidence
Arch of Claudius, 223, 240, 241, *241*
army
    economic impact on Britain, 270–3
    plebeians in, 40
    under Romulus, 15–16
Arsinoe, 154, 157, 158, 173, 183, 186, 204
Atrebates, tribe, 248, 249
augury, 10, 29
Augustus (Octavian), 182, *183,* 194, 196, 199, 200, 218, *see also* Octavian
    Res Gestae, 229
Aulus Plautius, 233, 235, 236, 240, 244, 252, 258
Aureus of Claudius, 242, *242*

B

Berenice, 154, 156
Boii, tribe 97, 98, 100
Bolsena Mirror, 9, *9*
Boudicca, 252, 253–5
Brigantes, tribe, 246, 247, 256, 257
Britain
    effects of Roman rule, 260–7
    political situation before Romans, 227–31

bronze coin of Cunobelinus, 230, *230*
Brutus, Lucius Junius, 42, 43, *44,* 46, 58

C

Caesar, Gaius Julius, 167, 170, *170,* 174, 179
    attempts to invade Britain, 217–18, 225–7
    Gallic War, 226–7
    relationship with Cleopatra, 171–7, *173,* 178–9
Caesarion, 165, *165,* 167, 177, 183, 202
Calgacus, 269–70, 281
Caligula (Gaius), 218, 223, 231–2, 233
Camulodunum (Colchester), 229, 236, 237, 244, 246, 247, 253, 254, 260–2, *261*
Cannae, battle, 109–12, *110,* 116, 118–19
Capitoline, She-wolf, *9*
Capua 83, 93, 109, 112, 114, 123, 130, 131
Caratacus, 249–50, 256
Carthage, 7, *85, 126,* 136
    Hannibal's defence, 129, 132–6
    loss of Iberia, 114, 124–5
    and Rome, 84–5, 87–8, 91, 132
Cartimandua, 248, 256
Cassius Dio, 88
    History of Rome, 228, 231, 235, 236, 239, 244, 253
    Roman History, 174, 175, 232, 233, 234, 240
Cassivellaunus, 227
Catuvellauni, tribe, 227
Celtic tribes, 97–8, 100, 101, 105, 106, 108, 109, 110, 111
census, 31–2, 35
Cicero, *Letters to Atticus,* 178, 179
Circus Maximus, 27, *27,* 28, 35, 37
civil war, Cleopatra and Ptolemy XIII, 170, 171
class system, 31–2, 40
Claudius, 223–31, *228,* 233–6, 239–43, *241, 242,* 244
Cleopatra
    character, 160–2
    expansion of Egyptian territory, 158–9
    family and early life, 154, 155–6
    and Isis, 160, 163–5, 192
    as Queen of Egypt, 157–65
    relationship with Antony, 186, 187–91
    relationship with Caesar, 171–7, *173,* 178–9
    representations of, *162,* 162–3, *163, 164,* 164–5

    suicide, 202–3, 204
    visit to Rome, 178–9
client-kings, 168–9, 170, 237, 246, 248
Cloaca Maximus, 28, 35, 37, 76
Cloelia, 48–9
coins
    Antony and Cleopatra, 191, *191*
    British kings, *228,* 228–9, *229,* 230, *230*
    Claudius, 241–2
    Cleopatra, 162, *162,* 163
    Cleopatra and Caesarion, *164,* 164–5
    Ptolemaic, 155
Comitia curiata 14, 36
Conflict of the Orders, 4, 51–2, 53–4
consuls, roles, 13, 39, 41, 42, 44, 45
Coriolanus, Marcius, 59
Cornelius Scipio, 97, 98, 99–100, 104–5, 107, 114, 117
Cunobelinus, 229, *229,* 230, *230*

D

Decemvirates, 61–2, 63, 65, 66
democracy, 13–14
dictators (magistrates), 41, 45, 49, 57, 179
Didius Gallus, 251, 252, 258
Dionysius
    early Republic, 40, 41, 44, 49, 57, 58
    Etruscan kings, 34, 35
    legendary kings, 13–14, 18
    literary tradition, 3, 7
    Roman Antiquities, 13, 15, 26–7, 32, 38, 44
Donations of Alexandria, 159, *159,* 191–2, 195

E

Ebro, Treaty of, 89, 94, 96
Egypt
    Antony and Cleopatra's relationship, 189–90
    expansion of territory, 158–9
    Rome's involvement, 169–70
elephants, 94, 98, 100, 104, 106, 107, 134, 135
emperors, influence on British occupation, 273–4
Etruscan civilisation, 9, 20, 25, *25,* 26, 28, *28,* 40
Etruscan Kings, 25–38

Index

F
Fabian strategy, 109, 119–21, 131
Fabius Maximus, 109, 110, 114, 118, 119–23, 125
    dedication, 122, *123*
Fabius Pictor, 3, 6, 8, 12, 35, 54, 88, 89, 90, 112
First Punic War, 84, 85
First Secession, 54–8
First Triumvirate, 183
Fishbourne, 248–9, *249,* 262–5, *263, 264, 265*
Flaminius, Gaius, 107–9, 117–18, 119–20
Forum, during Rome's foundation, 11, 17, 19, 28, 40
Fosse Way, 237, 257, *257*
foundation myths, 6–8, 10–12

G
Gabinians, in Rome and Egypt, 157, 170
Gaius (Caligula), 218, 223, 231–2, 233
Gaius Canuleius 66, 67
Gaius Mucius Scaevola, 48
Gaius Terentilius Harsa 60
Gallic tribes, *see* Celtic tribes
Gaul, 97, 113
Gauls, in Hannibal's invasion, 105, 106, 107
Geronium, battle, 122–3
gold staters
    Cunobelinus, 229, *229*
    Verica, 228, *228*
governors, policies and achievements in Britain, 250–8, 267–9
Gracchi 52

H
Hamilcar Barca, 85–6, 87–8, 89, 90, 143
Hannibal, 88
    crossing the Alps, 100–4, *102*
    defence of Carthage, 128–9, 132–6
    leadership, 95–6, 97–100, 103, 104
    motivation for invasion of Italy, 90–1
    supply routes, 113, 129, 130
    war with Rome, 104–14, 120–23, 130–1
    withdrawal from Italy, 129
Hanno the Elder 85, 113, 123, 129, 130
Hasdrubal Barca, 97, 114, 123, 124, 130, 131, 143
Hasdrubal the Fair, 88–90, 91, 94, 96
head of Cleopatra, 163, *163*
historical evidence
    Etruscan Kings period, 26, 28, 32–3, 37
    foundation of Republic period, 40, 44, 47
    legendary kings period, 7, 8, *8, 9,* 11, *11,* 13, *15, 19,* 20
Homer's *Iliad* 7
Horace, *Odes,* 162, 203
Horatii 20, 21
Horatius Cocles, 47, *48*
Horatius, Marcus, 46, 62, 63, 64, 65

I
Iberia, 87–8, 89, 90, 94, *94,* 97, 98
    Carthage's loss, 114, 124–5
Iceni, tribe, 246, 253–4
Isis, 160, 163, *see also* Cleopatra and Isis

J
Josephus
    Antiquities, 224
    Jewish War, 237
Julius Frontinus, 252, 257, 258

K
kings, British, political situation, 228–31

L
Lake Regilius, battle, 49, 54
Lapis Niger Stele, 11, *11*
Lapis Satricanus, 47, *47*
Lars Porsena, 46, 47–9
Latin League, 46, 48, 49
leadership, Hannibal's, 95–6, 97–100, 103, 104
legal initiatives, foundations of Rome, 21, 65, 66
legendary kings, 6, 9–22
lictors, 13, 45
literary tradition, 3, 4, 7, 26
Livy, *History of Rome*
    early Republic, 42, 52, 54, 58, 63, 64, 73
    Etruscan kings, 31
    Hannibal's invasion of Italy, 94–100, 101, 103–7, 109, 110–13
    legendary kings, 6, 9, 10, 14, 17, 18
    Rome's defeat of Carthage, 129, 130, 132, 134–5, 138
    Rome's response to Hannibal, 117, 118, 119, 120, 121, 124, 125
Londinium (London), 253, 261, 262
Lucius Aemilius Paullus, 109, 110, 112, 118
Lucius Valerius Potitus, 62, 63, 64, 65
Lucumo (Priscus), 26–7
Luni Sul Mignone, 8, *8*
Lutatius, Treaty of, 85, 87, 88, 96, 100

M
magistrates, 12, 13, 41, 45, 46
Mago Barca 83, 105, 107, 114, 115, 123, 124, 126, 128, 131
Maharbal, 109, 112
Marcellus, Marcus Claudius, 113, 114, 123, 131, 187
Marcus Horatius Barbatus, 46, 62, 63, 64, 65
Masinissa (Massena), 132, 134, 136
Masinissa of Numidia 87
    alliance with Rome 125
    role in defeat and destruction of Carthage 126, 128
Master of the Horse, 45, 49
Medway, river, 234
Menenius Agrippa, 58
military initiatives, foundations of Rome, 4, 15–16, 30, 31, 37, 40
military tactics, Britons', 226
Minucius, Marcus, 119, 121–3

N
Nero, 273–4
Numa, 6, 17–19
Numitor, King of Alba Longa 9, 10

O
Octavia (Antony's wife), 187, 188, 189, 190, 191
Octavian (Augustus), *183*
    and Antony, 182–3, 187, 188, 190, 192, 201
    Battle of Actium, 195, 196–200
    and Cleopatra, 162, 202, 203
    significance of suicides, 204
    war with Antony and Cleopatra, 195
orders (patricians/plebeians), 39–40, *see also* Conflict of the Orders
Ostorius Scapula, 246, 247, 249, 252, 258
ovations, 240

P
patricians, 13, 39, 41, 53, *see also* plebeians
patron-client relationship, 53, 168
Paullus, Lucius Aemilius, 109, 110, 112, 118
Perusine War, 187
Petilius Cerialis, 252, 256, 257
Petronius Turpilianus, 252, 255
pharaohs, 154
Plautius, Aulus, *see* Aulus Plautius
plebeians, 13, 35, 39–40, 41, 46–7
    causes of unrest, 52–3
    Conflict of the Orders, 51–2, 53–4
    tribunes, 52, 58, 59–60, 61
Plutarch
    Life of Caesar, 161, 170, 171–2
    Life of Fabius Maximus, 121
    Life of Mark Antony, 172
        Antony's character, 185, 187, 188, 190, 191
        Battle of Actium, 196–7
        Cleopatra and Antony, 185–6, 192
        Cleopatra's character, 156, 160, 161, 162, 166
        Octavian and Antony, 188, 195
political initiatives
    early Republic, 58, 59–61, 65–6
    legendary and Etruscan kings, 12–14, 21, 28, 31–2, 35
Polybius, *Histories*
    account of Punic Wars, 86–7
    causes of 2nd Punic War, 85, 87–9, 90–1, 143
    Hannibal's invasion of Italy, 94, 95–7, 101–5, 106, 108–10, 112, 113
    Rome's defeat of Carthage, 129, 132
    Rome's response to Hannibal, 117, 118, 120
Pompey the Great, 167, 170–1
Potter, T. W., 'The Transformation of Britain', 225
Prastagus, king, 246
Priscus, Tarquinius, 24, 26–30, 41, 45
Ptolemy XII (Auletes), 154, *155,* 156, 157, 169–70, 173

Index

Ptolemy XIII, 156, 157, 158, 167, 170, 171, 173, 174
Ptolemy XIV, 154, 158, 160, 173, 174, 178
Publius Valerius Publicola, 44, 46–7, *47*, 57

Q

Quintus Fabius, 60

R

Raiding Parties, battle, 99
Rape of Lucretia, 41–2, *42*
'Rape' of the Sabine women, 16–17
relief of Cleopatra and Caesarion, 165, *165*
religious initiatives
    Etruscan kings', 28, 33, 37
    legendary kings', 14–15, 17, 18, 19, 22
Remus, 9, 10
resistance, Britons vs Romans, 249–50, 252–5, 256, 257, 258
Rhone Crossing, battle, 98–9, *99*
Roman army in Britain, economic impact, 270–3
Roman governors in Britain, 250–8
Romanisation, 260–7
Rome, impact of Antony and Cleopatra's relationship, 189
Romulus, 6, 9–17
    conflicts with Sabines, 16–17
    foundation myth, 9–10
    military initiatives, 15–16
    political initiatives, 12–14, 32, 39
    religious initiatives, 14–15, 18

S

Sabines, 16–17, 29–30, 62
Sack of Rome, 54
Sacred Mount occupation, 57–8
Saguntum, 89–90, 94, 97, *see also* Siege of Saguntum
Scipio Africanus, 123–6, 129, 132–6
Second Punic War, 83–137
    impact on Carthage and Rome, 136–7
    reasons for outbreak, 84–91
Second Secession, 52, 56, 62, 64–5
Second Triumvirate, 183
Sempronius, Tiberius, 97, 105–7, 112, 117
Senate, role and development, 13, 21, 28, 35, 45
Servian reforms, 31–3
Servian wall, 32–3, *33*
Servilius, Gnaeus, 107, 108, 112, 117–18
Servilius, Publius, 55–6
Servius Tullius, 24, 30–3

Sextus Valerius Genialis, 237–8
Sibylline Oracles, 36
Sicily, 84, 85, 86, 96, 97, 113, 125
Sicinius Bellutus, 57, 58
Siege of Saguntum, 91, 95–6
Silures, tribe, 249
silver denarius of Antony and Cleopatra, 191, *191*
silver didrachma of Claudius, 241–2, *242*
Silvia Arsia, Battle, 46
social changes, Etruscan Kings, 28, 32, 37
Sosylus, historian 101
Spurius Cassius, 59
Stoicism, 6
subsistence farming, 8, 52
Suetonius (historian), 224
    Caligula, 231–2
    Claudius, 224, 240, 243
    Life of Divine Julius, 174, 176, 177, 179, 180
    Vespasian, 237
Suetonius Paulinus, 252, 253, 254, 255, 258, 274
Superbus, Tarquinius, *see* Tarquinius Superbus
Syphax of Numidia 125–6

T

tables of laws, 61, 62
Tacitus
    Agricola, 216–17, 217–18, 248
    Annals, 233, 241, 246–7, 250, 252, 253, 255, 260, 261
    Calgacus' campaigns, 269–70, 281
    governors and Britons, 251–3, 255, 256, 257, 258, 267
    Histories, 252, 255, 256, 274
Tarentum 111, 112, 113, 114, 122, 123, 131
Tarentum, Treaty of, 188
Tarquin conspiracy, 44
Tarquinius Priscus, 24, 26–30, 41, 45
Tarquinius Superbus, 24, 34–7, *36*, 38
    removal of, 43, 44, 45, 46, 47, 49
Tarsus, 185, 186
Temple of Diana, 31, 33
Temple of Janus, 19, *19*
Terentilius Harsa, Gaius, 60, 61
Thames, river, 235, 236
Ticinus, battle, 104–5, 117
timelines
    Cleopatra, 151–2
    invasion of Britannia, 219–21
    Rome's foundation, 4
    Second Punic War, 83

Togidubnus (Cogibudnus), 247, 248
Togodumnus, 235, 236
tombstones
    Rufus Sita, 238, *239*
    Sex. Valerius Genialis, 237–8, 239, *239*
Trasimene, battle, 107–9, *108*, 117–18
Trebellius Maximus, 252, 255, 256
Trebia, battle, 105–7, *106*, 115, 116, 117
tribes, British resistance to Romans, 218, *218*, 219, 228, 246–7, 253–5, 256
Trinobantes, tribe, 228, 229, 253–4, 261
Troy, 7, *7*
Truceless War, 85, 87
Tullus Hostilius, 6, 20–1, 21
Twelve Tables, 54, *54*, 65–6
tyrants, 13, 35, 44, 45, 59, 61

V

Valerio-Horatian Laws, 65, 66
Valerius Potitus, Lucius, 62, 63, 64, 65
Valerius, Publius, 44, 46–7, *47*, 57
Varro, Gaius Terentius, 109, 110, 118–19
Veii, 20, 28, *28*, 29, 46, 58
Velleius Paterculus, *Roman History*, 199, 202
Venutius of the Brigantes, 246, 247, 256
Veranius, Quintus, 252
Verginius, Lucius, 56, 62, 63, 64, 65, 73
Verica ('Berikos'), 228, *228*, 231, 233, 234
Verulamium (St Albans), 253
Vespasian, 218, 235, 236, 237
    as emperor, 248, 255, 257, 267, 274
Vestal Virgins, 9, 18, 19, 28
Vettius Bolanus, 252, 255, 256
Villanovan civilisation, 8, *14*, 15, *15*
Vindolanda tablets, 270–3
Virgil, *Aeneid*, 199–200, 250
Virginia, abduction of, 56, 62–3, *63*, 64, 73
Volcae, tribe 98–9
Volero Publilius, 59–60

W

warfare, 4
    early Republic, 47, 52
    Etruscan kings, 29–30, 37, 46
    legendary kings, 16–17, 20–1, 22
war, Octavian vs Antony and Cleopatra, 195–200
Wars of Independence, 45–9, 52
war veterans, 52, 55, *55*, 56

Z

Zama, battle, 132–6